God's Own Party

God's Own Party

DANIEL K. WILLIAMS

The Making of the

Christian Right

OXFORD

UNIVERSITY PRESS

2010

OXFORD
UNIVERSITY PRESS

Oxford University Press, Inc., publishes works that further
Oxford University's objective of excellence
in research, scholarship, and education.

Oxford   New York
Auckland   Cape Town   Dar es Salaam   Hong Kong   Karachi
Kuala Lumpur   Madrid   Melbourne   Mexico City   Nairobi
New Delhi   Shanghai   Taipei   Toronto

With offices in
Argentina   Austria   Brazil   Chile   Czech Republic   France   Greece
Guatemala   Hungary   Italy   Japan   Poland   Portugal   Singapore
South Korea   Switzerland   Thailand   Turkey   Ukraine   Vietnam

Published by Oxford University Press, Inc.
198 Madison Avenue, New York, New York 10016

www.oup.com

Oxford is a registered trademark of Oxford University Press

Library of Congress Cataloging-in-Publication Data
Williams, Daniel K.
God's Own Party : the making of the Christian right / Daniel K. Williams.
      p.   cm.
Includes bibliographical references and index.
ISBN 978-0-19-534084-6
1. Evangelicalism—Political aspects—United States—History—20th century.
2. Christian conservatism—United States—History—20th century.
3. Republican Party (U.S. : 1854–)—Religion.
4. United States—Politics and government—20th century.
5. United States—Church history—20th century. I. Title.
BR1642.U5W535   2010
322'.10973—dc22   2010009146

9 8 7 6 5 4 3 2 1
Printed in the United States of America
on acid-free paper

11/03/10

ACKNOWLEDGMENTS

THIS PROJECT REQUIRED ME to spend the better part of a decade researching, writing, and talking about the two subjects—politics and religion—that one is advised never to discuss in polite company. I am therefore especially grateful to the many scholars and friends who not only listened patiently to my findings, but also encouraged me in this journey and helped me adopt a dispassionate historical perspective on topics that are the subject of contentious public debate.

I would like to thank Jim Campbell, Joe Crespino, and Bruce Schulman for reading the manuscript in its entirety and offering lengthy, detailed comments. Jim, in fact, read the manuscript three times—twice during the dissertation stage and once in its early incarnation as a book manuscript, when it was more than six hundred pages long. His detailed critiques, insightful suggestions, and unflagging enthusiasm for the project prompted me to rethink some of my ideas, consider different perspectives, and sharpen my writing.

Jim Patterson, my dissertation adviser at Brown University, offered crucial support and guidance during the first three and a half years of this project. His thoughtful critiques, encouraging words, and genuine interest in my work meant more to me than he probably realized. As a skilled historian, Jim schooled me in the art of historical objectivity and provided a superb model of that in his own work.

Numerous historians reviewed my work at various stages of the project. During the first year of my research, when I was an inexperienced graduate student, Ed Harrell, Ken Heineman, and Lisa McGirr read early drafts of my dissertation prospectus and offered valuable suggestions that helped me avoid fundamental missteps at the outset of my research. Later, Darren Dochuk, Kevin Kruse, Steven Miller, Matt Sutton, and Mike Vorenberg read my dissertation and offered encouragement as I embarked on the task of bringing the work to its next stage. Martin Durham and Sally Gordon read individual chapters and gave me helpful feedback. David Courtwright read the entire manuscript shortly before its publication. Jack Bass, David Chappell, Don Critchlow, Kari Frederickson, Matt Lassiter, Nancy MacLean, and Randall Stephens offered insightful comments on my conference papers and journal articles, and helped me refine my ideas. Many colleagues and scholars in the field, including Shani Bechhofer, Sam Brenner, Robert Fleegler, Monte Hampton, Barclay Key, Alan Petigny, Kim Phillips-Fein, Stephanie Rolph, Bryan Thrift, Josh Zeitz, and Ann Ziker, as well as numerous others, shared conference panels with me, gave me new perspectives on my research topic, suggested additional sources to examine, or enriched my life with their supportive friendship.

I am grateful for the support of all of my colleagues in the history department at the University of West Georgia, especially the department chair, Steve Goodson, whom I respect not only as a colleague and supervisor but also as a mentor and friend. Steve was kind enough to review my initial book proposal and offer useful suggestions for framing my argument, and his constant support of my teaching and scholarship has helped me in more ways than I can possibly list in a few short sentences. Keith Pacholl read parts of the manuscript, listened to several of my conference paper presentations, and offered constant encouragement throughout the project. I have appreciated our many conversations about American religious history. I am also grateful to several other colleagues, including Michael de Nie, Chuck Lipp, and Tim Schroer, for all of the many intellectually stimulating conversations about religion, politics, and history that we have enjoyed.

I would like to thank my students—both undergraduates and graduates—at the University of West Georgia for the experiences they shared with me and for the conversations that helped me better understand the complex interaction between religion, politics, and race in the South. I owe special thanks to two graduate students for their help on this project. The many conversations that I had with Rick Primuth, who read my dissertation in the course of his own research on Ronald Reagan's presidential campaigns, challenged me to reexamine some of my ideas. Kyle Owenby served as my extremely able graduate research assistant for an entire academic year and saved me hours of work by retrieving articles and other materials that I requested, sometimes on very short notice.

I am grateful to the many people who assisted me in locating source material for this project. Librarians and archivists are the best friends of any historian, and I consider myself fortunate to have made the acquaintance of many able members of that profession who guided me to sources that I would never have found without their assistance. I owe a special debt of gratitude to Chip Berlet of Political Research Associates, Bill Sumners of the Southern Baptist Historical Library and Archives, Patrick Robbins and Mark Sidwell of the Fundamentalism File at Bob Jones University, Abigail Sattler of Liberty University Archives, and Wayne Sparkman of the Presbyterian Church in America Historical Center for going the extra mile in helping me to find the sources that I was seeking. I also received helpful assistance at the American Heritage Center at the University of Wyoming, the Bancroft Library at the University of California at Berkeley, the Bentley Historical Library at the University of Michigan, the Billy Graham Center Archives, the John Hay Library at Brown University, the archives of People for the American Way, Special Collections at Clemson University, the Nixon Presidential Library, the Gerald R. Ford Presidential Library, the Jimmy Carter Library, and the Ronald Reagan Presidential Library. I am grateful to the many archivists who devoted hours of their time to tracking down sources for me or who agreed to extend their facilities' hours of operation during my visits so that I could make the most of my research trips.

Bill Martin sent me copies of the interview transcripts that he had made for his book, *With God on Our Side*, and graciously allowed me to quote from this material. Jim Price and Jim Hershman shared copies of rare sources from their private collections that would have been difficult to obtain elsewhere. Sylvester Jacobs, Phyllis Schlafly, Baptist Press, the *Sword of the Lord*, and the Special Collections of the University of Arkansas granted me permission to reproduce photographs that were not in the public domain. Terry Frala of the *Sword of the Lord* answered my questions about John R. Rice and corrected a few factual errors in an initial draft section of my manuscript, and Tim LaHaye did the same for sections of the manuscript pertaining to his ministry. I would also like to thank the staff of the Florence Baptist Church in South Carolina for sending me their file on the Moral Majority, and Pastor Charles Gaulden of the Evangel Cathedral in Spartanburg, South Carolina, for his willingness to be interviewed about his church's role in politics during the 1980s.

I am also grateful to the organizations that provided me with research funding. The University of West Georgia and the Brown University Graduate School gave me research fellowships. The Southern Baptist Historical Library and Archives awarded me a Lynn E. May, Jr., study grant that helped me finance a research trip to Nashville, and the Gerald R. Ford Presidential Library gave me a grant to conduct research at that presidential library in Ann Arbor.

No book project makes it to completion without the assistance of a capable editor, so I am especially grateful to Theo Calderara of Oxford University Press for helping to transform my manuscript into a publishable work. Theo's detailed line critiques taught me to tighten my prose and sharpen my arguments, and his prompt responses to all of my queries ensured the timely publication of this book. I am particularly thankful for his unwavering belief in the value of the project. I am also grateful to all of the other editorial staff at Oxford University Press who guided this book through the publication process.

Finally, I would like to thank my parents, Ken and Linda Williams, for encouraging my earliest intellectual interests, fostering my critical thinking skills, and giving me the education that made this project possible.

CONTENTS

God's Own Party

Introduction

T HE REPUBLICANS WHO GATHERED IN July 1980 to nominate Ronald Reagan as the party's standard-bearer included many of the nation's prominent senators, congressional representatives, and governors. But the real power broker at the convention was neither a delegate nor a politician; he was a Baptist pastor from Lynchburg, Virginia. Jerry Falwell had launched the Moral Majority only the previous year, but the organization's rapid growth and political influence had already made him a household name. Falwell met with Reagan and the platform committee during the convention, and ensured that the platform included endorsements of constitutional amendments to restore prayer in schools and prohibit abortion, as well as a denunciation of the Equal Rights Amendment, which the GOP had officially supported for forty years. Journalists were astounded. "The political commandments endorsed by the Republican Party here this week may not be chiseled in stone," the *Washington Post* observed, "but, as one preppy-looking California Christian put it, 'they ought to be. It's right down the line an evangelical platform.'"[1]

As pundits struggled to explain what had happened, they arrived at a narrative that eventually became conventional wisdom. Evangelicals, they said, had long been Democrats, or had opted out of politics altogether. In the early twentieth century, conservative Protestants had made a brief bid for political influence with their antievolution campaign, but the Scopes trial had put an end to that. As historian William Leuchtenburg said, the fundamentalist political activities of the 1920s were the "last stand in a lost cause." After that, they had retreated to their churches, and did not emerge again as a political force until liberal Supreme Court decisions on school prayer, pornography, and abortion induced them to reenter the public square in the 1970s. A few historians complicated this narrative by suggesting that evangelicals had mobilized not in response to *Roe v. Wade*, but as a reaction to a 1978 IRS ruling that penalized Christian schools for not complying with civil rights policy. But whether they emphasized race or abortion as a catalyst for the Christian Right, most historians believed that its origins could be found in the events of the 1970s.[2]

The reality is otherwise. Conservative Christians had been politically active since the early twentieth century, and they never retreated from the public square. Their commitment to political activism and conservatism was much deeper and more long-standing than most analysts realized. What was new in 1980 was not evangelicals' interest in politics but, rather, their level of partisan commitment. Evangelicals gained prominence during Ronald Reagan's campaign not because they were speaking out on political issues—they had been doing this for decades—but because they were taking over the Republican Party. It was an event more than fifty years in the making.

The journalists who were surprised at the influence of evangelicals on the 1980 Republican convention could have found a parallel in the 1920s, when conservative Protestants attempted unsuccessfully to mobilize the Democratic Party in defense of Prohibition, and when three-time Democratic presidential candidate William Jennings Bryan led a national campaign against evolution. The fundamentalist movement, which emerged in opposition to theological liberalism, attempted to use politics to restore the nation's Christian identity. The fundamentalists claimed to be concerned primarily with defending the "fundamentals" of the faith, such as biblical inerrancy and the Virgin Birth, against the onslaughts of modern biblical scholarship, but they quickly began to combat cultural liberalism as well. Alarmed at the widespread teaching of human evolution in the nation's high schools, the growth of Catholic political influence, and the changes in public attitudes toward sexuality and gender roles, fundamentalists attempted to reclaim the nation's public institutions, including schools and government, and make them a force for Protestantism and public morality. Fundamentalists came from various denominational traditions, but they were united by a common belief that America was rapidly losing its Christian moorings and needed to repent. In short, they were committed to the idea of a Christian nation with a Protestant-based moral code—and they turned to politics in order to realize that vision.[3]

Despite their fervor, fundamentalists had only limited success in their political campaigns, mainly because neither of the nation's major political parties was receptive to their demands. The Democrats repudiated fundamentalist politics by nominating a Catholic, Al Smith, as their presidential candidate in 1928, and the Republicans showed little interest in the culture wars. In the 1930s, fundamentalists lost their campaign to maintain Prohibition. Though they did not abandon their interest in politics, they began to feel alienated from the nation's political institutions. While mainline Protestants and Catholics had representatives in Washington, fundamentalists did not. Instead, they turned to prophetic speculation, viewing the political developments of the 1930s as portents of an imminent divine judgment.

Yet fundamentalists never lost sight of the political vision that they had formed in the 1920s—the vision of reclaiming America's Christian identity through politics. In the early 1940s, they returned to the political sphere by creating a lobbying organization in Washington. This time, they met with more success. The fundamentalist campaigns of the 1920s had failed partly because fundamentalists had not secured control over a political party. Only when conservative Protestants united in support of a comprehensive program that included not only moral legislation, but also economic and foreign policy, could they create the partisan alliance that would give their movement national influence. And conservative Protestants began doing that in the 1940s.

Their alliance with the Republican Party developed in two stages. During the first stage, which lasted from the 1940s through the 1960s, conservative Protestants began to identify the GOP as the party of anticommunism and a Protestant-based moral order. They cultivated close relationships with Republican leaders, especially President Dwight Eisenhower and Vice President Richard Nixon. But they did not exercise a controlling influence in the GOP. Their power was limited by their lack of political skills and by religious divisions within their own movement.

During the second stage, which began in the late 1960s, conservative Protestants succeeded not only in making alliances with Republican politicians, but in changing the agenda of the party. This time, they focused more on the culture wars than the Cold War. Conservative Protestants who mobilized against feminism, abortion, pornography, and gay rights acquired control of the Republican Party, partly because of their long-standing alliances with Republican politicians, but perhaps more important because of the united front that they presented, and because of demographic and political shifts that favored evangelicals. By the beginning of the twenty-first century, the Christian Right was the most powerful interest group in the GOP.

Cold War conservative Protestant political mobilization began with the formation of the fundamentalist movement's first Washington lobbyist group, the National Association of Evangelicals (NAE), in 1942. After a string of fundamentalist political failures, conservative Protestants realized that they needed a voice in Washington at a time of rapid government expansion. The NAE initially held great promise. Northern and southern Protestants came together to lobby the federal government for Christian-based moral legislation, including protection of evangelical broadcasting rights, restrictions on liquor advertising, and limits on Catholic political influence. They abandoned the pejorative name "fundamentalist" in favor of the more optimistic-sounding "evangelical." Like the fundamentalists of the 1920s, the "new evangelicals" of the 1940s believed in the "fundamentals" of the faith and the necessity of reclaiming the nation's Christian heritage, but they were willing to make more broadly based religious and political alliances than the fundamentalists had, and were thus more politically influential. Because the NAE made fighting communism a priority from its inception, the Cold War enhanced the organization's political power.[4] By the early 1950s, evangelicals began to identify the GOP as the party most likely to take the strongest stance against communism and to offer public support for religion, so they created alliances with Republican politicians. Billy Graham became a regular visitor at the Eisenhower White House. Though evangelicals continued to worry about juvenile delinquency, alcohol use, and sexual promiscuity, they were confident that the nation's political leaders supported their causes, and they took heart whenever Congress passed anti-vice legislation. Fundamentalists of the 1920s had been politically marginalized, but the evangelicals of the postwar era sensed that they had power in Washington. By the late 1950s, many evangelicals were convinced that the Christian nation that they had long dreamed of creating was finally within reach.

But their political gains were short-lived. Fissures within conservative Protestantism weakened their political coalition. In the late 1950s, self-identified fundamentalists—a group that included Bob Jones, Jr., Jerry Falwell, and several prominent southern radio evangelists—broke with Billy Graham and the NAE and forged their own political alliances. Officially, fundamentalists repudiated Graham because he was willing to cooperate with mainline Protestants who did not accept the doctrine of biblical inerrancy. But the two groups also differed in their politics, especially in regard to civil rights. While evangelicals such as Graham took a moderate position on issues of race, giving cautious support to civil rights legislation, southern fundamentalists lambasted the civil rights movement as a communist plot. While evangelicals were forging alliances with centrist Republicans such as Dwight Eisenhower and Richard Nixon, fundamentalists supported more conservative figures, such as Strom Thurmond and Barry Goldwater. Fundamentalists' opposition to civil rights alienated them from centrist politicians and prevented them from attaining political influence. It also fragmented the fledgling evangelical political coalition. Northern evangelicals, along with leaders of the Southern Baptist Convention, were embarrassed by the overt defenses of segregation that came from their southern fundamentalist counterparts. In 1964, conservative Protestants split their vote, with southern fundamentalists strongly supporting Barry Goldwater and moderate evangelicals backing Lyndon Johnson.

But by that point, evangelical political influence had already been severely curtailed by John F. Kennedy's election. In 1960, Southern Baptists, northern evangelicals, and independent fundamentalists had come together in a rare moment of unity to try to stop a Catholic from being elected president and thereby to preserve Protestant influence in Washington. When they failed, they lost their connection to the White House, and they spent the rest of the decade as political outsiders. Conservative Protestants were alarmed by Kennedy's election, but shortly thereafter, they decided that secularism, rather than Catholicism, posed a greater threat to the country. By redefining their vision of a Christian nation as antisecular, rather than explicitly Protestant, they launched their second phase of political mobilization, one based on the culture wars. In the early 1960s, Supreme Court rulings against school prayer and Bible reading alarmed many conservative Protestants who began to see the secularization of the country—an idea that had been unimaginable in the 1950s—as a distinct possibility. Evangelicals and fundamentalists were unsure at first how to respond to these rulings, because many of them feared that a campaign for school prayer, which Catholic clergy supported, would further Catholics' political causes. But by the end of the 1960s, their fear of cooperating with Catholics had dissipated in the midst of their concerns over secularism and moral decline. The sexual revolution, sex education, race riots, the counterculture, increases in drug use, and the beginning of the feminist movement convinced them that the nation had lost its Christian identity and that the family was under attack. At such a time, evangelicals—and eventually many fundamentalists, as well—decided that it was imperative to unite with socially conservative allies, even if they happened to be Catholic.[5]

The creation of the "New Christian Right," which emerged at the end of the 1970s, was not an instantaneous process, because it required the political mobilization of disparate factions of conservative Protestantism that had not often cooperated. Mainstream evangelicals, associated with Billy Graham, began leaning toward the Republican Party in the early years of the Cold War, but fundamentalists pursued a different political course until the end of the 1960s. Even in the late 1970s, Jerry Falwell's Moral Majority, which appealed predominantly to fundamentalist Baptists, had limited appeal to many northern evangelicals and Southern Baptists. Many Pentecostals and charismatics—evangelicals who believed in modern-day miracles and who "spoke in tongues"—did not become politically mobilized until Pat Robertson brought them into the Republican Party. Ultimately, the success of the Christian Right depended on the political mobilization of the nation's largest Protestant denomination, the Southern Baptist Convention, which did not become a force in Republican politics until the 1980s. But by the end of Ronald Reagan's presidency, the Christian Right had become a united coalition that would remain a powerful political juggernaut for the next two decades. The divisions between southerners and northerners, and between fundamentalists and evangelicals, which had long impeded conservative Protestants' political influence, had disappeared. The culture wars had trumped denominational differences.

The end of the civil rights movement facilitated the formation of a new Christian political coalition, because it enabled fundamentalists and evangelicals who had disagreed over racial integration to come together. After the passage of federal civil rights legislation and the end of nationally publicized civil rights marches, fundamentalists such as Jerry Falwell accepted the reality of racial integration and began forging political alliances with mainstream Republicans who would have been embarrassed by their segregationist rhetoric only a few years earlier. At the same time, moderate evangelicals who had once cautiously supported the civil rights movement reacted in horror to the race riots and began taking more conservative stances on civil rights. Both fundamentalists and evangelicals embraced Richard Nixon's call for "law and order."[6]

Changing demographics also favored the creation of a politically influential Christian Right. For most of the twentieth century, evangelicals lagged behind mainline Protestants in wealth and education, but in the early 1970s, they began to close the gap. They created their own educational institutions, launched nationally syndicated television shows, and wrote best-selling books. By the beginning of the 1970s, mainline Protestant churches had begun to decline in membership, while evangelical congregations enjoyed rapid growth. The nation's most successful televangelists operated multimillion-dollar budgets and attracted millions of viewers. By the end of the decade, evangelicals realized that they had the voting power and financial resources to change national politics.

The growth of the Sunbelt enhanced evangelicals' influence. While evangelical churches exist in every part of the country, the movement has been disproportionately strong in the Bible Belt for more than a century. Today, for instance, 52 percent of American evangelicals live in the South, even though this region accounts for only 31 percent of the national population.[7] Thus, when southern states entered a period of rapid population growth in the 1970s, replacing the declining northern "Rust Belt" as a center of economic and political influence, southern evangelicals were poised to become political power brokers. For nearly a century, the South had been a reliable Democratic stronghold, but in the 1970s, a robust two-party system developed in the region, prompting both parties to vie for southern votes in presidential elections. Republicans quickly realized that they could win evangelical votes—and thus win the South—by adopting culture war rhetoric. Politicians of the 1960s had won white votes in the segregated South by opposing racial integration, but in the aftermath of the civil rights movement they had to find other issues that would appeal to culturally conservative voters, and they looked to evangelical leaders to tell them what those issues were.

Though the Christian Right was the creation of conservative Protestant grassroots activists, not Republican politicians, national Republican leaders did play a role in encouraging it. Had they not been receptive to the Christian Right's demands, the movement would probably not have gained national influence as quickly as it did. The GOP was a minority party in the 1970s. In order to win, Republicans had to siphon votes from the Democrats, and the Republicans' political strategists believed that a shift to the right on social issues would be the easiest way to do that. The Democrats at the time were becoming a more secular party by embracing culturally liberal stances on abortion, feminism, and gay rights, which alienated some of the conservative Catholics and southern evangelicals who had once been loyal members of the New Deal coalition.[8] In response, Republican leaders of the 1970s decided that adopting more conservative positions on abortion and other cultural issues would be a wise strategic move. Such a move seemed to make sense for a party that had already succeeded in attracting social conservatives through the public support of religion in the 1950s and an endorsement of a school prayer amendment in the 1960s. But what began as a temporary political ploy quickly became irreversible, and the party found itself increasingly controlled by the Christian Right.[9]

The election of Ronald Reagan, who allied himself with the Christian Right, gave conservative evangelicals the political influence that they needed to increase their control over the Republican Party, especially in the South. By the mid-1990s, the Christian Right exercised a dominating influence in one-third of the nation's state Republican parties, and it used its position to elect socially conservative congressional representatives in the Sunbelt and

Midwest, pulling the party further to the right. The GOP became increasingly dependent on its evangelical constituency. At the time that George W. Bush took office, evangelicals accounted for one-third of the Republican vote in presidential elections, but that figure increased to nearly 40 percent by the end of his term. It became impossible for any Republican presidential candidate to ignore the Christian Right's demands on abortion, gay rights, and other social issues.

But the Christian Right's political power did not produce the substantive legislative gains that evangelicals had expected. At the end of Bush's presidency, abortion was still legal and school prayer was not. Same-sex marriage and civil unions were legal in a few states, and Americans were more supportive than ever of gay rights. The majority of Americans did not want to turn back the clock to a prefeminist era when abortions were illegal, gays were closeted, and premarital sex was taboo. Conservative evangelicals found that they could win elections, but not change the culture. They had captured a party, but failed to reclaim a nation.

After observing the failures of the Christian Right and the collapse of several of its leading organizations, pundits in the last two years of the Bush administration proclaimed the movement dead. Evangelicals were becoming more moderate in their politics, they claimed. Their vote was up for grabs. The culture wars were reaching a truce. It was true that one-quarter of white evangelicals were Democrats—as had been the case for years—and some of them began attracting increasing media attention. But the convictions of the majority of white evangelicals—the ones who had been culture warriors for decades—were unchanged. Pundits who had expected the collapse of the Christian Right were unable to explain why Republican presidential candidate John McCain felt obliged to choose a strongly conservative evangelical as his running mate, or why evangelicals accounted for an even higher percentage of the Republican vote in 2008 than they had four years earlier.[10]

Evangelicals voted Republican in 2008 because they had nowhere else to go. They had linked their political fortunes to the Republican Party. They still believed in the possibility of restoring the nation's Christian identity through politics, and the GOP offered them the only hope of doing that. Even if it had been a largely futile quest so far, they still had faith that they could prevail. Christian Right leaders could rise and fall, but the core ideas of the movement remained. The fear of secularism that had produced the fundamentalist political movement of the 1920s continued to mobilize conservative evangelicals in the twenty-first century.

This book presents a chronological history of the Christian Right. An accurate understanding of this history is critical for understanding America itself. Its influence spanned nearly the entire twentieth century and affected every Republican president from the early postwar era to the present. The movement transformed the Republican Party, the national political agenda, and evangelical Christianity. Its history has been intertwined with the civil rights movement, the rise of the Sunbelt, southern political realignment, and American foreign policy. And it continues to affect American politics today. Millions of Americans still believe in the fundamentalist dream of restoring America's Christian identity. To make sense of their political influence, we have to understand the development of their religious vision and the reasons for its enduring power.

As this book goes to press, news reports are once again filled with discussions of populist anger on the right, much of it centered on cultural issues. A Democratic Congress complied with the demands of Christian lobbyists by agreeing to include a prohibition on federal funding of abortion in its health care bill. Voters in Maine surprised the pundits by banning same-sex marriage. Those who believe in blending faith with conservative politics have pushed recent books by Glenn Beck and Sarah Palin to the top of the best-seller lists. Even with the White House and Congress under Democratic control, the Christian Right has been remarkably resilient.

For those who are aware of the Christian Right's history, these news reports have a familiar ring. The Christian Right of the late twentieth century was not a passing fad. Nor is evangelicals' commitment to the Republican Party a recent development that can easily be reversed. Conservative Protestants have been campaigning since the 1920s for changes in moral legislation. And since the mid-twentieth century, they have identified those campaigns with the Republican Party. They cannot turn back from either their Republican partisanship or their political campaigns. To give up would mean acquiescing to the forces that they believe are destroying American families and American society.

Evangelical leaders and their political organizations will come and go, and their political styles will change, but the underlying rationale for their political campaigns is not likely to go away. And just as conservative evangelicals have been frustrated in their past efforts, they are likely to once again find it impossible to reverse the country's cultural direction through politics. Though they have largely succeeded in turning the GOP into "God's Own Party," they have not yet been able to make America God's own nation. Their ninety-year quest continues.

ONE | From Isolation to Influence

THE CULTURE WARS AT THE 1924 Democratic National Convention were the opening salvo in fundamentalists' attempt to reclaim the nation through politics. As conservative Protestants clashed with Catholics over Prohibition, moral legislation, and the nation's religious identity, the convention appeared on the verge of fracturing. Believing that the future direction of their party and nation was at stake, fundamentalists came in force to the New York convention hall. Bob Jones, Sr., a southern evangelist who would later found the South Carolina fundamentalist college that bears his name, showed up to cheer on the delegates who supported Prohibition and opposed the "wet" Catholic governor of New York, Al Smith. Some of Smith's supporters, who were mostly northerners and Catholics, booed the fundamentalist speakers and suggested that the party moderate its stance on the liquor question.

At the center of the religious polarization was three-time presidential candidate William Jennings Bryan, who was arguably both the nation's most famous Democrat and the fundamentalists' most talented orator. Bryan came to New York prepared to lead "the defenders of the home" in "resistance" against Smith. The stakes in the contest were nothing less than the preservation of the family and the maintenance of the nation's moral order, he argued. "Does Governor Smith expect the fathers and mothers to be inactive while those who make money out of the manufacture and sale of alcoholic drinks conspire against the strength of the boys and the virtues of the girls?" Bryan asked. "He cannot lead the nation back to wallow in the mire."[1]

Despite Bryan's efforts, fundamentalists lost the culture wars of the 1920s, and they were unable to secure control of the Democratic Party. Al Smith won the Democratic nomination in 1928, and a few years later, a Democratic administration repealed Prohibition. It would be several decades before fundamentalists returned to a political convention. They had failed in their campaign to reclaim the nation's government for Protestant Christianity.

But fundamentalists were undaunted. In 1942, they returned to the political arena by creating the National Association of Evangelicals (NAE), which established a permanent lobbying office in Washington to campaign for morally conservative legislation. "Millions of evangelical Christians, if they had a common voice and a common meeting place, would exercise under God an influence that would save American democracy," New York pastor William Ward Ayer declared.[2]

This time, conservative Protestants partly succeeded in their effort to Christianize the nation through politics. The Cold War, with its civil religious rhetoric and its identification of anticommunism with the purposes of God, made politicians more receptive to conservative Protestant demands than they had been a generation earlier. Conservative Protestants began exchanging their political isolation for political influence. And they discovered that the Republican Party of Dwight Eisenhower, rather than the Democratic Party that had scorned William Jennings Bryan, offered them their greatest chance of political victory.

The Ineffectiveness of Fundamentalist Politics in the 1920s and 1930s

The Christian Right's political ethos originated in the fundamentalist movement of the early twentieth century. Fundamentalism was a defensive movement intent on reclaiming a dominant societal influence for conservative Protestantism. For most of the nineteenth century, evangelical Protestants—that is, those who believed in personal salvation through a Christian conversion experience and who accepted the Bible as their supreme authority—had enjoyed a strong influence in religion, politics, and society. Eighty-five percent of American congregations were evangelical in 1860.[3] The Bible was a touchstone of American culture. But evangelicals began losing their cultural influence in the late nineteenth century. The arrival of millions of Catholic and Jewish immigrants in northern cities, the growth of a liberal Protestantism that rejected a literal faith in the Bible, and the challenge of science to traditional evangelical beliefs weakened conservative Protestant influence. In the early twentieth century, changes in sexual mores presented yet another challenge to evangelicalism.

Conservative Protestants decided to fight back. In 1919, they formed the World's Christian Fundamentals Association, choosing the name "fundamentalist" to signify their adherence to "fundamental" doctrines such as the Virgin Birth and biblical inerrancy. A literal adherence to the Bible, they believed, was the answer to the liberalism that threatened both church and society. In addition to fighting against theological liberalism in their own denominations, they campaigned against movies, drinking, and Darwinism in society, and they were not afraid to use state power to attack secular practices they opposed. Although most of their political battles were aimed at specific vices or educational practices, fundamentalists had a larger goal: the preservation of a Christian moral order in American society.

Fundamentalists of the early 1920s found many signs that America was losing its Christian identity. For the first time in the nation's history, more Americans lived in urban than in rural areas. Many young people who moved from the farm to the city embraced the hedonism of the era. They danced the Charleston, frequented the movie theater, and abandoned their "Victorian" sexual mores. Public profanity was no longer taboo. Traditional notions of femininity were under attack. Women cut their hair into chic bobs, exchanged their long skirts for short dresses, and started smoking cigarettes. College graduates—a group that was rapidly growing—began justifying the new morality with appeals to Sigmund Freud or evolutionary biology. Some exchanged the "old-time religion" for liberal Protestantism. A few quit going to church altogether. For many Americans who moved to the cities, these changes were a sign of the nation's degeneracy. The most politically active fundamentalist pastors of the 1920s were men who had moved to the nation's largest cities from rural areas in the South and Midwest. The cities in which they lived were full of sin, and they intended to clean them up through politics.[4]

Fundamentalists also sensed a growing secularization of the educational system. During the late nineteenth and early twentieth centuries, most of the nation's colleges abandoned their traditional emphasis on theology and moral education. Public school districts in California discontinued their traditional practice of devotional Bible reading in the early 1920s. Fundamentalists reacted with a campaign to restore Christian teaching to public schools and restrict the teaching of evolution. "Drive God and his Christ from the educational program of our children and you have made complete the wrecking of the greatest Republic on the earth," Los Angeles Methodist pastor Robert Shuler stated in 1923.[5]

Like Shuler, most fundamentalists viewed their political campaigns as a way to save their erstwhile "Christian nation" from divine destruction. They were obsessed with the image of a decadent nation aping the vices of ancient pagan empires. Fundamentalist pastor Joseph Larsen wrote in the *Moody Monthly* in July 1929, "The gravest danger is that America shall go *the same route that the ancient nations of Babylon, Greece, and Rome went*—into sinful pleasures, unchristian philosophy, heathen practices and pagan art, which will bring sudden destruction from a living God of justice."[6] To preserve the nation's conservative Protestant identity, fundamentalists tried to maintain Prohibition and the Volstead Act, regulate dancing, and, in 1928, prevent Al Smith, a Catholic presidential candidate, from winning the White House.

The family was the key to saving the republic. Movies and dancing, fundamentalists believed, were an attack on sexual morals, the foundation of the Christian home. Changes in women's fashion symbolized a new female liberation that they viewed as an assault on patriarchal marriage. Evolution threatened to corrupt their teenage children and destroy their faith in God.[7]

Even at the height of their political activities in the 1920s, fundamentalists never identified their causes with a particular political party. Some Midwestern fundamentalists, such as Billy Sunday, were conservative, pro-business Republicans, but many others, like William Jennings Bryan, were Democrats who staked out positions on the political left on matters of economic policy. As Bryan once told a reporter, he was both "a progressive in politics and a Fundamentalist in religion." He urged his fellow Democrats to wage a "progressive fight" to maintain Prohibition while simultaneously attacking the moneyed interests that had "enriched the few and made homeless the many." He conducted his political warfare with a "double-barreled shotgun," he explained, with one barrel aimed "at the elephant as he tries to enter the treasury and the other at Darwinism—the monkey—as he tries to enter the schoolroom."[8] But Bryan's economic views never became a part of the fundamentalist political program, and his cultural conservatism never had much influence on the Democratic Party. The Republican Party was similarly unresponsive to fundamentalist demands. As long as fundamentalists remained politically divided, unable to agree on an economic program or a partisan commitment, their influence in Washington was limited.

The movement's partisan divisions continued through the 1930s, when Southern Baptist papers supported the New Deal, while northern fundamentalist magazines condemned Roosevelt's programs as dangerous arrogations of state power. John R. Rice, a Baptist pastor in Fort Worth, Texas, whose *Sword of the Lord* later became the most widely circulated fundamentalist paper in the South, urged his congregants to vote against the Democratic Party because of Roosevelt's legalization of alcohol. Yet most Southern Baptist ministers could not bring themselves to vote against a man who had provided so many economic benefits for their impoverished flocks.[9]

Perhaps partly due to their partisan divisions, the fundamentalists of the 1920s experienced only limited success in their political campaigns. They convinced a few southern states to prohibit the teaching of evolution in their public schools, but in the process, their movement became a laughingstock in the North. They temporarily succeeded in maintaining Prohibition, and they rejoiced at Al Smith's landslide defeat. But when President Franklin Roosevelt repealed Prohibition in 1933, and when Catholic politicians gained an increased influence in Washington in the 1930s, fundamentalists worried that there was nothing more they could do to save the country from divine judgment.[10]

Instead, they turned to prophetic speculation, convinced that the imminent return of Jesus would deliver them from the nation's "impending doom." Most northern fundamentalists, as well as an increasing number of those in the South, had adopted a strain of end-time belief called "premillennial dispensationalism," which taught that the world would become increasingly corrupt until Jesus returned for his thousand-year reign. The nation's economic perils, along with the rise of fascist dictatorships in Europe, convinced many fundamentalists that the cataclysmic events of the "last days" were about to occur, so they were more likely to interpret news headlines as portents of the end of the world than to debate how policy-makers should respond.[11]

The National Association of Evangelicals

The Second World War made fundamentalist political alienation seem like a relic of a bygone era, a notion as out of date as the isolationism that American politicians abandoned after Pearl Harbor. After America entered the war, Americans could no longer avoid the federal government's influence. Fifteen million of the nation's young men, and an additional 1 million young women, served in the military, while most of the rest of the country's 131 million citizens fought for America's cause on the home front by recycling tin, planting "victory gardens," and following the government's mandate to forgo basic staples such as nylon stockings and new tires. The federal government expanded enormously in this era, and few Americans seemed to object. Even fiscal conservatives who had once expressed reservations about the $3 billion national deficits of the New Deal era unhesitatingly endorsed the government's new $50 billion deficits as a wartime necessity. When the Internal Revenue Service (IRS) began withholding income taxes from Americans' paychecks and extending the tax to cover wage earners to whom it had never before been applied, hardly anyone complained. A movement of political and religious separatism seemed out of step with the rest of the country at a time of national unity and governmental expansion.[12]

In such a milieu, fundamentalists decided that the federal government, which they had traditionally viewed as hostile to their interests, might be the key to defending themselves against mainline Protestants. The battle was over broadcasting. Nearly every major fundamentalist leader of the late 1920s and 1930s had a local radio program, and a few were able to purchase airtime on multiple stations, so it was vital to their movement's success to maintain access to the nation's airwaves. Charles Fuller's *Old-Fashioned Revival Hour* was on 456 stations in the early 1940s, reaching an estimated 20 million listeners a week. A host of lesser-known radio evangelists were popular in regional markets. But fundamentalist radio preaching aroused the opposition of the Federal Council of Churches, which considered it religious grandstanding and hate-filled rhetoric. In 1928, this ecumenical organization, which included representatives from Methodist, Presbyterian, Lutheran, and other mainline Protestant denominations, convinced the National Broadcasting Corporation (NBC) to eliminate paid religious shows and instead work with the Federal Council to allocate slots for free public service programming. If fundamentalists could not purchase airtime, they were likely to have to stay off the air. In 1931, CBS followed suit. By the early 1940s, Mutual Broadcasting Corporation remained the only network willing to sell airtime to fundamentalist preachers, and the Federal Council began pressuring them to put an end to paid religious programming.[13] If the Federal Council succeeded, Fuller's program, which was Mutual's most popular show, would have to leave the network. Fundamentalists believed that if they lobbied the Federal Communications Commission (FCC), they might be able to prevent this. To do that, they would need a national lobbying association to counter the influence that the Federal Council already had in Washington.

The conservative Protestants who gathered in St. Louis to create the NAE thought they had lost influence after the 1920s by retreating too quickly from the political sphere. At a time when George Cardinal Mundelein, Rabbi Stephen Wise, and representatives of the Federal Council of Churches were enjoying White House visits, fundamentalists lacked a representative in Washington. As a result, the nation now faced "a tidal wave of drunkenness, immorality, corruption, dishonesty, and utter atheism." The NAE's first president, Harold J. Ockenga, told the assembled ministers in St. Louis, "It is up to us to make sure that the Christian church will return to a new leadership, producing new statesmen for our government circles, influencing education, and rebuilding the foundations of society."[14]

Abandoning the traditional term "fundamentalist" in favor of the more optimistic-sounding "evangelical," the ministers who created the NAE looked forward to a time of ecumenical cooperation across regional and denominational boundaries. Baptist, Presbyterian, Methodist, and Pentecostal ministers were there, as were a few theologically conservative ministers who still remained in liberal mainline denominations, such as the Congregational Church. The organization included a few southerners, but most of its members, including seven of the nine initial board members, were residents of the North. The cities of the Northeast and Midwest—where large Catholic populations and a proliferation of bars and dance halls provided conservative Protestant ministers with clear evidence that they had lost the early rounds of the culture war—provided the ideal recruiting grounds for an organization that promised to reclaim the culture for conservative Protestantism.[15]

One of the NAE's first acts was to create a subsidiary, the National Religious Broadcasters Association, to secure federal protection for evangelical radio preachers' broadcasting rights. It took evangelicals eighteen years to get the FCC to declare that radio and television stations could count paid religious broadcasts as public service time, but it was worth the wait. The FCC's declaration resulted in the gradual demise of the mainline Protestant radio and television broadcasts that the National Council of Churches endorsed, and a sudden surge in the number of paid broadcasts from fundamentalist and evangelical preachers, paving the way for the evangelical media empires of the late twentieth century.[16]

The NAE also launched campaigns to restrict liquor advertising, Sunday commerce, and sexually provocative literature. Evangelicals argued that the Constitution was inherently "benevolent toward religion," rather than religiously neutral, and they engaged in efforts to make that alleged benevolence even more pronounced. In the late 1940s, the organization supported a campaign for a "Christian amendment" to recognize Jesus as Lord in the American Constitution, an idea that Congress had rejected in the late nineteenth century.[17]

Despite their confidence that the federal government could help them achieve their goals, evangelicals also feared that secularists in Washington were trying to erode the nation's religious heritage. In 1945, when Congress debated two bills that would have provided federal aid to education, the

NAE spoke out against the proposal. The "professional educators" who supported federal funding wanted to "centralize control in Washington, capture our educational processes and proceed to educate the rising generations along 'liberal' lines," the NAE warned. "They know that decentralization of authority leaves the schools in the hands of local citizens who still believe in the Constitution and the Holy Scriptures and who know how to deal with subversive propaganda when it rears its head in the classroom."[18]

The issue arose again in 1948, when the Supreme Court ruled in *McCollum v. Board of Education* that the Champaign, Illinois, school district's policy of giving public school students "released time" during the school day to attend religious classes taught by clergy violated the First Amendment's prohibition of the "establishment" of religion. Using arguments that foreshadowed those that they would employ after the school prayer and Bible reading court cases fifteen years later, the NAE said that nonbelievers had the right to exempt their children from religious classes, but that it was unfair for a minority of atheists to prevent religious parents from providing Christian instruction for their children during the school day.[19]

In all of these campaigns, evangelicals were fighting defensive battles against government interests that they perceived as hostile. But another evangelical cause—anticommunism—brought them into closer alliance with the government.

The Christian Campaign against Communism

Conservative Protestants, especially those in northern cities, had always viewed communism as an implacable enemy. The nation's first fundamentalist conference met in 1919, the same year as the Palmer Raids, against the background of fears of communist infiltration. Even in the early 1930s, when most Americans considered the nation's economic downturn a more urgent political crisis than communism, fundamentalists continued to proclaim their anticommunist message. "Atheists, modernists and communists have formed a deadly alliance against God, Christ, the Church, and the Bible," a Minneapolis pastor wrote in 1933. When the Roosevelt administration extended diplomatic recognition to the Soviet Union and then treated the country as an ally in the Second World War, some fundamentalists warned that the United States had compromised with evil. Looking to the Bible for prophetic guidance on current events, they declared that the Soviet Union was the sinful nation of "Gog" that the Hebrew prophet Ezekiel had predicted was doomed for destruction.[20] With Americans worried about other matters, such messages reinforced fundamentalists' sense of political alienation.

Fundamentalists' political fortunes changed as soon as the Cold War began, because they suddenly found that their opposition to communism brought them into closer alliance with the federal government and the prevailing national mood. In the 1940s and 1950s, fundamentalists and evangelicals largely abandoned their prophetic speculation of a coming judgment on the nation, and adopted a new patriotism that manifested itself in "Americanism" conferences and political endorsements. They eagerly followed politicians' attacks on alleged communist subversives, and even launched a few investigations of their own. In the early 1940s, the Church League of America, a politically conservative organization founded by Presbyterian businessmen in Wheaton, Illinois, in 1937 (the same year that the House Committee on Un-American Activities—HUAC—was created), began collecting files on suspected communists in the United States, which it offered to sell to investigators and employers for a nominal fee.[21]

The NAE's influence on the federal government was bolstered by its claim that it had been in the vanguard of the anticommunist movement at a time when few religious organizations considered anticommunism a priority. In 1943, only a year after its formation, the NAE declared that its nemesis, the Federal Council of Churches, was "blind to the menace which the infiltration of Russian Communism presents to our liberties at the present time." In 1950, the NAE accused the United Nations of being soft on communism, and passed a resolution condemning the UN as an organization that could usher in an age of "world socialism and dictatorship." During the 1950s, the NAE advocated governmental "investigations of subversive activities" and the "enactment of legislation protecting the nation and its citizens from the menace of Communism." The NAE's president in the early 1950s, Frederick Fowler, simultaneously served as vice chairman of the All-American Conference to Combat Communism, and warned that there were more than twice as many communists in the United States as there had been in Russia at the time of the Bolshevik Revolution.[22]

The NAE found a receptive audience for its views in Washington partly because some of the nation's representatives and senators shared their faith. A 1951 *Christian Life* survey found that more than one hundred members of the Eighty-second Congress were "born-again Christians." Many of them taught Bible classes and attended weekly prayer groups. Several congressmen began attending private prayer sessions that Abraham Vereide, a Methodist minister from Seattle, organized for government leaders through his International Christian Leadership. In the early 1950s, the vice president of his organization was the conservative Democratic congressman A. Willis Robertson (D-VA), whose son Pat later became one of the principal leaders of the Christian Right. The Republican leader in the Senate, Frank Carlson (R-KS), a devout Baptist, also developed a close relationship with Vereide and assisted him in convening the first annual National Prayer Breakfast in 1953. Representative Walter Judd (R-MN) maintained a close association with evangelical leaders, who shared his view that Christian devotion and Christian mission work could be key weapons in the struggle against communism. Senator Edward Martin (R-PA) may have expressed the sentiment best: "America must move forward with the atomic bomb in one hand and the cross in the other."[23]

Initially, Christian anticommunism was bipartisan. Although some leaders of the NAE began moving toward the GOP at an early date, many evangelicals, especially Southern Baptists, continued to vote for Democrats. In 1948, only 38 percent of evangelical voters supported Republican presidential candidate Thomas Dewey in his contest against President Harry Truman. Not only did the Democratic Party offer social welfare and pro-labor legislation that many working-class evangelicals favored, but it could also plausibly claim to be just as hawkish and anticommunist as the GOP. Martin Dies, the first chair of HUAC, was an aggressively anticommunist Democratic congressman from Texas who outdid most Republicans in denouncing alleged internal communist subversives. Truman promised American support for "free peoples who are resisting attempted subjugation" and created the North Atlantic Treaty Organization to bolster Western Europe's defenses against the threat of Soviet expansion. He doubled the percentage of federal revenues allocated to defense spending, authorized the development of the hydrogen bomb, and sent American troops to the Korean peninsula to prevent the communist North Korean government from taking over the noncommunist South. "Our allies are the millions who hunger and thirst after righteousness," Truman said in his inaugural address, adding that "with God's help," the United States could help assure a world of "justice, harmony, and peace" by opposing the communist threat.[24]

But some conservative Protestants decided that Truman's anticommunist measures were insufficient. When Truman objected to General Douglas MacArthur's attempt to take the Korean War into China, and then relieved the general of his command, many evangelicals were outraged at the president's unwillingness to confront the largest communist country in the world. The NAE passed a resolution that offered a "stinging rebuke of the Truman Administration." The NAE president Frederick Fowler called upon Dean Acheson, whom conservatives from both parties blamed for "losing China" to communists in 1949, to "reverse his mistaken policy and support our friend

Chiang Kai-shek and the Nationalist government of China." For evangelicals, the "loss" of China to atheistic communists was particularly galling because the country had long been a center of American mission work. Some of the leading voices in the evangelical movement had done mission work in China, and they bitterly resented the expulsion of Western Protestants after Mao Zedong's takeover. They also worried about the fate of the Chinese Christians that they had been forced to leave behind.[25] Such concerns made them more sympathetic to the claims of Republican anticommunist politicians such as Richard Nixon and Joseph McCarthy, who blamed the loss of China and the advance of international communism on Democratic subversives in the State Department.

By the early 1950s, the NAE had so closely aligned its anticommunist campaign with the GOP that it was sometimes difficult to distinguish between the statements of evangelical ministers and those of the Republican politicians that they supported. "We have had New Dealism and its neo-socialism which permitted Communists to move into the highest echelons of government," one article in the NAE's newsletter complained in 1953, a line that closely echoed Republican congressman Karl Mundt's earlier denunciation of "New Dealers, Fair Dealers, Misdealers, and Hiss Dealers" who had "shuttled back and forth between Freedom and Red Fascism like a pendulum on a kukoo clock."[26] But it was not only the NAE that sounded like an arm of the Republican Party. In fact, the most politically prominent, anticommunist, evangelical minister of the era was not a leader of the NAE, but was instead a young Baptist evangelist who had already landed several invitations to the White House.

Billy Graham's Christian Americanism

Communism, Billy Graham told the sixty-five hundred people who had come to his "Canvas Cathedral" in Los Angeles one night in 1949, was "a religion that is inspired, directed and motivated by the Devil himself." At a time when Americans were still adjusting to the uncertainties of the Cold War and the atomic age, the thirty-one-year-old evangelist provided his listeners with the assurance that they could gain the victory over communism through faith in Christ because God was on America's side. The message struck a chord. Graham began the Los Angeles crusade as a fundamentalist with a reputation confined only to his own religious circles, but he ended the campaign as an emerging national celebrity—a young, dynamic speaker who could draw crowds by offering the spiritual antidote to communism. Graham continued to preach a staunchly anticommunist message throughout the 1950s and 1960s, and he quickly became the best-known evangelical in America, as well as the leading proponent of a politicized religion that linked the gospel with the purposes of the state.[27]

Graham was raised in a devout Southern Presbyterian family focused on cultivating piety rather than promoting political change. He had grown up attending church and revival meetings, and like most southern conservative Protestants, he was "born again" in a teenage conversion experience. When he felt the call to preach, he enrolled at Bob Jones College, one of the leading fundamentalist schools in the South, at a time when its founder, Bob Jones, Sr., was preaching against becoming too entangled in politics. Graham did not object to Jones's political abstention, but he did chafe under the college's strict rules regulating student conduct, so after a semester at BJC he transferred to the Florida Bible Institute in Tampa, where he exchanged his Southern Presbyterianism for a Southern Baptist faith. From there, he moved to Wheaton College on the outskirts of Chicago, the center of a new evangelical movement.

In Chicago, Graham discovered that northern Protestants were beginning to shed their traditional separatism and adopt a new engagement with the world. His experiences transformed him from a southern fundamentalist into a "new evangelical." When he came to Wheaton, the school was already advertising itself as a center of anticommunism, while the surrounding town had become the headquarters of the politically conservative Church League of America. Graham was at Wheaton when the NAE held its first annual meeting in downtown Chicago, only twenty-five miles away from the campus, and though he probably did not attend that session at which Harold Ockenga gave a speech in favor of Christian participation in politics, he quickly came to share the NAE president's vision of cultural and political engagement with the world. Shortly after his graduation, Graham became one of the leading speakers in a new organization called Youth for Christ, one of the most innovative and successful northern evangelical ministries of the 1940s. Youth for Christ evangelists tried to distance themselves from fundamentalist stereotypes by presenting the gospel message to teenagers through contemporary slang, lively swing music, and flashy dress, all of which suited Graham's style. His youthful visage, combined with his rapid-fire delivery and dynamic presence, helped him draw crowds. He quickly expanded his ministry beyond high school students and began holding large urban revivals in stadiums and open squares.[28]

In 1949, Graham received his lucky break or, as he viewed it, his blessing from God. After William Randolph Hearst, America's leading newspaper magnate, heard about Graham's stirring condemnations of communism at the Los Angeles crusade, he recognized the potential of the young evangelist's message to foster the socially conservative values and staunch anticommunism that the publisher favored. "Puff Graham," he told his reporters, and they did. Graham became a national celebrity overnight. Harold Ockenga noticed the young evangelist's success and arranged for him to hold his second major crusade on the Boston Commons, outside the former NAE president's church. From that point on, Graham became closely identified with the brand of evangelicalism that Ockenga and the NAE were trying to promote, but his fame—and ambition—extended far beyond evangelical circles. He pressed for, and received, an invitation to meet with President Harry Truman at the White House. During the next decade, Graham attracted international press coverage as he preached in the great cities of the world, drawing thousands of respondents wherever he traveled. His "My Answer" column appeared in papers throughout the United States, and his radio program reached far and wide.

Graham's message was simple: he asked people to commit their lives to Christ and become "born again." Revivalists had preached this theme for decades. Yet Graham's interpretation of the traditional evangelical call provided a new twist on old revival themes. He came to call not merely sinners, but an entire nation, to repentance. America, Graham believed, was a chosen nation that had experienced a moral lapse. The nation needed a spiritual revival in order to become a beacon of light and a leader in the fight against communism.

Graham's crusade in Los Angeles came less than two months after a shocked nation had learned of the Soviet Union's possession of the atomic bomb, so when the evangelist warned of the "judgment hand of God over Los Angeles," his audience had little difficulty conjuring up images of their city being vaporized. Graham tapped into these fears. The City of Angels had become a "city of wickedness and sin" not only because of its drunkenness, materialism, and sexual immorality, but also because of the city's communist subversives. "Communists," the evangelist claimed, "are more rampant in Los Angeles than in any other city in America."[29]

Graham infused America's anticommunist struggle with an underpinning of evangelical theology. Fighting communism was a religious duty, and the American government was engaged in the work of the Lord when it opposed the Soviet Union. The "American way of life" was therefore the Christian way of life, and a threat to one was a threat to the other. By turning to God, Americans could avert an imminent Soviet attack. "Soviet Russia may well be the instrument in the hands of God to bring America to her knees in judgment," Graham told an audience in South Carolina in 1950. "God may well do it today unless America repents of her sins of immorality, drunkenness, and rebellion against God."[30]

In listing the sins that would make America vulnerable to a communist attack, Graham placed a special emphasis on threats to the home, especially those involving illicit sex. In each case, Graham condemned such behavior not only as an attack on the family or a violation of God's moral law, but also as an attack on the nation. "Communism works from without; delinquency bores from within," he said. Divorce "could ultimately lead to the destruction of our nation," he stated in another sermon. "The home," he declared, using the words of FBI director J. Edgar Hoover, "is the citadel of American life. If the home is lost, all is lost."[31]

But even as Graham issued such dire warnings, he remained confident that Americans would answer his call to repentance and that God would in turn give the nation ultimate victory over the communists. Many politicians shared this view, so they publicly supported Graham's ministry and passed legislation restricting pornography. A Senate subcommittee on juvenile delinquency held hearings to determine ways to discourage teenage vice and curb the distribution of pornographic books and photographs. For one month in the fall of 1958, the government attempted to prohibit *Playboy* magazine from being sent through the U.S. mail. Such measures bolstered Graham's optimistic assessment of the nation's spiritual health. As he looked out on the tens of thousands of people who came to hear him preach each night of his crusades, he was confident that a spiritual revival was occurring that would ward off the threat of communism. "A lot of people say, 'Do you think communism is going to win the world?'" Graham told a North Carolina audience in 1958. "They might win it temporarily, but it will only be temporarily. Because the Bible says that Jesus Christ is going to establish His kingdom, and the church will some day triumph."[32] Despite their sins, Americans were still people of faith who were ultimately on the Lord's side.

Graham's identification of Christianity with American ideals earned him widespread acclaim. Senators and governors sought out prominent seats at Graham's crusades whenever the evangelist came to their states. In 1958, Graham placed fourth in a national poll to determine "America's most admired man."[33] Mainstream newspapers that had ignored or lampooned fundamentalists a few decades earlier lauded Graham's efforts and portrayed evangelicals as quintessential American patriots. For Americans eager to find a religious justification for their struggle against the "atheistic" Soviet Union, Graham offered an inspiring message.

Graham tried to position himself as a representative of a broad religious and political consensus, and thus attempted to remain (or at least appear) above partisan politicking. In 1954, he declared himself "completely neutral in politics." That may have been his public stance, but unbeknownst to most of his admirers, Graham was intensely political in private, and developed a close relationship with Republican leaders in Washington. Graham was a registered Democrat, as were most Southern Baptists from North Carolina, but during Truman's second term in office, he, like many other Americans, lost patience with the president. In 1951, after he had publicly criticized Truman's handling of the Korean War and complained about the "staggering national debt," he decided that only General Dwight Eisenhower could provide the leadership necessary to reassert the nation's dominance in the Cold War. The evangelist wrote to the general in late 1951, urging him to run for president. "Upon this decision could well rest the destiny of the Western World," Graham told Eisenhower. The general was not persuaded. He insisted that he was going to stay out of politics. Graham held out hope that Eisenhower might change his mind, but he also began signaling that evangelical voters would be open to overtures from the GOP in 1952—if the Republicans agreed to back their views on foreign policy and moral legislation. "The Christian people of America are going to vote as a bloc for the man with the strongest moral and spiritual platform, regardless of his views on other matters," Graham said in October 1951. "I believe we can hold the balance of power."[34]

When Eisenhower finally entered the race, Graham was elated. The popular five-star general projected the image of a strong leader who would stand up against international communism, which would have been enough to endear him to Graham. But when the evangelist learned that Eisenhower's Democratic opponent, Adlai Stevenson, was a divorced Unitarian, he had even more reason to promote Eisenhower's candidacy. He used the Republican campaign slogan, "Clean up the mess in Washington," in a few of his sermons in 1952, and he spoke of the need for a "new foreign policy" issued by a "strong spiritual leader." He also met with Eisenhower on several occasions before and after the election, and developed a lasting friendship with the former general and his stridently anticommunist running mate, Richard Nixon. He viewed Nixon as "most sincere" and a "splendid churchman," while Eisenhower was a "man who believes in prayer."[35]

At a time when American religiosity was at an all-time high, Eisenhower recognized the importance of having a spiritual adviser of Graham's stature.

Although the general had grown up in a devout family—he had been named after the late-nineteenth-century evangelist Dwight L. Moody—he had strayed somewhat from his childhood faith and had not lived a particularly pious life. At the time of his election to the presidency he did not belong to a church. Eisenhower's campaign staff urged him to find a church to attend, but he rebuffed their entreaties, saying that to begin going to church in the middle of a campaign would be hypocritical. Yet as soon as Eisenhower won the election, Graham persuaded the new president to begin attending a Presbyterian church in Washington, a practice that soon became a weekly habit for him. Less than two weeks after the inauguration, Graham baptized the new president in a private White House service.[36]

Realizing the power of religious devotion to unify the nation in the Cold War, Eisenhower stepped eagerly into his new, unofficial role as high priest of America's anticommunist civil religion. The Cold War, he told the press a few days before his inauguration in January 1953, was a "war of light against darkness, freedom against slavery, Godliness against Atheism." As the nation's new leader of the fight against "atheistic" communism, Eisenhower took the unprecedented step of personally leading a prayer at his own inauguration—rather than asking a member of the clergy to do it—and at the suggestion of his Mormon secretary of agriculture, he began every Cabinet meeting by invoking the favor of the Almighty. In 1953, he inaugurated a new tradition by becoming the first president to attend the National Prayer Breakfast. When he met with NAE president Frederick Fowler and other members of the organization at the White House, Eisenhower used the occasion to call for "national reaffirmation of faith in God, the Author of man's freedom, repentance from sin and a new dedication of the task of bringing freedom to the world."[37]

Eisenhower's legislative actions gave credence to his claim that he was, as he told Graham, leading "America in a religious revival." When the pastor of the Presbyterian church that Eisenhower attended suggested that Congress needed to add the words "under God" to the pledge of allegiance in order to differentiate American schoolchildren from "little Muscovites," Eisenhower immediately embraced the idea, and members of Congress from both parties quickly passed a bill in time for Eisenhower to sign it on Flag Day in 1954. "This modification of the pledge is important," Homer Ferguson (R-MI), the bill's sponsor in the Senate, told his colleagues, in language that expressed a widespread view in Washington, "because it highlights one of the real fundamental differences between the free world and the Communist world." Using similar reasoning, Congress passed—and Eisenhower signed—legislation in 1955 requiring the words "In God We Trust" to appear on all of the nation's coinage and printed currency. The following year, they made the phrase a national motto.[38]

At a time of unprecedented cooperation between the federal government and the nation's religious leaders, Graham believed that the Eisenhower administration offered evangelicals a chance to effect a moral and religious revival in the nation through the office of the president. On several occasions Graham discussed with Eisenhower the chief executive's duty to "contribute to a national spiritual awakening." After one such meeting in 1954, Graham could hardly contain his joy. "Millions of Americans thank God for your spiritual leadership," he told Eisenhower. Near the end of Eisenhower's second term in office, Graham compared the president to Lincoln, saying that he would "go down in history as one of our greatest presidents," because he had "put a spiritual emphasis in the White House."[39]

Eisenhower was never a full-fledged evangelical, despite his association with Graham. He believed in religious devotion as a foundation of American freedom, but he conceived of religion in far more ecumenical terms than evangelicals did. As the first American president to participate in a ceremony dedicating a Muslim mosque, and as a proponent of "Judeo-Christian civilization" at Jewish cultural events, Eisenhower had no interest in endorsing evangelicals' belief that Jesus was the only way to salvation. He considered all religions equally valid, as long as they supported American democracy and anticommunism. "Our government makes no sense unless it is founded on a deeply felt religious faith," Eisenhower said on several occasions, "and I don't care what it is." Eisenhower's generic endorsement of faith was hardly a controversial statement, of course. But that did not mean that it was meaningless. Eisenhower, as a Cold War president, spoke about the link between religion and democracy on so many occasions that it seems clear that he viewed himself as a national pastor in a troubled time—a person who, if he did not lead a spiritual revival in the way that Graham expected, at least tried to bolster the nation's spiritual life in order to promote national unity.[40]

Although the president was wary of becoming too closely associated with Graham's particular religious views, he recognized that the evangelist could be politically useful for his reelection campaign. When Graham sent Eisenhower a letter shortly after the 1956 Republican convention, offering to "do all in my power during the coming campaign to gain friends and supporters for your cause," the president forwarded it to the chair of the Republican Party. "It occurs to me that some time during this campaign we might want to call on him for a little help," Eisenhower noted.[41]

Evangelicals gave Eisenhower strong support in 1956, just as they had four years earlier. At least 60 percent of evangelical voters supported

Eisenhower in each campaign. *Christianity Today*, which Billy Graham founded in 1956 and which quickly became the nation's leading evangelical magazine, found that 85 percent of Protestant ministers supported the president's reelection, while only 11 percent intended to vote for Stevenson. A 1960 *Christianity Today* survey showed that of the subscribers who provided their political affiliation, 1,977 were Republicans and 658 were independents, while only 482 were Democrats. Evangelicals—at least those in the North—were feeling very comfortable in the Republican Party.[42]

At times, Graham thought that he should not only campaign for the president, but also play a role in shaping his policies, particularly urging him to take an even more aggressive stance against international communism. "I have been praying a great deal for you in the last few days as you wrestle with the Indo-China problem," Graham wrote to Eisenhower in May 1954, when the president deliberated over America's role in Vietnam. "Whatever your ultimate decision, I shall do my best through radio and television to make my contribution in selling the American public. My private opinion is that Indo-China must be held at any cost."[43]

Eisenhower may not have given much credence to Graham's unsolicited advice on foreign affairs, but members of his administration recognized the value of Graham's services as an international diplomat. Vice President Nixon arranged meetings between Graham and various world leaders. One reporter asked Eisenhower in 1957 if he was spending time with Graham because he wanted to use his services in "mobilizing the religious countries of the world against communism."[44] Eisenhower brushed off the reporter's question, but he could not easily dismiss the idea behind it—that Graham had come to symbolize, in the minds of many Americans, the religious battle against communism.

GRAHAM AND CIVIL RIGHTS

Graham's centrist position on civil rights also positioned him for influence in the Eisenhower administration. Like the president, Graham endorsed a cautious strategy of gradual racial integration that he hoped would result in substantive gains for African Americans without antagonizing southern whites. Beginning in 1953, he insisted that seating at all of his crusades be racially integrated, even in the South. When the Supreme Court ruled in *Brown v. Board of Education* (1954) that "separate but equal" schooling was unconstitutional, Graham lauded the decision and praised African Americans who were involved in the struggle to integrate public schools. "The Bible speaks strongly against race discrimination," he said in October 1956.

He invited Martin Luther King, Jr., to lead a prayer at his New York crusade. When King led the mostly white, evangelical audience of nearly one hundred thousand people in a prayer for "a brotherhood that transcends color," it sent a message to the world that Graham endorsed a change in race relations.[45]

In the midst of the Eisenhower administration's greatest test on civil rights, Graham gave the administration a strong show of support. In September 1957, after Arkansas governor Orval Faubus defied the president by refusing to follow a federal court order to admit African American students to Little Rock's Central High School, Eisenhower became the first president since Reconstruction to send federal troops to the South to enforce the civil rights of African Americans. Graham tried to defuse the tension by appealing to white southerners to comply with federal policy. He was confident that "all thinking southerners" opposed the violent reaction against integration in Little Rock, and he hoped that the violence would soon end. That same month, he sent a letter of encouragement to Dorothy Counts, an African American high school student in his hometown of Charlotte, North Carolina, who had braved the threat of physical danger and harassment by enrolling in a previously all-white high school. "This is your one great chance to prove to Russia that democracy still prevails," Graham wrote.[46]

As his letter indicated, Graham thought of the civil rights movement primarily in terms of the Cold War. Like many politicians in both parties, he was embarrassed by the Soviet Union's exploitation of America's racial problem in its propaganda, and thought that the promotion of civil rights would improve the nation's image abroad. He genuinely desired advances for African Americans, but because his view of civil rights was so closely linked to his perception of the government's interests, he could not countenance King's strategy of civil disobedience. "We have the responsibility to obey law no matter what the law may be," Graham said in 1960.[47]

Despite his support for civil rights legislation, Graham worried that the Supreme Court could provoke a white backlash in the South if it pressed too forcefully on integration. He thought that gradual, rather than immediate, desegregation provided the best hope for a "sensible program for better race relations." "If the Supreme Court will go slowly and the extremists on both sides will quiet down, we can have a peaceful social readjustment over the next ten-year period," he told President Eisenhower in 1956.[48] He was worried that his endorsement of civil rights might lead him into too close an association with "socialists," as other southerners and fundamentalists labeled the liberal politicians who favored civil rights for African Americans. Even though Graham prayed with King, he never marched with him, and he continued to insist that individual conversions, rather than political activism, offered the best hope of improving American race relations.

Eisenhower recognized that Graham had earned the respect of many Protestants across the political spectrum and was thus ideally situated to defuse racial turmoil in the South. In March 1956, as the president prepared for his reelection campaign, he urged Graham to meet privately with religious leaders to persuade them to temper the pulpit rhetoric on both sides of the school segregation issue. Graham happily complied with this request. "I had several private meetings with outstanding religious leaders of both races, encouraging them to take a stronger stand in calling for desegregation and yet demonstrating charity and, above all, patience," Graham reported to Eisenhower in June 1956. "I met with excellent and overwhelming response."[49]

Although Graham was willing to talk with Christian pastors about civil rights, he cautioned the president against saying or doing much on the issue until after the elections, because he worried that any forceful action would have dire consequences for fledgling southern Republican parties. "I am somewhat disturbed by rumors that Republican strategy will be to go all out in winning the Negro vote in the North regardless of the South's feelings," Graham told Eisenhower. "Again I would like to caution you about getting involved in this particular problem. At the moment, to an amazing degree, you have the confidence of white and Negro leaders. I would hate to see it jeopardized."[50]

Graham had reason to worry. Although the leadership of the South's two major regional denominations, the Presbyterian Church (US) and the Southern Baptist Convention, endorsed the Supreme Court's ruling in *Brown v. Board*, several influential pastors in those denominations dissented. Graham's father-in-law, L. Nelson Bell, a North Carolina pastor, responded to the *Brown* decision with an article titled "Christian Race Relations Must Be Natural, Not Forced," a phrase that summarized the sentiments of most racial conservatives. W. A. Criswell, the pastor of the twelve-thousand-member First Baptist Church in Dallas, where Graham had placed his membership, likewise opposed the Supreme Court's decision in spite of his own denomination's endorsement of the ruling.[51]

But Graham distanced himself from the views of southern conservative pastors and instead allied with northern evangelicals. Although some leaders in the NAE dissented, the organization as a whole endorsed civil rights, at least in the abstract. In 1951, the NAE adopted a resolution advocating "equal opportunities" for all races in housing, education, wages, and commerce—and singling out "the American negro," in particular, as deserving of these rights. *Christianity Today* endorsed civil rights, but also published pieces suggesting that Christians did not have an obligation to support racial integration. Most northern evangelicals favored gradual integration as long as it was not socially disruptive, a stance that accorded well with the Eisenhower administration's position.[52] As if to signify that he did not intend for his view on civil rights to challenge the Eisenhower administration, Graham arranged for Vice President Nixon to speak at his New York crusade only two days after Martin Luther King prayed at the event.

As the vice president looked out on the crowd of one hundred thousand people who had filled every seat in Yankee Stadium and spilled out into the outfield, he marveled at the preacher's ability to draw such a crowd—the largest in the stadium's history. Nixon agreed with Graham that something greater than mere talent had drawn these people together and that not only this crusade but the success of the nation itself was dependent on Americans' "deep and abiding faith in God." "We as a people," Nixon told the crowd, "can be only as great as the faith we have in God."[53]

Nixon's appearance at Graham's crusade was a sign that evangelicals had succeeded in making their personal faith a political religion for the nation. Only two decades before, conservative Protestants had been politically isolated, waiting for divine deliverance from a morally corrupt nation that they believed they had little ability to influence. But now, thanks to the Cold War, they had become full participants in the political system, linking their gospel preaching to the aims of the state and finding a welcome reception in the White House. Their moderate position on civil rights facilitated their alliance with the Eisenhower administration, but above all, their opposition to communism made it possible for them to view the president as a spiritual leader. Never before had conservative Protestants become so closely allied with a presidential administration. The formation of the New Christian Right was still two decades away, but by the end of the 1950s, evangelicals had already begun to think of the United States as a Christian nation and the Republican White House as an ally in a righteous cause.

B ILLY GRAHAM DID NOT REPRESENT every conservative Protestant. A year after Graham invited Martin Luther King, Jr., to pray at his crusade and publicly supported school integration, Jerry Falwell, the twenty-five-year-old pastor of a newly formed, rapidly growing fundamentalist Baptist church in Lynchburg, Virginia, preached his own sermon on race. Falwell assured segregationists that God and the nation were on their side. "The true negro does not want integration," Falwell told his nine-hundred-member congregation. "He realizes his potential is far better among his own race. Who then is propagating this terrible thing? . . . We see the hand of Moscow in the background." Racial integration was the product of the "Devil himself."[1]

The contrast between Graham and Falwell's messages signaled a fault line in conservative Protestantism that would divide mainstream evangelicals from self-identified fundamentalists for the next generation. In the early 1950s, conservative Protestants had been united in their promotion of an anticommunist civil religion, and even the most conservative members of the National Association of Evangelicals (NAE), including southerners such as Bob Jones, Jr., and John R. Rice, had endorsed Graham's message and supported mainstream Republican politicians such as Dwight Eisenhower. But in the late 1950s, Jones and Rice publicly broke with Graham, because he accepted support from liberal clerics who did not accept the inerrancy of the Bible. By 1965, the acrimony between the two groups had become so pronounced that Jones accused Graham of "disobeying the word of God" by "building the Church of the Antichrist and aiding and abetting apostasy." This theological disagreement extended to nomenclature: while evangelicals associated with Graham abandoned the use of the term "fundamentalist" because of its pejorative connotations, Jones, Rice, Falwell, and others of their doctrinal persuasion embraced it.[2]

Fundamentalists viewed themselves as defenders of the "old-time" gospel who resisted the political and religious compromises of evangelicals, but in reality, they appropriated aspects of the modern world as readily as evangelicals did. Most of the fundamentalist leaders of the late 1950s had earned college degrees and were rapidly advancing in socioeconomic status. Most had traveled widely, and some had spent time in northern cities during their youth. After returning to the South, they built colleges, launched national radio ministries, and became experts in large-scale fund-raising and political organizing. They were keenly interested in politics. In contrast to their parents' generation, they identified the gospel with American patriotism, and the anticommunism they preached was closely tied to partisan politics.

Despite their increasing prominence, fundamentalists, in contrast to evangelicals, viewed themselves as an embattled minority, estranged from a government that they feared was filled with communist sympathizers. In the early 1950s, they viewed most politicians as "soft" on communism. In 1954, their suspicions were further confirmed when the Supreme Court mandated school integration. In a quest to reclaim their nation, fundamentalist leaders in the South cultivated alliances with staunchly conservative, segregationist politicians, and used their radio broadcasts to denounce the United Nations, civil rights, and, above all, communism. While Graham used anticommunism to forge an alliance with a moderate Republican presidential administration, the emerging fundamentalist right employed the same issue to create a regional political movement that was often at odds with the Eisenhower administration over civil rights and foreign policy.

The Partisan Politics of John R. Rice

One of the earliest southern fundamentalists to embrace a conservative political program was Texas-born *Sword of the Lord* editor John R. Rice. Rice had gotten his start as a Baptist preacher under the mentorship of J. Frank Norris, one of the most politically active fundamentalists of the early twentieth century. During the 1920s, when Rice was a young Baylor University graduate who had just taken his first pulpit assignment in Dallas, he watched Norris take on the state's liquor interests, racetrack gambling, the teaching of evolution in public schools, and Catholic politicians. Norris testified before the state legislature on behalf of his favorite political causes, and he used his pulpit and the pages of his weekly paper to campaign against Texas governor James Ferguson, whom he called a "bootlegger" allied with "Rum, Romanism, and Russianism." In 1928, Norris became so worked up over Al Smith's presidential bid that he embarked on a two-month campaign across the South to defeat the Catholic presidential candidate. The church, he said, needed "political preachers."[3]

Rice followed this advice even after he broke off contact with Norris in the 1930s. But his political views were more consistently conservative than Norris's were. While Norris had occasionally championed economic progressivism and had never entirely abandoned the Democratic Party, Rice developed an aversion to the New Deal in his youth and became a lifelong Republican. He launched the *Sword of the Lord* magazine in 1934 and did not hesitate to use it for political purposes. Even though half of his congregants were receiving public relief through programs that the Roosevelt administration had created, Rice urged his readers to vote against the Democrats in the 1934 midterm elections, because they were responsible for repealing Prohibition. Indeed, he soon focused his ire on New Deal social welfare spending, which he considered an ominous extension of federal power and a step on the road to communism. Like other premillennial dispensationalists, he associated centralized governmental control with the Antichrist, a view that at the time was more common among northern, rather than southern, fundamentalists. In a move that brought him closer to other conservative Protestants who shared his opinions, Rice left Dallas in 1940 and moved to Wheaton, Illinois, the home of a conservative Christian college where Billy Graham was then a student and the headquarters for the staunchly anticommunist Church League of America.[4]

At first, Rice welcomed the new evangelical movement that was developing. He supported the NAE in its early years, and he had a close relationship with Billy Graham in the late 1940s and early 1950s. But by the mid-1950s, he decided that the northern evangelical movement had become far too theologically inclusive, and he broke fellowship with Graham. Ironically, Rice, who had left the South after breaking with regional tradition by denouncing the New Deal and the Democratic Party, discovered that southerners were more receptive than northern evangelicals to his religious and political messages. In the early 1960s, he left Wheaton and moved *Sword of the Lord* to Murfreesboro, Tennessee. For the next two decades, *Sword of the Lord*, with a circulation of 150,000, was the leading periodical among southern fundamentalists, influencing a generation of conservative pastors with scriptural exegesis, moral advice, sermon reprints, and—especially in election season—political commentary.[5]

By mixing politics with scripture, Rice introduced southern fundamentalists to the idea that the GOP was the party of Christian anticommunism. "The New Deal put America in the greatest danger it has ever been in," Rice wrote in September 1948. "Roosevelt's leadership sold out to Russia so far that now it seems nearly impossible to keep Russia contained, that is, to keep Russia from taking over the rest of the world without war. . . . We must, by all means, put an end to the New Deal. And the only chance to do that is through the Republican party."[6]

Most southerners ignored Rice's plea to support a New York Republican governor over Truman, a folksy, Southern Baptist incumbent with strong working-class appeal. And while some may have been willing to follow his lead in voting for General Dwight Eisenhower in 1952, most fundamentalists, especially those of an older generation, were reluctant to accept Rice's wholesale denunciation of Democratic Party policy as "wicked, un-Christian and un-American." Yet Rice's editorials had an effect on a younger generation of southern fundamentalists who were ready to break with their parents' brand of politics. Jerry Falwell was one such pastor who became one of Rice's friends and a *Sword of the Lord* contributor. Another was Bob Jones, Jr.[7]

The "Christian Americanism" of Bob Jones, Jr.

Rice found a kindred spirit in Jones, the son of the Alabama evangelist who had founded one of the South's best-known fundamentalist colleges. Like Rice, Jones had grown up in the South, and both had spent a few years living in Chicago. Jones, too, had initially supported both Billy Graham and the NAE before becoming disillusioned with northern evangelicalism in the 1950s.

While Rice had learned his preaching skills from a politically minded pastor, Jones came from a family that was somewhat more cautious about political involvement. His father had supported William Jennings Bryan in his youth and had joined the anti-Catholic campaign against Al Smith in 1928. But after the failure of Prohibition, he had given up hope of reforming the nation through politics. The son, in contrast, emerged from the Second World War with an optimistic view of the nation's future. Unlike his father, who had received all of his schooling in Alabama, the younger Jones pursued graduate education at the University of Pittsburgh and Northwestern University, and he emerged from the experience with a worldly sophistication. In contrast to most fundamentalists, who denounced the theater and movies, Jones became an amateur Shakespearean actor and started a film company called "World's Most Unusual Films" in order to make movies that met conservative moral strictures. His views on politics reflected his desire to meld conservative theological beliefs with a new engagement with the world.[8]

In the early 1950s, as president of his father's college, Jones became an ardent crusader against communism and political liberalism. He supported the NAE, serving for a year as its vice president. He resigned from the organization shortly after that because of the group's willingness to accept members from churches he thought insufficiently fundamentalist, but his falling-out with the NAE did nothing to dissuade him from adopting the conservative political philosophy that many northern evangelicals were beginning to endorse.[9]

Jones's first foray into political activism came in December 1950, when his university hosted a week-long convention featuring speeches by dozens of foreign diplomats "from all parts of the non-Communist world." To cap off the extravaganza, he gave a keynote speech lambasting the federal government's unwillingness to take a firm stand against international communism. "Those who shape the policies of our State Department, either in inexcusable stupidity or vicious betrayal, tossed the forces of democracy in China to the raving wolves of the Kremlin," Jones told his students. "The blood of American youth smokes on the snows of Korea as a result." The solution, he thought, was a forceful military policy that brooked no compromise with communist nations.[10]

Jones's sympathies were with the conservative wing of the Republican Party, but that did not preclude him and his allies from supporting the more centrist policies of Dwight Eisenhower. In 1952, when the university conducted a straw poll of its three thousand students to find out which presidential candidate they supported, 80 percent favored Eisenhower over Adlai Stevenson. Even among the 216 students who came from South Carolina, a state that Stevenson carried in the general election, Eisenhower received 79 percent support.[11]

But during the next decade, Jones and the university gave increasing support to a more reactionary form of conservatism. Although the 1950 conference had included a speech by South Carolina governor Strom Thurmond on "states' rights," most of the speeches made no reference to debates over domestic policy. In contrast, the 1951 edition focused on the theme of "Americanism" (a code word for rightist politics at the time) and included speeches such as "Santa Claus, M.D.," an indictment of Truman's proposal for federally funded national health insurance. In the early 1960s, the university strengthened its alliance with Thurmond and began inviting Representative L. Mendel Rivers (D-SC), an ultraconservative segregationist who advocated withdrawing the United States from the United Nations, to speak at its conferences.[12] By that point, Jones's early flirtation with northern evangelicalism and centrist Republicanism was all but forgotten, and his university's name had become almost synonymous with right-wing politics.

Carl McIntire's Campaign against Communism

While Jones was forging ties between his college and the conservative movement, right-wing radio preachers were reaching a broader fundamentalist audience with a similar anticommunist message. Carl McIntire's educational background made his choice of a career as a fundamentalist radio preacher a surprising one. Born in Michigan to Presbyterian parents in 1906 and then raised in Oklahoma, McIntire received the training that one might have expected for an intelligent, middle-class young man of his generation who had his eyes set on a Presbyterian pulpit. He enrolled in the nation's most prestigious Presbyterian school of higher learning, Princeton Theological Seminary. But McIntire found Princeton too liberal, and he soon transferred to fundamentalist Westminster Theological Seminary in Philadelphia. There he joined other young fundamentalists, such as Harold Ockenga, who were looking for a place to engage in intellectually rigorous theological discussion without compromising their faith. McIntire might have seemed headed toward a promising career as a northern evangelical preacher, just as Ockenga was, but he quickly became more fundamentalist than any of his colleagues. As the northern evangelical movement coalesced around Ockenga, McIntire renounced it over doctrinal disputes about end-times theology and other matters. He formed his own fundamentalist denomination, the Bible Presbyterian Church, centered around his fifteen-hundred-member congregation in Collingswood, New Jersey, and in 1941 he created his own association of fundamentalist churches—the American Council of Christian Churches (ACCC)—which served as a much smaller rival to the more inclusive NAE.[13]

McIntire was a capable writer, and in the mid-1930s he began publishing a nationally circulated fundamentalist periodical, the *Christian Beacon*. In its first few years, McIntire's paper largely avoided the political subjects that were later to become the central focus of his career; instead, he focused on theological disputes. But as his war of words against theologically liberal Protestants escalated, he seized upon the issue of communism as a way to discredit the mainline Protestant Federal Council of Churches (which in 1950 became the National Council of Churches). In 1945, he published *The Rise of the Tyrant: Controlled Economy versus Private Enterprise*. God had sanctioned capitalism, McIntire said, so when the Federal Council supported the welfare state, it was not only advocating "near-Communism" but was also endorsing a deviation from the divine order. McIntire disavowed any interest in "partisan politics," but his book gave clear evidence of his political sympathies. The ACCC began echoing the policy positions of the conservative wing of the Republican Party. In 1949, the organization denounced Truman's health-care plan as "socialized medicine" and called for an investigation of the State Department to determine whether treason had contributed to America's failure to prevent China from becoming communist.[14]

While Billy Graham and the NAE cultivated a close relationship with the Eisenhower administration, McIntire, who denounced Eisenhower for welcoming liberal Protestants to the White House, chose instead to work with the House Committee on Un-American Activities (HUAC). The HUAC's investigations of suspected communists offered a unique opportunity to strike back at the allegedly socialistic National Council of Churches (NCC). McIntire traveled to Washington and testified before Congress that several prominent liberal Protestant leaders had communist sympathies, and he became a close associate of J. B. Matthews, a McCarthy staffer who shared his suspicion of the mainline Protestant clergy. McIntire enlisted Matthews to do most of the research for the *Christian Beacon* tract *How Red Is the National Council of Churches?*[15]

McIntire brought an anticommunist, right-wing consciousness to southern fundamentalists who had not formerly shared the political views of northern evangelicals. In the 1930s, most southern ministers had supported the New Deal even though many northern fundamentalists had opposed it. In the early 1950s, the South had given less support to Senator McCarthy than any other region of the country had. Many southern ministers were reluctant to preach about communist subversion from the pulpit. But McIntire convinced many southern fundamentalists of the gravity of the internal communist danger and the necessity of supporting right-wing anticommunist politicians. Two years after his appearance before Congress, McIntire launched a national radio ministry that had particular appeal in the South, a region that accounted for 45 percent of the five hundred stations that carried his broadcasts. Although McIntire was a Presbyterian, the pages of his *Christian Beacon* were filled with letters from admiring Southern Baptists who expressed alarm that the internal communist threat was far more ominous than they had thought. In 1953, Bob Jones University awarded him an honorary doctorate.[16] McIntire's campaign against communism went far beyond his own denomination or ministry, and his work helped to transform fundamentalists into purveyors of a uniform anticommunist creed.

Billy James Hargis's Christian Crusade

The other leading anticommunist radio preacher in the South, Billy James Hargis, had grown up in a poor family in a small town in northern Texas, where he and his parents had attended congregations affiliated with the conservative wing of the Disciples of Christ (Christian Church). Hargis looked and talked like the son of a truck driver that he was. In later years, journalists commented on his large frame and his ongoing battle with obesity, and they noted the lack of sophistication in his sermons and pamphlets. But while he did not live up to the urbane standards of a middle-class minister, Hargis never doubted that he was called to preach to a national audience. In his late teens, he enrolled in a small denominational college in Bentonville, Arkansas, but dropped out after a year and a half. Nevertheless, he received his ministerial ordination in 1943, when he was only eighteen years old, and became pastor of a Christian church in Tulsa.[17]

Hargis's interest in politics was awakened in 1948, when a traveling evangelist gave him some anticommunist tracts. Hargis was shocked by what he read. At the age of twenty-three, he began speaking out against the communist threat. Initially, he was primarily concerned about the presence of communist sympathizers in the Protestant clergy; like McIntire, he believed that the World Council of Churches was "soft on communism." But he soon began to fear that communism's potential for evil extended far beyond religious circles. Communism, he said, was Satan's tool to destroy America. His sermons became fifty-minute monologues against Marxism, with ten minutes of fundamentalist doctrine thrown in for good measure. Hargis came across as earnest and dynamic, even if his ungrammatical speech betrayed his lack of education. When his own denomination shunned his message, Hargis bought a tent and began preaching to the crowds who wanted to hear about the dangers of communism. In 1949, he launched his own radio show.[18]

Two promoters, Carl McIntire and the advertising expert L. E. White, recognized Hargis's abilities and decided to use their influence to support his ministry. White had used his publicity skills to launch the career of another young Tulsa tent preacher, Oral Roberts, and he did the same for Hargis. When McIntire heard about Hargis's interest in anticommunism, he recognized the Oklahoma evangelist as a kindred soul, and recruited him to head a project that promised to send thousands of balloons carrying Bibles across the Iron Curtain to the communist countries of Eastern Europe.[19]

The project never quite achieved the results that McIntire had envisioned, but the effort earned Hargis a moment in the national spotlight. Never one to shy away from publicity, Hargis promptly announced that he would tour the world to become acquainted with communism on a firsthand basis. He traveled to Taiwan and met with Madame Chiang Kai-shek in 1957, then returned to the United States to enlarge his anticommunist ministry through his newly formed Christian Crusade organization. He began broadcasting on several hundred radio stations; by the time he reached the peak of his influence, in the late 1960s, he reached 500 radio and 250 television stations, most of them in the South and Midwest. He was also mailing out 250,000 copies of his books and pamphlets each month, and his monthly magazine had 130,000 subscribers.[20]

Hargis's working-class and rural audiences provided him with a steady flow of small contributions, averaging only four dollars per person. The notes that arrived with these donations told stories of penny-pinching Southern Baptist and Christian Church members, many of whom were elderly widows and pensioners who scraped together funds to support his ministry. Although Hargis's followers were not wealthy, they were numerous. By 1961, he could plausibly claim to have the "the largest and most active organization in America devoted solely to combating Socialism and Communism."[21]

Hargis preached a brand of anticommunism that directly echoed Joseph McCarthy's, so it was not surprising that he supported the Wisconsin senator. A few months after McCarthy shocked the nation by announcing that he had a list of 205 known communists in the federal government—a number that kept changing over the next few weeks—Hargis lauded the senator for his "courage and patriotism." For Hargis, McCarthy offered salvation from the New Deal liberals who had been blind to the dangers of communism. Communists in the State Department, he said, were betraying America's interests abroad, and "fellow travelers" in the news media were supporting their treachery. United Auto Workers president Walter Reuther wanted to "convert the entire nation into a 'Soviet America.'" The *New York Times*, *Life*, and columnist Walter Lippman "glorified Communist claims and objectives, and have fought bitterly against the efforts of conservative, patriotic Christian Americans to take steps to counteract Communist aims." Even William Randolph Hearst, Jr., whom few Americans would have considered a leftist, had "filled his papers with nonsense about Russia."[22]

Like Bob Jones—as well as evangelicals such as Billy Graham—Hargis linked his political views to a version of Christian nationalism that presented a politically conservative interpretation of America's religious heritage. "America is a Christian country," Hargis wrote in 1960. "The men and women who braved an uncharted wilderness to carve out this Republic, were rich in faith. With a Bible under one arm, and a musket under the other, they were willing to fight for their faith and their freedom."[23] Hargis's proposal to save the United States from communism closely paralleled this myth. If Americans were going to maintain their freedom, he said, they must embrace fundamentalist Christianity and oppose arms negotiations with the Soviet Union.

Hargis's views appealed to some southern fundamentalists, but many others repudiated him, viewing his political efforts as incompatible with his calling as a gospel preacher. The only denomination that regularly opened its doors to Hargis during his early preaching years was the Baptist Bible Fellowship (BBF), a small association of independent Baptist churches to which Jerry Falwell belonged. Although Rice, Jones, and McIntire had embraced partisan politics, many conservative Protestants in the South still believed that overt politicking on the part of a minister was inappropriate. Mindful of this criticism, Hargis claimed that communism was a moral, rather than a political, issue. "Communism is simply Atheism," he wrote in 1950. "I fight Communism . . . because it is part of my ordination vows, part of my creed," he told an interviewer. He had no party affiliation, and until 1960, he said almost nothing about domestic elections or partisan issues. He claimed that he had no interest in running for office. But most conservative Protestants were not convinced of Hargis's protestations, and many churches, including those of his own denomination, refused to invite him to speak. By the 1960s, many Southern Baptist leaders were trying to move their church in a more socially progressive direction, shedding the racist, reactionary image that had plagued them. They had no use for politically polarizing radio broadcasters such as Hargis. Northern evangelicals likewise had little respect for a preacher they viewed as a paranoid extremist.[24]

Nor was there any reason for politicians to pay attention to the anticommunist movement that McIntire and Hargis represented, because neither preacher had legislative influence in Washington or among voters. Hargis, like McIntire, was a premillennialist, and he occasionally hinted in his writings that he expected Jesus to return to earth at any moment. As a result, his approach to communism was often fatalistic. Some fundamentalists declared that communism would continue to claim adherents until Christ annihilated it at the battle of Armageddon, but Hargis did not go quite that far. Instead, he said that the Lord could defeat communism at any time, but that he would do so only for a righteous people. Thus, the best way to end the threat of communism was to do what fundamentalists had always proposed: live godly, upright lives, and encourage others to do the same. Such fatalist thinking did not lend itself to an organized program for political change.[25]

Hargis's only policy proposals in the late 1950s and early 1960s were that Congress should outlaw the American Communist Party and that the United

States should withdraw from the United Nations. "The United Nations, which severely threatens the sovereignty of our nation, was conceived in subterfuge and was clearly the result of careful Kremlin planning," he said.[26] The only recourse for the United States was to abandon the organization in order to protect its own interests. While most politicians viewed such advice as bizarre, it reflected Hargis's theological tradition of separation from evil. Fundamentalists came from a theological tradition of separation from religious "apostasy"; in the 1920s and 1930s, they had left mainline Protestant denominations in order to separate themselves from religious liberals, and in the 1950s and 1960s, they continued to abstain from "worldly" activities, such as drinking, dancing, and movies, and refused to cooperate with theological modernists. It thus came as no surprise that they asked the U.S. government to take similar measures by separating itself from communists.

Jerry Falwell and the Fundamentalist Churches of the 1950s

In addition to the national radio evangelists, there were many local pastors throughout the South who infused their Sunday sermons with anticommunist exhortations and found a way to blend religion and politics in their communities. One of the most important was Jerry Falwell.

Falwell was born in 1933 in Lynchburg, Virginia, a small town that had never recovered from an economic downturn following the Civil War. His alcoholic father, a small-town businessman who was wracked by lifelong guilt for killing his own brother in self-defense, died of cirrhosis of the liver while Falwell was still in his teens. His pious mother, by contrast, tried to inculcate a sense of religion in her children by dutifully bringing them to Sunday school at a local Baptist church and requiring them to listen to Charles Fuller's *Old-Fashioned Revival Hour* every Sunday morning. Falwell initially resisted the influence of both of his parents, and instead set his sights on leaving Lynchburg. In a thriving, postwar American economy with a rapidly growing military-industrial complex, this was a realistic goal for an intelligent young man like Falwell, who dreamed of becoming an engineer. As the captain of his high school football team, class valedictorian, and the top student in his math classes, he hoped to secure a scholarship to study at Virginia Tech as soon as he completed his preliminary coursework at a local junior college. But instead, during his sophomore year, he "got saved" at a fundamentalist Baptist church, and immediately felt a divine call to the ministry. He completed his education at the Baptist Bible College in Springfield, Missouri, an institution associated with the strongly anticommunist Baptist Bible Fellowship.[27]

When Falwell returned to Lynchburg in 1956 and launched a new fundamentalist Baptist church, he discovered that the town had become an industrialized center far different from the community in which he had grown up. The year before Falwell started his church, two industrial giants—Babcock & Wilcox and General Electric—built new plants in Lynchburg, bringing thousands of new jobs to the community. Other corporations followed, and by 1980, Lynchburg had two hundred factories, making it a thriving contributor to the country's military-industrial complex. Its residents became wholehearted supporters of the nation's Cold War capitalist economy. The northern-born managers who came to Lynchburg to supervise some of the new factories revitalized the local Republican Party. The blue-collar workers who arrived from rural regions in Tennessee, Virginia, and the surrounding area were much more likely to be Democrats, but they shared their managers' strong opposition to communism and belief in the possibility of upward mobility.[28]

Falwell recognized the potential for evangelistic outreach among his town's Appalachian transplants. He launched a weekly radio program within one month of his church's first service, and a few months later, he added a television program in an era in which local TV preaching was still a novelty. His media presence, combined with many hours of door-to-door evangelism, allowed him to reach the unchurched citizens of Lynchburg. By the end of Falwell's first year as pastor of Thomas Road Baptist Church, his congregation's size had increased from 35 to 864, and the twenty-four-year-old pastor was preaching four sermons every Sunday.[29]

Falwell considered the growth of his church a "miracle," but it reflected a national trend in which young, dynamic pastors could create colossal church empires in metropolitan areas by reaching out to recent southern migrants who had come to the city in search of industrial jobs. During the 1950s, the percentage of southerners living in urban areas increased from 44 to 58 percent, largely because of the construction of new military-industrial plants in southern cities. Many of the workers who came to the city from rural areas wanted to belong to a congregation, and they were searching for one that shared their conservative theology. Young, upwardly mobile blue-collar workers were often attracted to churches that combined fundamentalist or Pentecostal preaching with television ministries and social programs. During the decade in which Falwell launched his radio and TV programs, Rex Humbard built the Cathedral of Tomorrow and launched a national television show from Akron, Ohio; Robert Schuller began attracting thousands of people to his new drive-in church in Los Angeles; and Oral Roberts became a nationally known television preacher by telling audiences in Tulsa and elsewhere that they should "expect a miracle."[30]

All of these preachers presented a version of the gospel that appealed to Americans in an era of consumerism. Falwell avoided the miraculous claims of the Pentecostal and charismatic TV preachers, and his message was more fundamentalist than Schuller's, but his television preaching reflected the preferences of his target audience in the same way that other televangelists' sermons did. Televised worship services required carefully choreographed musical programs, precisely timed sermons, and an upbeat worship style that appealed to the public. In 1958, two years after his initial television broadcast, Falwell's church hired its first music minister. In 1960, shortly after his program added a second station in Roanoke, the church launched a gospel quartet to perform on the air. Falwell's preaching style likewise reflected the needs of television. Instead of shouting at his audience, as many fundamentalist preachers had done in the past, Falwell spoke in calm, reassuring tones, delivering messages filled with personal anecdotes and promises of comfort. His sermons emphasized the personal happiness and improved life that a person could gain from becoming a Christian and accepting God's love.[31]

Unlike many fundamentalists of the previous generation, Falwell viewed the church as a purveyor of social services that could bring poor whites into the middle class. In 1959, he launched a home for alcoholics, and four years later, he constructed a youth camp for two thousand children. By the end of the 1960s, his church had a ministry to bring over one thousand poor children from Lynchburg and distant rural areas to Bible classes, an outreach program to help drug addicts, a day school for parents who wanted a Christian-centered education for their children, and a Sunday school program that was the ninth largest in the United States. Falwell preached that capitalism was a divinely ordained system and that hard work was the key to success, and he exemplified those virtues by logging nineteen-hour workdays to turn his church into an ecclesiastical business empire.[32]

Falwell's church offered an alternative to secular society, but it was never quite as disengaged from the world as Falwell liked to think. Falwell preached the imminent return of Jesus, an event that he expected to occur within his lifetime, but he said that first the gospel would have to be preached to every person in creation in order to prepare the world for Christ. In his evangelism, he took full advantage of all of the modern resources at his disposal, including television preaching, corporate advertising techniques, the latest theories of business management for his ministerial organizations, and fund-raising contests that at times had more in common with game shows than with traditional tithing. His evangelistic emphasis also pulled him into politics, because in his view, communism was an impediment to global evangelism and a satanic conspiracy that had to be stopped.[33]

When the civil rights movement reached his home state of Virginia, he charged it with being communist-inspired. Although many postwar liberals viewed civil rights legislation as a way to prevent the spread of communism, southern fundamentalists such as Falwell considered it a communist plot. If civil rights activists were influenced by Marxist ideology, their cause was anti-Christian, regardless of whether they organized in churches or wore clerical collars. Similarly, if civil rights activism caused the nation international embarrassment, it aided the Soviet cause and was therefore contrary to God's will. "The communistic forces are laughing up their sleeves," Falwell said in 1958, in a sermon against school integration. "Russia has made our racial problems her top ammunition in her propaganda scheme of proving the fallacies of capitalism to the world. . . . If Chief Justice Warren and his associates had known God's Word and had desired to do the Lord's will, I am quite confident that the 1954 decision would never have been made."[34]

Falwell's defense of segregation alienated him from his state's political moderates and branded him as a conservative advocate of "Massive Resistance" to *Brown v. Board*. Only a few weeks before his sermon, the governor of Virginia had required three counties to close their schools rather than admit African American students. For a while, it seemed that Virginia might be able to resist court-ordered school integration, especially after proponents of Massive Resistance, with the support of Senator Harry F. Byrd, Sr. (D-VA), organized the Defenders of State Sovereignty and Individual Liberties to maintain segregation. But in January 1959, Governor Lindsay Almond, Jr., retreated from his original support for Massive Resistance and agreed to comply with court-ordered school integration. There was little that the Defenders could do to stop him, and public support for the organization began to wane. In Lynchburg, more than five hundred citizens, including the manager of the General Electric plant and many of the city's business leaders, who were worried that closing public schools would hurt the economy, organized a local chapter of the Virginia Committee for Public Schools to resist the Massive Resisters and keep the public schools open. Falwell fought them. When the Defenders opened a Lynchburg chapter, Falwell was its first chaplain. A week later, at the Robert E. Lee School auditorium, Falwell led a prayer after a South Norfolk school superintendent gave a speech encouraging opposition to school integration in the name of states' rights.[35]

All this increased Falwell's political influence among his region's fundamentalists, but only at the cost of national marginalization. His defense of segregation defied the Eisenhower administration, the national Democratic and Republican parties, and his own city's business leaders. Although southern fundamentalists were advancing in socioeconomic status and becoming more politically active, they were unable to create a nationally influential political movement, primarily because their defense of segregation ran counter to the nation's increasing acceptance of civil rights and left them regionally isolated.

The Division between Fundamentalists and Evangelicals on Civil Rights

Southern fundamentalists' stance on segregation also separated them from most evangelicals. While Graham and his northern evangelical supporters took a moderate stance on civil rights, and while Southern Baptists practiced a cautious silence on the issue, southern fundamentalists broke with many of their fellow Christians by openly defending segregation. In Little Rock, Arkansas, for instance, the only pastors who openly endorsed Orval Faubus's defiance of federal authority in order to uphold school segregation were fundamentalist, independent Baptist ministers who operated outside the Southern Baptist Convention. Billy James Hargis likewise championed racial segregation, and in 1960 he invited Faubus to give the keynote address at the Christian Crusade's annual convention.[36]

Like many other white southern segregationists, Hargis believed that most African Americans were content to live in a segregated society, and he blamed the civil rights movement's early campaigns for desegregation in Montgomery and Little Rock on the agitation of outside communist agitators, including the NAACP, which he said was a "pro-communist movement to destroy the unity of a nation."[37] Speaking out against civil rights was therefore a way to defend American values and protect the country from communism.

Some fundamentalists admitted that without the alleged connection between communism and the civil rights movement, they would have no grounds on which to defend racial segregation, because the scriptures gave them little support. Immediately after the Supreme Court issued its ruling in *Brown*, John R. Rice wrote that "there is no Bible basis for inforced [*sic*] segregation of the races as far as I know." He then perhaps surprised his readers by giving the Court's decision his cautious approval, saying that since "Christians must be good citizens and must obey the law . . . they must accept the fact that Negroes are to vote, are to have the same privileges as white people in busses, trains and schools as the law requires." But Rice concluded his editorial by indulging in some red-baiting at the expense of civil rights activists: "Socialists, communists, new-dealers, well-meaning left-wingers like Eleanor Roosevelt and certain labor leaders, have constantly stirred up trouble when they did not understand the situation," Rice wrote. "The greatest threat to peace in the South are these same left-wing socialists who would force an employer to hire Negroes when they might want to employ white people, who would set out to change customs, not by careful education but by the interference of the federal government in matters best attended to under the authority of states and local citizens."[38] Such sentiments were hallmarks of the fundamentalist reaction against civil rights in the 1960s.

As sit-ins, boycotts, and marches throughout the South increased in the early 1960s, fundamentalists escalated their charges against Martin Luther King, Jr., and his allies. Noel Smith, editor of the BBF's *Baptist Bible Tribune*, repeatedly charged civil rights advocates with communism, raising the specter of interracial marriage as a threat if they were to succeed. "To make intermarriage between Whites and Negroes as commonplace as black tomcats squalling in back alleys is the supreme goal of this integration campaign," he wrote in 1961. Fundamentalists also complained about King's liberal theology, a charge that resonated with preachers who remained loyal to the "fundamentals" of the faith. "Rev. M. L. King Confesses to Apostasy," one headline in G. Archer Weniger's *Blu-Print* proclaimed in 1962.[39]

As fundamentalists observed the support that the civil rights movement was receiving from federal officials and the national media, they, like many white southerners, began to view themselves as a beleaguered minority, the lone defenders of a vanishing constitutional order. "In a day when rascals in clerical garb join hands with anarchists in mob violence and law breaking, Bob Jones University sends out men and women who stand for the fundamental principles of Constitutional Americanism," Bob Jones, Jr., told his incoming class of freshmen in September 1963.[40]

At the beginning of the 1950s, fundamentalists could have joined the evangelical alliance with Republican centrist politicians, but their deep fear of communist influence, their refusal to cooperate with evangelicals, and their uncompromising opposition to civil rights prevented them from doing so, relegating them to the margins of American political life. By the end of the decade, when Graham was enjoying a close relationship with the president and vice president of the United States, fundamentalists such as Jones, Falwell, Hargis, McIntire, and Rice had almost no influence on national politics. The mainstream press mostly ignored them. But in the South, the fusion of Christian nationalism, militant anticommunism, and opposition to civil rights formed the basis for an emerging regional movement that would eventually give fundamentalists such as Falwell the national influence they sought.

| God and Country during
the Kennedy Presidency

FIVE DAYS BEFORE VOTERS WENT to the polls to choose between Richard
Nixon and John F. Kennedy in 1960, Billy Graham stood beside the
Republican presidential candidate on a platform in Columbia, South Carolina—
underneath a banner that said, "Dixie Is No Longer in the Bag"—and delivered
an invocation. Graham's presence at one of Nixon's final campaign rallies
before the election was a sign of evangelicals' growing political influence.
Graham was so important to the Republican campaign that a reporter asked
Nixon at a press conference if he was considering the evangelist for a Cabinet
position. Nixon brushed off the question, but conservative Protestants were
indeed some of his most loyal supporters.[1] He received unofficial endorsements not only from Graham but also from the National Association of Evangelicals (NAE), the Southern Baptist Convention, several Protestant denominations,
and southern fundamentalists such as Bob Jones, Jr., and John R. Rice. In a
rare moment of political ecumenism, fundamentalists and evangelicals were
united in a campaign to keep a Catholic out of the White House.

But their power vanished with Kennedy's victory. Over the next five
years, evangelicals saw every major gain of the previous decade evaporate.
They lost their influence at the White House. They failed to stem the cultural
liberalism and sweeping social changes of the decade. They watched in
dismay as the federal government appeared to become increasingly secular. In
response, conservative Protestants had to reexamine their notion of American
national identity and their place in the political sphere. Evangelicals who had
been allies of the Eisenhower administration began to think of themselves as

beleaguered defenders of traditional American values attempting to reclaim their nation from hostile political institutions.

The Presidential Election of 1960

Evangelicals and fundamentalists' campaign against Kennedy, which was an attempt to maintain the nation's explicitly Protestant identity, put them at odds with an increasingly pluralistic nation. A generation earlier, Protestants from across the theological spectrum had united against the nation's first Catholic presidential nominee, Al Smith. By the 1940s, such overt anti-Catholicism was already beginning to weaken, and the NAE was fighting a difficult battle against Catholic political influence. The Cold War gave Catholics a chance to prove their American patriotism, further integrating them into the mainstream. In 1955, Will Herberg's widely circulated *Protestant, Catholic, Jew* argued that religious differences were no longer a divisive force in America and that the nation's three major religious traditions championed the same basic American values.[2] By 1960, many Americans thought that the nation had become sufficiently tolerant to elect a Catholic president.

Conservative Protestants, however, argued that a Catholic president was a threat to religious liberty. The nation's founding documents were products of a Protestant religious heritage, they thought. A Catholic president would take orders from a church hierarchy opposed to religious freedom. By connecting constitutional liberties to their own religious faith, conservative Protestants posed as guarantors of American democracy.

In the early stages of Kennedy's campaign, even some liberal Protestants agreed with the evangelicals. Protestants and Other Americans United for the Separation of Church and State refused to criticize Kennedy by name, but the organization repeatedly questioned the ability of a Catholic president to govern free of church influence. In April 1960, G. Bromley Oxnam, a Methodist clergyman and leading figure in the National Council of Churches, said that while he did not oppose the idea of a Catholic president per se, he felt uneasy about the prospect. He would demand that any Catholic presidential candidate make a convincing case that he would not be influenced by the Catholic Church's official position on such policy matters as the federal funding of birth control distribution or aid to parochial schools. In an unabashed display of anti-Catholicism, Norman Vincent Peale, a mainline Protestant minister from New York, joined with evangelicals from *Christianity Today* to form Citizens for Religious Freedom, whose sole purpose was to declare Kennedy a threat to the separation of church and state.[3]

Kennedy assuaged the doubts of mainline Protestants by meeting with prominent ministers in Houston in September 1960 and answering a battery of questions about the way in which his faith would influence public policy. Several leading Protestants responded by withdrawing their earlier criticisms of the senator's religion. Peale resigned from Citizens for Religious Freedom and announced that there was no reason why a Catholic should not be president. Most mainline Protestant ministers did not want to appear to be anti-Catholic bigots.[4]

Evangelicals, by contrast, increased their criticism of Kennedy as Election Day approached. Churches that had not previously engaged in partisan activities were transformed into centers of a grassroots campaign against Kennedy. The NAE's official publication, *United Evangelical Action*, urged pastors to conduct voter registration drives outside their churches. Pastors should not hesitate to use their sermons to impress upon church members the responsibility of voting, the magazine suggested, and they should ask for a public show of hands to find out how many people in their congregation had not yet registered to vote. The premier northern evangelical institution of higher education, Wheaton College, gave free mailing privileges to students who wished to send campaign literature for Nixon. *Christianity Today* tried to maintain an appearance of balanced reporting, but few readers could have had any doubt that the editors intended to vote for Nixon in November, especially after they signed a statement saying that the religious issue was a "major factor" in the presidential election and that any Catholic would face "extreme pressure" from the Vatican to make America's foreign policy conform to the desires of the Catholic Church.[5]

Separatist fundamentalists also joined the campaign against Kennedy, arguing that a Catholic posed a danger to the "Americanism" that they had been championing for the last decade. "If Kennedy is a good Catholic, his religion requires him to owe first allegiance to the Pope, and not to the United States," Bob Jones, Jr., said. "I am tolerant enough to believe that a Catholic has the constitutional right to be president, but I will not compromise my convictions by voting for him or refusing to speak out against him."[6]

Southern denominations that had traditionally eschewed political pronouncements joined the fray. Most of the leading magazine editors of the historically nonpolitical Churches of Christ expressed opposition to Kennedy, and in October 1960, NBC filmed one of the denomination's Nashville preachers delivering a sermon on the dangers of Catholicism and its threat to religious liberty. Pentecostals, who had once been among the most apolitical evangelicals, likewise took public stands against Kennedy. The International

Pentecostal Assemblies and the General Presbytery of the Assemblies of God both passed resolutions opposing the election of a Catholic.[7]

Perhaps the Protestant campaign against Kennedy had its most pronounced political effect on the Southern Baptist Convention (SBC). Southern Baptists had avoided the increasing political activities of other evangelicals and fundamentalists during the 1950s, but the denomination's leaders launched an all-out offensive against the Kennedy campaign. In May 1960, the denomination passed a thinly veiled anti-Catholic resolution warning that "a candidate's affiliations, including his church, are of concern to the voters in every election." SBC president Ramsay Pollard said that he could not "stand by and keep my mouth shut when a man under control of the Catholic Church runs for Presidency of the United States." In July 1960, W. A. Criswell, pastor of the nation's largest Southern Baptist church, distributed one hundred thousand copies of his sermon warning that Kennedy's election would "spell the death of a free church in a free state and our hopes of continuance of full religious liberty in America."[8]

In keeping with his role as a national evangelist who was allegedly above the political fray, Billy Graham tried to maintain a veneer of nonpartisanship in the election, but behind the scenes, he played an important role in the Nixon campaign. For Graham, Nixon's election was imperative—not only to keep a Catholic out of the White House, but also to perpetuate the civil religion and evangelical political alliance that President Eisenhower had promoted. As a result of Graham's frequent visits to the Eisenhower White House, Nixon had also become his friend, a man with whom he regularly corresponded and played golf. Accordingly, he began an unofficial campaign for Nixon months before the actual campaign started. In the fall of 1959, he made an unprecedented partisan statement on Nixon's behalf by telling the press that Nixon was the "best qualified and best trained man for the presidency." In May 1960, he gave the press another strong hint of his presidential preference by alluding to Nixon's eight years of experience in the Eisenhower administration. "This is a time of world tensions," he said, "and I don't think it is the time to experiment with novices."[9]

Graham was far more overt in his private correspondence with Nixon. Throughout the campaign, he sent Nixon frequent letters and telegrams suggesting political strategies that might appeal to evangelical voters, nearly always beginning them with the friendly salutation, "Dear Dick." Nixon should "attend church regularly and faithfully from now on" in order to appeal to the "religious minded people in America," Graham told the vice president in November 1959. He suggested ways in which Nixon could "recapture the farm vote," appeal to southerners, and avoid controversy on foreign policy. He polled religious and political leaders to ask what their concerns were, and he reported these to Nixon. His frequent letters to Nixon reflected a constant worry about Kennedy's lead in the polls, and he often speculated about what Nixon could do to close the gap.[10]

Most of all, Graham gave Nixon updates on how he thought the "religious issue" would play among the nation's voters. He felt that the open attacks on Kennedy's Catholicism that came from fundamentalists and Southern Baptists were counterproductive, because they had "the effect of solidifying a much stronger Catholic vote." Instead, he advised Nixon to spend more time discussing his own religious faith, saying that he could solidify his standing among Protestants by presenting himself as a devout Christian and a man of conviction without appearing to be a religious bigot. Graham knew that Nixon's appeal to Protestants offered him the only hope he had of carrying the traditionally Democratic South.[11]

Nixon seemed to welcome Graham's input. He responded promptly to all of his letters, usually agreeing with his suggestions. He accepted Graham's invitation to appear at one of his crusades in the summer of 1960. Yet in practice, Nixon rarely acted on Graham's advice. After he increased the frequency of his churchgoing in the summer of 1960, as Graham had been urging him to do for months, he grumbled that his opponents were now charging him with "deliberately injecting the religious issue into the campaign by allowing my picture to be taken going to church." As he told Graham in a letter, "This shows that you just can't win on that issue!" On nonreligious issues, he gave even less weight to the evangelist's suggestions. Early in the campaign, for example, Graham encouraged Nixon to choose as his running mate Representative Walter Judd (R-MN), a former missionary to China who was a darling of politically active Republican evangelicals. "It becomes imperative for you to have as your running mate someone the Protestant church can rally behind enthusiastically," Graham told Nixon in June. "With Dr. Judd I believe the two of you could present a picture to America that would put much of the South and border states in the Republican column and bring about a dedicated Protestant vote to counteract the Catholic vote."[12] But Nixon instead selected Henry Cabot Lodge, Jr., a name that Graham had not even mentioned in his correspondence.

What Nixon wanted from Graham more than advice was an endorsement, but Graham was reluctant to appear too political, and he resisted some of the Nixon campaign's overtures. Throughout the summer of 1960, he continued to tell journalists that he was not making an official endorsement of Nixon's candidacy, and he bristled whenever the press implied otherwise. "I emphatically deny that I plunged into American politics as stated in *Time*," he complained in a letter to the editor of the magazine. Torn between his loyalty to Nixon and his desire to retain his nonpartisan image and national influence as an evangelist, Graham agonized over whether an endorsement of Nixon was appropriate. He skipped the Republican National Convention in order to hold an international crusade, despite receiving an invitation from the Nixon campaign to lead the convention's opening prayer. And after writing a pro-Nixon article for *Life* in October 1960, he decided, at the last minute, to take the advice of some of his friends and cancel its publication. Several times throughout the campaign, he promised Nixon that he would make an official endorsement of his candidacy, but each time, he backed off. In the spring, he said that he would make the endorsement on *Meet the Press* in early June. When he failed to do so, he told Nixon that he would probably come out for him officially in October, but then in late September, he decided against a direct endorsement. "We have already witnessed what the Press did to [Norman Vincent] Peale," he told Nixon. "I cannot possibly get involved in the religious issue. Not only would they crucify me, but they would eventually turn it against you, so I must be extremely careful." Yet he assured Nixon that even though he was trying to avoid indications of partisanship while in public, "privately I intend to do all in my power to help you get elected."[13]

Graham kept his promise to work "privately" on Nixon's behalf. He sent a letter to the 2 million people on his mailing list to encourage them to "organize their Sunday school classes and churches to get out the vote." He met individually with key evangelical leaders with whom he thought he had some political influence. He cornered Martin Luther King, Jr., at the Baptist World Alliance, and tried to dissuade him from voting for Kennedy, as the civil rights leader apparently intended to do. King proved to be a tougher sell than white evangelicals, but Graham felt that after three days of conversation with him, he had made some progress. "I think I at least neutralized him," Graham reported to Nixon. "If you could invite him for a brief conference it might swing him. He would be a powerful influence."[14]

At the urging of NAE leader J. Elwin Wright, Graham arranged for twenty-five anti-Kennedy evangelical ministers to meet him in Montreux, Switzerland—a location safely removed from prying journalists. The group, which included NAE founder Harold Ockenga, as well as L. Nelson Bell, discussed political strategy. If Nixon's Protestant religious identity were publicized among ministers, particularly in the South, the Republican candidate might be able to line up an evangelical voting bloc large enough to secure a victory, they decided. To accomplish this end, the NAE formed Citizens for Religious Freedom in Washington, DC, in early September.[15]

Publicly, Nixon distanced himself from any attempt to inject religion in the campaign, but privately, his campaign encouraged endorsements from Protestant ministers. In 1959, near the beginning of his presidential campaign, Nixon met with Ockenga in Boston after receiving a pledge of his support. In early 1960, the Nixon campaign also hired a lesser-known evangelical, Representative Orland K. Armstrong (R-MO), to reach out to Protestant ministers. Armstrong was on hand for the Southern Baptist Convention's annual meeting in May, where he encouraged its anti-Catholic resolution, and he convinced ministers in several other Protestant denominations to begin speaking out against Kennedy. Nixon had the private support of many evangelicals, but more than anything, he wanted a public endorsement from Graham. Nixon finally got his wish in the last week of the campaign, when Graham decided to compromise his nonpartisan image by publicly appearing with the Republican candidate at a campaign rally in Columbia, South Carolina, where he delivered an invocation.[16]

The election was closer than many had predicted. Kennedy barely eked out a victory, and some election surveys indicated that opposition to the senator's religion may have hurt the Democratic candidate in heavily Protestant areas of the country. A poll showed that 66 percent of Protestant voters nationwide voted against Kennedy. Even in the traditionally Democratic "solid South," 53 percent of Protestant voters cast their ballots for Nixon, according to a Gallup survey.[17] With such strong opposition to a Catholic candidate, it was not surprising that Nixon won the electoral votes of several states on the South's periphery.

Nevertheless, Kennedy's win delivered a shocking blow to the thousands of conservative Protestant pastors who had united in a campaign against him. Some were at first unable to accept the reality of a Catholic president. Three weeks after the election, G. Archer Weniger, a Conservative Baptist pastor in San Francisco and a member of the board of directors of Bob Jones University, urged readers of his fundamentalist newsletter to continue to pray that election officials would declare a Republican victory based on a favorable recount. When that did not happen, the California pastor contented himself with publishing occasional articles denouncing Kennedy for his profane language and speculating about what might have happened had events gone differently during the presidential campaign. Bob Jones, Sr., blamed Billy Graham for Nixon's defeat. Even though Graham had worked tirelessly on Nixon's behalf and had joined him on the campaign trail in South Carolina, Jones claimed that the evangelist's unwillingness to issue a direct endorsement had cost Nixon the election. "A straightforward statement by Billy would have influenced enough votes to have made the difference," Jones grumbled.[18]

Graham himself may have felt that way too. Several months after Nixon's defeat, he wrote a long, agonizing letter to Nixon in which he came close to reproaching himself for not having done more to help his favored candidate. On election night, he said, he had felt "a deep sense of remorse and almost guilt that somehow I had failed."[19]

But most evangelicals soon stopped blaming themselves or each other for Nixon's defeat and instead prepared for a long-term loss of Protestant influence in government. "We have felt like [a] death of a loved one has taken place—not the death of an individual, but the death throes of a nation," L. Nelson Bell said immediately after the election. The country now faced "a slow, completely integrated and planned attempt to take over our nation for the Roman Catholic Church." As Bell looked back on the campaign, he could not help but think of it as a heroic last stand against the forces of evil. "You, Dick, stood for the things which have made America great, while Mr. Kennedy appealed to the most venal elements in individuals and society as a whole," Bell told Nixon a few days after the candidate conceded defeat. "I feel that the judgment of God hangs over a people to whom He has given so much and who have rejected spiritual values for those which are material."[20]

The Fundamentalist Reaction against the Kennedy Administration

Having lost their influence in the nation's capital, conservative Protestants prepared for a long-term political offensive to take it back. Immediately after the election, the NAE's executive director said that given the Catholic Church's growing influence, evangelicals needed to devise their own "Protestant strategy for the sixties." With only a vague sense of a political program, and little hint of a partisan commitment, northern evangelicals spoke of the desirability of voting for people who shared their religious beliefs, since they assumed that evangelical candidates, no matter what their political platform, would work to keep America "Christian." *Moody Monthly* abandoned its decades-old fatalistic doom-and-gloom perspective and began advocating politics as a suitable career for Christians. "Should Christians go into politics?" the November 1960 issue asked, and it offered a decisively affirmative answer. Noting the increased political consciousness among northern evangelical pastors, *United Evangelical Action* remarked in December 1960, "This is good. It must continue. . . . Already we know of certain pastors who have taken the cue. Whereas they once regarded political activity as a somewhat 'worldly' pursuit, they are now encouraging their laymen to *make the plunge into civil affairs* in their own communities."[21]

Fundamentalists also increased their political activity in the early 1960s, partly by attacking Kennedy's policy decisions almost immediately after he took office. During the campaign of 1960, they had argued that Kennedy was a threat to the nation's liberties because he was a Catholic. After his inauguration, they began arguing that he was a threat to the nation's security because he was soft on communism. Such charges had little basis in fact, because the young Democratic president made the fight against international communism his highest priority immediately after taking office. Yet fundamentalists who viewed Kennedy's religion as un-American found it easy to believe that he would compromise American security, and they looked for signs of incompetence or subversion in his administration. Kennedy's decision to send a covert military force to invade the Bay of Pigs in Cuba in an unsuccessful attempt to oust communist leader Fidel Castro from power was "the rankest kind of stupidity," Bob Jones, Jr., said in May 1961. Jones had not criticized the Eisenhower administration for its foreign policy errors, but the Bay of Pigs fiasco caused him such concern that he devoted a university chapel talk to Kennedy's incompetence. "This cost us prestige among the nations of the world," he said. "Unhappy {are} the people whose government is in the hands of a child."[22]

When the Kennedy Defense Department rebuked Major General Edwin Walker, a member of the far-right John Birch Society, for telling his soldiers that Eleanor Roosevelt and Dean Acheson were communist sympathizers and that they should vote for conservative candidates in order to stop the threat of international communism, fundamentalists seized upon the action as an example of the administration's alleged left-wing sympathies. Carl McIntire accused the Defense Department of "muzzling the military." When Walker resigned his commission over the dispute, Billy James Hargis recruited him for a speaking tour and championed him as a victim of the Kennedy administration's persecution. "I'm convinced that the Kennedy administration is trying to neutralize the anti-Communist efforts of the United States," Hargis told a gathering of students and faculty at Bob Jones University.[23]

During his first nine months in office, Kennedy increased military spending by 14 percent and Minuteman missile production by 100 percent, but fundamentalists accused the Kennedy administration of entertaining the idea of disarmament. They also lambasted his domestic policies as a step toward socialism. "Our tax money is even being used to send so-called foreign aid to our mortal enemies, the communist conspiracy, in addition to being wasted shamefully in America on various crackpot socialistic schemes," Hargis said during his Independence Day broadcast in 1961.[24]

With the White House in enemy hands, some fundamentalists developed a closer relationship with Senator Strom Thurmond (D-SC), a conservative Democrat who had temporarily broken with his party and run for president as a Dixiecrat thirteen years earlier and who had spent the ensuing decade establishing himself as a principal opponent of civil rights. Thurmond had little party loyalty and even less respect for the president. Fundamentalists loved him. When he delivered a scathing denunciation of the Defense Department's handling of the Walker case on the floor of the Senate in August 1961, McIntire reprinted the speech as a pamphlet. Bob Jones University, which had already made Thurmond one of its trustees, invited him to give a speech airing his objections to Kennedy's allegedly soft policy toward communism. Thurmond obliged with an address entitled "Shall We Survive?" which expressed nostalgia for the McCarthy era. "The greatest danger we face is not the external enemy—it is Communism from within," Thurmond told the Bob Jones students.[25]

Seeking to broaden the anti-Kennedy coalition, Billy James Hargis launched a nonpartisan political campaign in 1962 to elect conservative candidates to Congress throughout the nation. He expressed hope that Arkansas governor Orval Faubus, a staunch segregationist, would challenge the state's more liberal senator, J. William Fulbright, in the Democratic primary, and that conservative candidates would likewise oust liberal incumbents in other states. At the presidential level, the Republicans seemed far more likely than the Democrats to adopt the conservative platform that Hargis favored, but at the state level, the Oklahoma radio evangelist insisted that party labels were no indication of ideology. "In the South you've got to elect conservative Democrats and in the North conservative Republicans," Hargis told a group of his supporters in Tulsa.[26]

As the first fundamentalist minister to launch a nationwide effort to influence congressional elections, Hargis pioneered a concept that would later appeal to other Christian Right activists, including Jerry Falwell, Pat Robertson, and Ralph Reed. But the idea failed in 1962. Even in socially conservative Arkansas, Hargis had far less influence than he had expected. Faubus decided not to challenge Fulbright for his seat.[27]

Hargis's campaign may not have succeeded in the short term, but it had the important effect of introducing the concept of "conservatism" as a rallying cry for fundamentalists. Hargis announced his intention to endorse "conservative" candidates, and he began to describe his own program as "conservative." "Christ is the heart of the Conservative cause," Hargis said in

1962, and the next year he claimed that "there is a sound scriptural basis for the position taken by the political conservative." The fight against the "softening, putrefying Liberalism of Washington" on the domestic front was simply an extension of his other anticommunist activities, he said, since American liberalism was in reality "a broad, slick runway straight into Communism."[28] In the 1950s, fundamentalists had struggled to define their brand of anticommunism with such terms as "Americanism" or "Christian Americanism," which were not explicitly partisan. "Conservative" was a term that was much more closely identified with a political faction, and when fundamentalists began using the word, they signaled their willingness to ally with self-identified conservative politicians such as Strom Thurmond and Senator Barry Goldwater (R-AZ). Their new choice of nomenclature identified them as part of a grassroots movement associated with William F. Buckley's *National Review*, Young Americans for Freedom (YAF), the John Birch Society (JBS), and the campaign to draft Goldwater to run for president in 1964. When fundamentalists became "conservatives" in opposition to the Kennedy administration, they took a step toward ending their political isolation and becoming part of a rising national movement. At the time, the alliance gave them little additional political influence, because conservatism—especially the far-right version that the fundamentalists adopted—was still a reactionary ideology with a narrow following. But the alliance would serve fundamentalists well in the future.[29]

In a move away from the fundamentalist separatist tradition, Hargis accepted a leadership role in several nonfundamentalist organizations on the political right. In the early 1960s, he became a member of the board at Liberty Lobby, joined Edwin Walker on a national speaking tour, served on the advisory board of the JBS, and served as president of the right-wing organization We the People! The organizations with which Hargis allied were thriving, rapidly growing entities, and it appeared that by making these alliances, he was heading for even greater success. YAF had far more members on college campuses than the left-wing Students for a Democratic Society did in the early 1960s, and it played a leading role in the "Draft Goldwater" movement. The "far right," consisting of organizations such as the JBS (which taught that even President Dwight Eisenhower had been an agent of the communist conspiracy), reached the height of its influence in the early 1960s. Many of these right-wing organizations drew most of their membership from mainline Protestants and Catholics, so fundamentalists who allied with them reached a far larger audience than they had before.[30] Hargis's attempts to coordinate efforts among the Birchers, YAFers, fundamentalists, and conservative politicians suggested that he was looking for a way to translate the groundswell of opposition to the Kennedy administration into a coherent political strategy that could result in electoral victories.

Hargis's associations with nonfundamentalists caused some conservative Protestants, including Bob Jones, Jr., to question his fundamentalist bona fides. In a letter to Jones in 1968, Hargis responded to the charges by admitting that he had welcomed conservative Catholic Fred Schlafly, whose wife Phyllis would later become a household name in conservative circles for her STOP-ERA campaign, on his radio program, but he denied that he had compromised with Catholicism. "I don't think that anyone could accuse me of failing to discuss the Catholic issue because I have," he wrote.[31]

Jones was hardly in a position to complain about Hargis's activities, because he, too, was actively involved in secular politics in the 1960s, often in conjunction with Hargis himself. The speaking roster for his university's 1962 Americanism Conference speaking roster was a "who's who" of the far right. Hargis gave an address titled "The President—Ignorant or Untruthful? The Facts on the Danger from Communist Infiltration"; right-wing radio commentator Dan Smoot spoke on "liberalism"; and We the People! president Harry T. Everingham delivered a talk titled "The United Nations: Socialist Trap for American Freedom." The two national politicians who appeared, Representative Dale Alford (D-AR) and Representative L. Mendel Rivers (D-SC), were among the most pro-segregationist, arch-conservative figures in Congress.[32]

The university's new conservative political activities were "entirely natural," Jones said, because "a good, Bible-believing Christian is by nature a good, patriotic American." As a patriot, it was necessary to oppose the Kennedy administration, because of the presence of "Communist infiltration into our government, and the tolerance of the administration toward radicalism, and the weakness shown in dealing with the Communist threat." Together the fundamentalists and their arch-conservative allies crafted a new vision for American policy that offered a militaristic alternative to the Kennedy administration's proposals. If they had had their way, the U.S. government would have withdrawn from the United Nations, launched a full-scale military invasion of Cuba in order to liberate it from communism, increased its investigations of alleged communist subversives within the United States, and rescinded its civil rights initiatives.[33]

Evangelicals generally avoided fundamentalists' overt identification with the far right, but many of them joined anticommunist organizations that were only slightly more moderate than the ones that fundamentalists favored. The Christian Anticommunism Crusade, an organization that the Baptist layman and medical doctor Fred Schwarz had founded at Billy Graham's urging in 1953, reached the height of its influence in the early 1960s. Conservative political activists such as Phyllis Schlafly, William F. Buckley, Jr., and Ronald Reagan signed up for the doctor's "schools," which featured long, detailed analyses of Marxist ideology, followed by a warning that communists would take over the United States by 1973 if the country did not adopt a more vigilant defense against the Red menace. In 1962, Schwarz held a rally in New York's Madison Square Garden to warn the nation that the president needed to adopt a more aggressive stance against the Soviet communists even if it meant risking nuclear war. Pat Boone, a popular singer and Hollywood actor who was a devout member of the Church of Christ, told the crowd, "I have four lovely young daughters, and I'd rather see them blown to Heaven in a nuclear war than to live in slavery under Communism."[34] When it came to communism, fundamentalists and evangelicals shared a similar critique of the Kennedy administration, even if they did so in separate organizations.

Like fundamentalists, evangelicals created political organizations to effect electoral changes. During the 1950s, evangelicals had not needed new lobbying groups, because they had good relations with the White House and could count prominent congressmen in both parties among their number. But by the early 1960s, that was no longer the case. Although the Cold War was still intense, government officials no longer relied on the overt religious rhetoric that they had employed in the 1950s, and some of the prominent evangelical voices of the 1950s, like Representative Brooks Hays (D-AR) and Walter Judd, were no longer in Congress. Evangelicals decided that it was time to reclaim their influence. With some initial encouragement from Judd, as well as from Bill Bright, a Presbyterian evangelical who had founded the widely successfully organization Campus Crusade for Christ a decade earlier, Southern Baptist businessman Gerri von Frellick launched Christian Citizen in January 1962 in order to assist evangelicals running for public office. Within a month, it had two thousand members scattered across seventeen states.[35]

Von Frellick was a political conservative who admired the John Birch Society and the Christian Anticommunism Crusade, and he took it for granted that any evangelical politician, regardless of party affiliation, would be staunchly anticommunist. But he was more interested in electing born-again Christians to office than in any candidate's position on the issues. "We don't care if he's liberal, conservative, Democrat, Republican, black, white or Jew—if he is converted," von Frellick told the press. "Just so long as he gives a public commitment to a fundamental belief in Christ." Yet even though his organization was not explicitly partisan or ideological, von Frellick's support came primarily from conservative Republicans who were trying to shift their party to the right and make inroads in the once solidly Democratic South. At the organization's inaugural banquet, Senator John Tower (R-TX), a business-oriented conservative who had recently been elected to Lyndon Johnson's former seat as the first Republican senator from Texas since Reconstruction, gave an address, as did conservative commentator Paul Harvey.[36] Evangelicals had not yet worked out the details of their political program, but they knew that Kennedy's election had caused them to lose their influence in Washington, and an alliance with conservative Republicans seemed to offer a way to recapture it.

School Prayer

Conservative Protestants' anxiety about their loss of influence was exacerbated in 1962, when the Supreme Court ruled in *Engel v. Vitale* that the recitation of a state-composed prayer in the classroom was unconstitutional. It was unclear whether this ruling forbade all classroom prayer—as later court decisions stated—or whether, as many Americans of the time thought, it applied only to state-composed, recited prayers. But many Americans saw even that small step as a threat to their country's civil religious tradition.

The prayer in question—endorsed by Catholic, Protestant, and Jewish clergy—reflected a nondenominational, Judeo-Christian consensus that Americans had promoted as a bulwark against "godless communism." Many thought that atheists and agnostics had no right to challenge this tradition, which was an intrinsic part of national identity even for those who rarely attended church or synagogue. Only eight years before the *Engel* decision, Congress had added the words "under God" to the Pledge of Allegiance. Yet while politicians in the 1950s had bolstered American civil religion by equating religious faith with patriotism, the Supreme Court had been moving in the opposite direction and had, since the late 1940s, attempted to shore up the wall between church and state. That put it directly at odds with national sentiment. A Gallup poll taken immediately after the *Engel* ruling showed that 79 percent of the nation's citizens supported religious exercises in public schools.[37]

Riding a crest of popular opinion, politicians of both parties denounced the decision. Among Democrats, opposition ranged from conservative southerners such as Representative John Bell Williams (D-MS) to northern liberals such as Senator Eugene McCarthy (D-MN). Senator Prescott Bush (R-CT), a moderate Republican, called *Engel* "most unfortunate," while conservative

Senator Barry Goldwater denounced the Court for ruling "against God." Public disgruntlement was so strong that President Kennedy felt that he had to protect the reputation of the Supreme Court by making a public appeal for Americans "to pray a good deal more at home" rather than protest the school prayer decision, and to "support the Constitution and the Court's responsibility in interpreting it."[38]

Catholic clerics argued that the Court's decision challenged America's traditional reverence for God in the public sphere and weakened the nation's defense against communism. "This decision puts shame on our faces, as we are forced to emulate Mr. Khrushchev," James Francis Cardinal McIntyre said. Francis Cardinal Spellman concurred. "This is the establishment of a new religion of secularism," he said. "This should be ruled unconstitutional."[39]

One might have expected fundamentalists and evangelicals to join other Americans in condemning the Court's ruling. But this was not the case. Most evangelicals had little reason to fear that the Court decision would turn their fellow citizens into secularists. The Court, they thought, had ruled not against classroom prayer in general, but only against state-composed prayers, a form of religious devotion for which they had little use. Because evangelicals and fundamentalists emphasized spontaneous prayers in their church services, they were uncomfortable with the practice of recited prayer in the classroom, especially when the school prayers had been composed by state-appointed ecumenical coalitions of Jews, Catholics, and liberal Protestants. *Christianity Today* supported the Court's prayer decision and noted its disdain for the New York Board of Regents' "corporate prayer," which promoted a "least-common-denominator type of religion." *Eternity* and *Moody Monthly* likewise expressed their support for *Engel* and argued that a state that was incapable of promoting genuine religious devotion should leave religious instruction and prayer composition to churches and parents. Many fundamentalists agreed with evangelicals on this point. "Prayer itself without the name of Jesus Christ was not a non-denominational prayer—it was simply a pagan prayer," Carl McIntire wrote. "No Government agency or power in the United States can be used to establish a religion."[40]

Many evangelicals welcomed the Court decision as a way to counter the political influence of Catholics. At the time of the ruling, Catholic leaders were in the midst of a prolonged political fight to secure federal funding for parochial schools, and Southern Baptists and the NAE were engaged in a counteroffensive. Evangelicals who were involved in this fight lauded *Engel* because it gave them a legal precedent for opposing government aid for religious education. "We should all thank the Supreme Court for this decision," the editor of the *Alabama Baptist* wrote in July 1962. "This ruling will do more than anything else to thwart the efforts of those who believe their religious schools should be supported by tax monies."[41]

But evangelicals and fundamentalists also worried that the Court decision might circumscribe religious influence in public schools and the federal government. The NAE vacillated on the issue. Two consecutive issues of the NAE's newsletter ran editorials endorsing the ruling, but in August the newsletter warned that "the decision opened a Pandora's box of secularistic influences which would be turned loose on every reference to God and religious in public life." Recognizing the debate among fundamentalist Baptists on the issue, Noel Smith's *Baptist Bible Tribune* published opposing editorials on the Court ruling.[42] Ultimately, evangelicals and fundamentalists were uncertain how to respond to *Engel* because they did not know whether Catholicism or secularism posed a greater threat to Protestant influence in public life.

Bible Reading in Public Schools

Many evangelicals who cautiously endorsed the Court's stance on school prayer in 1962 changed their tone the following June when they received word of the ruling in *Abington v. Schempp* (1963), which forbade devotional Bible reading in public schools. Devotional Bible reading from the King James Version had been a hallmark of the nation's Protestant-designed public school curriculum since the early nineteenth century, when Protestants had instituted the practice over the objections of Catholics and other religious minorities. Evangelicals interpreted the Court's decision as a personal affront. Because evangelicalism was based on faith in the Bible as the authoritative word of God, and because evangelicals believed that the Bible was instrumental in leading people to Christ, a ruling that forbade the reading of scripture in public schools seemed to strike at the heart of evangelical beliefs and the nation's Protestant identity in a way that the Court's ruling against the recitation of school prayers had not.

Although the NAE had hesitantly accepted *Engel*, the organization's leaders had no intention of acquiescing to the Court's verdict in *Schempp*. In the NAE's official publication, columnist Don Gill denounced the ruling, saying that it "augment[ed] the trend toward complete secularization" and "veer[ed] away from our national heritage of reverence." The organization that only a few months earlier had adopted a wait-and-see attitude toward the school prayer ruling decided in the summer of 1963 to advocate a constitutional amendment to restore prayer and Bible reading to public schools.[43]

In the process of protesting *Schempp* and defending America's Protestant Christian identity, evangelicals adopted rhetoric that was nearly identical to that of Catholic clerics who had criticized *Engel* the previous year. "A neutral or secular state, while preserving the nation from dominion by a denomination, leaves America in the same position as Communist Russia," argued Harold Ockenga. To some conservative Christians, the Court's verdict was nothing less than an attack on the nation. "In handing down the decision that it is unconstitutional to read the Bible in public schools, the Supreme Court is doing its utmost to destroy the United States of America," evangelical pastor Oswald J. Smith said in 1963.[44]

Like evangelicals, fundamentalists began to view the national government as a secularizing force that was hostile to Christians, and they were determined to fight back. "We understand that a greater issue is at stake than simply Bible reading in the schools," Carl McIntire wrote in 1964. "At stake is whether or not America may continue to honor and recognize God in the life of the nation." McIntire, along with Billy James Hargis, urged political parties to endorse a constitutional amendment to restore classroom prayer and Bible reading. Hargis's Christian Crusade also urged social conservatives to run in school board elections in order to influence educational policy at the local level. "Shall we sit meekly by and accept the anti-God decisions of the liberals that rule God out of public life or shall we obey the Lord?" Hargis asked in August 1963.[45]

With more than 70 percent of the American electorate favoring school prayer, politicians knew that the move to overturn the *Engel* and *Schempp* decisions enjoyed widespread support. Some congressmen reported that half of the correspondence that they received from their constituents in 1963–1964 focused on school prayer, and those letters initially ran 20–1 in favor of a constitutional amendment. Between June 1962 and May 1964, 111 congressmen submitted 147 proposals for school prayer constitutional amendments.[46]

The issue became an important one for Republicans who hoped to secure the support of socially conservative voters. Republican representative Frank Becker of New York submitted the leading school prayer amendment proposal in 1964, and Republican Senate Minority Leader Everett Dirksen (R-IL) introduced a similar amendment two years later. In 1964, the Republican Party officially endorsed a constitutional amendment to circumscribe the Court's *Engel* and *Schempp* rulings. Highlighting the contrast between the parties, Republican presidential candidate Barry Goldwater accused his opponents of showing "an utter disregard for God." Some fundamentalists noted the difference as well. "In the minds of a large number of Americans, the Democratic Party is the party of opposition to the Bible in the schools," Carl McIntire said in August 1964. Using a strategy that the Christian Coalition would employ a generation later, McIntire's American Council of Christian Churches distributed leaflets that showed where political candidates stood on the school prayer issue, a move that the organization's leaders presumably thought would help northern Republicans and southern conservative Democrats, both of whom tended to support school prayer amendments. Several Republican politicians in the South, including Tennessee senatorial candidates Howard Baker and Bill Brock, also made support for school prayer a central focus of their successful campaigns in the late 1960s and early 1970s.[47]

But the Southern Baptist Convention supported the Court's ruling in *Schempp*, just as it had with *Engel*. Ever since the colonial era, when their denominational forebears had encountered persecution from established churches, most Baptists had placed a greater primacy on religious freedom than on public displays of faith. In a continuation of this tradition of church-state separation, the SBC passed a resolution in 1964 opposing a constitutional amendment to overturn either *Engel* or *Schempp*. Not all Southern Baptists agreed with this position, and in 1966, some of the denomination's pastors voiced their dissent by joining with nearly four thousand other Protestant ministers in signing a petition that urged the Senate to vote on a school prayer constitutional amendment.

But Southern Baptists who were still more concerned about Catholic political influence than about secularization warned their fellow church members that if they opposed *Schempp*, they could give the Catholics a political advantage in the battle over federal funding for parochial schools. Readers who "had an emotional reaction to the Supreme Court's decision," the *Alabama Baptist* said, needed to "remember the strenuous efforts being made by the Catholic Hierarchy to get legislation passed making available tax monies to operate their institutions." The editorial concluded, "If these laws [requiring the reading of the Bible in public schools] had been upheld, then the Catholics would have a right to insist that we erect the statues of their saints in our public schools in order to be reverent, and other religious groups would have a right to bring their non-Christian or atheistic views into the classrooms."[48]

At the denominational level, Southern Baptist opposition to school prayer amendments remained strong throughout the 1970s. In 1971, the Southern Baptist Convention joined other denominations in lobbying against a school prayer amendment, helping to ensure the amendment's defeat in Congress. As late as 1979, SBC president Jimmy Allen publicly opposed Senator Jesse

Helms's (R-NC) attempts to restore prayer to the public school classroom. With the exception of Billy Graham, no nationally known Southern Baptist preacher of the 1960s and early 1970s spoke against the Supreme Court's rulings on school prayer and Bible reading.[49]

Evangelicals were reluctant to support a school prayer amendment partly because in many parts of the country, school prayer and Bible reading continued into the 1970s in spite of the Supreme Court's rulings. Americans United for Separation of Church and State estimated that in 1972, 25 percent of the nation's schools were not complying with the *Engel* and *Schempp* verdicts. In the South, the rate was even higher. One study found that in 1970, 43 percent of public school teachers in Tennessee continued to read the Bible to their classes, and in other southern states, violations of the Court's rulings were just as common. A Mississippi school administrator told a reporter in 1972, "We never did cut out prayers. Teachers still have them whenever they want to."[50]

The Southern Baptist position gradually became the dominant one among evangelicals in the late 1960s and 1970s. The uproar with which some evangelicals had greeted *Schempp* quickly subsided. Although fundamentalists continued to decry the Court's ruling on school Bible reading as a sign that the judiciary had rejected religious values, most evangelical leaders decided that the Court had acted wisely in putting an end to a tradition that violated the Constitution's establishment clause. No denomination passed a resolution in the 1960s objecting to either *Engel* or *Schempp*. *Christianity Today* and *Eternity* likewise accepted both decisions.[51]

In the 1960s, only a minority of conservative Protestants, such as fundamentalist radio preachers and the NAE, were ready to wage a campaign against the Supreme Court. The conservative Protestant political unity that had brought evangelicals and fundamentalists into a common coalition during the presidential election of 1960 had disappeared. After losing their fight to maintain Protestant control over the nation's governing institutions, conservative Protestants struggled to adjust to their new role as a beleaguered minority. They had no idea how to regain the political influence that they had lost with Kennedy's election. By 1964, they were more politically divided than they had been in at least twenty years.

| The Christian Silent Majority

O N THE EVE OF THE 1964 presidential election, Billy Graham told the
press that his own family was "politically divided." His sixteen-year-
old daughter Anne had recently gone to a rally for Republican presidential
candidate Barry Goldwater and had endorsed the Arizona senator, but the
nation's best-known evangelist insisted that he did not support his daughter's action. "President Johnson will get my prayers day and night," Graham
said. He refused to issue an endorsement in the election, and he advised
churches to "stay out of straight politics."[1]

The divide in Graham's family was replicated on a national scale. The
coalition of conservative Protestants that had supported Richard Nixon
in 1960 had disintegrated into competing factions. Some evangelicals,
including Graham, supported civil rights legislation, but many southern
fundamentalists staunchly opposed such measures, and they championed
Goldwater's candidacy as a way to fight the combined evils of communism,
secularism, and civil rights. Although the term was not yet in use, a Religious Right seemed to be developing among southern fundamentalists,
who argued that the Republican Party's platform promoted Christian
values. But opposing them was an even larger group of religious liberals
who believed that the civil rights activists were on God's side and that
Goldwater was not. Mainstream evangelicals such as Graham fell between
these two positions. Before a Christian "Silent Majority" could take shape,
evangelicals and fundamentalists had to come to an agreement on issues of
race and politics.

Fundamentalists and Civil Rights

Fundamentalists had preached against the civil rights movement almost since its inception, but until the early 1960s, they had directed their rhetoric primarily against civil rights activists, not the federal government. That changed in June 1963, when President John F. Kennedy endorsed a civil rights bill that promised to bring more substantive gains for African Americans than any previous piece of twentieth-century legislation. Appealing to the nation's Christian consciousness, the president declared the problem of racial discrimination "a moral issue . . . as old as the Scriptures and . . . as clear as the Constitution."[2]

Civil rights were a moral issue for southern fundamentalists as well, but not in the way that Kennedy had suggested. They saw the movement as an attack on the nation's well-being and a threat to the right of private institutions, including churches, to exclude anyone they wished. In 1963 Noel Smith wrote in his *Baptist Bible Tribune* that if Kennedy's proposed civil rights bill passed, any segregated church would lose its tax exemption, and the increased governmental control that would result from such legislation would soon lead down the slippery slope toward a full-fledged communist regime in America. "Mr. Kennedy is demanding that Congress enact legislation that will make the Federal government the absolute master of all stores, hotels, motels, restaurants, and theaters," Smith wrote. "By the same logic, by the same principle of law, the Federal government can become the master of the churches of this country. Not only can, but will. And what kind of a government will we then have? A Communist government."[3]

Nearly every fundamentalist preacher who wrote against the civil rights movement argued at length that he did not harbor any animosity against "the Negro" and that he knew many fine black Christians. But the civil rights "agitators" were in a different category because their demands were opposed to fundamental American values, such as the rights of free association and private property and the rule of law. "The basic proposition of these Negro agitators is that they should have what they want; not on the basis of character, of respect for law and order and the basic rules of personal and community health, but solely on the ground that their skin is black," Smith wrote. "Which means that they are contending for the very thing they profess to condemn: progress on the basis of the color of the skin." But Smith had confidence that their campaign would fail. "Mr. Kennedy, the Supreme Court, and the mobs are not going to succeed in forcing people to associate themselves against their mutual will and their mutual interests," he said.[4]

Southern fundamentalists were aghast in the spring of 1964 when President Lyndon Johnson, Kennedy's successor, succeeded in doing what they had thought impossible—securing a strong civil rights act that abolished legalized segregation in America. They had disliked Kennedy, but they discovered that Johnson, a fellow southern Democrat, was even worse. Bob Jones, Jr., announced that because of his opposition to interracial marriage and dating, his university would refuse to admit African Americans, in defiance of the law. If that resulted in a loss of the university's tax exemption, he would consider it religious "persecution," a stance that set him on a religiously inspired campaign against the president. "You can't preach today without preaching against the Administration," he said.[5]

Alienated from the government, some fundamentalists turned to politicians on the right whose campaigns centered on attacking Washington bureaucrats. Jones awarded Alabama's segregationist governor, George Wallace, an honorary doctorate from his university in May 1964, while the governor was in the midst of an unsuccessful challenge to President Johnson for the Democratic Party's presidential nomination. Wallace's opposition to civil rights legislation, Jones said, provided confirmation that there still remained "at least some hope for the preservation of our constitutional liberties." At a time when fundamentalists such as Jones were becoming increasingly testy about their representation in the media, they took heart that Wallace, too, had been "slandered, maligned, and misrepresented" by biased journalists, but had boldly maintained his defense of the principles he believed in. Such courage, Jones said, made the governor "a David warring against the giant, Tyranny."[6]

The close alliance between fundamentalists and the southern racist right worried political analysts. The assassination of a popular liberal president, an event that some people blamed on the influence of right-wing extremism in Dallas, and the unexpected success of the ultra-conservative Senator Barry Goldwater in the Republican Party presidential primaries seemed to be signs of a rejuvenated "radical right," a movement many thought had died with Joe McCarthy. Combining fears of internal communist subversion with opposition to the United Nations and civil rights, the "radical right"—a term that political analysts of the time used to describe groups ranging from the John Birch Society to the anticommunist radio broadcasters—was on the rise in the early 1960s. A flood of books published in 1964, including Arnold Forster and Benjamin Epstein's *Danger on the Right*, Brooks Walker's *The Christian Fright Peddlers*, and Harry and Bonaro Overstreet's *The Strange Tactics of Extremism*, argued that the "far right" was irrational and antidemocratic, a charge that echoed the arguments that Columbia historian Richard

Hofstadter had made the previous year in Daniel Bell's edited volume *The Radical Right*. Hofstadter blamed the paranoia of the right on fundamentalist religion. "To understand the Manichaean style of thought, the apocalyptic tendencies, the love of mystification, the intolerance of compromise that are observable in the right-wing mind, we need to understand the history of fundamentalism," Hofstadter wrote."[7] Such vilification from the intellectual establishment ensured that whatever political influence fundamentalists enjoyed would be regionally or religiously isolated, but it also increased fundamentalists' feelings of alienation and their determination to make their voice heard in a society that seemed increasingly hostile.

Fundamentalist Support for Goldwater

Fundamentalists who thought that Washington had abandoned American values considered Barry Goldwater a godsend. In a Republican Party that was still heavily influenced by northeastern business interests and moderate liberals, Goldwater's straight-shooting conservative rhetoric, southwestern heritage, virulent anticommunism, and hostility to almost all federal social spending put him on the far right of the nation's political spectrum. For many young Republicans, including the campus activists in the staunchly conservative Young Americans for Freedom, that was exactly what they wanted. Goldwater was especially popular among conservative activists in southern California, a center for the Sunbelt conservatism that later became the dominant political ideology in the Republican Party. But the GOP's northeastern wing held Goldwater in low esteem and expected the liberal New York governor Nelson Rockefeller to win the party's presidential nomination.[8]

Fundamentalists had not traditionally taken an interest in presidential primaries, but they showed an unusual concern about Rockefeller because of his recent high-profile divorce and remarriage. In 1962, after thirty-one years of marriage, the New York governor had divorced his wife, and a year later, he had married a woman who had left her husband and four children only a month before. With this scandal fresh on their minds, fundamentalists viewed Rockefeller's candidacy as a threat to the country's morals and a symbol of an ominous secular trend. "How can the decent, respectable people of the United States possibly place in the White House a man whose conduct is so obviously contrary to the moral standards of the Holy Scriptures as they pertain to holy matrimony[?]" the *Sword of the Lord* editorialized in July 1963. "May there be enough God-fearing people left in the United States to see that Nelson Rockefeller is not elected to the highest office in the government of this Republic!" The conservative Protestant reaction against Rockefeller was especially strong in California, because of the importance of the state's primary. As Rockefeller and Goldwater competed for votes in the nation's largest state, conservative Protestants rallied against the New York governor.[9]

One of the pastors who was particularly perturbed at the thought of Rockefeller winning the nomination was Tim LaHaye, a thirty-eight-year-old Baptist pastor in suburban San Diego. LaHaye had grown up in a working-class, single-parent home in Detroit. After serving in World War II, he had studied the Bible at Bob Jones University, a school that reinforced his family's fundamentalist Baptist religion. While LaHaye was at BJU, Bob Jones, Jr., was beginning to lead the school into anticommunist politics. But LaHaye said little in public about politics during the 1950s. After pastoring churches in rural South Carolina and urban Minneapolis, LaHaye and his wife, Beverly, moved to San Diego in 1956. The area was home to many southern evangelicals who shared the LaHayes' religious values, but it was also a region where cultural liberalism, represented by easy divorce and casual sex, coexisted in an uneasy tension with more traditional moral standards. In this environment, LaHaye became involved in an emerging conservative movement that was deeply suspicious of communism, social welfare spending, and cultural permissiveness, and that viewed Barry Goldwater as a hero. He began giving talks at meetings of the John Birch Society.[10]

In May 1964, shortly before his state's Republican primary, LaHaye sent a letter to evangelical pastors throughout California, urging them to vote against Rockefeller. "A wife stealer, who divorced his wife of 30 years, broke up another man's home, and took a mother from her four children, stands a good chance to win the approval of Republican voters in California," LaHaye wrote. "If he is elected it will be the same as public approval of his wicked actions, and [it will] help to skyrocket our divorce rate." He announced that he intended to deliver a Sunday morning sermon against Rockefeller, and urged other pastors to do the same. "The cost of being silent is just too great!" he warned.[11]

Goldwater defeated Rockefeller for the nomination and quickly won the support of many of the South's leading fundamentalists. They endorsed most of Goldwater's political positions, especially his hard-line anticommunism and opposition to civil rights. At a time when most of the nation's political leaders were becoming increasingly concerned about the dangers of nuclear weapons and welcomed antiproliferation treaties with the Soviet Union, Goldwater, like many fundamentalists, opposed such negotiations. And the senator's laissez-faire, libertarian ideals were good news for fundamentalists who feared state power.

Fundamentalists' devotion to Goldwater was so great that they overlooked some faults that ordinarily might have disturbed them. When the Arizona senator selected a New York Catholic to be his running mate, fundamentalists did not protest the choice, even though they had vehemently opposed Kennedy only four years earlier. Nor did they say anything about Goldwater's frequent profanity or lack of sympathy for evangelical religion. Instead, they focused on the senator's conservative ideology. Goldwater "seems to be the only anticommunist running," Carl McIntire said.[12]

Billy James Hargis was effusive in his praise for the Arizona senator. If Goldwater were elected and, with him, a conservative Congress, it would "be the millennium," he said. He hung a large picture of Goldwater behind the speakers at his August 1964 annual Christian Crusade convention and announced that he would "do everything in my power to help him." After the election, Hargis lamented the fact that he could not legally do more for the Goldwater campaign. "As an individual, I did everything I could for Senator Goldwater," he wrote. "I wished a thousand times that I could use my broadcasts . . . our publications . . . to inform our people of my personal reasons for backing Goldwater. But, I couldn't. The Internal Revenue Service would never forgive me if Christian Crusade had taken a stand for the Senator."[13]

Bob Jones, Jr., followed the lead of McIntire and Hargis, and publicly spoke out against Johnson's candidacy. He blamed the Democrats for liberal Supreme Court decisions, antibusiness policies, civil rights programs, and a weak military, and decided that it was time to repudiate the party. Other administrators at Bob Jones University concurred. Although he expressed concern that Goldwater was "not conservative enough," Laurence Lautenbach, the dean of Bob Jones University's College of Business, said that the Arizona senator's election would be a "step in the right direction." Inspired by the political stance of administrators at their school, a group of Bob Jones University students and faculty members took to the road in a "Goldwater bus" emblazoned with a banner that said, "Turn Back America! Only a Divine Miracle Can Save Us Now!"[14]

Southern fundamentalists' support of Goldwater placed them squarely at odds with liberal Protestant ministers. Many mainline Protestant leaders who had not previously been politically outspoken mobilized on behalf of the civil rights movement in the early 1960s, and developed a new interest in politics as a result. Goldwater represented everything that they opposed. He had voted against the Civil Rights Act of 1964, and he was opposed to social welfare programs and arms limitation treaties. To many liberal clergy, a vote for

Goldwater was un-Christian and immoral. "Goldwater has set himself against the overwhelming consensus of Christian social doctrines enunciated by the churches," a publication of the Council for Christian Social Action of the United Church of Christ declared in September 1964. "Christians when they vote should know that." The minister at the liberal Riverside Church in New York preached against Goldwater's failure to take the correct stand on civil rights, "one of the biggest moral issues before the nation." For the first time in its twenty-five years of publication, *Christianity and Crisis* issued a presidential endorsement, supporting Johnson. One of the nation's leading theologians, Reinhold Niebuhr, joined several of his colleagues in explaining that such an action was appropriate because "a vote for Mr. Goldwater is a vote for irresponsibility, recklessness, and reaction."[15]

The liberal clergy's opposition to Goldwater prompted a backlash among conservative Protestants, who objected to being called un-Christian. The anti-Goldwater denominational leaders, they claimed, were "so far out of touch with the thinking of both clergy and laity as to constitute an unrepresentative minority," and they had no right to claim that the collective Christian church—or even their own denominations—opposed Goldwater. *Christianity Today* accused liberal ministers who issued political endorsements of transgressing the boundary separating church and state. "Despite their tax-exempt status that is based on non-participation in politics and non-sponsorship of legislation, some religious publications editorially promoted the defeat of one candidate and the election of another," the magazine's editors complained. Liberal ministers had abandoned the kingdom of God for "a kingdom at whose entrance stood a polling booth."[16] Conservative Protestants who had once loudly denounced Kennedy from their pulpits became upset when liberal clerics did the same to Goldwater.

Appealing to religious conservatives, Goldwater highlighted his party's support for school prayer, though it contradicted his own libertarian ideals. Although many politicians of both parties supported a constitutional amendment to restore classroom prayer in public schools, the Republicans had taken the leadership on the issue, not only by authoring the leading amendment proposal in Congress, but also by officially endorsing such an amendment in their party platform. "The moral fiber of the American people is beset by rot and decay," Goldwater declared in a speech in Salt Lake City shortly before the election. "Is this the time in our nation's history for our federal government to ban Almighty God from our school rooms?" In the face of this "moral rot," the Democrats had ignored God, Goldwater charged. "You will search in vain for reference to God or religion in the Democratic platform," he said.[17]

Republican campaign commercials discussed rising juvenile delinquency, the proliferation of pornography, and even the president's personal vice of drinking beer while speeding around in his Lincoln Continental during vacations on his ranch. Rus Walton, an advertising agent who would become active in the Christian Right a decade later, produced a half-hour film entitled *Choice* that depicted the Democrats as the party of social disorder and moral decay. Many fundamentalists believed Republicans' claim that their party held the moral high ground. "I never heard one of Johnson's supporters ever fail to admit he is a crook," Bob Jones, Jr., told a group of political conservatives.[18]

Evangelical Ambivalence in the Election of 1964

Fundamentalists did not receive much support from evangelicals in their campaign for Goldwater. Most of the nation's evangelical leaders supported President Johnson's civil rights measures, so they had little reason to oppose his bid for reelection. The Southern Baptist Convention endorsed the Civil Rights Act of 1964, as did some evangelical preachers in the North. *Christianity Today*'s editorials from the summer of 1964 indicated the editors' frustration with southern fundamentalists who were determined to oppose civil rights. It was time, the magazine said, for Christians to give up their attraction to "strange, reactionary political ideas and groups that embarrass Christ's Church."[19]

Billy Graham avoided taking a specific stance on the Civil Rights Act of 1964 while it was being debated in Congress, but after it passed, he gave the cause of civil rights a general endorsement. "I think that many of the peaceful [civil rights] demonstrations have aroused the conscience of the nation," Graham said in 1965. "Demonstrations have brought about new, strong, tough laws that were needed many years ago." Unbeknownst to much of the public, Graham's once friendly relationship with Martin Luther King, Jr., had cooled in the early 1960s. Graham had been unwilling to support civil disobedience, and some black civil rights activists had begun to view him as a traitor to their cause. But Graham's cautious public endorsement of racial integration made him more useful than ever to racially progressive and centrist politicians who needed his influence to win over conservative southern whites and evangelicals.[20]

In July 1964, two months after the passage of the Civil Rights Act, President Lyndon Johnson, who was fully cognizant of Graham's national influence, asked him to chair a citizens' committee to oversee the implementation of the legislation. Graham was reluctant to serve as chair, but he did agree to become a member of the committee and to lend his imprimatur to civil rights law. A month later, Johnson showed his appreciation by inviting Graham and his wife to spend a night at the White House. Not even Eisenhower had given Graham such treatment. Fearful that Graham might be tempted to endorse Goldwater, Johnson began hosting the evangelist at the White House on a regular basis, and frequently sought both his spiritual and political counsel. He asked him for advice on a running mate, and questioned the preacher about what he should do after one of his close aides resigned following a homosexual affair. On some of Graham's visits, he swam with the president in the White House pool, or reminisced with him about life in the South. The two men developed a close friendship, but Johnson never lost sight of his ultimate goal in winning Graham to his side. "Now Billy, you stay out of politics," he told the evangelist, worried that he might succumb to the temptations of the Republican Party.[21]

In 1964, Graham followed this advice, as did many of his fellow evangelicals. By the fall of 1964, it had become clear that Goldwater's support came mainly from opponents of the civil rights movement, self-identified political conservatives, and the most extreme anticommunists—groups that many evangelicals, unlike southern fundamentalists, wanted to repudiate. Thus, even though Graham received 1 million telegrams urging him to endorse Goldwater, he refused to do so, and many suspected that he cast his ballot for Johnson. In a survey of evangelical publishers, *Christianity Today* found that 62 percent supported Johnson, while 38 percent favored Goldwater, a ratio that roughly approximated the sentiments of the general populace.[22]

But even if many evangelicals voted for Johnson, they gave his campaign only tepid support. Evangelical magazines such as *Christianity Today* refused to tell their readers how to vote in the upcoming election, a position that contrasted markedly with fundamentalist periodicals' enthusiastic endorsements of Goldwater and liberal Protestant magazines' equally strong denunciations of the Republican candidate. Wayne Dehoney, president of the Southern Baptist Convention, said that the presidential candidates of both parties championed values that he considered "basic in our Baptist tradition." Billy Graham summarized the feelings of many evangelicals who felt little inclination to become politically active in 1964. "I represent the kingdom of Heaven, and whatever government we have, I must support it," the evangelist said. He added, "I think the church sometimes becomes too involved in politics."[23]

The political division between evangelicals and fundamentalists reflected a larger regional divide. Goldwater won the electoral votes of only six states, five of which were in the Deep South. The rest of the country supported Johnson. Similarly, southern fundamentalists who opposed civil rights celebrated Goldwater's candidacy, while evangelicals who did not want to be tagged as "extremist" eschewed his campaign. The unified political coalition that conservative Protestants had created to oppose John F. Kennedy in 1960 was now only a memory. By 1964, conservative Protestants were politically factionalized over the issue of civil rights.

The Vietnam War and the Political Transformation of Evangelicals

The Vietnam War erased some of the political tensions between evangelicals and fundamentalists. As American military involvement in Vietnam escalated after 1965, an emerging Religious Left—mainline Protestant clergy from the World Council of Churches (WCC) and religious antiwar activists such as Catholic priest Daniel Berrigan and Yale chaplain William Sloan Coffin—denounced the war as immoral.[24] But evangelicals and fundamentalists were united in supporting the war, and their political divisions over civil rights no longer seemed as important as they had in 1964. Evangelicals' stance on the war also increased their influence in Washington, as hawkish politicians needed the support of conservative Christian ministers to counter criticism they faced from mainline Protestant clergy.

Fundamentalists, in keeping with their long tradition of anticommunism, supported the Vietnam War from the beginning. In 1966, John R. Rice wrote that he had "no doubt that if there is ever holy and righteous cause for war, it is to prevent godless communism." Two years later, as the tide of public opinion began to turn against the war, Bob Jones, Jr., said that he favored escalating the war effort and that he hoped the military would "drop an atomic bomb on Hanoi in order to end the war" if it were "necessary." Some fundamentalists condemned antiwar protestors by citing scriptural passages that commanded obedience to the government. When the National Guard killed four Kent State University students at a campus protest in 1970, Jones exclaimed, "Those young people got exactly what they were entitled to and what they ought to get out in Berkeley, too."[25]

While fundamentalists may have been the most active proponents of the war, moderate evangelicals were not far behind. In 1968, 54 percent of students at Chicago's Moody Bible Institute said they favored an increase in the level of bombing in North Vietnam, while only 21 percent of students at other American universities held that opinion. When the WCC called on President Johnson to halt the bombing of North Vietnam in the spring of 1966, *Christianity Today* denounced the resolution. For good measure, one of the magazine's editors, L. Nelson Bell, wrote a letter to President Johnson in late 1965 to tell him that he had nothing to fear from the antiwar Religious Left, because pro-war evangelicals greatly outnumbered liberal pacifists.[26]

Johnson recognized the value of evangelical support on the war, particularly when it came from Billy Graham. As early as 1954, Graham had told Eisenhower that "Indo-China must be held at any cost," and he continued to hold that view. "I think that the U.S. has a moral obligation to defend freedom in Southeast Asia," Graham told the press in September 1965. As liberal ministerial opposition to the war escalated, Johnson increasingly relied on Graham to fend off such attacks. He encouraged the evangelist to take a tour of Vietnam as General William Westmoreland's guest in December 1966, which Graham did. "I have no sympathy for those clergymen who [urge] the U.S. to get out of Vietnam," Graham said. "Communism has to be stopped somewhere, whether it is in Hanoi or on the West Coast. The President believes it should be stopped in Vietnam."[27]

As he had during the campaign of 1964, Johnson continued to rely on Graham for support of some of his domestic policies, including his antipoverty and civil rights initiatives. But it was on Vietnam that Graham proved of greatest service to the president. In addition to publicly supporting the war effort, Graham offered the president personal encouragement, urging him to stay the course in the fight against international communism. "No man has worked harder for his country than you," Graham told Johnson in July 1965. "I want to reassure you of my support, friendship, and personal affection. . . . The Communists are moving fast toward their goal of world revolution. Perhaps God brought you to the kingdom for such an hour as this—to stop them. In doing so, you could be the man that helped save Christian civilization."[28]

Graham's support for the war estranged him from the emerging antiwar wing of the Democratic Party. In December 1967, he criticized the antiwar message of Democratic presidential candidate Eugene McCarthy and suggested that he might support Republican candidate Richard Nixon. When Senator Robert Kennedy launched his campaign for the Democratic Party's presidential nomination on an antiwar platform, it did nothing to endear Graham or other evangelicals to the Democrats. Even though the party's nomination ultimately went to Johnson's vice president, Hubert Humphrey, rather than to an antiwar candidate, large numbers of Democrats at the party's convention in Chicago spoke out against the war, alienating voters who wanted victory in Vietnam. Some Democrats expressed alarm that the nation's most influential evangelical preacher was making no secret of his Republican sympathies in such an environment. James Rowe, a presidential campaign adviser, told Johnson in a memorandum in July 1968 that Democrats "are most disturbed because they understand that Billy Graham is getting ready to come out for Nixon." He noted that Johnson's "close relationship with Graham" had deterred the evangelist from speaking out against the Democrats in 1964, and he urged the president to use his influence to stop Graham from hurting the party among religious voters. "There must be some way or suggestion you can make on how to prevent Billy Graham from doing this," Rowe said.[29] But Johnson did nothing to dissuade Graham from supporting Nixon, leaving the evangelist to become more overt than ever in his support for the Republican Party.

The Christian Silent Majority

Shocking cultural changes swept the United States in 1967. Thousands of hippies converged on the Haight-Ashbury neighborhood of San Francisco for a summer of drugs, sex, music, and countercultural protest. During that same summer, angry African Americans in Detroit destroyed thirteen hundred buildings in a spontaneous eruption of rage against racist oppression. In Washington, DC, fifty thousand protestors descended on the Pentagon to denounce the Vietnam War.[30] Young men followed the example of the Beatles and began growing their hair out in opposition to their parents' wishes. Young women openly flouted the prevailing sexual norms in order to engage in "free love." Society, many Americans believed, was being torn apart from within. No one felt this sense of unease more keenly than fundamentalists and evangelicals.

Nearly all of the major fundamentalist publications of the late 1960s were filled with warnings about the nation's moral disintegration. In Oakland, California, Baptist pastor G. Archer Weniger filled his newsletter with warnings about the sexual revolution, the alleged "communist" lyrics in rock music, and crime. From his office in Springfield, Missouri, Noel Smith, the editor of the *Baptist Bible Tribune*, lamented America's national sins, ranging from the Supreme Court's decisions on school prayer and Bible reading in the early 1960s to the perceived breakdown in law and order at the end of the decade. John R. Rice gave his readers a similar diet of doom-and-gloom pronouncements. The social upheaval related to the civil rights movement, the urban race riots, sex education, and the nation's high-profile assassinations alarmed him. As *Sword of the Lord* proclaimed in 1968, the crises had brought the country "to the brink of civil war."[31]

Evangelicals were just as alarmed. In 1966, Billy Graham's *Hour of Decision* radio program included sermons such as "A Nation Rocked by Crime" and "Victory over Despair," while in early 1967, he preached on "Hope in Days of Evil," "Students in Revolt," "Conquering Teenage Rebellion," and "Obsession with Sex." By the summer of 1967, nearly all of Graham's sermons dealt with the national crisis that America was facing. Sermon titles such as "The Shadow of Narcotics Addiction," "Flames of Revolution," and "Rioting, Looting, and Crime" told evangelicals what they already sensed—that the nation was on the verge of disintegration. The title for Graham's radio sermon during the first week of August in 1967 summarized evangelicals' fears in one succinct phrase—"America Is in Trouble." The following year, the message was even more dire: "Can America Survive?"[32]

Conservative Protestants were especially disturbed by the nation's rapid changes in sexual morals. In the 1950s and early 1960s, most Americans had believed that people, and especially women, should reserve sex for marriage, a standard honored as much in the breach as in the observance. But by the late 1960s, a sexual revolution had largely erased the "double standard" in sexual behavior between men and women and had encouraged premarital sex without guilt. The birth control pill, which the FDA approved for public distribution in 1960, allowed young women to enjoy sex without worrying about getting pregnant. Books such as Helen Gurley Brown's *Sex and the Single Girl* (1962) directly challenged the traditional notion that women should maintain their virginity until marriage. By the end of the decade, several of the nation's leading universities had abandoned their traditional rules against male visitation in female dorms, and at a few places, college students had begun to openly cohabit with members of the opposite sex. Public opinion surveys revealed a rapid shift in college students' beliefs about sex. In the early 1960s, most college women believed that they should save sex for marriage, but by the end of the decade, many of them saw nothing wrong with premarital sexual affairs devoid of long-term commitment. In accordance with society's new openness about sexual behavior, educators called for a new sex education curriculum for the public schools.[33]

Pornography had also become more widely available. In the 1950s, social conservatives had been outraged by the popularity of Hugh Hefner's *Playboy*, and they had worked with Congress to restrict its circulation through the U.S. postal system. But a series of Supreme Court decisions upheld the right of risqué magazine publishers to produce erotic literature and limited the ability of social conservatives to restrict pornography in the name of public decency. As a result, by the mid-1960s, not only were drug stores and newsstands selling "girlie" magazines with nude centerfolds, but publishers were also free to produce homosexual pornography. In response, evangelicals allied with conservative Republican politicians to attack pornography through state legislation and referenda. In California, a state that produced 60 percent of the nation's pornography in the mid-1960s, Richard Barnes, a Methodist minister and Republican state legislator, joined with his fellow conservative state legislator William Dannemeyer and San Diego Baptist pastor Tim LaHaye to found the antipornography organization California League Enlisting Action Now (CLEAN). In 1966, CLEAN introduced Proposition 16, a state referendum to limit pornography in California. Even though it failed at the polls, it gained the endorsement of Republican gubernatorial candidate Ronald Reagan, and it brought evangelical pastors such as LaHaye into contact with wealthy conservative activists such as Walter Knott, whose Knott's Berry Farm fortune partially funded CLEAN's campaign.[34] Instead of retreating from the political sphere after their campaign was over, the social conservatives involved in CLEAN turned their attention to other related issues, particularly sex education.

Sex education became a controversial issue after 1964, when the Sex Information and Education Council of the United States (SIECUS), a creation of Dr. Mary Calderone and other medical experts, produced the nation's first comprehensive sex education program. At a time when the birth control pill was leading many young people to believe that their parents' concerns about teen sexual activity were outdated and irrelevant, Calderone and others hoped to give students a scientifically accurate perspective on sex that avoided moralizing and helped students draw on their personal values to make informed choices about sexual behavior. Educators across the nation welcomed Calderone's approach, and by 1968, nearly half of the country's schools had a sex education program.[35]

Social conservatives objected to the nonreligious and amoral context of Calderone's curriculum. In 1968, Eleanor Howe, a Catholic mother who had children enrolled in a public school in Anaheim, California, enlisted her neighbors in a grassroots campaign against sex education that not only succeeded in getting a new, conservative school board elected, but also gained the attention of conservative Republican state legislators in Sacramento. California state senator John Schmitz, a veteran of CLEAN and a socially conservative Catholic Republican, succeeded in passing a law that made it illegal for public schools to require students to take sex education. The campaign spread to other communities throughout the United States in 1969. In the South, organizations such as Association of Volunteers for

Educational Responsibility in Texas (AVERT) fought against sex education, and in the North, grassroots organizers in Racine, Wisconsin, and Minneapolis, Minnesota, blocked the introduction of sex education programs. A host of new single-issue organizations led the fight in many communities, while the Christian Crusade, the John Birch Society, and the American Education Lobby fought at the national level. In an unprecedented showing of political and religious ecumenism, fundamentalist Protestants, socially conservative Catholics, right-wing organizations, and conservative Republican legislators united in fighting sex education.[36]

The campaign against sex education transformed anticommunist organizations into defenders of a broader, socially conservative agenda. In 1969, when the John Birch Society launched the Movement to Restore Decency (MOTOREDE), an anti-sex-education affiliate, the society was in decline, unable to attract new recruits with dire warnings of a communist conspiracy. Sex education, which the society's members believed was a product of a communist plot, offered a more tangible enemy for social conservatives.[37]

Billy James Hargis's Christian Crusade, which had grown rapidly in the early 1960s through its aggressive campaign against communism, began campaigning against sex education in the summer of 1968. In a move that brought some needed talent to his organization, Hargis recruited Gordon Drake, a socially conservative Michigan educator, to coordinate a national campaign against sex education. The battle began with the publication of Drake's *Is the Schoolhouse the Proper Place to Teach Raw Sex?* which became the chief reference for those seeking a succinct denunciation of SIECUS. By 1969, sex education seemed to eclipse communism or the Supreme Court as the focus of the Christian Crusade's ire.[38]

At a time when politicians such as Ronald Reagan were building conservative political coalitions by denouncing government bureaucracy as hostile to the nation's families, social conservatives began to employ similar arguments in their defense of parental rights against the power of an increasingly secular state. Fundamentalists argued that SIECUS was a "usurpation of the authority of parents." Although they conceded that young people needed to learn about sex, they insisted that such teaching should occur "only by the proper parties at the proper time, when the youth are at the proper age." Fundamentalists and evangelicals produced sex education literature for use in their own homes during the late 1960s, but as one Denver fundamentalist publication stated, "All such sex teaching is the prerogative and the responsibility of the parents."[39]

By the late 1960s, many conservative parents realized that sex education was not the only sign of secularization in the public schools. Some social conservatives focused their ire on "situation ethics," a philosophical view that liberal theologian Joseph Fletcher popularized in a 1966 book. Employing an argument designed to appeal to a youth-oriented culture and a society experiencing rapid social change, Fletcher suggested that children had a right to determine their own values. Moral values, he said, were not absolute, so people should abandon the idea of universal moral codes. Not surprisingly, fundamentalists reacted negatively to Fletcher's ideas, and for the next two decades, they charged public schools with propagating his philosophy in classroom "values clarification" discussions that required children to engage in exercises in moral decision-making. Such discussions, they thought, were a blatant rejection of God's standard. "This so-called 'new morality' is nothing but immorality garbed in different terminology," an American Council of Christian Churches resolution proclaimed in April 1967. "'Situation ethics' is a revolt against God's law and His authority over the affairs of men."[40]

Sometimes fundamentalists linked their critique of "values education" to a broader conservative political program. Mel and Norma Gabler launched a nationwide campaign against the textbook industry in the 1960s and 1970s. The Gablers, who were devout Southern Baptists and ranchers from Longview, Texas, held conservative views in politics and religion, and they expected their local schools to do the same. They were therefore unpleasantly surprised in 1961 when their son alerted them to an allegedly liberal political bias in his high school history textbook. Much to their dismay, they discovered that their son's textbook praised the New Deal and the growth of the federal government in the twentieth century, and it depicted the Constitution as a document designed to promote, rather than limit, federal power. Their suspicions aroused, the Gablers began combing through other textbooks and became increasingly distressed by the passages that they read. High school economics textbooks taught Keynesian theory instead of the classical free-market model, history books neglected to mention the religious beliefs of America's founders, and biology texts presented Darwinian evolution as a fact rather than a mere hypothesis. The Gablers became so incensed by modern school curricula that they decided to make reviewing textbooks a full-time occupation.

Capitalizing on the fact that textbook publishers could not afford to ignore the demands of the huge Texas market, the Gablers painstakingly reviewed all textbooks that the Texas State Board of Education considered adopting each year, and then submitted a detailed list of the books' factual errors or bias in an attempt to influence the state's textbook selection. By 1981, their home-based organization had become a nationally known conservative pressure group with a mailing list of twelve thousand members.[41]

While some fundamentalists protested public school curricula, others, including Jerry Falwell, withdrew their children from the public education system and started private Christian schools, a move that increased their feeling of alienation from the government. Catholics and Lutherans had had their own parochial schools for generations, but until the mid-twentieth century, most fundamentalists, with the exception of Bob Jones, had given little thought to creating a system of private primary and secondary education. Now, having lost faith in the public school system, evangelicals and fundamentalists began constructing new private schools at the rate of two a day. By the late 1970s, there were at least five thousand Christian schools in the United States. With a few notable exceptions, these schools were small operations affiliated with an independent Baptist, charismatic, or conservative evangelical church. Many of them were nonaccredited, but that did not seem to matter to parents who wanted to give their children a conservative religious education coupled with strict discipline. From 1965 to 1975, enrollment in Christian schools grew by 202 percent, and by 1979, they had more than 1 million students.[42]

Some of the fundamentalist schools were clearly "segregationist academies" designed to escape the court-ordered racial integration of the public schools. But by the late 1960s, fundamentalists who opened such schools were often just as angry about sex education or the lack of classroom prayer as they were about integration. Jerry Falwell's Lynchburg Christian Academy offered a case in point. The school opened its doors in the fall of 1967, the same year in which Virginia's commissioner of education had ordered the immediate desegregation of all of the state's schools. Lynchburg Christian had a student body comprised entirely of whites, although it admitted its first African American student only two years later. But when Falwell spoke of his reasons for opening the school, he did not mention school integration, even though he had been an active proponent of maintaining segregated schools less than a decade earlier. Instead, he focused his attention on the Supreme Court's rulings against school prayer and Bible reading. "When a group of nine 'idiots' can pass a ruling down that it is illegal to read the Bible in our public schools, they need to be called idiots," he told his congregation in 1967. "Our nation was built upon Christianity and Christian principles, and no nine men have the power to undermine and rock that which God has built up."[43]

Falwell's eagerness to talk about secularization, rather than segregation, reflected a wider shift. Although Bob Jones University still refused to admit African American students, other fundamentalists were no longer as willing as they once had been to defend racial segregation. Falwell said in his autobiography, written twenty years after the events of the 1960s, that he had first been convinced of the injustices that African Americans experienced in 1963, when a black shoe shiner in Lynchburg asked him when he was going to be able to join the pastor's all-white church. Falwell claimed that he had been so touched by that remark, as well as by his experiences with blacks during a mission trip to the Dominican Republic that same year, that he began to change his thinking on race and decided to open his summer camp to black children.[44] Although his conversion on the subject was probably not as instantaneous or as complete as he made it appear, it was true that after 1963, he opposed the civil rights movement without defending segregation, a distinct contrast with the sermon that he had preached against integration in 1958. Instead of arguing that liberal ministers who supported civil rights were wrong because they violated God's rules about the separation of races, he argued that they were wrong because they had compromised their ministerial calling by becoming involved in political agitation.

Falwell's denunciation of all ministerial political activity—a position that he would later come to regret—was a sign of his desperation as he searched for an excuse to condemn the liberal clergy's participation in civil rights marches. "Believing the Bible as I do, I would find it impossible to stop preaching the pure saving gospel of Jesus Christ, and begin doing anything else—including fighting Communism, or participating in civil-rights reforms," he announced in March 1965 in a sermon titled "Ministers and Marches." "Preachers are not called to be politicians but to be soul winners."[45]

This may have seemed unusual coming from a minister who had already shown a proclivity for politics by becoming a leader in a campaign to maintain school segregation, but Falwell's stance was hardly unique. Even some of the nation's most vocal anticommunist preachers, such as Carl McIntire, were willing to resurrect the doctrine that preaching and politics should not mix after they heard about the hundreds of liberal ministers participating in civil rights demonstrations. "People have asked me what I thought about all these preachers going down to Mississippi and Alabama," he said in 1965. "I said they ought to stay home and preach the Gospel and set this country on fire with the message of salvation."[46] For fundamentalists, preaching against communism and liberalism was part of a Christian minister's calling, because communism was anti-Christian, but marching for civil rights was "meddling" and consisted of nothing more than "politics." Yet what was noticeably absent from these fundamentalist messages of the mid-1960s was any hint that segregation was morally right; most fundamentalists were no longer willing to make that argument.

John R. Rice went so far as to publish an editorial in 1964 stating that he supported the gradual desegregation of public schools and the right to vote for "Negroes who qualify." He was by no means endorsing King's campaign for social justice, but at the same time, he clearly differentiated himself from segregationist politicians, who were fighting a losing battle. "I think it is time for the 'Jim Crow' laws to be repealed," Rice wrote. After 1964, the difference between fundamentalists and evangelicals on racial issues began to narrow, as fundamentalists slowly began to accept the inevitability of civil rights reforms. In 1968, shortly after the assassination of Martin Luther King, Jr., Falwell admitted the first African American family to his church.[47]

But if fundamentalists reluctantly accepted integration, they continued to speak out against the Black Power movement, as did many evangelicals. The urban race riots of the late 1960s brought fundamentalists and evangelicals closer together, because both groups strongly opposed inner-city looters and Black Power activists who advocated violence as a solution to the nation's racial conflict. Fundamentalists blamed the urban riots on the agitation of nonviolent civil rights demonstrators and the acquiescence of liberal politicians. "The lawlessness of Martin Luther King and others, and the pussy-footing politicians who want the Negro vote, have made possible the treason of the Rap Browns and Carmichaels," John R. Rice wrote in April 1968, immediately after King's assassination. "We are sorry for the death of Martin Luther King. However, he who sowed lawlessness and thus brought about the death of others, reaped lawlessness." Bob Jones, Jr., shared Rice's view, and when the civil rights leader was assassinated, his university refused to lower its flags to half-mast.[48]

Billy Graham refused to speak against King in those terms, but he, too, condemned the race riots and supported a tough-minded attitude toward African Americans who engaged in violence. "There is no doubt that the rioting, looting and crime in America have reached the point of anarchy," Graham told *Hour of Decision* listeners in 1967. A decade earlier, Graham had taken a leading role among white evangelicals in supporting integration efforts, and he had endorsed King's moral leadership during the Montgomery bus boycott. But his position had gradually become more conservative. As a strong proponent of a brand of anticommunist religion that closely identified God's purposes with those of the state, he had objected to the civil disobedience of the early 1960s. In 1965, he had expressed concern that "some of these demonstrations have gotten out of hand and are getting more and more violent," even though he continued to laud King and other civil rights leaders for their achievements. By the late 1960s, he was issuing unqualified denunciations of urban riots. "We've got to have law and order, no matter how much power and force it takes," he said in November 1968, in an indirect endorsement of Richard Nixon. By that point, civil rights activists no longer considered the evangelist an ally, because Graham's rhetoric on the subject of race had become barely distinguishable from that of conservative Republican politicians.[49]

Graham's change in opinion reflected a larger shift in the American public that benefited the Republican Party. In 1966, after a year of race riots, polls showed that for the first time since Kennedy's civil rights proposals in 1963, a majority of white Americans thought that the government was moving "too fast" on civil rights. In the midst of this backlash, the open housing legislation that Johnson had proposed to allow African Americans to move into middle-class white neighborhoods stalled in Congress. Martin Luther King, Jr., met a hostile reception in Chicago in 1966, and his influence with the administration began to wane. Several Republican politicians replaced the national call for civil rights legislation with a demand for punitive measures against rioters. Partly as a result of the public's desire for "law and order," Republicans picked up forty-seven seats in the House of Representatives in the midterm elections of that year and also won several governorships. In California, the political neophyte Ronald Reagan won a gubernatorial election by calling for tougher action against crime, militant Black Power activists, and long-haired campus protestors who, he said, "act like Tarzan, look like Jane, and smell like Cheetah."[50]

But no national politician combined the themes of opposition to campus protests, race riots, and alleged cultural decline as successfully as Richard Nixon. By 1968, the year that Nixon launched his second campaign for president, 81 percent of Americans believed that the nation had failed to maintain "law and order."[51] At a time of such great social unrest, Nixon made "law and order" not only a campaign slogan, but also a path to his own political rehabilitation. In Nixon, evangelicals and fundamentalists found a candidate who understood their dismay at the moral decline of the nation. In 1960, they had rallied around Nixon as the candidate of Protestant America who could save them from a Catholic presidential candidate. Eight years later, as part of Nixon's "great, silent majority," they looked to the Republican presidential candidate to save their country from secularization, moral disintegration, and social anarchy, and in the process return the nation to its traditional religious and moral values.

FIVE

Nixon's Evangelical Strategy

ONE YEAR BEFORE THE PRESIDENTIAL election of 1968, Richard Nixon launched a political comeback as a social conservative with an article in *Reader's Digest*. At a time when many were alarmed at the nation's rising sexual libertinism, race riots, illicit drug use, and campus protests, Nixon positioned himself as a champion of public morality who would return the nation to its bedrock values of religious faith, strong families, and public decency. "Does America have the national character and moral stamina to see us through this long and difficult struggle?" Nixon asked. "We must face up to an unpleasant truth: A nation weakened by racial conflict and lawlessness at home cannot meet the challenges of leadership abroad."[1]

Nixon's message resonated with evangelicals who had believed for at least two decades that the fight against international communism depended on the maintenance of a public faith and morality at home. Like the evangelicals, Nixon proclaimed that the keys to public morality were personal responsibility and stable families. "Of what value to our community is one of our federal programs that provides money for dependent children—only as long as the fathers stay away from the home?" he asked. Instead of honoring its families, Nixon said, the nation had jettisoned traditional values, and as a result, there had been a "decline in respect for public authority and the rule of law in America."[2]

A cynic might have questioned Nixon's sincerity. After all, it was not the first time he had tried to reinvent himself. Nixon had been an aggressive, conservative anticommunist in the late 1940s and early 1950s; a mature, centrist candidate in 1960; an embittered, defeated politician in 1962; and, in the elections of 1964 and 1966, a loyal Republican foot soldier campaigning for GOP candidates regardless of ideology. But while Nixon may not have been ideologically consistent, he was always politically astute. With his instinctive feel for the political anxieties of "Middle America," he guessed that an emerging "silent majority" wanted a champion of public morality as its president. Nixon found the role a natural one. A lapsed Quaker who had little personal religious faith, he sometimes winced at the pietistic pronouncements of his evangelical supporters, but he relished the thought of a socially conservative campaign that attacked Ivy League–educated liberals and their long-haired, radical children. Nixon's motives may have been cynical, but evangelicals were so eager to find a champion of traditional morality that they did not doubt that Nixon was a true believer.

The Election of Richard Nixon

Nixon's outreach to evangelicals began even before he announced his candidacy. Billy Graham had maintained a correspondence with Nixon after his defeat in 1960, so the former vice president found it easy to call on the evangelist for some political help. Three months after his article appeared in *Reader's Digest*, he summoned Graham to his vacation home in Key Biscayne, Florida. It was during the Christmas holidays, and Graham was sick with pneumonia, but Nixon felt that it was imperative to have the evangelist's blessing before he entered the presidential race. During Graham's three-day visit, they read scripture and talked about football and religion, but Nixon was most interested in discussing his proposed presidential bid. Graham listened politely, but he avoided giving Nixon the direct encouragement that he wanted. "What should I do?" Nixon asked Graham at the visit. Graham responded that if Nixon did not run, he would spend the rest of his life wondering whether he could have won the presidency. Then—at least in Nixon's telling—Graham gave him the blessing that he had been seeking. "Dick, I think you should run. . . . You are the best prepared man in the United States to be President."[3]

Graham later denied giving Nixon such a direct endorsement, saying only that he had offered to pray that God would give Nixon "wisdom to make the right choice." But even though Nixon had begun making plans for his presidential bid long before his walk on the Florida beach with Graham, he found it politically useful to claim that the evangelist had pushed him into running. Throughout the campaign, Nixon continued to use his ties to Graham for political advantage. In September, he attended a Graham crusade in Pittsburgh, and then flew to Charlotte, North Carolina, to visit Graham's mother, who proudly wore a Nixon campaign button for the reporters who spoke with her afterward. When Graham let it slip in late October that he had cast his absentee ballot for Nixon, Nixon's campaign ran a television ad announcing the fact. Anticipating a close race, the Nixon campaign depended on the evangelist's support to pick up votes in the upper South and suburban areas, where conservatives were receptive to a call for "law and order" and a return to "traditional" values.[4]

Despite Graham's protestations of nonpartisanship, he proved more than willing to give Nixon the support that he craved. Only a few days after his meeting with Nixon in Key Biscayne, he told a crowd in Atlanta that Nixon was the "most experienced Republican" running for president. As the campaign progressed, Graham began to speak of the candidate in even more glowing terms. "There is no American that I admire more than Richard Nixon," he told a crusade audience in May 1968. In September, he assured the press that Nixon's reputation as "tricky Dick" was completely undeserved and that he was a "man of high moral principles." Even when Graham was not discussing Nixon directly, he often echoed his campaign themes. At one crusade, he praised the "great unheard-from group" that were "not out carrying placards and demonstrating," saying that they would "be heard from loudly at the polls."[5]

Although Graham had refused to take sides in 1964, he decided that the nation's rapid moral decline made it impossible for him to remain neutral in 1968. "I feel that the very survival of the country may be at stake in this year's election," he said. He feared a coming judgment of God on the nation. As his wife, Ruth Bell Graham, told the press, "If God does not punish America for its sins, He will have to apologize to Sodom and Gomorrah." Nixon was the candidate who would bring moral order to the country and adopt policies representing the conservative social values of evangelical Christians, Graham believed. At the Republican national convention, the evangelist attempted to shore up support for Nixon among southern delegates and convince wayward conservatives not to cast their ballots for Ronald Reagan.[6]

Graham and Nixon both knew that if they did not present a united front, the Republicans would likely lose critical southern states to Alabama governor George Wallace, a third-party candidate whose "law and order" rhetoric was so tough that he promised to run over any antiwar demonstrator who lay down in front of his car. As a candidate who had achieved national notoriety by defying federal court orders to desegregate his state's schools, Wallace appealed to social conservatives who disapproved of the civil rights movement and who distrusted the "pointy-headed intellectuals" in Washington's federal agencies. But while Wallace did well among laypeople in rural Southern Baptist and Methodist precincts, he received his strongest support from non-churchgoers rather than from pastors. Northern evangelicals repudiated Wallace, and none of the major fundamentalist leaders in the South endorsed him. Billy James Hargis and John R. Rice supported Nixon.[7]

Fundamentalists' relatively cool reception of Wallace was partly a reflection of their desire to distance themselves from the overt racism that had characterized their churches for much of the decade. In the late 1960s and early 1970s, some fundamentalist churches that had resisted the civil rights movement accepted a few African American members, and as they did so, their pastors quickly became embarrassed by the blatant racism associated with their movement. In 1969, the American Council of Christian Churches, a fundamentalist organization that had long followed the lead of its founder, Carl McIntire, voted not to renew McIntire's seat on the executive committee because of his support for Georgia's openly racist governor, Lester Maddox. In 1970, Moody Bible Institute, a flagship school of northern fundamentalism, canceled John R. Rice's speaking invitation after Rice published an editorial in *Sword of the Lord* condemning interracial marriage and defending Bob Jones University's refusal to admit African American students. Rice had endorsed racial integration several years earlier, but by 1970, some fundamentalists considered that stance no longer sufficiently tolerant if it was coupled with opposition to interracial marriage. Dallas Baptist pastor W. A. Criswell, who became president of the Southern Baptist Convention in 1968, apologized to the SBC for endorsing segregation a decade earlier, and announced his unqualified support for racial integration in churches and society. In such a climate, Nixon was a more attractive candidate than Wallace. In October 1968, *Christianity Today* published an editorial denouncing the Alabama governor, an unusually partisan move on the part of an editorial board that generally tried to be more subtle in its political statements.[8]

By moving beyond the blatant racism of their past, evangelicals and fundamentalists positioned themselves for national political influence. Wallace, despite his national aspirations, was only a regional candidate; he carried only five states in the Deep South in 1968, and many northerners scorned him. Nixon, on the other hand, was a national candidate who carried states in every region of the country, from the southern perimeter to the West Coast, by employing a new conservative rhetoric of "law and order" that avoided a direct discussion of race. While Wallace carried the rural counties of the South, where overt racism was still prevalent, the South's suburban counties, with rapidly growing, conservative evangelical churches, voted for Nixon.

Nixon carried Jerry Falwell's Campbell County in Virginia, Billy Graham's Buncombe County in North Carolina, W. A. Criswell's Dallas County in Texas, and Bob Jones's Greenville County in South Carolina. Other southern suburban counties that would later become Christian Right strongholds, such as Cobb County, Georgia, likewise voted for Nixon.[9] Conservative Protestants' political choice in 1968 marked their rejection of the regional isolationism of the rural South and made them a vital component of Nixon's political coalition and of the Republican Party.

Shortly after Nixon's victory in 1968, political scientists began speaking of the Republican-leaning counties of the rapidly growing metropolitan South and West as the "Sunbelt," a region that they said stretched from Virginia to California and included such metropolitan areas as Atlanta, Houston, Dallas, Phoenix, and Los Angeles. Although no one could define the precise parameters of the Sunbelt, since the term described more a cultural and political attitude than a geographical concept, it was easy to see how its political effects benefited Nixon and the GOP. The mostly white, college-educated workers who moved to Sunbelt suburbs to take high-tech jobs in the region's rapidly growing defense industries favored Republican politicians who supported a strong military. They worried about the effect that rising crime might have on the safety of their neighborhoods, so they were receptive to calls for "law and order" from conservative politicians. They disliked the overt racism and economic populism of southern Democrats such as Wallace, but they supported Republicans such as Nixon and Reagan who knew how to denounce crime, drugs, and welfare without mentioning race.[10]

Many of the new residents of the Sunbelt joined evangelical churches, shifting the nation's religious balance of power from northern mainline Protestant denominations to predominantly southern evangelical churches. Before the late 1960s, mainline Protestants, represented by the National Council of Churches (NCC), had enjoyed more political influence, wealth, and education than evangelicals had. During Franklin Roosevelt's administration, representatives of mainline Protestant denominations had frequently visited the White House and Capitol Hill, while fundamentalists and evangelicals had no representatives in Washington. Evangelicals had acquired an increased influence in the nation's political life in the 1950s, but even during that era, the NCC attracted more political attention than the National Association of Evangelicals (NAE) or any evangelical denomination did. But in the late 1960s, membership in mainline Protestant churches declined rapidly, while evangelical congregations grew. Americans in the mainline-Protestant bastions of New England and the mid-Atlantic no longer went to church as frequently as they once had, while

Americans in the South and Southwest began pouring their increased wealth into building larger churches that combined an array of social services, such as youth programs and marriage counseling, with a traditional evangelical theology. By the early 1970s, the nation's ten largest churches were located in the South, West, and socially conservative Midwest, and nearly all of them were evangelical.[11] The growth of Sunbelt evangelicalism offered Nixon a political boost. At a time when the NCC and the nation's mainline Protestant clerics were denouncing his foreign policy in Vietnam, he could rely on the support of politically conservative, evangelical ministers.

President Nixon and the Evangelicals

Immediately after taking office, Nixon bolstered his support among the religiously devout by inaugurating a series of Sunday morning White House church services. Nixon's close associates knew that church worship bored him and that he tried to avoid going whenever possible. But the administration could not let Americans know about the president's lack of personal piety. The White House services offered an ideal way to present a devout image to the public while simultaneously politicking with the invited guests, whom the White House staff carefully selected for their political influence and potential usefulness to the administration. "Develop a list of rich people with strong religious interest to be invited to the White House Church services," a White House memo directed Charles Colson.[12]

Each week, White House aides arranged for a different visiting pastor and choir to appear, and they treated both the music and the sermon as politically significant. In July 1970, when Tennessee Republican candidate William Brock, a Presbyterian, was challenging the Southern Baptist Democratic incumbent, Senator Albert Gore, for his seat in the U.S. Senate, the Nixon White House invited a Memphis Presbyterian choir to the White House in order to show its support for a home state representative of Brock's denominational tradition. "This would supposedly be *very* helpful to Bill Brock in his attempt to unseat Albert Gore in the Senate Race," a White House aide noted.[13]

Two weeks later, when the administration found itself in trouble with the Southern Baptist Convention for appointing an ambassador to the Vatican, it extended a White House preaching invitation to SBC president Carl Bates to make amends. Bates was a "staunch Republican, a good friend of Billy Graham," one White House staff member noted. "It would be very good politics . . . that he be invited to preach at a White House Church Service."[14]

Nixon aides also attempted a direct manipulation of the politics of the Southern Baptist Convention. In late May 1970, the administration faced a wave of negative criticism as students across the country demonstrated against Nixon's secret bombing of Cambodia. But fewer than 12 percent of Southern Baptist pastors opposed the president's policy in Vietnam, and more than 80 percent supported it. Charles Colson decided that a show of support from the 11-million-member Southern Baptist Convention could give the president the political cover he needed to deflect criticism from more liberal denominations. In order to encourage the SBC to pass a resolution endorsing the president's foreign policy, Colson suggested that the president send a telegram congratulating the SBC's Foreign Mission Board on its 125th anniversary, and then have Fred Rhodes, the deputy director of the Veterans Administration, make an appearance on the floor of the Convention's annual meeting. The tactic worked: the SBC gave the president the resolution that he wanted.[15]

Unaware of Nixon's political machinations, evangelicals basked in the attention that they received from the White House. They were ecstatic that Nixon relied on one of their own—Billy Graham—to facilitate his White House services. Previous presidents had, for the most part, attended mainline or theologically liberal churches, but Nixon chose an evangelical minister as his preacher. Graham officiated at the first White House worship service, and then, at the invitation of the White House, submitted a list of suggested speakers for future services. The new practice of church in the White House benefited both men, offering Graham an opportunity to promote the civil religious ideals that he had preached since the Eisenhower years, and Nixon a chance to engage in an unprecedented political manipulation of religious groups. Even if Nixon was not an evangelical, conservative Christians thought of him as a fellow Christian because of his connection with Graham.[16]

Graham, for his part, was fully willing for the White House to use him as a political operative in order to bring evangelicals into the Nixon coalition. He let White House aides know which Southern Baptist pastors were politically conservative—and therefore good candidates for a White House speaking invitation—and which ones might be most helpful to Nixon in his reelection campaign. He arranged for the president to send telegrams of support to key evangelical meetings, such as Explo '72 in Dallas, and invited him to make conspicuous appearances at his crusades. He also worked to sell White House policy to his fellow believers. As the nation was experiencing a cultural rift over the Vietnam War, Graham preached conservative patriotism and national unity, a message that closely echoed the president's. He spoke out in favor of Nixon's war strategy, saying that the president was "motivated by a desire for peace." When southern whites objected to Nixon's efforts to enforce court-ordered school desegregation, Graham, at Nixon's request, taped a series of television public service announcements urging southerners to comply with White House civil rights policy.[17]

Nixon also tapped Graham, who had been traveling internationally for two decades and had contacts in many high places overseas, for unofficial ambassadorial duties. When the administration began making plans for a historic goodwill trip to China, America's long-standing ally in Taiwan, General Chiang Kai-shek, became enraged and refused to discuss the matter with Nixon administration officials. Billy Graham, he declared, was the only American he was willing to see. Seizing this opening, Nixon's advisers brought Graham to the White House for foreign policy briefings, and then sent him off to Taipei. White House Chief of Staff H. R. Haldeman assured Henry Kissinger that the evangelist would "try to explain things to them in whatever way we want them explained."[18]

Graham also helped the president sell his new China policy to skeptical evangelicals and fundamentalists. When the president announced his plans for a trip to communist China and began arms limitation talks with the Soviet Union, many of his fundamentalist supporters were aghast. "The Suicide of a Nation—Ours!" proclaimed a headline in Billy James Hargis's *Christian Crusade Weekly* in October 1971. Subsequent issues of Hargis's publication grumbled about the "Leftist direction taken by the Nixon administration." Nixon used Graham to mute such criticism by encouraging him to bring twenty or twenty-five "highly influential people within the conservative ranks" to meet with Henry Kissinger for a briefing on the rationale for the president's trip to China. Later, Graham invited a group of nationally known evangelicals, including W. A. Criswell, Oral Roberts, *Christianity Today* editors Harold Lindsell and Harold O. J. Brown, and Campus Crusade founder Bill Bright, for another session with Kissinger on "China policy."[19]

Evangelicals such as Graham supported the president even when he deviated from their policy goals because they feared that they were losing control of their country, and they longed for someone to restore public piety and morality. A Gallup poll showed that in 1970, 75 percent of Americans thought that the influence of religion in America was declining, compared to only 14 percent of Americans who had believed that in 1957. Evangelicals' fear of secularization permeated the letters they sent to the White House. They complained about the "atheists or communists" who were "actually running the country," and public school curricula's "atheistic and faith-snatching ideas," which had produced "so many delinquents and the sort of hippies and young people we have." But Nixon gave them hope that the nation could be saved. "There is no doubt in my mind that you are a sincere, born-again Christian," Billy James Hargis declared after seeing the president's worship services. As one Baptist pastor in Wichita, Kansas, told the president in a letter, "With your God-fearing attitude and spiritual insight I believe our nation is on the right track."[20]

Nixon's efforts to manipulate evangelical political opinion occasionally backfired when he was too tactless in his effort to turn Christians' religious meetings into political gatherings. When the White House, at Billy Graham's urging, tried to secure an invitation for Nixon to speak to a Campus Crusade event in Dallas in 1972, some members of Campus Crusade protested, and the president abandoned the idea. Similarly, the White House tentatively arranged for the president to address the Southern Baptist Convention during his reelection campaign, but several Southern Baptist pastors complained. Nixon again found an excuse to cancel. For a brief while, Southern Baptists enjoyed a respite from the Nixon administration's attempts to use them for political gain.[21]

The respite would indeed be brief. Nixon did not personally attend the meeting, but White House aides attempted to acquire even greater influence over the Convention through a political coup to install one of their own, deputy Veteran Affairs administrator Fred Rhodes, as the Convention's president. Having a member of the administration as head of the SBC was "obviously in the President's interest," Colson told a White House official. In addition to inviting Rhodes to preach at the White House, Colson decided to "run a little campaign" to convince Southern Baptists to elect Rhodes.[22]

The plan failed. The SBC elected one of the most politically liberal presidents that it had had in years—the pro–civil rights Democrat Owen Cooper, a friend of Georgia governor Jimmy Carter. One year later, Cooper used his annual Convention address to rebuke the Nixon administration for the Watergate scandal.[23] Cooper's presidency did little to shift the Southern Baptist Convention away from its growing social conservatism or its general support of Nixon, but his election did indicate the limits of the administration's evangelical strategy.

Nixon was unable to control the Southern Baptist Convention partly because he had little understanding of evangelicals' specific political or religious concerns. His conversations with White House aides about strategies to win the evangelical vote revealed significant gaps in his knowledge. He frequently called evangelicals "fundamentalists," even though they had abandoned that moniker more than two decades earlier. He thought that they were still virulently anti-Catholic, even though many evangelicals, including Graham, were beginning to accept Catholics as socially conservative allies. He knew the names of hardly any national evangelical leaders besides Graham.

But he had a sense that the evangelicals were on his side, and that feeling often made up for his ignorance of evangelical theology. Evangelicals were the "decent people of America," he said. At a time when most mainline religious leaders—a group that he called a "terrible bag"—were rejecting his policies, he knew that he could depend on evangelicals to support the socially conservative values that he championed. "The only character you find in religion in this country happens to be among the fundamentalists," he mused in an Oval Office conversation with conservative writer Russell Kirk. "The Billy Grahams and all the rest, the Southern Baptists and so forth, they've got character. They've got guts to believe in something."[24]

Billy Graham's Role in Nixon's Reelection Campaign

Nixon and his aides decided that their best chance of winning reelection was to reach out to socially conservative voters in the suburban areas of the Sunbelt and Midwest. Two political science studies—Kevin Phillips's *The Emerging Republican Majority* (1969) and Richard Scammon and Ben Wattenberg's *The Real Majority* (1970)—became their campaign bibles. The books argued that the Republican Party was poised for future electoral dominance if it continued to gain voters in the rapidly growing, culturally conservative regions of the country. But Republicans would win this area only if they continued to emphasize "law and order" and conservative social values. Guided by these arguments, Nixon spoke often about crime, moral values, and the "silent majority." He highlighted his efforts to restrict pornography and his opposition to campus protestors. And to increase his share of the southern and Midwestern evangelical vote, he turned to Billy Graham.[25]

Immediately after the midterm elections of 1970, the president sent a memo to White House aide H. R. Haldeman outlining the way in which Graham could lock up the conservative Protestant vote for the Republicans. "He was enormously helpful to us in the Border South in '68 and will continue to be in '72," Nixon wrote. "We have to remember that our primary source of support will be among the fundamentalist Protestants, and we can probably substantially broaden that base of support."[26]

At the president's request, Haldeman held regular meetings with Graham from February 1972 through the election in order to discuss strategy and the way that the campaign was playing out among evangelicals in the nation's heartland. As a lapsed Christian Scientist, Haldeman had little direct knowledge of American evangelical political views, so he peppered Graham with questions. How much negative campaigning would they tolerate? What could Nixon do to defuse Democratic candidate George McGovern's appeal to left-wing evangelicals who were concerned about social welfare? "Should the President attack McGovern or should he carry on the theme of 'Bring Us Together?'" Haldeman asked Graham. Haldeman also floated the idea of a more direct cooperation between the Nixon campaign and American evangelicals. Would it be appropriate, he asked Graham, for members of the Committee to Re-elect the President (CREEP) to work with the staff of Bill Bright's Campus Crusade for Christ? The Nixon White House even tried unsuccessfully to secure Graham's mailing list. "We were scheming to win their support," Charles Colson recalled in an interview years later. "We were looking at the conservative Evangelical votes as the political [movement] that actually did emerge in the eighties."[27]

Graham encouraged Nixon campaign strategists to look at conservative evangelicals as an emerging voting bloc. "I have been pointing out to you in a number of conversations that we have had that there is an emerging evangelical strength in this country that is going to have a strong bearing on social and political matters probably for a generation to come," Graham told the president in August 1972. In Graham's view, an alliance between evangelicals and the president would not only advance evangelicals' social status, but would also be the key to promoting the president's vision of "law and order" and public morality. To achieve that goal, Graham had to convince the White House to begin looking at white evangelicals as a voting constituency, and he had to become a political strategist himself as he worked to secure the president's reelection. Graham gave Nixon an official endorsement in 1972—the first time that he had ever directly endorsed a candidate for president, though in most previous elections, he had left little doubt about his political sympathies.[28]

Although Graham faced some public criticism for his association with Nixon, he could take comfort in the fact that most evangelicals seemed to relish the thought of an evangelical preacher in the White House, since it gave their movement unprecedented access to the corridors of power. "We grant that there is risk involved when a clergyman becomes a confidant of powerful figures in the secular world," a *Christianity Today* editorial noted in March 1972. "But is not the risk far outweighed by the opportunity? Have not many evangelicals long prayed for an entrée without compromise into the affairs of state? . . . In the case of Graham, there is no evidence that he has watered down his convictions to gain access to the White House."[29]

Graham's identification with the president probably cost him influence outside Republican circles and compromised his ability to pose as a nonpartisan national evangelist. Graham was eager to reach out to young people, minor-ities, and the "unchurched" in the early 1970s, and he appeared at evangelism conferences with young black evangelicals who were critical of the Nixon administration. But despite his stated desire to reach out to those outside the conservative fold, the audiences at his crusades consisted almost entirely of white, conservative, middle-class Americans who shared his view of America's place in the world. In July 1972, when Graham preached in Cleveland, a majority-black city that had recently elected an African American mayor, his audience was 99 percent white. Many African Americans saw him as a lackey of the conservative establishment, a symbol of the racism of the Republican White House.[30]

A few northern evangelical academics who disapproved of Graham's pres-idential alliance decided to rally behind George McGovern, a Methodist minister's son. The young founders of Evangelicals for McGovern believed in a political program that emphasized concern for the poor, the disfranchised, and the oppressed, and they objected to their elders' unquestioning support for the Vietnam War and the Republican Party. Some had written provoca-tive critiques of mainstream evangelicalism, and they viewed Evangelicals for McGovern as another challenge to evangelicals' blithe acceptance of the status quo. In a mass mailing to other liberal evangelicals, Walden Howard, the organization's chair, wrote, "Let's end the outdated stereotype that evangel-ical theology automatically means a politics unconcerned about the poor, minorities, and unnecessary military expenditures."[31]

Howard agreed with Graham and many other evangelicals that Christians should support candidates whose policies they thought most closely reflected the views of Jesus—they just disagreed on who those candidates were. "Pol-icies, however camouflaged, which are designed to slow down or reverse racial progress grieve the One whose eternal Son became incarnate in the Middle East. . . . If Amos is right in declaring that God disapproves when the rich live in luxury at the expense of the poor, then surely evangelicals should help McGovern close the [tax] loopholes and make the rich pay their fair share," Howard wrote. He contrasted McGovern's "courageous stand" for school busing with Nixon's attempt to "profit from a white backlash," and he praised McGovern's opposition to the war, a stance that he credited to the "honesty" that McGovern's "Wesleyan Methodist parents" had instilled in him.[32]

Howard and his associates sent out mass mailings, held interviews with major news magazines, and made phone calls to raise funds for McGovern's campaign, but their biggest coup came when McGovern made a campaign stop at Wheaton College, the nation's premier evangelical institution of higher education and the alma mater of both Graham and Howard. With less than one month to go before the election and with an abysmally low rating in public opinion polls, McGovern used the occasion to reach out to evangelicals and frame his political positions in religious terms. He was an evangelical minister's son, a former student minister, and a fervent believer in social morality, he said. His candidacy was a fight for "moral and spiritual values." In a speech laden with biblical quotations and references to Jesus' teachings, he talked about the importance of feeding the hungry, promoting social justice, and caring for others through the political system. It was time, he said, for the presidency to return to moral leadership and for the country to recover the spiritual values on which it was founded. "The wish of our forebears was to see the way of God prevail," McGovern told the Wheaton students. "We have strayed from their pilgrimage, like lost sheep. But I believe we can begin this journey anew."[33]

Some younger evangelicals were hopeful that Graham's version of evangelical politics might give way to McGovern's. "The days when the old-line evangelist spoke for all of us are gone," remarked a twenty-four-year-old Jim Wallis, editor of the recently created leftist evangelical newspaper the *Post-American*. "I personally think that the strongest single source of change and prophetic witness in America is going to come from evangelical sources."[34]

But Wallis's prediction was far off the mark. Few evangelicals embraced McGovern's ideology. Even at Wheaton, many students attended his speech armed with Nixon campaign signs. McGovern spoke the Christian language of social compassion, but he failed to deliver the evangelical message of American patriotism, which, by the 1970s, had become crucial to winning votes among conservative Protestants. At Explo '72, a national convention for young evangelicals that Billy Graham helped to organize, only 11 percent of the attendees expressed support for McGovern.[35]

But the prospect that even a small contingent of evangelicals might defect to McGovern alarmed fundamentalists. Leaders of Billy James Hargis's Christian Crusade viewed a few professors' endorsement of the Democrat as a sign that many of America's Christian colleges were drifting from their foundations. When members of Evangelicals for McGovern published *The Cross and the Flag*, a critique of the evangelical civil religion of patriotism, Hargis associate David Noebel denounced the work as a sellout in the Cold War. "The evangelical authors of the work have gone off to institutions of higher learning only to have their minds washed with a heady solution of liberalism or worse," Noebel wrote. "Instead of converting their humanistic, left-leaning professors to Christianity, the professors have converted the flower of Christian youth into left-leaning depth charges."[36]

To offset these defections, some conservative Protestants who had not been overtly partisan stepped up their support for the president. Harold Ockenga, the first president of the NAE and then president of Gordon-Conwell College and theological seminary, endorsed Nixon shortly before the election, citing the concerns of the Cold War as a reason for doing so. In November, 84 percent of evangelicals voted for Nixon.[37]

Shortly after the election, Graham assured evangelicals that Nixon's second term would bring "a lot more emphasis on moral and spiritual affairs," a promise that other evangelicals found reassuring. *Eternity* said that Nixon's "close association with Billy Graham and his conservative Quaker upbringing give us hope that the reelected President will not be known simply as a pragmatic politician who has achieved diplomatic success in thorny international issues, but one who by precept and example guided the nation out of its ethical morass."[38]

Instead, Nixon plunged the nation into an unprecedented presidential scandal. For most of 1973, evangelical leaders refused to believe reports suggesting the president's complicity in Watergate. Nixon's "moral and ethical principles wouldn't allow him to do anything like that," Graham said in February 1973. Privately, he had his doubts, but he was momentarily reassured in April when the president told him that "no one in the White House" was involved in the scandal. The next month, he reiterated his support of the president. "I hope that our judicial system will not be jeopardized by newspaper and television headlines based on rumors," Graham said.[39]

The next year, when the Senate Judiciary Committee released partial transcripts of the White House tapes, Graham was so dismayed that he became physically sick. Nixon, whom Graham had thought he could trust as a Christian leader, was revealed as a foul-mouthed, conniving politician. He had never had a genuine interest in a moral revival, and he had used Graham merely as a political tool. Years later, the evangelist said that he "felt like a sheep led to the slaughter."[40]

Graham's relationship with Nixon haunted him for decades. In the early twenty-first century, when evidence surfaced showing that Graham had assented to one of the president's anti-Semitic rants and had shared a few of his own negative feelings about Jews, he was again taken aback, and apologized profusely for a conversation that he said he no longer recalled. Even the evangelist's admirers felt that he had tarnished his reputation by associating so closely with Nixon. "If there were times when Graham made Nixon better, there were also times when Nixon made Graham worse," two of the evangelist's sympathetic biographers noted. Senator Mark Hatfield felt that Watergate confirmed his judgment about the danger of linking the gospel with a political program. "We must distinguish between civil religion and biblical faith," Hatfield wrote in 1976. "The more I observe contemporary America while reading the Scriptures and the history of the Church, the more I sense how dangerous it is to mix our piety with patriotism."[41]

In reaction to his experiences, Graham distanced himself from political causes. He rarely visited the White House during the Ford and Carter administrations, and he refused to issue another presidential endorsement for the rest of the twentieth century. When the Christian Right emerged in the late 1970s, Graham did not lend it his support. Instead, he focused on the gospel message and the unity of the faith, and he dismissed efforts to ally evangelicals with a particular political party. "There are going to be political differences among evangelicals," he said in 1976. "Some will be more right or more left than others sociologically and economically and for other reasons. This should not bring about a break in spiritual fellowship, which transcends all peripheral differences."[42]

Other evangelicals ignored Graham's warnings against political partisanship and continued to cultivate ties with the GOP. The cultural trends that Nixon had exploited to win election continued to push evangelicals into the Republican Party. Some conservative Protestants continued to admire Nixon even after Watergate. Jerry Falwell kept a portrait of Nixon in his office for years, and occasionally spoke of his admiration for the former president.[43] Falwell probably recognized the critical role that Nixon played in the formation of the Christian Right by bringing evangelicals and fundamentalists together with the promise of "law and order." If it had not been for Nixon's evangelical "silent majority," Falwell's task of mobilizing a "moral majority" might have been much more difficult.

| The Grassroots Campaign to Save the Family

T HE TWENTY-FIVE HUNDRED WOMEN GATHERED at the Texas state-house in the spring of 1975 hardly looked like harbingers of the American political future. Instead of pantsuits, they wore pink dresses. Their idea of women's roles was more June Cleaver than *Maude*. And at a time when only 40 percent of Americans regularly attended church, 98 percent of them were church members.

Their political cause—opposing the Equal Rights Amendment (ERA)—seemed to be equally anachronistic in an era when sweeping majorities in Congress and both political parties had endorsed the measure. The women were considered so out of touch with current political opinion that the *New York Times* did not even cover their campaign.[1]

They also lacked a leader to represent their views in Washington. Richard Nixon's resignation had brought an end to White House church services. His successor, Gerald Ford, showed little interest in evangelicals' political concerns. Billy Graham rarely visited the White House anymore, and he made few comments about national political issues. Fundamentalists also lost some of their own political leaders. Billy James Hargis resigned from his ministry in 1974 following a sex scandal, and Carl McIntire became increasingly marginalized in the late 1960s and early 1970s.[2] So evangelicals turned to local campaigns.

The issues that Nixon had campaigned on transcended his administration, so his downfall did not mark the end of the "silent majority." A rapidly rising divorce rate, the public acceptance of sex outside of marriage, and the national legalization of abortion convinced evangelicals that the two-parent family was endangered. The evangelical activists who organized grassroots campaigns to save the "traditional" family were, for the most part, amateurs who had no prior experience in political campaigns. When they joined forces with conservative Catholics, they faced opposition from some of their own pastors. They met resistance from national Republican leaders, including the chair of the Republican National Committee, the First Lady, and the vice president, because of their stances on the ERA and abortion. Nevertheless, they succeeded in getting national politicians to pay attention to their cause, because their campaign reflected deeply rooted anxieties about the family that appealed to a far larger number of Americans than politicians and pundits had imagined.

The socially conservative women in Austin lost their fight to prevent Texas from ratifying the ERA, but they succeeded in their national campaign. Yet that was only the beginning of their political activism. Within one year of their stand in Austin, many of these women became involved in a comprehensive grassroots campaign to reshape the Republican Party and the national political agenda.

Campaigning against the ERA

Conservative Protestants had argued since the 1920s that the security of the nation depended on the strength of its home life. In the 1950s, Billy Graham had been confident that the nation's politicians—and a majority of the American people—supported his proscriptions against premarital sex and pornography, and his belief that fathers should be leaders in their families. But by the 1970s, this could no longer be assumed.

To some Americans, the "traditional" family appeared to be on the verge of disintegration. The divorce rate doubled between 1965 and 1975, and the out-of-wedlock birth rate increased by more than 50 percent. State universities abandoned their regulations against student cohabitation. Marriage and birth rates declined, while the abortion rate increased.[3]

Instead of discouraging such trends, the media and the government seemed to support them. Television shows such as *Maude* and *Rhoda* suggested that a single career woman could have a thriving sex life. The X-rated film *Deep Throat* became a blockbuster hit. The federal government, restrained by the Supreme Court, did nothing. Evangelicals realized that if they were going to save the nation's families, they would have to launch a sweeping campaign against these social and political trends. The nation was facing "an assault on marriage such as man has never known," Graham warned in 1972. If that assault was not stopped, America would be "finished."[4]

Who was to blame for the family's disintegration? Evangelicals looked squarely at the feminist movement. At no other time in the nation's history had women achieved such sudden advances toward social and legal equality. As late as 1963, the year that Betty Friedan published *The Feminine Mystique*, federal law did not protect women from discrimination in hiring or employment. Airlines were free to fire their female flight attendants as soon as they married, and corporations were free to exclude women from managerial positions. But Friedan's book, which encouraged women to pursue professional careers, contributed to a social revolution in gender roles that was already developing. Women achieved a milestone with the passage of Title VII of the Civil Rights Act of 1964, which prohibited companies from practicing employment discrimination on the basis of sex. Two years later, Friedan and other concerned women created the National Organization for Women in order to initiate legal action against businesses that failed to comply with Title VII.[5]

As other legal barriers to women's equality came down, feminists realized that the nation might at last be ready to enshrine women's legal equality in the Constitution. The ERA, which stated that "equality of rights under the law shall not be denied or abridged by the United States or any State on account of sex," passed in Congress by overwhelming margins and received the endorsement of both parties. Jubilant feminists expected that the thirty-eight states whose votes were needed for ratification would quickly approve the amendment.[6]

Yet the ERA ignited an unexpected backlash from social conservatives—including many women—who were concerned that it would subject women to the draft and end other legal privileges that they enjoyed. Even worse, the ERA was an assault on social conservatives' traditional notions of femininity and the importance of "separate spheres" for men and women. Social conservatives of the early 1970s saw that Americans were becoming increasingly comfortable with the idea of women in professional careers. Television networks had replaced the previous decade's socially conservative programs, such as *Andy Griffith*, with culturally innovative fare, such as *The Mary Tyler Moore Show*, a sitcom focusing on a professional woman. In addition to traditional domestic magazines such as *Good Housekeeping* and *Better Homes and Gardens*, supermarkets and bookstores now carried far more daring female-oriented publications, including *Ms.* and *Cosmopolitan*. *Ms.*, which adopted as its title the controversial prefix that symbolized the liberation of women from their husbands' identity, celebrated the feminist movement's achievement of

securing women a place in the professional world, and earned the oppro-
brium of moral traditionalists because of its outspoken editor, Gloria Steinem.
The sweeping changes in gender roles during the early 1970s shocked social
conservatives, and they had no intention of giving feminists a symbolic constitutional victory, especially when they feared that the Supreme Court would
use the ERA as a basis to enforce additional changes in gender relations.[7]

Conservative Protestants had long believed that the health of the family
depended on the preservation of traditional gender roles. In the 1920s, conservative Protestants cited the Apostle Paul to protest against short hemlines
and the proliferation of contraceptives. In 1945, John R. Rice published a
book on marriage in which he exhorted husbands to take the leadership role
in their marriages, women to submit to their husbands, and couples to refrain
from the use of birth control. As American gender norms became more egal-
itarian in the early 1970s, conservative evangelicals continued to emphasize
that God had created men and women with different roles and that he
intended for married women to find fulfillment in the home, rather than in a
professional career.[8]

Socially conservative women who viewed the ERA as an attack on their
feminine identity led the protest against the amendment. They did not want
to become equal to men, they said; instead, they wanted to accentuate God-
given gender differences. Within months of the ERA's passage, conservative
Christian women in Louisiana formed a local organization to denounce the
ERA as an affront to God, who, they said, had not "made a mistake" when he
had created men and women biologically different. Maxine Secrest, a columnist for Billy James Hargis's *Christian Crusade Weekly*, devoted many of her
articles in 1972 to a defense of traditional hierarchical marriage and women's
domestic role. In accordance with her position that husbands should defend
their wives against assaults from the political arena, her own spouse, Charles
Secrest, assailed the ERA in *Women's Lib: One Way Street to Bondage*. "Let
no woman forget that the drive to take her out of the home is anti-family,
anti-children, and pro-abortion," he wrote.[9]

Although fundamentalists and conservative evangelicals from many denominations spoke out against the ERA, the woman who translated that sentiment into political action was a conservative Catholic whose résumé hardly
looked like that of the stereotypical housewife she wanted to protect. Phyllis
Schlafly, the founder of STOP-ERA, had, at the age of twenty, earned a master's degree in political science from Radcliffe College, where, by all reports,
she had been a brilliant student. Schlafly's professors had urged her to apply
for Ph.D. programs in her field, but instead of following their advice, she
married a lawyer and entered politics, running for Congress from Illinois in

1952 on the slogan "A Woman's Place is in the House." Schlafly lost the election, as she would twenty years later when she again ran for that office, but she became an activist in the conservative wing of the Republican Party. She served as a delegate from Illinois at several Republican National Conventions and became a leader in the Federation of Republican Women. Her first book, *A Choice Not an Echo*, promoted Barry Goldwater's bid for the Republican presidential nomination in 1964. Goldwater's defeat did nothing to hurt Schlafly's popularity, and in 1967, she began publishing an anticommunist, staunchly conservative newsletter titled the *Phyllis Schlafly Report*.[10]

Schlafly paid little attention to the ERA when it began moving through the House and Senate in 1971. She was far more worried about liberal spending initiatives and foreign policy failures. Only at the end of 1971, when a friend convinced her that the ERA was a dangerous proposal, did she begin to focus on it.[11] Since it was already too late to mobilize opposition in Congress, Schlafly took her campaign to state legislatures, attempting to convince them that the ERA posed a threat to the social order.

In view of Schlafly's lack of previous concern about the ERA, some accused her of insincerity, suggesting that her campaign was merely an attempt to build a conservative power base. They could not comprehend why a highly educated professional woman opposed women's quest for legal equality. But these opponents did not understand Schlafly's deeply held conservative beliefs about gender relations. Between running for Congress and embarking on a career as a political activist, Schlafly had been a full-time homemaker and had raised six children. She held traditional notions about familial organization, and she distrusted the expansion of federal power into the private realm. She became convinced that the liberal Supreme Court would probably use the ERA to require state funding of abortions and the legalization of homosexual marriage. In addition, she believed that the ERA threatened protective legislation for women.[12]

At first, Schlafly's STOP-ERA appeared to be a quixotic fight. With both major political parties and a solid majority of the public expressing support for the ERA, and few politicians opposed to it, Schlafly faced a formidable challenge. But she understood that the traditional image of womanhood had a powerful hold not only on large numbers of American men, but also on millions of women who were insulted when they perceived that liberal elites were denigrating homemakers. For conservative evangelical women, submission to the protection of male leadership and the acceptance of a domestically oriented life were intrinsic to feminine identity. By portraying the ERA as a symbol of feminism, Schlafly transformed the debate over the amendment into a national referendum on "women's lib." "No more radical piece of legislation could have been devised to force women outside of the home," she declared. Women who wanted to enjoy the life of a traditional homemaker would find it difficult to do so. They would no longer be entitled to alimony and exemption from overnight shifts or arduous labor. They might have to face the draft and be sent into combat. "What about the rights of the woman who doesn't want to compete on an equal basis with men?" Schlafly asked. "Doesn't she have the right to be treated as a woman—by her family, by society, and by the law?"[13]

Schlafly's campaign for the "right to be treated as a woman" appealed to evangelical women, who began publishing a spate of books that glorified traditional concepts of femininity. Evangelical women of the early 1970s were willing to accept a few tenets of the feminist movement, such as the idea that women could pursue careers and that women's sexual drives were just as strong and important as men's. But at the same time, they argued that God had created men and women with distinct emotional and biological natures, which was why women had a duty to be "helpmeets" to their husbands. "The woman who is truly Spirit-filled will want to be totally submissive to her husband," wrote Beverly LaHaye, the wife of San Diego Baptist pastor Tim LaHaye, in her widely distributed book *The Spirit-Controlled Woman* in 1976. Other books, such as Anita Bryant's *Bless This House* (1972), Helen Andelin's *Fascinating Womanhood* (first published in 1965, and then reissued in 1974), and Elisabeth Elliot's *Let Me Be a Woman* (1976), propagated a similar message. Marabel Morgan's *The Total Woman* (1973), which made the *New York Times* best-seller list, stated that "it is only when a woman surrenders her life to her husband, reveres and worships him, and is willing to serve him, that she becomes really beautiful to him. She becomes a priceless jewel, the glory of femininity, his queen!"[14]

Schlafly had little trouble enlisting conservative women in her anti-ERA campaign. The number of subscribers to her monthly newsletter increased from 3,500 in 1972 to 50,000 by the end of the 1970s. Schlafly's organization was strongest in the South, Southwest, and Midwest, and it drew heavily from the ranks of conservative evangelicals. A survey of women who testified before the Texas state legislature in opposition to the ERA in 1975 showed that 98 percent of the amendment's opponents were church members, and 66 percent of them described themselves as "fundamentalist Protestants."[15]

Ironically, by mobilizing to preserve their own submissive roles, evangelical and fundamentalist women became political leaders of an ecumenical movement and convinced male pastors to follow their lead. In the fights against the ERA in Oklahoma and Texas, Schlafly depended on Lottie Beth Hobbs, a Church of Christ Bible class teacher and author from Abilene, Texas.

In the West, Schlafly worked closely with Mormons. In the Southeast, she worked with Baptists. By the late 1970s, fundamentalist pastors who had not previously considered the possibility of cooperating with Catholics or Mormons decided to follow the lead of the women in their congregations. Jerry Falwell, who had once refused to ally with nonfundamentalists, made an exception for Schlafly, calling her "one of the most knowledgeable people I know" and "the greatest leader Illinois has produced since Abraham Lincoln."[16]

Schlafly's campaign also turned evangelical women into Republican Party activists, which contributed to the conservative takeover of the GOP. The Republican Party had endorsed the ERA at every convention since 1940. But Schlafly, as an experienced leader in the conservative wing of the party and a strong supporter of Governor Ronald Reagan's bid for the GOP presidential nomination in 1976, was determined to change the party's direction. Partly due to her efforts, the delegation for Ronald Reagan, a candidate who opposed the ERA, included a higher percentage of women than President Gerald Ford's, even though Ford and his wife supported the ERA and were moderately sympathetic to the feminist movement. In 1972, Republican feminists had succeeded in passing a platform plank supporting government-financed daycare, and they expected to make additional gains in 1976, but to their dismay, they were forced to devote all of their effort at the convention to stopping Schlafly's forces. The platform committee turned down Schlafly's proposal to rescind the party's endorsement of the ERA only by a vote of 51–47, a sign that conservatives held far more influence in the party than the Republican women's rights advocates had imagined.[17]

Abortion

Prior to the mid-1970s, no one would have associated the GOP with opposition to abortion. Republican politicians spearheaded some of the earliest efforts to liberalize abortion laws in California, Colorado, and New York. Even one of the party's conservative icons, Barry Goldwater, supported abortion rights, perhaps partly because he had once secretly arranged an abortion for his daughter.[18]

If Republicans were reluctant to restrict abortion in the late 1960s and early 1970s, so were most evangelicals. They greeted the first state abortion legalization laws with silence and apathy. For years, they had ignored America's thriving underground abortion industry, because state laws officially proscribed the practice, even though millions of American women found ways to terminate their pregnancies in the pre-*Roe* era. Before the 1960s, most states allowed women whose lives were at stake to obtain an abortion. The Catholic Church condemned abortion even in these circumstances, but because the availability of abortion services was rarely publicized, neither Catholic nor Protestant religious leaders campaigned against hospital abortions. John R. Rice noted in 1945 that abortion was "a crime prohibited by law and condemned by all decent people."[19] As long as conservative religious leaders believed that most Americans shared their opposition to abortion, they saw little need to address the subject.

But in the 1960s, many Americans began to rethink abortion. State abortion laws, they felt, needed to be updated to reflect changing medical practices and social mores. In the nineteenth century, when most states passed laws restricting abortion, primitive prenatal care was often unable to reduce the serious health complications that many women faced during pregnancy, and women sometimes had to resort to abortion in order to protect their health and even their lives. The laws therefore allowed for these situations. By the mid-twentieth century, such cases were rare. Yet many women expressed a desire to terminate their pregnancies in cases where they suspected that they were carrying deformed fetuses, and they were often surprised to discover that state laws did not allow them to do so.[20]

In 1962, Sherri Chessen Finkbine, star of a children's television show and an Arizona mother of four children, faced this dilemma when she sought an abortion. Finkbine had become pregnant while taking a thalidomide-laced tranquilizer, which she learned might endanger her baby's health. Her hospital board refused to give her permission for an abortion, and she and her husband had to fly to Sweden to find a doctor willing to perform the procedure. When American news magazines publicized her story, some people were outraged that Finkbine had chosen to have an abortion, but many others sympathized with her plight. Even many churchgoing women who ordinarily might have condemned abortion felt that they could identify with a middle-class, happily married, conservative mother who believed that she and her husband were not ready to care for a disabled child. While these women did not advocate legalizing abortion in all circumstances, they wanted to protect women in Finkbine's situation, so they joined a grassroots movement to legalize "therapeutic" abortion, a term that described abortions in cases of fetal deformity, rape, incest, or risks to a mother's health. Finkbine's case transformed Americans' attitudes toward abortion; according to polls, after 1962, a majority of the population supported "therapeutic" abortion.[21]

A birth control revolution also contributed to Americans' changes in attitude on abortion. In 1960, the birth control pill became available in the

United States, giving women the opportunity to control their own fertility. In 1965, the Supreme Court decision in *Griswold v. Connecticut* overturned the last vestiges of state legislation against birth control distribution. As an increasing number of Americans accepted the idea that women should have the right to control their own fertility, they became more supportive of the liberalization of state abortion laws. In 1967, Colorado's Republican governor signed into law the nation's first abortion liberalization bill. Later that year, California governor Ronald Reagan signed the Beilenson bill, which gave women the right to terminate their pregnancies in cases of rape or incest, or when a pregnancy endangered their health. Several other states quickly passed similar legislation.[22]

The legalization of "therapeutic" abortion perturbed many Catholic clerics. Catholics drew on a tradition of antiabortion church teaching dating back to the first centuries of Christianity. They also cited a succession of nineteenth- and twentieth-century papal decrees, culminating with Vatican II in 1964, all of which condemned abortion. Yet when the Catholic hierarchy denounced Finkbine's decision and the subsequent shift in public opinion on "therapeutic" abortion, many Americans refused to listen. On four separate occasions in the early 1960s, Catholic priests in California successfully pressured the state legislature to vote against liberal abortion legislation. But in 1967, they found that they were powerless to stop the Beilenson bill from becoming state law. Devout Catholic Democrats in the state legislature voted against the measure, but most Protestants, including some of the state's most conservative Republican legislators, did not. Francis Cardinal McIntyre met with Governor Reagan in a vain attempt to try to convince him that the bill was morally wrong, but Reagan, who personally opposed abortion, felt politically obligated to sign the bill, a move he later regretted.[23]

Catholics found little public support for their campaign against abortion in the 1960s. Neither the Democratic Party nor the Republican had taken an official stance on abortion, and several leading politicians in both parties supported campaigns for the liberalization of state abortion laws. Few mainline Protestant ministers were willing to join Catholics in their campaign against abortion, partly because they viewed Catholics' attempt to prohibit abortion as another manifestation of their decades-long fight to restrict legal access to birth control, a campaign that had attracted the opposition of many Protestants. Yet the lack of allies did not dissuade Catholics. Calling the move toward less restrictive abortion laws "an infamy that poisons society," Catholic bishops, with support from a few conservative Lutheran pastors, formed the Right to Life League, the nation's first antiabortion organization.[24]

Although evangelicals remained silent while the Catholic Church protested the liberalization of California's abortion law, the wave of abortion policy revision that followed in other states in the late 1960s made it impossible for them to ignore the issue. Yet they disagreed on how they should respond. While Catholics could rely on a centuries-old antiabortion church tradition for guidance, Protestants had no such resource. The Bible, which evangelicals used as their authoritative guide to every aspect of life, did not offer clear instruction. Despite this, some conservative Protestants, including Billy Graham, insisted that abortion was sinful in most cases, although they conceded that women could legitimately resort to the procedure if their lives were in danger. Other evangelicals took a more liberal stand, and allowed for "therapeutic" abortion. "Personally, I certainly do not condemn those who terminate pregnancy to save the mother's life or when rape or incest is involved," the physician S. I. McMillen noted in his article on abortion in the September 1967 issue of *Christian Life*. Yet he conceded that "the Bible does not give a direct answer" on the subject and that the issue of abortion's acceptability was murky. He had no wish to see abortion become widespread. "Rape, incest, deformed babies or a risk to the mother's health . . . should be the only reasons for abortions," he wrote.[25]

In August 1968, two of the most prominent evangelical leaders in America—Harold Ockenga and Harold Lindsell, editor of *Christianity Today*—tried to resolve this debate by inviting twenty-five evangelical scholars to the Protestant Symposium on the Control of Human Reproduction. They concluded that "abortion-on-demand" was sinful, but that "therapeutic" abortion might be acceptable in some cases. The following month, *Christianity Today* continued this trend of evangelical equivocation. "Therapeutic Abortion: Blessing or Murder?" the article's title asked, but there was no clear answer. After fetal viability, abortion was wrong, the author said, but before viability, some medically necessary abortions might be acceptable.[26]

In the early 1970s, after several more states had liberalized their abortion laws, northern evangelicals strengthened their opposition to the procedure. The "therapeutic" abortion laws allowed for far more abortions than many people had envisioned in the late 1960s. In 1968, the year after California passed a "therapeutic" abortion bill, 5,000 Californians obtained legal abortions, but by 1972, the number of legal abortions in the state had increased to 100,000 per year. Several states, including New York and Hawaii, passed abortion laws that were even more liberal than California's, so by the early 1970s, American women who had the ability to travel could almost always obtain an abortion during their first trimester of pregnancy. In the face of the nation's rising number of legal abortions, Carl F. H. Henry, the founding editor of *Christianity Today* and an early leader in the evangelical movement, wrote a staunchly pro-life editorial for the February 1971 issue of *Eternity*. In *Christianity Today*, articles such as "The War on the Womb," which appeared in the June 1970 issue, replaced the vague and equivocating statements on abortion that the magazine had made only two years earlier. When *Roe v. Wade* was decided in 1973, the pro-life movement was still largely Catholic, but many northern evangelicals were joining the cause.[27]

Southern Baptists were more tolerant of abortion than northern evangelicals were, partly because they were suspicious of a Catholic cause and partly because abortion law did not become a political issue in the South until several years after it had begun polarizing northern state legislatures. Southern Baptists lacked a clear theological tradition on abortion, so for most pastors, the safest response to the issue seemed to be silence. They did not protest in 1967 when 90 percent of North Carolina's state senators voted for a bill that legalized abortion in cases of rape, incest, fetal defect, and dangers to a woman's health. SBC publications did not begin to discuss abortion until 1969, and when they finally broached the subject, they gave no indication that abortion was a moral evil tantamount to murder. Although Southern Baptists objected to using abortion as a means of birth control, they were generally willing to tolerate it in cases of medical necessity, which they defined quite broadly. In 1970, a *Baptist View* poll showed that while 80 percent of Southern Baptist pastors opposed "abortion-on-demand," 70 percent favored allowing abortion to protect the physical or mental health of a woman, and 64 percent thought that state laws should permit abortion in cases of fetal deformity. Seventy-one percent had no objection to abortion in cases of rape and incest.[28] Thus, while only a minority of Southern Baptist pastors countenanced abortion in all cases, the vast majority favored legalizing "therapeutic" abortion.

In fact, the Southern Baptist Convention passed a resolution in 1971 that urged states to liberalize their abortion laws. While affirming a "high view of human life, including fetal life," the Convention's resolution urged "Southern Baptists to work for legislation that will allow the possibility of abortion under such conditions as rape, incest, clear evidence of severe fetal deformity, and carefully ascertained evidence of the likelihood of damage to the emotional, mental, and physical health of the mother." Not all Southern Baptists favored the resolution, and Convention president Carl Bates received several letters from Southern Baptists who were outraged that their denomination had officially endorsed a medical procedure that they considered "murder." But he deflected such criticism by arguing that there was room in the SBC for a diversity of opinion on the issue.[29]

On the other hand, self-identified fundamentalists outside the mainline denominations did not hesitate to take an unequivocal stand against abortion. While many Southern Baptists viewed their Convention as a "mainline" denomination, only slightly more conservative than Methodist and Presbyterian churches in the South, fundamentalists saw themselves as a small, faithful "remnant" living in a corrupt society. For them, liberalized abortion laws served as confirmation of the wickedness of American society and the corruption of the Protestant churches that supported such legislation. In 1967, when California passed its liberal abortion bill, the *Baptist Bible Tribune*, which spoke for independent Baptists who were more theologically conservative than those in the SBC, reacted with horror. "There is no difference between murder of life in the womb and murder of life in the crib," one editorial stated. "And there is no doubt that an outraged Holy God is going to judge us—now, down here on this earth."[30]

John R. Rice viewed the abortion legalization campaign as the latest liberal assault on morality in a rapidly escalating culture war. "It is not surprising that the people who are eager to legalize abortion and murder more unborn babies, are the same crowd that do not want the death penalty for murder in other criminal cases," he wrote in 1971. "They are usually the same crowd, the left-wing, the demonstrators, the socialists, the civil rights lawbreakers. They are against censorship of pornographic literature and filthy movies. They are for the 'new morality' and license. The people who are strongest for abortion are not good people and they are not good citizens of America."[31]

Despite their pro-life beliefs, fundamentalists were unable to mount an effective protest against abortion, because they were still politically and religiously isolated. They refused to join predominantly Catholic pro-life organizations, so their protests against abortion never reached beyond their own circles. Meanwhile, the advocates of legalizing abortion continued to gain ground. Between April 1967 and January 1973, nineteen states liberalized their abortion laws. Pro-life Catholics turned back the tide of abortion legalization in a few northern states, including Pennsylvania, and they created a national organization, the National Right to Life Committee (NRLC), to coordinate their state campaigns. But they could not help noting the lack of help that they received from Protestants in these endeavors. "The only reason we have a pro-life movement in this country is because of the Catholic people and the Catholic Church," the executive director of the NRLC said in 1973.[32]

Then came *Roe v. Wade*. In a 7–2 decision, the Court declared that women's "right to privacy" gave them a constitutional right to abortion during the first and second trimesters of pregnancy, up to the point of fetal viability. When the Court issued its decision, only four states had abortion statutes that were liberal enough to satisfy the Court's demands; the other forty-six, including California, had to revise their abortion laws in order to comply with *Roe*.[33]

Roe v. Wade shocked the pro-life movement and galvanized it into action. Fundamentalists who had condemned abortion before the *Roe* decision began to make more concerted efforts on behalf of the pro-life cause. Billy James Hargis created a new pro-life organization, Americans against Abortion, and entrusted its leadership to David Noebel, whose authority in the Christian Crusade ministry was second only to Hargis's. Only four months after the Court's ruling in *Roe*, Noebel published *Slaughter of the Innocent*, a denunciation of the Court's decision, and spent the rest of the year writing articles and giving speeches against abortion. Articles with such provocative titles as "Murder of Babies: It's a Major Issue in New York," "Does a Woman Have a Right to Murder?" and "The Sacrifice of Human Life Goes On" appeared in fundamentalist publications shortly after *Roe*, leaving readers little doubt as to where they stood on the abortion issue.[34]

Southern Baptists, on the other hand, were not so quick to condemn the ruling. In April 1969, the Texas *Baptist Standard* had conducted a poll on abortion and had found that 90 percent of its readers thought their state's abortion law was too restrictive. Thus, Texas Baptists were hardly in a position to protest the Court's decision. Even one of the state's most politically and theologically conservative pastors, W. A. Criswell, who had served as president of the SBC from 1968 to 1970, lauded the Court's ruling in *Roe*. "I have always felt that it was only after a child was born and had life separate from its mother, that it became an individual person, and it has always, therefore, seemed to me that what is best for the mother and for the future should be allowed," he said.[35]

When Southern Baptists realized that abortion legalization had furthered the cause of the feminist movement and the sexual revolution, they withdrew some of their earlier support for abortion rights, but stopped short of complete opposition. In 1973, the Texas Christian Life Commission, which had argued for the liberalization of the state's abortion law only two years earlier, encouraged the Texas state legislature to pass a bill that would place some restrictions on abortion. In 1974, the SBC passed a resolution reaffirming the resolution on abortion that it had adopted in 1971, which Southern Baptists believed "reflected a middle ground between the extreme of abortion on demand and the opposite extreme of all abortion as murder."[36]

As head of the SBC's Christian Life Commission, Foy Valentine kept his denomination from taking sides in the culture war that was developing over abortion in the 1970s. Because he viewed abortion as an "extremely complex problem" rather than a clear-cut moral issue, he focused most of his attention as head of the CLC on other social issues, such as poverty. In 1977, he signed "A Call to Concern," an interdenominational manifesto that objected to "the absolutist position that it is always wrong to terminate a pregnancy." Valentine explained that while he held that "all life is sacred including fetal life," he did "not believe that all abortions are murders," and that in a few situations he considered abortion "the lesser of the available evils." He viewed the pro-life movement as a Catholic cause. "The Roman Catholic bishops have been pushing very hard with a well organized and well financed campaign to enact their absolutist position about abortion into law in this country," he said, and he wanted no part of their campaign.[37]

A few younger Southern Baptist pastors launched a campaign to change their denomination's position on the subject. Robert Holbrook, pastor of the First Baptist Church in Hallettsville, Texas, began his campaign against abortion immediately after *Roe*, a decision that outraged him. He was even more upset to discover that most Southern Baptists considered liquor laws and gambling policies more important political issues than abortion. "Surely the killing of the unborn is a more pressing issue of morality than 'betting on a horse,'" he wrote in May 1973. Holbrook founded Baptists for Life in 1973 and began campaigning for the rights of the unborn. In addition to mailing letters to the fifteen thousand Baptists who attended the annual conventions, he testified before Congress in favor of a human life constitutional amendment and created a politically active advisory committee of professionals and political leaders that included Senator Jesse Helms (R-NC), a conservative politician who was emerging as a leader of the fledgling "New Right" movement within the GOP.[38]

Holbrook's campaign to convince the Southern Baptist Convention to pass a strong antiabortion resolution at its annual meeting in 1974 did not succeed, but he tried again two years later. By then, Southern Baptists had become increasingly uncomfortable with abortion. Yet instead of endorsing Holbrook's position, the SBC adopted a compromise measure that tried to appease people on both sides of the debate. The Convention recognized the "limited role of government in dealing with matters related to abortion," while also condemning "abortion as a means of birth control" and "abortion for selfish non-therapeutic reasons," all of which were phrases designed to please denominational leaders such as Valentine. At the same time, the SBC offered a concession to the denomination's pro-lifers by declaring that "every decision for an abortion, for whatever reason must necessarily involve the decision to terminate the life of an innocent human being."[39]

Pro-life Baptists did not consider the concession sufficient, so they turned to Catholics for support. As a theologically conservative Southern Baptist, Holbrook had once opposed interdenominational cooperation with Catholics, but after *Roe*, he began speaking to Catholic groups about abortion and accepted money from predominantly Catholic organizations in order to launch Baptists for Life. In 1974, he joined four Catholic cardinals to testify against abortion before Congress. John Wilder, a Missouri Baptist who founded Christians for Life in 1977, likewise found that Catholics were his closest allies. After mailing antiabortion literature to thirty-five thousand Southern Baptist churches, Wilder was disappointed when only a few Baptists responded to his call to lobby the SBC for a strong pro-life resolution. He blamed his co-religionists' lack of interest on their anti-Catholic biases. "The assumption was that it must not be right if Catholics backed it, so we haven't. Unfortunately, it's a conclusion based on prejudice," Wilder said.[40]

While Southern Baptists remained on the sidelines, northern evangelicals proved somewhat more willing to view *Roe v. Wade* as an assault on the family and the nation's Christian identity. "We deplore, in the strongest possible terms, the decision of the U.S. Supreme Court which has made it legal to terminate a pregnancy for no better reason than personal convenience or sociological considerations," the National Association of Evangelicals (NAE) stated in 1973. *Christianity Today* echoed the charge. "Christians should accustom themselves to the thought that the American state no longer supports, in any meaningful sense, the laws of God, and prepare themselves spiritually for the prospect that it may one day formally repudiate them and turn against those who seek to live by them," the magazine stated.[41]

In 1975, Ruth Bell Graham, the wife of America's best-known evangelist, helped organize a pro-life conference of Protestant ministers. Only twenty-five ministers and lay leaders attended, but among them were some of the most prominent Protestant pro-life activists, including Holbrook. Ruth Graham and two other attendees volunteered to create a task force to mobilize Protestant women in the pro-life cause. That same year, Harold O. J. Brown, a *Christianity Today* editor, organized the Christian Action Council to prove that antiabortion activism was not "wholly a Catholic" cause. By this time, Protestants had already secured leadership positions in several national antiabortion organizations. A Methodist headed the traditionally Catholic National Right to Life Committee, while another Protestant presided over American Citizens Concerned for Life.[42]

The pro-life movement was still overwhelmingly Catholic, but evangelical opponents of abortion, along with anti-ERA activists, exercised enough political influence to gain national attention. In 1976, they launched a campaign to change the dynamics of the presidential election and force the Republican Party to the right on issues of cultural politics.

Bill Bright and Conservative Politics

One evangelical who sensed that the moment had come to mobilize evangelicals and transform the Republican Party was Bill Bright. Bright had long had a vision of transforming American society through Christianity. In the early 1950s, when he was a young California businessman and Presbyterian layman, he felt a call from God to preach the gospel to the unconverted. In response to that divine imperative, Bright started a student Christian association at the University of California in Los Angeles in 1951, and then took that ministry nationwide as Campus Crusade for Christ. Bright planned to evangelize the entire world within a generation, he said, and he intended Campus Crusade to be the first step. In 1965, Bright condensed evangelical theology into a seventy-seven-word statement that he called the "four spiritual laws," which trained volunteers could present to potential converts in less than five minutes. By 1976, Campus Crusade reported that its staff was personally presenting the "four spiritual laws" to nearly 2 million non-Christians every year and that about 8 percent of these people were responding with a profession of faith in Christ.[43]

Yet as Campus Crusade continued to grow, its founder became increasingly worried that his organization would be unable to stop the secular trends that were destroying American society. "Our nation is in grave trouble," Bright told *Christianity Today* in September 1976. "Morally and spiritually, we have reached the point of bankruptcy. Our entire society is becoming increasingly secular, humanistic, and materialistic. Anti-God forces largely control education, the media, entertainment, and government." Bright launched a new organization (Here's Life, America!) that he hoped would "saturate our nation with the Gospel." Here's Life used Bright's audiovisual programs to train four hundred thousand volunteers to spread the Christian message in their communities. But even as Bright engaged in this new evangelistic outreach, he decided that that effort was not sufficient to stem the tide of secularism in America. He thought that politics might offer another venue in which Christians could save America from moral "bankruptcy."[44]

As a former businessman, Bright had been a politically conservative, strongly anticommunist Republican throughout his adult life. During the 1950s and 1960s, he had occasionally contributed to the conservative political causes that were popular in southern California. But never before had he made a concerted effort to bring evangelicals into politics. The sexual revolution, the feminist movement, and the nation's declining sense of patriotism led him to believe that the nation was facing an unprecedented moral crisis that could be solved only with a change in national leadership that replaced secular liberals with Christian conservatives.

Seeking a way to bring Christians into politics, Bright joined forces with John Conlan, a conservative Republican congressman from Arizona who was also an evangelical. In 1974, they launched Third Century Publishers to distribute books encouraging Christians to become involved in politics. One of their publications, Rus Walton's *One Nation under God*, offered a brief history of the American republic from a conservative Christian perspective. Walton argued that God approved of free-market economics and limited government, and he said that the Founding Fathers had envisioned a small federal government when they created the republic. With chapter titles and subheadings such as "Taxes and the Power to Destroy," "Caesar Demands Too Much," and "Inflation Is Killing America," he traced the precipitous decline of America since the presidency of Franklin Roosevelt. If *One Nation under God* offered a diagnosis of America's problems, Third Century's *In the Spirit of '76: The Citizen's Guide to Politics* provided the prescription. Billed as a "handbook for winning elections," *In the Spirit of '76* taught Christian conservatives how to run effective campaigns and get elected to office.[45]

Third Century quickly became a more explicitly political organization than Bright had originally envisioned. Even though Bright was an unabashed political conservative, he hesitated to link his name, which was widely identified with the apolitical Campus Crusade, with a partisan cause. Conlan, on the other hand, tried to turn Third Century into a voter mobilization effort for the conservative wing of the Republican Party. He did not hesitate to ask pastors to endorse specific candidates or set up voter registration tables on church property. He directed local Third Century chapters to screen born-again Christians who applied for training in political skills, and to turn away all who seemed politically liberal. Those who supported Ronald Reagan would be welcome in the organization, he said, but if anyone approved of Vice President Nelson Rockefeller, that person's application would be rejected. Conlan had no respect for liberal evangelical senators such as Mark Hatfield (R-OR) and Harold Hughes

(R-IA). "These are not the kind of people we want in government," he said.[46]

To help the Christian public decide which candidates to support, Third Century issued an "index" of congressional voting records that evaluated all members of the House and Senate on the basis of their votes on welfare policy, deficit spending, foreign aid, and other issues. "At this time, there are at least 218 people in the House [of Representatives] who follow in some degree the secular humanist philosophy which is so dangerous to our future," Conlan said. "If you don't elect (this) year more people who will be God's men and women, who will support legislation to insure the continued freedom to proclaim the gospel, it may be too late."[47]

To a much greater extent than earlier Christian organizations, Third Century envisioned an evangelical voting bloc that could be mobilized to change the course of American politics. "The evangelical Christian community is a sleeping giant," Rus Walton, Third Century's editor in chief, told *Newsweek* in the summer of 1976. "There are between 40 and 50 million evangelical fundamentalists in the U.S. If even one-tenth of them became active in politics—wow!" In an effort to awake that "sleeping giant," Intercessors for America, a closely related organization whose founders also sat on the board of Third Century Publishers, sent letters to 120,000 American pastors urging them to purchase copies of Bright's book *Your Five Duties as a Christian Citizen*.[48]

Some evangelicals listened, but others were alarmed by Bright's unprecedented involvement in politics. Billy Graham, who had been closely associated with Bright's earlier evangelistic efforts, publicly rebuked the Campus Crusade founder for his involvement with Third Century Publishers, and withdrew his support from Here's Life. Campus Crusade staff members also urged Bright to refrain from politics. When an exposé in the left-wing evangelical magazine *Sojourners* embarrassed Third Century's founders by portraying them as conservative partisans and political operatives, Bright discontinued his political activities.[49]

Third Century Publishers represented a new awakening of evangelical political consciousness. Never before had evangelicals made such a concerted, partisan effort to effect political change. But in 1976, evangelicals, though becoming increasingly politically conservative, were not yet ready to give a religious blessing to an explicitly partisan agenda. They did not yet see the connection between their grassroots, single-issue moral campaigns and a national political program. They largely ignored or repudiated Bright and Conlan's political activities and refrained from committing themselves to the Republican Party.

Sexual Politics in the Presidential Election of 1976

Evangelicals' initial lack of enthusiasm for Gerald Ford mirrored the rest of the nation's. Ford had taken office in circumstances that would have been difficult for anyone, but his pardon of Richard Nixon, his failure to end a cycle of stagflation that was crippling the national economy, and his reputation as an ineffective bumbler confirmed the image of mediocrity that many Americans had of a man who had once described himself as "a Ford, not a Lincoln." Social conservatives had even more reason to dislike Ford. During his brief term in the White House, he had done more than any other Republican president to push the GOP toward a progressive stance on women's issues. He had selected Nelson Rockefeller, a liberal, pro-choice Republican, as his vice president, and he had appointed Mary Louise Smith, another pro-ERA, pro-choice member of his party, as the first woman to chair the Republican National Committee. In August 1975, he had said nothing in opposition when his wife, Betty Ford, told the nation on 60 *Minutes* that *Roe v. Wade* was the "the best thing in the world . . . a great, great decision," and that she would not object if her daughter had premarital sex or if her children experimented with marijuana. Both Fords strongly supported the ERA.[50]

With this record of cultural liberalism, the president should not have been surprised by the vilification that he received from the country's most theologically conservative Protestants. "In Washington, we have some men who do not have any better experience or any better comprehension of truth than a snail crawling along, leaving his slime behind him," Bob Jones, Jr., wrote in July 1976. "Any man who cannot control his wife better than he does Betty is not fit to run the nation."[51]

Conservative evangelicals and fundamentalists in the South were delighted when Ronald Reagan, the former governor of California and the best-known figure on the right wing of the Republican Party, challenged Ford for the GOP presidential nomination. They shared Reagan's strong opposition to communism and to the policy of détente with the Soviet Union. They appreciated his denunciation of the Panama Canal Treaty. But they were especially pleased when Reagan indicated that he would be their ally in the culture wars over sexual behavior. Even though Reagan was a divorced Hollywood actor who attended church only occasionally, he knew how to appeal to evangelicals' sense of moral propriety. As governor of California, he had signed tough antiobscenity legislation, as well as a measure allowing parents to remove their children from sex education classes, and he had prided himself on his ability to stand up to left-wing protestors on college campuses. He also had a keen awareness of the evangelical belief that America was a

"Christian nation" that had forsaken its God. When someone in North Carolina asked him to name his favorite Bible verse, he responded by quoting 2 Chronicles 7:14, the verse that evangelicals had long used to call the nation to repentance: "If my people, which are called by my name, shall humble themselves, and pray, and seek my face, and turn from their wicked ways; then will I hear from heaven, and will forgive their sin, and will heal their land."[52]

Reagan's delegation at the Republican National Convention in Kansas City included conservative evangelicals such as Pat Boone, a Christian singer and head of California Christians Active Politically. Reagan also picked up delegates from some of the staunchest fundamentalist churches in the South. Bob Jones University faculty had not participated in a presidential campaign since Barry Goldwater's in 1964, but they reentered the political arena in order to support Reagan. Several Bob Jones faculty members, as well as one of the university's deans, participated in a voter registration drive to register new Republican voters, and six hundred fundamentalists from the college and its neighboring churches attended Greenville County's Republican convention to make sure that their region's delegates went to the former California governor.[53]

Recognizing the potential of the conservative Christian vote, and hoping to revive a flagging campaign, Reagan agreed in June 1976 to an interview with California evangelical radio talk show host George Otis, a long-standing political supporter and friend. Reagan used the interview to portray himself as a religious conservative who could identify with his audience's values. He had had "an experience that could be described as 'born again,'" he said. He considered prayer an important aspect of his life, he said, and had "never had any doubt" that the Bible was of "divine origin." Though he had signed an abortion liberalization bill nine years earlier, he was now firmly opposed to the practice. "You cannot interrupt a pregnancy without taking a human life," he declared. He favored the restoration of school prayer and recognized the problems that the proliferation of pornography and illicit sex had caused. He said that if he had had the opportunity, he would have vetoed legislation decriminalizing homosexuality. Reagan summed up his views on moral legislation in language that would have been familiar to any evangelical who had been involved in the morality campaigns of the 1970s. "There has been a wave of humanism and hedonism in the land," he said. "However, I am optimistic because I sense in this land a great revolution against that. . . . The people of this country are not beyond redemption."[54]

Reagan lost to Ford in a tight race that did not end until the convention. Evangelicals were left with a choice between the incumbent president and his

Democratic challenger, Georgia governor Jimmy Carter. When Carter declared in early 1976 that he was a born-again Christian, many of his co-religionists, particularly those in the South, viewed him as the answer to their prayers. As a devout Southern Baptist, Carter read the Bible daily, taught a men's Sunday school class, and faithfully attended church. In his keynote address at the Southern Baptist Convention in June 1976, Bailey Smith, who later became president of the SBC, could not resist including a Carter campaign pitch in his sermon. The United States needed a "born-again man in the White House," Smith said. "And his initials are the same as our Lord's!"[55]

Carter's campaign excited evangelicals partly because they had been searching for a born-again candidate to carry out a "Christian" agenda, and partly because they were proud of the new respectability that Carter's candidacy gave born-again Christianity. His acceptance of the evangelical label implied that born-again Christians had finally clawed their way to the top echelons of American society and had earned a right to be heard. "There was great pride to think that 'one of us' might be in the White House," one pastor said. In recognition of the publicity that Carter's campaign had provided for evangelicalism, a *Newsweek* cover story declared 1976 the "year of the evangelical."[56]

Evangelicals quickly responded with Democratic endorsements. An evangelical publisher issued a book titled *The Miracle of Jimmy Carter*. Citizens for Carter, an evangelical organization, placed an ad in *Christianity Today* that highlighted Carter's spiritual experiences.[57]

Yet many of the evangelicals who relished the new respectability that Carter's candidacy gave their religion were disappointed to learn that the Democratic candidate took the "wrong" positions on many issues. Carter was moderately pro-choice and supported the ERA, and his stances on social and economic issues were only slightly more conservative than those of most Democratic politicians. Some feared that he would legalize marijuana. Carter also alienated some conservative Baptists with his liberal theological views. He told the press that Reinhold Niebuhr, a Union Theological Seminary professor who had disdained Billy Graham's ministry as too conservative and superficial, was his favorite theologian. He did not know if the Garden of Eden had ever really existed, he told a reporter, and he was not sure that he accepted the Apostle Paul's injunctions about women's roles. Early on, a Gallup poll predicted that the Georgia governor would receive 75 percent of the Southern Baptist vote, but as southern conservative Christians learned more about Carter's religious and political views, their support for his candidacy diminished. At the end of the summer, Third Century Publishers published a critique of Carter's theological and political liberalism titled *What about Jimmy Carter?* which concluded that the Democratic nominee was unfit to be president.[58]

The real falling-out between Carter and his erstwhile evangelical allies came in September, when the Georgia governor made a critical misstep by consenting to an interview with *Playboy*. Carter attempted to use the interview to refute *Playboy's* charge that he might set a "puritanical tone" in the White House. He assured the reporter that he was just as much a sinner as any *Playboy* reader. Even if he had not slept with a woman other than his wife, he had "committed adultery in my heart many times," a phrase derived from Jesus' Sermon on the Mount. His Christian faith required him to maintain a nonjudgmental attitude toward hedonists and sexual libertines, he argued. "Christ says, don't consider yourself better than someone else because one guy screws a whole bunch of women while the other guy is loyal to his wife," Carter said.[59]

Many evangelicals were shocked. The Democratic candidate clearly had a very different idea of Christianity than many evangelicals did, and in their view, he had positioned himself on the wrong side of the culture wars. W. A. Criswell, pastor of the nation's largest Southern Baptist church, denounced Carter from his Dallas pulpit and said that there was no need for a presidential candidate to grant an interview for a "salacious, pornographic magazine." "We're totally against pornography," Bailey Smith, the pastor who had endorsed Carter in June 1976, told the press in September. "And, well, 'screw' is just not a good Baptist word." An evangelical constituency that had once seemed to be firmly in Carter's camp now threatened to bolt.[60]

Independent fundamentalist Baptists in the South were even more ready to criticize the Democratic nominee. Carter's moderately progressive views on civil rights did not impress the fundamentalists, and they were upset that he made favorable references to Martin Luther King, Jr. For many fundamentalists, Carter was too liberal not only politically but also theologically. To preachers who had been criticizing Billy Graham as an "apostate" since the late 1950s, the Georgia governor's public proclamation of his born-again Christianity meant nothing, and some called the Democratic candidate a "pious fraud." In contrast to Southern Baptists, who could identify with Carter's faith even if they sometimes disagreed with his politics, fundamentalists outside the SBC did not share any affinity for Carter's religious beliefs. "On the basis of clear Bible teaching, Jimmy Carter is not a fundamental Christian," Bob Spencer, pastor of the independent Metropolitan Baptist Church in Atlanta, told the press.[61]

As soon as they heard about Carter's *Playboy* interview, fundamentalists who had been quietly criticizing Carter in the pages of their church bulletins went public with their rebuke of the presidential candidate. Bob Jones III told an audience of six thousand students that he could not support a candidate who used "barnyard language," and that if Carter were elected, "this nation cannot survive long." The pastor of Georgia's largest megachurch joined sixteen other independent Baptist ministers from the Atlanta metropolitan area in convening a conference to criticize Carter's "abuse of God" by claiming to be a Christian while interviewing with *Playboy*. Yet while claiming to be concerned primarily with Carter's *Playboy* interview, they also questioned the candidate's policy positions on issues of gender, sex, and abortion. Carter, they said, had "refused to take an unequivocal stand against the murder of unborn babies" and had expressed support for the Equal Rights Amendment (ERA), which the ministers strongly opposed as a threat to "the basic unit of our society, the home."[62]

Fundamentalist furor over Carter brought Jerry Falwell into the fray. In the early 1970s, Falwell had grown his church into one of the nation's largest, with a weekly attendance numbering in the thousands. He had also become increasingly interested in politics, and in 1976, he felt ready to plunge into the presidential race. Shortly after Carter's *Playboy* interview, Falwell spent a few minutes criticizing the Democratic candidate on his weekly radio program *Old-Time Gospel Hour*. By the next presidential election, such an action would no longer seem shocking, but this time, it created a firestorm. Never before had Falwell used his radio program to speak out for or against a presidential candidate, and when he did so, the Carter campaign demanded equal time to respond on Falwell's show. The Baptist preacher granted the request, but not on terms that satisfied Carter's aides. Some of the nation's leading independent Baptist pastors, including John R. Rice, rallied to the defense of their fellow pastor and denounced the Carter campaign's unwillingness to listen to "dissent."[63]

The squabble with the campaign solidified Falwell's commitment to the Republican Party. He had already endorsed Ford, but he considered the Carter campaign's effort to "squelch a preacher in the pulpit" confirmation of the Democratic Party's antipathy to conservative Christians. Carter, he said, needed to "apologize to the nation for this infringement of the basic freedoms of all Americans—freedom of religion and freedom of speech." Years later, a vice president of the Moral Majority said that the angry reaction that Falwell received from the Carter campaign was the "catalytic triggering event" that gave Falwell a sense of his own political influence and prompted him to enter national politics.[64]

With fundamentalists taking advantage of an opportunity to criticize a candidate whose politics and theology they had always considered suspect, and with conservative Southern Baptists and evangelicals abandoning their erstwhile political hero, Republicans saw an opportunity to pick up a few votes. In the spring of 1976, President Gerald Ford's campaign had written off "fundamentalist Protestants" and southerners as likely Carter supporters and had decided to focus its efforts on winning votes among Catholics, secular conservatives, and mainline Protestants in the "big industrial states" of the North. But by early summer, Ford's campaign team had begun to take another look at southern evangelicals. Ford accepted an invitation to speak at the Southern Baptist Convention's annual meeting in June 1976, becoming the first American president to address the SBC. Basing his speech on the biblical verse "Blessed is the nation whose God is the Lord," Ford spoke about the faith of America's founders and the importance of acknowledging God in public life—a message that evangelicals had been preaching for the previous two or three decades.[65]

Sensing that Ford was ready to reach out to conservative Protestants, Falwell sent the president an invitation to speak at his Thomas Road Baptist Church in Lynchburg, Virginia, on July 4. "We can offer [Ford] a special audience he can get no other place: 100,000 conservative, fundamental people in Lynchburg, Va., and another 15 million fundamental, conservative voters watching on national television," Falwell's public relations director told the White House. At first, Ford's staff was inclined to turn down the invitation, but when they heard that Falwell might extend a similar offer to Ronald Reagan, who was still threatening a convention floor fight for the nomination, the president's staff changed course. Attempting to hedge his bets, Ford did not appear before Falwell's congregation, but instead sent a videotaped address in which he discoursed on the role of religious faith in American history and the contributions that Baptists had made to the country's heritage.[66]

Ford had long viewed his religious beliefs as a private matter, but by the end of the summer of 1976, he realized that he could not appeal to conservative Christians without providing some type of religious testimony. In September, Ford invited some of the foremost evangelical leaders in America to the White House and announced that he, like Carter, had been "born again." It was the first presidential election in American history in which both major candidates made this claim. Ford told the group—which included the president of the NAE, an associate editor of *Christianity Today*, and the president of the National Religious Broadcasters—that he had a "relationship with Jesus Christ through my church and through my daily life." Like Carter, he claimed to read the Bible daily. The following month, Ford paid a visit to the nation's largest Southern Baptist congregation, W. A. Criswell's First Baptist Church in Dallas. Criswell preached a political sermon lambasting Carter for his *Playboy* interview, and gave Ford his endorsement.[67]

Unlike Carter, Ford's advisers knew that social conservatives cared about the politics of sex. They made sure that evangelicals knew that the president had refused to grant an interview to *Playboy*. They arranged for Ford's son, Michael, a ministerial student at evangelical Gordon Conwell Theological Seminary, to appear in a campaign commercial discussing his father's religious beliefs. In Ford's most significant bid for the votes of social conservatives, he began taking a more conservative position on abortion.[68]

The Abortion Issue in the Presidential Election of 1976

Ford wanted to keep the abortion issue out of presidential politics, a sentiment that many other leading Republicans shared. Five years earlier, when Richard Nixon was expecting a reelection contest against Edmund Muskie, a devout Catholic who had proclaimed his belief in the fetus's "sanctity of life," Nixon had tried to neutralize the abortion issue. He asserted that he shared Muskie's personal opposition to abortion, but that he also believed that abortion was the "province of the states, not the Federal Government," and therefore was not a suitable subject for presidential candidates to debate. Nixon briefly used the abortion issue to appeal to social conservatives during his campaign against George McGovern in 1972, but as soon as the election was over, he ignored the subject. When *Roe v. Wade* transformed abortion into a national political issue, the Nixon White House offered little comment. Ford, who at the time was the House minority leader, sponsored a constitutional amendment that would rescind *Roe*. But when that amendment proposal failed, Ford lost interest in the issue, and said nothing on the subject for the next three years. At a time when the First Lady, the vice president, and the chair of the Republican National Committee were advocates of abortion rights, many people assumed that the president was as well.[69]

In early 1976, antiabortion activists forced the president to end his silence on the issue. To the surprise of journalists who had underestimated the degree of popular opposition to *Roe*, antiabortion protestors dogged most of the major contenders for the Democratic Party's presidential nomination, making it the most contentious issue in the Democratic presidential primary. Ellen McCormack, a New York right-to-life activist who had never previously run for office at any level, gathered far more support than pundits had predicted in her bid for the Democratic presidential nomination. She received 9 percent of the vote in Vermont's presidential primary, 8 percent in South Dakota, and more than 5 percent in both Indiana and Kentucky.[70]

When a right-to-life rally brought sixty-five thousand antiabortion activists to the nation's capital on the third anniversary of *Roe v. Wade*, Washington reporters realized that a substantial minority of American voters cared about the issue of abortion, and they began badgering the White House press secretary with questions about the president's position. The presence of thousands of antiabortion protestors on the Washington mall might have been disconcerting for Ford, but even more troubling was the fact that Reagan had sent the marchers a telegram of support.[71]

When the president finally broke his silence on the issue, he took a position that was deliberately vague. "I do not believe in abortion on demand," Ford said in February 1976, but he believed that the law should permit women to obtain abortions to protect their health or in cases of rape or "any of the other unfortunate things that might happen." He also supported state control of abortion policy, suggesting that he would endorse a constitutional amendment to rescind *Roe v. Wade* and return the matter to the states, as he had in 1973. But by 1976, this was not enough to satisfy antiabortion activists, who favored a constitutional amendment to protect fetal life. "The President's statement is so negative and equivocating that it is useless as a basis for protecting the value and dignity of any human being's life," a director of the March for Life said in February 1976. "What he characterized as a 'moderate' position—presumably that translates into just a 'moderate' amount of killing preborn human beings."[72]

Pro-life activists began giving Ford's candidacy more serious consideration after the Democratic National Convention produced its first official platform statement on abortion rights in June 1976. In the early 1970s, some Democrats, most notably George McGovern's devout Catholic running mate, Sargent Shriver, had spoken out against abortion. Many Catholic pro-life activists of the late 1960s and early 1970s were liberal Democrats. But by 1976, feminists were moving the Democratic Party in a pro-choice direction. The party's platform did not directly endorse abortion rights or promise to defend them, but its opposition to an antiabortion constitutional amendment was enough to shock some Catholics. Archbishop Joseph L. Bernardin called the platform's abortion statement "morally offensive in the extreme." "The platform makes it official," Reverend Edward O'Connell wrote at the conclusion of the Democratic National Convention. "The Democratic Party doesn't want Catholics."[73]

When Republicans met for their national convention a few weeks later, shrewd strategists on the Ford campaign team decided to make pro-life Catholics feel welcome. At the same time, Ford's advisers were still worried about appeasing Reagan delegates. Reagan had promised to take his presidential campaign all the way to the convention floor, and one of his strategies for appealing to social conservatives was his support for a human life amendment. In order to counteract Reagan's strategy, Senator Robert Dole (R-KS), who became Ford's running mate, met with Ellen McCormack's campaign team to find out what platform language on abortion would be acceptable to activists in right-to-life organizations. Soliciting advice from a Democratic presidential candidate's campaign team might have been an unorthodox move for a Republican vice presidential candidate, but Dole, who had relied on graphic antiabortion advertisements from pro-life groups to retain his Senate seat in a close election two years earlier, realized the political value of the abortion issue, and he thought that McCormack's supporters represented a constituency that the GOP could attract. Acting on the advice of the McCormack supporters, Dole convinced delegates to adopt a platform that called for a constitutional amendment to "restore protection of the right to life for unborn children."[74]

It was a tougher stance than Ford had advocated, but Dole felt that it was necessary to appease the pro-life activists, and Ford embraced it as a way to lure social conservatives into the Republican camp. In his meeting with the National Conference of Catholic Bishops in September, the president underscored his opposition to abortion and pointed to the party platform as proof of his pro-life bona fides. After the meeting, Archbishop Bernardin told the press that the bishops were "encouraged," a statement that contrasted markedly with his earlier assessment of the Democratic Party's platform. As Ford's campaign team realized the benefits of appealing to religiously conservative voters, they made greater efforts in the final weeks of the campaign to highlight the party's platform on the abortion issue. In October, they hired Marjory Mecklenburg, president of American Citizens Concerned for Life, as an adviser. She arranged for Pat Boone, a former Reagan supporter, to make a radio commercial for the president. "President Ford has said he is against abortion on demand and he is willing to do something about it," Boone told the Christian radio audience.[75]

Ford's strategy seemed to work. Even though Ford had begun his campaign with a socially liberal record that few evangelicals or conservative Catholics could endorse, he ended his campaign as the preferred candidate of most of the leading figures in the pro-life movement. The Republican Party platform received endorsements from Mildred Jefferson, president of the National Right to Life Committee; Harold O. J. Brown, head of the Christian Action Council; and Dan Lyons, who led Christian Crusade's anti-abortion efforts. "The platform of the Democratic Party is unacceptable," the three pro-life leaders said in a statement that they released to the press. "If the candidates of the Republican Party honor the plank in their platform that supports the enactment of a right-to-life amendment, the Republican Party will constitute the Party of Life."[76]

Ford won a bare majority—51 percent—of the nation's evangelical vote, but he was unable to make substantial inroads into the southern, white, conservative Protestant constituency. He lost every southern state except Virginia, and did particularly badly among Baptists. A Harris survey showed that Ford received only 43 percent of the white Baptist vote nationwide, compared to Carter's 56 percent. Even Pat Robertson, a religious broadcaster who later became one of the nation's best-known Christian Right leaders, supported Carter. Most evangelicals were more interested in celebrating the Democratic candidate's religious faith than in debating the nuances of party platform language on abortion.[77]

But Carter's favorable standing with southern evangelicals would be short-lived. Within months of his inauguration, the cultural issues that Carter had tried to ignore in the campaign, such as abortion, feminism, and gay rights, would drive a wedge between conservative evangelicals and their president. The grassroots activists who had already begun to transform evangelical politics by mobilizing against the ERA and abortion would make Carter the target of their next campaign.

Harold Ockenga (1905–1985), first president of the National Association of Evangelicals. The formation of the NAE in 1942 inaugurated a new era of evangelical political activity. (Wheaton College Archives and Special Collections)

Dwight and Mamie Eisenhower leaving Sunday worship services. Eisenhower's public support of religion endeared him to evangelicals. (National Park Service / Dwight D. Eisenhower Presidential Library)

Billy Graham in New York City. Graham's crusade in New York's Madison Square Garden in 1957 featured an address from Richard Nixon and marked the peak of his political influence in the early years of the Cold War. (Southern Baptist Historical Library and Archives)

John R. Rice (1895–1980), editor of the *Sword of the Lord*. Rice, a friend of both Jerry Falwell and Bob Jones, Jr., combined conservative politics with biblical preaching in his widely circulated fundamentalist periodical. (Sword of the Lord)

Billy James Hargis (1925–2004), anticommunist radio preacher. Hargis's Christian Crusade mobilized southern fundamentalists for conservative political causes in the 1950s and 1960s. (Special Collections, University of Arkansas Libraries)

Billy Graham and Richard Nixon departing from the administration's first White House church service, January 1969. Nixon used his White House church services and relationship with Graham to build an evangelical political coalition. (Nixon Presidential Library and Museum)

Phyllis Schlafly addressing an International Women's Year counter-rally in Houston, 1977. Though Schlafly was a Catholic, her STOP-ERA campaign received the support of thousands of conservative evangelical women. (Photo permission of Phyllis Schlafly)

Anita Bryant with her husband, Bob Green, addressing the Southern Baptist Convention, 1978. Bryant's campaign against gay rights in Miami in 1977 launched the careers of many conservative evangelical political activists. (Southern Baptist Historical Library and Archives)

Francis Schaeffer (1912–1984) addressing a pro-life rally in London. Schaeffer's writings against abortion and secular humanism were a political inspiration for many evangelicals, including Jerry Falwell. (Photo copyright Sylvester Jacobs)

James Robison, Texas Baptist evangelist. Robison's protest against a Dallas station's refusal to air his sermons against homosexuality in 1979 was a pivotal moment in the formation of the New Christian Right. (Southern Baptist Historical Library and Archives)

Jerry Falwell leading an "I Love America" rally at the statehouse in Trenton, New Jersey, in 1980. Falwell's rallies, along with his Moral Majority, mobilized evangelicals on behalf of conservative political causes. (William E. Sauro / *New York Times* / Redux)

Paul Weyrich (1942–2008), New Right activist and ally of the Christian Right. Weyrich convinced Jerry Falwell to launch the Moral Majority in 1979. (American Heritage Center, University of Wyoming)

President Ronald Reagan addressing the National Association of Evangelicals, 1983. Reagan's speech at the NAE combined culture war themes with the Cold War in an effort to enlist evangelical support for his nuclear arms program. (Ronald Reagan Presidential Library)

Ronald Reagan frequently met with Christian Right leaders throughout his time in office. Here he is shown with Jerry Falwell (top), James Dobson (bottom), and Tim and Beverly LaHaye (right). (Ronald Reagan Presidential Library)

Randall Terry displaying a fetus to Operation Rescue volunteers at an abortion clinic blockade in Philadelphia, 1988. Terry's Operation Rescue, which used civil disobedience to shut down abortion clinics, attracted thousands of evangelical activists in the late 1980s. (AP Photo / George Widman)

Pat Robertson (right) and Ralph Reed, 1997. Robertson and Reed's Christian Coalition was one of the most powerful conservative political groups in the 1990s and helped move the Republican Party to the right on social issues. (AP Photo / John Bazemore)

President George W. Bush's televised address to the 2005 Southern Baptist Convention. Bush received strong support from Southern Baptists in 2004 and enjoyed a close relationship with several SBC leaders at the beginning of his second term. (Baptist Press / John Swain)

Rick Warren with presidential candidates John McCain and Barack Obama at the Saddleback Civil Forum, August 2008. Warren's outreach to both McCain and Obama represented a new style of evangelical politics and highlighted the importance of the evangelical vote. (Baptist Press / Meredith Day)

| Culture Wars in the Carter Years

J IMMY CARTER DID NOT EXPECT a conflict with evangelicals when he
entered the White House. At the beginning of his administration, he
gave every indication that he would be one of the most religiously devout
presidents that the nation had had in decades. Less than a week after his
inauguration, he transferred his church membership to Washington's First
Baptist Church and signed up to teach Sunday school. First Baptist was
racially diverse and socially tolerant, while also holding to the traditions
of the Baptist faith. In essence, the church represented the type of centrist
liberalism that Carter hoped to promote, proclaiming a vision of social betterment that was rooted in the traditional language of the Christian faith.[1]

But fundamentalists and conservative evangelicals quickly realized that
Carter's type of Christianity was far removed from their own. Carl McIntire,
now seventy years old, wrote, "The election of Governor Jimmy Carter to the
Presidency of the United States has shaken Christian people everywhere."[2]

Evangelicals' political mobilization in the late 1970s was the culmination
of a decade-long struggle to come to terms with the diminished influence of
a Protestant-based moral code in the nation. As conservative evangelicals
looked for an explanation for the continuing strength of the cultural liberalism that they opposed, many of them became convinced that all of the
trends that they found disconcerting, ranging from gay rights to abortion,
were the product of a single philosophy that they labeled "secular humanism."
Christian politicians, they thought, should devote themselves to opposing
secular humanism in the legislative arena, but Carter did not share that opinion.
His view of religion centered on personal piety, not public morality. He

continued to cling to a centuries-old Baptist tradition of church-state separation, arguing that he could not impose his moral beliefs on the rest of the nation. To conservative evangelicals and fundamentalists, Carter was on the wrong side of the culture wars.

Concerns about "Secular Humanism" in Education

Prior to the 1970s, few evangelicals or fundamentalists had been concerned about the small coterie of intellectuals who called themselves "humanists." When a coalition of Unitarians, atheists, and secular educators such as John Dewey organized the American Humanist Association in 1941 in order to promote a nontheistic value system and vision of social betterment, conservative Protestants paid no attention. At a time when an overwhelming majority of Americans believed in God and attended religious services, the humanists had little influence, and most conservative Protestants ignored them.

Yet when social conservatives became concerned about changes in school curricula in the late 1960s, they decided that objectionable programs such as sex education and values clarification classes might be an attempt by the National Education Association and, in the words of conservative Catholic journalist John Steinbacher, John Dewey's "coterie of sycophantic followers" to "make good little Humanists out of the kids." Parents who enrolled their children in Christian schools usually cited the pervasiveness of "secular humanism" in public schools as the major reason for doing so. "Secular humanism," the *Baptist Bible Tribune* said in 1975, appeared to be "an organized effort to take over the public schools of the United States." The arguments identifying a secular humanist conspiracy resonated with fundamentalists who were campaigning against "objectionable" textbooks, as well as with pastors who were concerned about the secularization of society. "It should come as no surprise that the godless ideas of Humanism would supplant prayer and Bible reading in the public school system," Steinbacher wrote.[3]

Conservative Christians' mobilization against "secular humanism" acquired national publicity and became an organized movement in the fall of 1974 in the coal-mining region of West Virginia. Fusing concerns about sex, race, and secularism in the new curriculum, Kanawha County school board member Alice Moore, the wife of a Church of Christ minister, convinced thousands of parents throughout the county to boycott their classes for a few weeks to protest the required literature selections. The new curriculum for high school students included inappropriate sexual themes and "negative references to Christianity and God," Moore explained. She was upset that the county's students would be required to read Allen Ginsberg's poetic description of a visit to a prostitute, e. e. cummings's sexually suggestive poem "I Like My Body," and Gwendolyn Brooks's profane references to God and Jesus. She was equally upset by one textbook's characterization of the story of Daniel in the lion's den as a "myth," and by "ghetto English" in selections from James Baldwin and Eldridge Cleaver. "There was lots of profanity and anti-American and racist anti-white stories," Moore said. "They presented a warped view of life."[4]

Moore gained the support of several fundamentalist and evangelical pastors in the community, as well as thousands of parents and other supporters who resented the attempt of educational "elites" to contravene their community's values. Their deep anger at the "giants who have mocked and made fun of dumb fundamentalists" resulted in violent protests. Sympathetic miners walked off their jobs to show their support for the boycott against the "dirty books." Several preachers went to prison for inciting angry crowds to blow up school buses and engage in vandalism against school buildings. The school board ultimately acquiesced to the social conservatives' demands, but not before several political conservatives, including Representative Robert Dornan (R-CA), textbook watchdogs Mel and Norma Gabler, and representatives of the John Birch Society came to Kanawha County to support the demonstrations. New Right activist Paul Weyrich's recently created Heritage Foundation offered legal aid for the fundamentalist preachers who had been arrested.[5]

Several of the New Right activists who came to Kanawha County were conservative Catholics who wanted to use the protests as a springboard for a larger movement for parental rights in education, a movement that quickly became linked to the conservative wing of the Republican Party. One of the leaders in the Kanawha County protests was Connaught "Connie" Marshner, a thirty-three-year-old education director at the Heritage Foundation and a speechwriter for conservative Republican congressmen, who traveled to West Virginia with her husband, a Catholic seminarian at the conservative University of Dallas, to provide organizational assistance to the protestors. Marshner encouraged angry parents to abandon the public school system altogether and enroll their children in newly created Christian schools. Under her auspices, the Heritage Foundation organized a series of "Citizens' Workshops" that brought nationally known conservative educational consultants to Kanawha County to defend the rights of parents to select their children's textbooks and to discuss the possibility of launching "parent-run schools." After spending several months in Kanawha County, Marshner returned to Dallas, where she began working with Mel and Norma Gabler to influence textbook selection in the Texas public schools, and she looked for other opportunities to aid the burgeoning Christian school movement.[6]

In late 1974, at the height of the Kanawha County protests, Marshner wrote a speech in defense of school vouchers for conservative Republican congressman Phil Crane to deliver on the House floor. Some of Crane's colleagues who knew the Illinois congressman as a hard-drinking, lapsed mainline Protestant may have been surprised by the references to obscure papal encyclicals and detailed philosophical defenses of parental rights that Marshner had inserted into the speech, but Crane's advocacy of private alternatives to the public school system probably came as less of a shock. Crane, who was one of the House's most ideological defenders of the free market and who would soon serve as president of the American Conservative Union, was a rising star in the conservative wing of the Republican Party. Although a plan for school vouchers had no chance of passage in a Democratic Congress, Crane's willingness to champion Marshner's proposal ensured advocates of private alternatives to the nation's public education system a continued voice in the GOP and the emerging New Right. Marshner's involvement in the Kanawha County protests also inspired her to write *Blackboard Tyranny* (1978), a book that gave socially conservative parents detailed instructions for starting their own Christian schools.[7]

Onalee McGraw, a conservative Catholic at the Heritage Foundation with a Ph.D. in political science from Georgetown, contributed to the debate by publishing the pamphlet *Secular Humanism and the Schools: The Issue Whose Time Has Come* in late 1976. "Humanistic education," she argued, "repudiates values taught in the home and at church" by encouraging children to create their own system of morality without regard for the religious teachings of their parents. As an assault on the family and Christianity, "humanism" was therefore a violation of the First Amendment's prohibition on governmental interference in religion.[8]

By the late 1970s, conservative Christians were no longer concerned only about individual components of the school curriculum, such as sex education or evolutionary biology. Instead, as McGraw had suggested, they believed that public educators had mounted a broad-based attack on their values with the deliberate aim of undermining their children's beliefs. The public school curriculum, they thought, was permeated with an alternative values system that conflicted with their fundamentalist Christian worldview. To a certain extent, they were correct. Many educators of the 1970s shared a positive view of the rights-based movements of the previous decade. The curricula and textbooks that they designed reflected their view that adolescents should be encouraged to think for themselves rather than blindly accept their parents' dogmatic teaching, and that children should read literary selections that reflected the nation's cultural diversity and challenged society's traditional assumptions about gender roles. But conservative Christian parents were bothered by elementary school reading texts that depicted fathers, rather than mothers, washing dishes, or that showed women, rather than men, doing construction work. Most of all, they were angry with educators who, they believed, had usurped the rights of parents in shaping the moral values of the nation's schoolchildren.[9]

Conservatives in the Republican Party were sympathetic to parents' complaints about educational "bureaucrats," because they, too, were opposed to what they considered undue governmental interference in the lives of the nation's citizens. At the 1976 Republican Party convention, Senator Jesse Helms encouraged the party to approve a platform statement opposing federal funding of "controversial" textbooks. The party did not do so, but it did adopt a lengthy statement complaining about the federal government's "restrictive regulations" of local schools, and it stated that responsibility for children's education belonged to "local communities and parents," not bureaucrats in Washington. In a concession to social conservatives, the platform advocated the right of communities to practice "non-sectarian prayers in their public schools." And in a bid for the support of the growing number of families who had decided to reject public schools altogether, the party called for tax credits for parents who were paying private school tuition.[10]

Francis Schaeffer

In 1976, Francis Schaeffer, a Presbyterian missionary in Switzerland, published the evangelical best-seller *How Should We Then Live?* and converted a new generation of evangelicals into culture warriors. An independent-minded missionary who had severed his ties with his own denomination and had been living abroad since 1948, Schaeffer was an unlikely candidate for a leader of the Religious Right, but his eclectic background made him uniquely suited to bring a broad spectrum of Christians into the campaign against secular humanism. He was an intellectual by temperament. He entered adolescence as an agnostic, but then converted to Christianity as a high school student in Pennsylvania in the early 1930s. In a preview of his later maverick tendencies, he attended an African American church while a student at Hampden-Sydney College in Virginia, and spent his spare time arguing theology with his less devout classmates. But although Schaeffer showed signs of a social consciousness during his college years, his graduate studies at the staunchly conservative

Westminster Theological Seminary led him into fundamentalism, and he became a conservative pastor and young leader in fundamentalist radio preacher Carl McIntire's Bible Presbyterian Church. Then he received a denominational commission to serve as a missionary in Switzerland. While preaching in Europe, Schaeffer experienced a crisis of faith that caused him to reject McIntire's denomination and its strict fundamentalism and instead adopt a more ecumenical evangelical theology.[11]

Schaeffer did not abandon his beliefs in biblical inerrancy and the necessity of evangelism, but his method of reaching others with the gospel differed radically from that of most American preachers. Instead of holding evangelistic crusades, he and his wife, Edith, opened their home to travelers and university students, and soon hundreds of young people made their way through the Swiss Alps to L'Abri (The Shelter), where they had the opportunity to debate existential questions with the preacher, who was quickly acquiring a reputation as an evangelical pop philosopher. His theology remained orthodox, but instead of merely preaching from the Bible, as fundamentalists had traditionally done, Schaeffer also drew on Sigmund Freud, Jean-Paul Sartre, and the Beatles for illustrations. Young evangelicals appreciated this fresh approach. By the late 1960s, Schaeffer had become an internationally known Christian thinker and a celebrated lecturer at American evangelical colleges. He sold 3 million copies of his twenty-four books in the United States alone, and his works were translated into twenty-one languages.[12]

To many young evangelicals, Schaeffer, who had exchanged his tie for Swiss hiking knickers and long hair, seemed a welcome alternative to the straitlaced preachers of traditional fundamentalism. L'Abri became a destination for young, left-wing iconoclasts who wanted to "buck the evangelical establishment," as Schaeffer urged them to do. Schaeffer's admirers included Larry Norman, a long-haired musician who pioneered "Jesus rock" in the early 1970s, and Jack Sparks, a leader in the socially radical Jesus Movement in Berkeley. Many non-Christians also respected Schaeffer, even if they disagreed with his theology, and they welcomed the chance to visit L'Abri. Schaeffer tolerated the drug users and hippies who made their way to his Alpine home, and in exchange, he gained the opportunity to discuss Christian philosophy with college-age rebels in quest of social liberation or personal nirvana. Even Timothy Leary visited.[13]

Politically, Schaeffer was hard to place, but many young evangelicals assumed that he was leftist in his thinking, since he wrote about Christians' social responsibility and published books such as *Pollution and the Death of Man* (1970), which urged evangelicals to become environmentally conscious.

In the early 1970s, he rebuked the church for its historic racism and its failure to advocate the "compassionate use of accumulated wealth." He spoke out about the dangers of nuclear war, and reprimanded Christians who equated the gospel with conservative politics. "One of the greatest injustices we do to our young people is to ask them to be conservative," Schaeffer wrote in 1970.[14]

In the early 1970s, politically conservative fundamentalists were wary of Schaeffer. Billy James Hargis admitted that he appreciated Schaeffer's biblical insights, but he criticized the theologian for his "mistake" in sympathizing with the "hippie / yippies."[15] But Schaeffer enjoyed an almost cultlike following among young evangelicals, many of whom viewed him as a modern Christian sage.

Schaeffer understood secular trends in a way that other conservative Protestants did not. While many American evangelicals of the 1960s and early 1970s assumed that their nation still supported Christian values at some level, Schaeffer had no doubt that secular society was hostile to Christianity. Because he lived in a highly secularized European academic community, he had an opportunity to engage the thinking of existentialists, structuralists and poststructuralists, behaviorists, and adherents of other philosophies that, in his opinion, were egregiously wrong. He came to the conclusion that a Christian's basic intellectual assumptions differed radically from those of contemporary society and that Christians now lived as aliens in a world that no longer accepted biblical truth.[16]

Yet instead of separating himself from the world, Schaeffer urged Christians to confront and infiltrate the cultural institutions of their society in order to transform them. Instead of telling Christian young people to eschew movies, he encouraged talented Christians to produce films. Instead of merely denouncing nude art as "dirty," Schaeffer analyzed its intellectual dimensions and social messages. Above all, Schaeffer urged Christians to go into politics. Only a few months before his death in 1984, Schaeffer summarized his life's message by saying, "Throughout my work there is a common unifying theme, which I would define as 'the Lordship of Christ in the totality of life.'"[17]

Schaeffer's belief in the necessity of extending Christian influence in society led him to attack "secular humanism" in the 1970s. His antipathy to humanism was partly the logical outgrowth of his long-standing opposition to existentialist and nihilist philosophies: for him, "secular humanism" was merely a shorthand term for a wide range of anti-theistic philosophies. But Schaeffer's opposition was also a reaction to the legalization of abortion. Schaeffer blamed this on the fact that Westerners, including Americans, had replaced God's moral standards with "secular humanism," which allowed people to make their own capricious moral rules or live by none at all. In this system, Schaeffer said, either anarchy, tyranny, or the imposition of the will of the majority—no matter how corrupt—would prevail, and minorities and the defenseless would have no protection from a society that no longer acknowledged the absolute value of human life. "In regard to the fetus, the courts have arbitrarily separated 'aliveness' from 'personhood,' and if this is so, why not arbitrarily do the same with the aged?" Schaeffer wrote. "So the steps move along, and euthanasia may well become increasingly acceptable. And if so, why not keep alive the bodies of the so-called no-morts (persons in whom the brain wave is flat) to harvest from them body parts and blood, when the polls show that this has become acceptable to the majority? . . . Law has become a matter of averages, just as the culture's sexual mores have become only a matter of averages."[18]

To bring his message to the world, Schaeffer produced a new tour de force—a book and film documentary titled *How Should We Then Live?* which offered a sweeping survey of the humanistic trends in Western thinking since the Renaissance. Schaeffer showed how the humanistic assumptions of many European and American philosophers had permeated popular culture and created a social and political milieu that no longer accepted the idea of an absolute standard of truth. Western societies faced a choice, he argued: they could return to a biblical standard of morality, or they could drift toward authoritarian governmental regimes that arbitrarily defined rights and laws in ways that would gradually deprive people of their liberties. He ended his book with a call to political action. After commending the examples of early-nineteenth-century evangelicals who spoke out against slavery and twentieth-century Christians who "acted against abuses in the areas of race and the noncompassionate use of wealth," he argued that it was time for Christians to follow their example and "act against the special sickness and threat of our age—the rise of authoritarian government."[19]

Schaeffer might have been content with a series of lectures and a book had it not been for his nineteen-year-old son, Franky, a serious amateur artist who was strongly opposed to abortion. Franky urged his father to make a thirteen-episode documentary that featured on-location filming at the great art museums of Europe to illustrate his historical and philosophical points. Schaeffer was reluctant at first. Although he was internationally known among evangelicals, he had never been a religious broadcaster or fund-raiser and did not have the financial connections to fund a project on this scale. But Billy Zeoli did. A young evangelist in Grand Rapids, Michigan, a director of Gospel Films, Inc., and a chaplain to several major-league sports teams, Zeoli had come to L'Abri in the early 1970s. He enjoyed connections with a number of well-heeled evangelicals, and he was also a spiritual adviser to Gerald Ford, the House minority leader who was on the verge of becoming vice president—and then president—of the United States. With Zeoli's help, the Schaeffers began soliciting money from wealthy conservatives, such as oil magnate Nelson Bunker Hunt and Amway founder Richard DeVos.[20]

As the film project progressed, Zeoli's own political influence expanded. When Ford became vice president, Zeoli began sending him weekly spiritual advice memos; and when Ford entered the White House, Zeoli began traveling to Washington on a regular basis to pray with him. He was on hand to offer spiritual comfort at moments of crisis in the president's life, such as the day of Betty Ford's breast surgery. Garry Wills, writing in the *New York Times*, referred to him as the president's "own private Billy Graham." Like Graham, Zeoli professed to be nonpartisan, but when he began giving Ford campaign advice about how to attract the evangelical vote in 1976, his political sympathies became evident.[21]

Zeoli introduced the Schaeffer family to the Fords. Michael Ford became a student at L'Abri while his father was vice president, and Michael's wife became a regular babysitter of Franky's young daughter. When Gerald Ford became president, he invited Francis and Edith Schaeffer to the White House. Schaeffer's work also attracted the notice of Representative Jack Kemp (R-NY), a Catholic, pro-life, conservative Republican who arranged for Schaeffer to speak to gatherings of conservative congressmen and senators.[22]

Schaeffer's documentary, *How Should We Then Live*, became a sensation among evangelicals, drawing audiences of up to five thousand in the churches that screened it. The accompanying book was a best-seller in the evangelical market.[23] Conservative evangelicals had been looking for an explanation for the secular drift of their country, and Schaeffer's diagnosis of contemporary cultural ills gave them a framework for understanding it. After 1976, many evangelicals who had once distanced themselves from the attacks of more conservative fundamentalists on secularism in the public schools decided that there really was a culture war taking place in America, and they determined to become active participants in it.

The same year in which Schaeffer published his book, H. Edward Rowe, a former pastor who was a leader in the Christian Freedom Foundation, published a critique of secular humanism that translated Schaeffer's ideas into a political program. "For too long Christians have demonstrated an almost complete lack of interest in government," Rowe wrote in *Save America!* "If our country is to be saved from a whirlwind of destruction brought about by evil forces within, Christian citizens must move decisively into the forefront of public leadership at all levels as rapidly as possible. Only they are equipped spiritually and morally to render the kind of public and political decisions which will be pleasing to God and which will lead to the strengthening of the fiber of our nation and civilization."[24]

Schaeffer had deliberately left his political advice vague enough to be applicable to Christians in almost any Western country from almost any political party, but Rowe's *Save America!* offered a political agenda that was unmistakably conservative Republican. Rowe argued that liberal economic policy, as well as liberal social morals, had resulted from the nation's turn toward secular humanism. "Godless men are running the country while men of God rest in peace or—at the most—complain mildly," Rowe lamented. "In morals, a climate of relativism, situation ethics, and the quest for selfish pleasure prevails. In economics, the picture is dismal—deficit spending, spiraling inflation, debasement of our currency, increasing federal controls, and skyrocketing taxes." In a further departure from Schaeffer, Rowe did not focus on the evils of abortion, but instead directed his ire against the rights revolutions of the 1970s, such as the feminist movement, and charged that those were a product of secular humanism.[25]

Rowe noted with approval that Christians were resisting secular humanism through Christian schools and local antipornography campaigns, but he argued that more concerted political action was necessary. "It appears that our Christian population nationally could—if properly trained—serve as a citizen bloc for the betterment of our political institutions and processes," Rowe wrote. "This vast resource of Christian manpower is a sleeping giant which needs to be aroused." Rowe advocated the formation of a Christian PAC that could "identify potential Christian political candidates, encourage them to run for public office, help them to gain election and undergird them throughout their term of service." Evangelicals needed a "Christian legislative action group" that would "provide Christian analysis of key bills before city, county, state, and national legislative bodies, reporting a clearly stated Christian position to the community through the press and other available media," he said.[26] Rowe's political program sounded ambitious at the time, but he was convinced that only such large-scale political activism could stem the advance of secular humanism.

Despite the urgency of his appeal, Rowe's call for a Christian political movement did not produce any results in the short term. Yet evangelicals continued to mount legal and political attacks on "secular humanism" through other means. As soon as Jimmy Carter became president, many conservative evangelicals and fundamentalists began watching him closely to see which side of the culture war he would choose. When Carter began promoting the ERA and endorsing the feminist movement, they decided that it was time to speak out against the administration.

Opposing the Carter Administration on Feminism

Conservative evangelicals' first major conflict with the White House began in March 1977, when Carter announced his appointments to the International Women's Year (IWY) state conferences—federally funded, UN-backed efforts to promote gender equality. Social conservatives were chagrined to find that most of the convention members were feminists who, like the president, supported the ERA. Heading the list was Bella Abzug, a liberal Democratic former congressional representative from New York. Her abrasive political style, which had earned her the sobriquet "Battling Bella," alienated even some liberals, so Carter's appointment of her to the women's commission was almost guaranteed to infuriate socially conservative evangelicals. Pat Robertson, founder of the Christian Broadcasting Network (CBN) and host of *The 700 Club*, was one of the offended parties. Robertson, the son of a conservative Democratic senator, had supported Carter in 1976, but that support ended after the newly elected president selected Abzug to head the series of state women's conferences. "I wouldn't let Bella Abzug scrub the floors of any organization I was head of," Robertson later told a reporter.[27]

In earlier years, fundamentalists and evangelicals probably would have been content to denounce the conferences and the Carter administration in their publications and radio broadcasts, but this time, they decided to take a different tack. "Because we represent the majority of women, we must take over these conferences and make sure they project a pro-family, pro-homemaker, pro-morality, pro-life image," Phyllis Schlafly told her socially conservative female readership in one of her newsletters.[28]

Conservative women turned out in impressive numbers for the state conventions: in New York, more than seven thousand people showed up at the state conference, when conference organizers had predicted a crowd of only three thousand. They turned the conventions into heated debates over the ERA, abortion, and gay rights. Tempers flared on both sides. Feminists believed that the socially conservative women were trying to hijack the conferences and thwart the progress of women's rights, while conservatives at the state conventions thought the feminists were trying to foist a secular humanist agenda on the nation and destroy the traditional family. Some of the conservative delegates who had seen Schaeffer's film the previous year came prepared to fight for the preservation of the nation's culture. "This is a war between God and the devil," one attendee at the New York women's conference exclaimed. But the conservative women were nevertheless disappointed with their lack of influence during the conference proceedings. They thought the conferences did not give adequate consideration to conservative viewpoints, and they believed that their opponents had unfairly discriminated against social conservatives in selecting official conference delegates. The few social conservatives who were allowed to vote at the conferences could not dissuade other delegates from endorsing the ERA, nor prevent the passage of resolutions supporting lesbian rights or abortion-on-demand. Many returned from the conferences with a renewed determination to oppose feminism.[29]

Opponents of the ERA prepared for a standoff with feminists at the national culmination of the IWY state conferences, the National Women's Conference in Houston, in November 1977. Since they had been able to secure only 20 percent of the seats at the Houston convention for their own side, conservative women knew that they would be unable to prevent the endorsement of the ERA and other feminist causes, but they were nevertheless determined to use the Houston gathering to their advantage. While pro-ERA women met across town at the National Women's Conference, fifteen thousand conservative women from across the United States traveled to the Houston Astro Arena for an emotional assault on feminism, sexual liberation, lesbianism, and abortion.[30]

The numerical strength that socially conservative women displayed in Houston energized the antifeminist movement. One Louisiana minister whose congregation sent sixty delegates to the Pro-Family Rally in Houston reported that "while the family-rights people were emphasizing our need of God's guidance, the IWY Conference opened its session without any recognition of God, and proceeded to push through its socialistic Plan of Action and to wildly and enthusiastically place its stamp of approval upon the killing of unborn children, lesbianism, ERA, and a host of other highly questionable resolutions. . . . Moral rottenness filled the hall with the stench of death."[31]

Fourteen months after the Houston conference, President Carter dismissed Bella Abzug from the women's commission, but it was too late for him to reconcile his differences with conservative evangelicals. Nor did he seem interested in trying. He continued to support the ERA, which he viewed as a human rights measure. And in November 1978, he selected Sarah Weddington, the lawyer who had secured a landmark abortion rights victory for "Jane Roe" in *Roe v. Wade*, as his assistant for women's affairs. With the approval of the president, Weddington made the campaign for ratification of the ERA her top priority.[32]

Only two months after Weddington's appointment, conservative evangelicals stepped up their activism against the ERA. For the previous seven years, most of the evangelical women who lobbied against the ERA had done so through Phyllis Schlafly's national STOP-ERA or through smaller state organizations that were affiliated with Schlafly's movement. But in January 1979, Beverly LaHaye incorporated a new national organization in Sacramento that offered evangelical women an opportunity to become involved in an explicitly evangelical Protestant effort to stop the ERA. LaHaye viewed the feminist movement as a direct assault on the family. The National Organization for Women (NOW) claimed to promote the interests of American women, yet LaHaye was sure that it did not represent her values or those of the women with whom she associated. Deciding that she and other homemakers needed a voice in Washington to counter the influence of NOW, LaHaye invited some of her evangelical friends to join her for an informal discussion about their reaction to the feminist movement. Twelve hundred people responded to her invitation. Together, LaHaye and her female allies formed Concerned Women for America (CWA), whose primary goal was defeating the ERA. Within five years of its founding, it had nearly half a million members and a lobbying office in Washington.[33]

The conflict between social conservatives and feminists reached a fever pitch in the summer of 1980, when both sides prepared for a showdown at the White House Conference on Families (WHCF), a government-sponsored, information-gathering series of three regional conferences on gender and family issues. The National Pro-Family Coalition, an organization that had emerged from the Pro-Family Rally in Houston, encouraged social conservatives to apply to be delegates to the WHCF. Social conservatives won an overwhelming number of elected seats, but since the majority of conference seats were allocated by gubernatorial or commission appointment, most of the conference attendees were social liberals whose goals accorded with those of the commission. The result was predictable: neither the conservatives nor their opponents were interested in engaging the other side in a meaningful dialogue on controversial issues, and since the conservatives did not have the votes to win, they walked out of the conference in protest, charging that the system of delegate selection was "rigged."[34]

As they had done with IWY, social conservatives who felt rejected at the WHCF staged counter-rallies. More than five thousand Christian conservatives attended America's Pro-Family Conference, which Tim LaHaye helped organize in Long Beach, California, in July 1980. Jerry Falwell and Senator Jesse Helms delivered keynote addresses exhorting the delegates to become politically active in order to promote pro-family causes.[35]

By the end of the 1970s, the anti-ERA movement had blossomed into a formidable force in the culture war. The seven-year time limit for the amendment's ratification expired in 1979, with only thirty-five, rather than the required thirty-eight, states ratifying it. At the time that Schlafly began her campaign against the ERA, the amendment's passage had seemed certain, but socially conservative women persuaded state legislators to vote against ratification. When Congress extended the time limit for ratification for another three years, the move merely fanned the flames of conservative opposition. The ERA was never ratified.

Gay Rights

The battle over feminism coincided with the emergence of an evangelical campaign against gay rights, which also widened the gap between social conservatives and the president. Evangelicals and fundamentalists had once been almost oblivious to the presence of homosexuality in America. In the 1960s and early 1970s, when Carter forged his political career, it was easy for him and other evangelicals to ignore homosexuality, since antisodomy laws were still in force in most states, and since many gays and lesbians concealed their identities in order to avoid job discrimination, social ostracism, familial rejection, and physical intimidation or violence. But there were signs that the culture was changing. In the 1950s, many gays and lesbians formed informal social networks and made a few gains through organizations such as the Mattachine Society and the Daughters of Bilitis. The sexual revolution of the 1960s resulted in increased toleration not only for premarital sex, but also for homosexuality. By the mid-1960s, some liberal clergy publicly endorsed homosexuality as an acceptable "lifestyle," a move that prompted some fundamentalists to denounce the "filthy vice" of homosexuality.[36]

The fledgling movement to protect gays from discrimination experienced one of its greatest triumphs in 1969, when patrons at a gay bar in Greenwich Village resisted arrest during a police raid and proclaimed their right to live lives free from harassment. Emboldened, more gays began to come out of the closet and demand respect from society. Gay rights parades soon followed. The National Gay Task Force began lobbying for legislative protection in 1973, and the following year Representative Bella Abzug introduced the first congressional gay rights bill. It did not pass, but gays secured legislative gains at the local level as cities across America began rescinding antisodomy ordinances. At its annual meeting in 1973, the American Psychiatric Association removed homosexuality from its list of mental disorders.[37] Since Americans could no longer view homosexuality as a disease, and since many were reluctant to think of it as a sin, a growing number of Americans began extending at least limited toleration to the country's gay minority.

Carter, who was mindful of the need to live up to the Democratic Party's newfound reputation for tolerance and diversity, used his presidential campaign to reach out to gay rights activists with promises of support. His campaign took out advertisements in gay and lesbian newspapers and received endorsements from gay rights leaders. Although he said that as a Baptist he opposed the homosexual "lifestyle," he also assured gays that he was on their side, telling them that he "oppose[d] all forms of discrimination on the basis of sexual orientation." Conservative evangelicals balked at this, but they became even more alarmed when Carter promised to sign Bella Abzug's gay rights bill. Socially conservative columnist William Willoughby noted in a Christian magazine in September 1976 that "the question over homosexuality for most evangelicals, if grass-roots samplings are any indication, is as politically damaging to Carter in their eyes as the Democratic stand on abortion is to the Catholic voters."[38]

Evangelicals began organizing a counterattack. In the early 1970s, they had been silent as thirty American cities, including Seattle and Los Angeles, passed gay rights ordinances. But the growing political prominence of the gay rights movement prompted them to fight back. After Bloomington, Indiana, enacted a gay rights policy at the end of 1975, more than twenty-five hundred social conservatives signed a petition urging residents of the city to "shun the sodomites and their supporters . . . and to rededicate our community to the standards set forth by God." In June 1976, Southern Baptists in Atlanta collected sixteen thousand signatures for a petition protesting the mayor's declaration of a Gay Pride Day. That same month, the Southern Baptist Convention passed its first resolution against homosexuality.[39]

The conflict escalated when Christian singer Anita Bryant led a campaign against gay rights that mobilized conservative evangelicals throughout the nation and launched the political careers of several future leaders of the Christian Right. By her own admission, the thirty-seven-year-old Bryant rarely read newspapers and was unconcerned about politics until she initiated a campaign against a gay rights ordinance in her hometown of Miami. She had had a conservative upbringing in Oklahoma, where she had won awards for her songs and her beauty, including a Miss Oklahoma title at the age of nineteen and second runner-up in the Miss America contest of 1959. Sales of her popular gospel albums enabled her to purchase a $300,000 mansion in Miami, but fame and fortune did not affect her religious outlook. Her ambition had always been to raise a family, so she married at the age of twenty, gave birth to four children, and dutifully submitted to her husband's leadership in accordance with her understanding of biblical doctrine. Even after moving to a Florida city known more for its vice than for its evangelical religion, Bryant attended Sunday services at a Southern Baptist church every week. When she was not singing gospel songs or writing Christian books, Bryant used her wholesome image to market Florida orange juice.[40]

Bryant was shocked when she heard her pastor announce in January 1977 that the Miami city council was considering an ordinance that would forbid schools—both public and private—from discriminating against homosexuals in hiring. Many evangelicals, including Bryant, considered homosexuals a threat to their children. Believing that male homosexuals were more likely than heterosexuals to molest children and to try to "recruit" young boys to their "perverted, unnatural, and ungodly lifestyle," Bryant thought it would be dangerous to allow them to teach in public schools. She began lobbying against the proposed ordinance. "If this ordinance amendment is allowed to become law, you will, in fact, be infringing upon my rights and discriminating against me as a citizen and as a mother to teach my children and set examples and to point to others of God's moral code as stated in the Holy Scriptures," she told the city commissioners. Her pleadings fell on deaf ears: the council passed the ordinance by a 5–3 margin.[41]

Undaunted, Bryant then took her campaign to the people, launching a citywide movement to rescind the city's gay rights policy through a popular referendum. Within a month, she persuaded sixty thousand people, six times the number required by law, to sign a petition to put a referendum on the ballot.[42]

Many gay rights advocates in Miami welcomed the chance to prove through the ballot box that popular opinion was on their side. Before Bryant made gay rights a political issue in Miami, the city's homosexual population had been less politically active than gays in many other American cities. Now they began organizing. With polls predicting a narrow defeat for Bryant's referendum, gay rights supporters were confident that Bryant had made a grave mistake by taking on their community. "The truth is that Anita Bryant is the best thing that has ever happened to us," said activist Robert Kunst a month before the scheduled vote. "This is a human rights fight and we're prepared to take it all over the country."[43]

But Bryant was equally determined to turn her own agenda into a national campaign. At the beginning of her crusade, she created the organization Save Our Children and began soliciting donations from supporters throughout the country. She went a tour to raise money from church groups and evangelical ministries in the South. As with other conservative grassroots fund-raising efforts that relied on large computerized mailing lists of potential supporters, many of the individual donations she received were small, but the total was not. More than half of her contributions came from Miami residents, but evangelicals and political conservatives in other areas also volunteered to help. Bryant was a registered Democrat, but when her local Democratic Party officially opposed her efforts, she reached out to conservative Republicans. She appeared alongside Ronald Reagan at the Florida Conservative Union's annual dinner, and used the organization's mailing list to recruit support. Senator Jesse Helms gave Bryant funds from his political PAC. Bryant eventually raised nearly $200,000—a smaller sum than her opponents' $300,000, but more than enough to mount a concerted advertising campaign.[44]

Meanwhile, the Carter White House assisted the advocates of gay rights. In February 1977, White House aide Midge Costanza met with two representatives from the National Gay Task Force, and in March, she arranged for another meeting with ten gay rights activists. The president, who continued to tell reporters that homosexual unions were not "a normal interrelationship," was more reticent than his aide to give an overt endorsement of gay rights, but he did tell the press in June that those who tried to limit the rights of homosexuals were in the wrong. "I don't see homosexuality as a threat to the family," Carter said. "I don't feel that society, through its laws, ought to abuse or harass the homosexual."[45]

As the Carter White House moved to the left in the culture wars, Bryant moved to the right, uniting evangelicals across the nation in a comprehensive campaign for social conservatism. She enlisted in the fight against the ERA by testifying before the Florida state legislature. For many social conservatives, the two causes were related, especially since Phyllis Schlafly insisted that the ERA would lead to the legalization of same-sex marriages. Bryant also transformed her local campaign into a national anti-gay-rights movement. Even before Miami residents had a chance to vote on Bryant's referendum, Save Our Children began lobbying against gay rights in Minnesota and other states. She promoted her cause on Pat Robertson's 700 *Club*, Jim and Tammy Bakker's *PTL Club*, and Jerry Falwell's *Old-Time Gospel Hour*. Two weeks before the scheduled vote, one hundred prominent pastors, including Falwell, converged on Miami for a "Christians for God and Decency" rally that attracted more than ten thousand supporters.[46]

In a vote that stunned gay rights advocates and exceeded the expectations of Bryant and her supporters, Miami residents approved the anti-gay-rights referendum by more than a 2–1 margin. Gay rights supporters throughout the country were horrified. In New York's Greenwich Village, thousands of demonstrators held a protest march. In Provincetown, Massachusetts, one popular restaurant removed orange juice from its menu to signify disapproval. But in Miami, a jubilant Bryant heralded this victory as a populist uprising of the "normal majority." "With God's continued help, we will prevail in our fight to repeal similar laws throughout the nation which attempt to legitimize a life style that is both perverse and dangerous," she declared.[47]

For a brief moment, conservative evangelicals had the illusion that the "people" of the nation would rise up against the liberal elite and turn back the tide of gay rights, just as it appeared that they had done with the ERA. Two days after the election, Bryant traveled to Norfolk, Virginia, where twenty-five hundred people gathered to hear her read biblical passages denouncing sodomy. That same month, the Southern Baptist Convention passed a resolution lauding Bryant's "courageous stand against the evils inherent in homosexuality." The Texas *Baptist Standard* ran an editorial titled "We Love You, Anita." "Miss Bryant is very controversial. We love her for it," the paper said. "Nobody is doing more to stop the homosexuals in their campaign for equal rights." Bryant's popularity among Southern Baptists remained so high that in 1978, some Southern Baptist pastors mounted a campaign to elect her as the Convention's first female vice president.[48]

Bryant lost the election, but she remained a popular figure not only among Southern Baptists, but also among social conservatives of various theological persuasions. Northern evangelicals portrayed her as a saintly hero. She was a David who had taken on the supposed Goliath of the gay-friendly media and government, but also a martyr who had suffered financial loss and personal vilification in order to wage a campaign for the cause she believed in. When a New York television producer denied Bryant a TV series contract because of her anti-gay-rights campaign, *Christianity Today* spoke up in her defense: "In today's topsy-turvy society this Christian is being penalized for her stand *against* evil, specifically the sin of homosexual behavior." Independent fundamentalists made favorable references to Bryant in their publications, and Carl McIntire preached a sermon in support of her cause. In a sign that her appeal also extended beyond fundamentalism and evangelicalism, Bryant took first place in *Good Housekeeping* magazine's "Most Admired Woman" poll in both 1978 and 1979.[49]

Building on her success, Bryant broadened the scope of her campaign, using Save Our Children (later Protect America's Children) to target pornography and promote the restoration of school prayer. She knew that her enemies were legion, but she remained confident that the cause of righteousness would prevail. "Together, you and I can openly face and attack the laws sheltering child pornographers, child molesters, sex and violence on TV—and so much more that pollutes the minds of our children," she told supporters.[50]

Despite her success, Bryant was miserable. The stress of her campaigns often drove her to tears, and she longed for a respite. When her performance bookings fell by 60–70 percent as a result of the negative publicity that she incurred during her campaign, she felt rejected. She interpreted her opponents' disagreements with her as a personal affront. Her marriage began to disintegrate, and she and her husband divorced in 1980, only three years after they had launched a campaign to preserve family values. Most pro-family advocates considered a divorced woman a political liability, and the Christian Right leaders who had flocked to Miami to help Bryant in 1977 treated her as a pariah in the early 1980s. Lonely, angry, and disillusioned, Bryant retreated from the political scene. "I've served my time in the front lines," she told the *Ladies Homes Journal* in 1980. "You won't believe this but I am really a very private person."[51]

Although Bryant ultimately viewed her campaign as futile, her cause energized the right, inspiring social conservatives to continue the battle against gay rights and social liberalism in other parts of the country. Mike Thompson, who handled Bryant's advertising in 1977, went on to produce nationally televised attack ads linking President Jimmy Carter with homosexual demonstrators. H. Edward Rowe, the director of Anita Bryant Ministries, became a leader in the national Christian Right organization Religious Roundtable in the early 1980s. Adrian Rogers, who supported Bryant at the "God and Decency" rally in Miami, later played a leading role in the conservative takeover of the Southern Baptist Convention, and was elected president of the SBC in 1979. As a result of his experiences in Miami, Jerry Falwell began preaching a nationally televised series of sermons against homosexuality, abortion, and other such issues.[52] Two years after he spoke at the "God and Decency" rally, Falwell founded Moral Majority and became the best-known Christian Right leader in America.

One Republican California state legislator, Representative John Briggs (R-Fullerton), returned from Bryant's Miami campaign with a determination to do more to stem the tide of gay rights. A conservative Catholic representing a traditionally Republican district in Orange County, Briggs was an ambitious legislator who hoped to run for governor. A statewide anti-gay-rights campaign that would win him support from conservative voters could launch him toward that goal. With the help of Reverend Ray Batema and Reverend Louis Sheldon, who preached at evangelical churches in southern California, Briggs introduced Proposition 6, a referendum that would not only rescind a 1975 California law that protected gay teachers from discrimination, but would also give school districts explicit authority to fire gay teachers or any teacher who publicly endorsed homosexual practices.[53]

The political climate in which Briggs introduced his referendum seemed to augur well for conservatives. Dozens of new conservative Republican congressional candidates defeated Democratic incumbents in 1978, and conservatives made important gains in the Senate as well. Californians defied public expectations and approved Proposition 13, an anti-tax referendum, in June 1978, inaugurating a nationwide tax revolt. That success gave many social conservatives hope that Briggs could pass his initiative. "One individual led the entire state to reduce its taxes," Falwell said. "What was done for taxes can be done for righteousness." Falwell traveled to California to support the initiative, which he believed was necessary to protect children from gay schoolteachers. "Homosexuals often prey on the young," he wrote. "Since they cannot reproduce, they proselyte [sic]." Falwell led rallies in support of Briggs's measure and sent letters to hundreds of California pastors, urging them to get out the vote for Proposition 6. "It is time that today's Christian generation stand up and speak out against the sin that is eating away at the very foundations of our nation," he wrote. In May 1978, Falwell preached a nationally televised sermon against homosexuality. "Like a spiritual cancer, homosexuality spread until the city of Sodom was destroyed," he said. "Can we believe that God will spare the United States if homosexuality continues to spread?"[54]

Tim LaHaye took a similar view. In *The Unhappy Gays*, which he published a few months before the vote on Briggs's referendum, he argued that homosexuality was a degenerative influence in American society and that gay school teachers would further that influence. "You can expect homosexual teachers single-handedly to double the homosexual community within ten years, not by recruiting, but by preparing youngsters mentally for the recruiters," LaHaye wrote. He denied that Proposition 6 was discriminatory. Rather, the issue was parental rights. "The Briggs initiative does not discriminate against homosexuals, but it does protect school children from being taught perverted sex by a homosexual," he wrote. "The school classroom is a privileged sanctuary where teachers are entrusted—by parents—with the minds of young people and children."[55]

Briggs's measure was more narrowly constructed than anti-gay-rights referenda that passed in other parts of the country in 1977 and 1978, and it received strong support from evangelical and fundamentalist churches, but it nonetheless suffered a crushing defeat. Two out of every three California voters who went to the polls in November 1978 cast their ballots against the initiative, and even in conservative Orange County the measure did not receive majority support. Perhaps the Briggs initiative lost because Californians, who had elected the socially progressive Democratic candidate

Jerry Brown as governor, were more liberal than voters in other states. More likely, voters rejected it because even the state's leading conservatives, including Howard Jarvis and Ronald Reagan, opposed the initiative as a threat to liberty and privacy rights. Reagan's public statements against the Briggs initiative proved particularly galling to Falwell, who had hoped for more support from secular conservatives. Reagan, Falwell said, had taken "the political rather than the moral route," and as a result, he would "have to face the music from Christian voters two years from now" during the 1980 presidential election.[56]

Despite its failure, the Briggs campaign, like Bryant's effort in Miami, had far-reaching effects. Evangelical pastors involved in the campaign continued their political activity, as well as their cooperation with conservative Republican politicians. Falwell created the Moral Majority a few months after the election, and LaHaye joined him as one of the organization's charter board members. Louis Sheldon founded the Traditional Values Coalition, which became one of the nation's leading anti-gay-rights groups in the late 1980s and early 1990s. Robert Grant, a former pastor from Los Angeles, united several anti-gay-rights organizations under the umbrella organization Christian Voice, the first comprehensive, national association of the incipient Christian Right. In 1980, Christian Voice promoted the campaigns of conservative congressional candidates throughout the nation.[57]

Conservative evangelicals were eager to support Republican candidates in 1980, partly because they strongly opposed Carter and the Democratic Party on the gay rights issue. The president's assurances that he viewed homosexuality as a sin meant little to them. "If the president is against homosexuality, let's see some evidence," Bob Jones III said. In March 1980, Jones and four other fundamentalist pastors collected seventy-four thousand signatures for a petition that called homosexuality a "perversion" and urged the White House to treat it as an "unlawful moral deviation" rather than a "protected minority normal lifestyle." To no one's surprise, the White House ignored the petition. When the 1980 Democratic National Convention adopted a platform that urged the elimination of discrimination on the basis of sexual orientation, it confirmed social conservatives' suspicions that Carter was a lackey of the gay rights lobby.[58]

The Evangelical Movement against Abortion

When Carter took office, his stance on abortion seemed decidedly moderate and likely to please the majority of centrist Americans. He personally opposed abortion, but he was committed to upholding national law and the Supreme Court's decision in *Roe v. Wade*. He opposed an antiabortion constitutional amendment, as did 55 percent of Americans in 1977.[59] During Carter's campaign, this stance had cost him the support of a few evangelicals, but not many. Yet during Carter's presidency, evangelicals became increasingly active in the pro-life movement, and by the end of his presidency, some of them were ready to make abortion a litmus-test issue for politicians in all future elections.

In his first year in office, Carter gave the pro-life movement some cause for optimism by supporting the Hyde amendment. After their unsuccessful campaign to overturn *Roe v. Wade* with a constitutional amendment, pro-life activists were jubilant when Representative Henry Hyde (R-IL), a Catholic, gave them their first legislative victory by blocking federal funding of abortion, and they were even more delighted when the Supreme Court upheld it.[60] But the White House did little after 1977 to retain the support of abortion rights opponents, and as evangelicals became increasingly pro-life, the differences between the two camps could no longer be ignored.

The pro-life movement achieved additional political victories in November 1978. Voters' widespread disillusionment with President Carter's apparent inability to control inflation or promote economic recovery led many of them to vote Republican in the midterm elections. Since the GOP was developing closer ties to the pro-life movement, many of the newly elected Republican congressional representatives and senators were right-to-life advocates. In some campaigns, conservatives used abortion as a campaign issue to win votes from pro-life Catholics who might otherwise have voted Democratic or stayed home. Iowa senatorial candidate Roger Jepsen, who had the endorsement of the National Right to Life Committee, was polling ten points behind his Democratic opponent, the incumbent Senator Dick Clark, until Iowans for Life, in cooperation with conservative direct-mail expert Richard Viguerie, mobilized on his behalf. On a Sunday morning two days before the election, the state's leading pro-life organization placed three hundred thousand anti-abortion, pro-Jepsen flyers on the cars parked outside Catholic churches. When Jepsen upset Clark with 51 percent of the vote, pundits attributed his victory largely to the pro-life movement. The National Right to Life Committee and other national pro-life organizations also supported several other Republican challengers, including Rudy Boschwitz of Minnesota, Gordon Humphrey of New Hampshire, and Larry Pressler of South Dakota, all of whom won their senatorial campaigns.[61]

Francis Schaeffer was largely responsible for mobilizing evangelicals against abortion during the Carter presidency. Evangelicals had become increasingly interested in what had once been only a Catholic issue, but their conversion to the pro-life cause was far from complete. The Southern Baptist Convention had voted down a proposal to repeal its official pro-choice stance in 1976, and few Protestants participated in antiabortion campaigns. Sensing that more needed to be done to energize evangelicals on the issue, C. Everett Koop, a Presbyterian elder and Philadelphia pediatrician who later became a surgeon general in the Reagan administration, approached Schaeffer and his son Franky with the idea of producing another film that would focus specifically on the pro-life cause. The result was a $1 million production entitled *Whatever Happened to the Human Race?* The four-hour documentary, released in 1979, featured both Koop and Francis Schaeffer describing the procedures of abortion and euthanasia in graphic detail. If Christians remained silent, Koop and Schaeffer argued, Americans would become increasingly desensitized to the horrors of killing, and infanticide, along with the involuntary killing of the elderly, would soon become as socially acceptable as abortion. In the most memorable scene, Koop inveighed against abortion while standing in the midst of hundreds of abandoned baby dolls strewn across the banks of the Dead Sea.[62]

Schaeffer and Koop's film toured twenty American cities, but Schaeffer was disappointed to find that many American churches were still not ready to accept his strongly antiabortion views. Some pastors discouraged their parishioners from attending the screenings, because they had no wish to see their churches become involved in a pro-life movement that they viewed as highly controversial and predominantly Catholic. At Wheaton College, where Schaeffer had received an enthusiastic welcome in the 1960s, administrators scheduled a mandatory chapel session during the film screening to prevent students from seeing Schaeffer's work.[63]

Despite the comparatively small audience sizes, which averaged between seven hundred and fifteen hundred per city, evangelicals who saw *Whatever Happened to the Human Race?* were often deeply moved. Many of those who saw the film came from churches where abortion was never discussed, so they came to the theater with no prior commitment to the pro-life cause. Some left resolving to join the antiabortion movement. In St. Louis, students at the conservative Presbyterian Covenant Theological Seminary began volunteering for pro-life demonstrations that previously had attracted only Catholics. Randall Terry, who would later found the militant antiabortion organization Operation Rescue, wept when he saw Schaeffer's film, and decided to devote his life to protesting abortion.[64]

Jerry Falwell had occasionally preached against abortion in the mid-1970s, but after reading one of Francis Schaeffer's articles on the issue, he embarked on a pro-life campaign in 1978 with a nationally televised sermon, a book, and a fund-raising letter that focused on abortion. "Abortion is a weapon that has annihilated more children than Pharaoh murdered in Egypt, than Herod murdered when seeking the Christ child, than the Nazis slaughtered of the Jews in World War II," he said during a May 1978 broadcast of the *Old-Time Gospel Hour*. Falwell frequently credited Schaeffer with introducing him to political activism, calling him "one of the greatest men of my generation" and a "man of courage."[65]

Schaeffer's writings convinced Falwell to cooperate with Catholics and to join the pro-life movement, but when Falwell began speaking out on the subject in 1978, he depicted his pro-life campaign not only as a campaign for human rights, which was Schaeffer's focus, but also as a fight against feminism and sexual promiscuity. Women who sought abortions were "pregnant because of sin," Falwell said. "I cannot understand a mother wanting to abort a child who was conceived with her husband." Many of them were also feminists who had "been caught up in the ERA movement and want to terminate their pregnancy because it limits their freedom and their job opportunities." "Some members of the 'jet set' do not mind a poodle dog around the apartment, but a baby would cramp their style," he added.[66]

Years after his father's death, Franky Schaeffer complained that Falwell and other Christian Right leaders had used "their power in ways that would have made my father throw up."[67] But in the late 1970s, Franky's father said nothing about his differences with Falwell. Francis was not interested in fighting against the ERA or feminism, but he considered any opponent of abortion a potential ally. Perhaps he also realized that if evangelicals had not connected abortion to the ERA, feminism, and cultural liberalism, they might not have shown much interest in waging a campaign against it.

The Conservative Takeover of the Southern Baptist Convention

The Southern Baptist Convention, which had rejected antiabortion resolutions as recently as 1976, reconsidered its position after the release of Schaeffer's film and book. The SBC had been reluctant to act on abortion partly because the Convention's leaders were a group of pastors later known as "moderates," who tended to be political centrists and who resisted northern evangelicals' increasing political mobilization over cultural issues. They were theologically conservative in maintaining the denomination's traditional respect for biblical authority and the necessity of a "born-again" conversion, but they did not want to get involved in an intradenominational fight over biblical inerrancy, and they were not necessarily opposed to women's ordination. They valued their denomination's long-standing belief in the "priesthood of the believer," which allowed individuals and local congregations to make up their own minds on controversial issues. In the face of an increasing evangelical affinity for the Republican Party, they maintained their denomination's tradition of church-state separation, which they thought would preclude the Convention from endorsing other evangelicals' right-wing political causes.

Southern Baptist moderates did not share the fear of secularization that gripped many conservative evangelicals in California, Florida, and the upper South and Midwest. As a result, they saw no need to follow their lead in making ecumenical alliances with Catholics, or to make a battle against gay rights, the ERA, and abortion a high priority. Many of the moderates paid little attention to evangelical theological developments outside of their own denomination. Most had barely heard of Schaeffer, and they had little interest in what was happening at Wheaton College or northern evangelical seminaries. "We're not evangelicals," Foy Valentine, director of the SBC's Christian Life Commission, insisted in 1976. "That's a Yankee word. They want to claim us because we are big and successful and growing every year. But we have our own traditions, our own hymns, and more students in our seminaries than they have in all of theirs put together. We don't share their politics or their fussy fundamentalism, and we don't want to get involved in their theological witch-hunts."[68]

But a cadre of self-styled "conservative" Baptists, many of whom were younger than Valentine and were poised to move into leadership positions during the next decade, viewed the moderates' stance on abortion and other cultural issues as weak and vacillating. Several of the leading members of the conservative faction had received their ministerial training in northern evangelical seminaries, and during their sojourns outside of the South, they acquired a northern evangelical consciousness of the culture wars. They imbibed the northern evangelical reverence for Schaeffer, and after reading his works, they became convinced that Christians needed to become active opponents of secular humanism and abortion. Southern Baptists who accepted Schaeffer's ideas were appalled that Valentine accepted the legitimacy of abortion in some cases, as had several past SBC presidents.[69]

In June 1979, a contingent of Southern Baptist "conservatives" launched a surprise takeover of the SBC and won election to the denomination's executive office. The election of Adrian Rogers, pastor of the eleven-thousand-member Bellevue Baptist megachurch in Memphis and a leading member of the group that the *New York Times* called the "ultraconservatives," was a stunning blow to the moderates. Officially, the conservatives won on a platform requiring the denomination's seminary professors to believe in biblical inerrancy. But as outside observers noted, hardly any Southern Baptists could be characterized as theological liberals. One of the leading moderates told the conservatives that he had "no problem believing Jonah was swallowed by a fish." The moderates were unwilling to require seminary professors to teach a fundamentalist or literal view of the Bible, as the conservatives wanted, but conservative disagreement with the moderates went far beyond that issue. The conservatives were upset that the moderates were rarely willing to take a stand in the nation's culture wars. "Abortion was the stick of dynamite that exploded the issue," Southern Baptist conservative leader Al Mohler said years later. "It was the transparent issue that brought clarity at least on one side."[70]

The moderates considered their election loss a temporary defeat, but to their dismay, they continued to lose elections in the 1980s, and eventually realized that they would never be able to regain control over the denomination. Under conservative leadership, the Southern Baptist Christian Life Commission's journal shifted its focus from poverty to abortion and homosexuality. In 1980, the Convention passed resolutions denouncing pornography, homosexuality, human evolution, and the White House Conference on Families, along with a resolution on the role of women that noted that "the Convention does not endorse the Equal Rights Amendment." Most important, conservatives reversed the moderate stance on abortion that the denomination had officially held since 1971 by calling for "appropriate legislation and / or a constitutional amendment prohibiting abortion except to save the life of the mother."[71]

The SBC resolutions of 1980 put the denomination officially in opposition to the Carter White House on nearly all of the major social issues that were of concern to conservative evangelicals. In June 1980, Tim LaHaye wrote an article that reviewed the Carter administration's record, and concluded that the president had consistently been on the wrong side of the nation's culture wars. "Is Jimmy Carter a Christian who is naïve about humanism and respects humanists more fully than he does Christians?" LaHaye asked. "Or is he a humanist who masqueraded as a Christian to get elected and then showed his contempt for the 60 million 'born agains' by excluding them from his government?"[72]

In 1976, Carter's self-identification as a born-again Christian had been sufficient to win over many of his fellow evangelicals, but by 1980, many conservative evangelical leaders wanted a candidate who publicly identified with their side in the culture wars. Carter was unwilling to take that role, so evangelicals began to search for a candidate who would.

"WE HAVE TOGETHER, WITH THE Protestants and the Catholics, enough votes to run the country," Christian broadcaster Pat Robertson announced in 1979. "And when the people say, 'We've had enough,' we are going to take over."[1]

The last two years of the Carter administration marked the beginning of a new era. Evangelicals who had previously been content to exercise their political influence merely by voting for conservative candidates or waging single-issue moral campaigns realized that they could change the nation's government by forming a comprehensive political movement allied with the New Right. Their religious groups were now larger and more influential than most mainline Protestant denominations. Evangelicals operated massive television, educational, and publishing empires. They were beginning to gain access to prominent political figures. No longer did evangelicals have to behave as a beleaguered minority, lamenting the "secular humanism" in the nation while longing for a political deliverance. Instead, evangelical leaders such as Jerry Falwell and Pat Robertson saw that conservative Christians had the prominence to dictate the terms of alliance to Republican politicians and force the Republican Party to begin paying attention to evangelicals' stances on abortion, gay rights, and the ERA. Falwell, Robertson, and other evangelical leaders transformed these single-issue campaigns into a comprehensive political agenda that they made part of the Republican Party platform. Their goal of reclaiming the nation by transforming the Republican Party might have seemed ambitious, but Falwell and his evangelical allies were confident that they would succeed, not only because God was on their side, but also because the voting numbers were. They were now the "moral majority."

Of course, despite the claims of some evangelical leaders, the "New Christian Right" that Falwell, Robertson, and others formed did not actually represent a majority of Americans, and their coalition was never as broadly based as they had hoped it would be. Falwell's Moral Majority appealed mainly to conservative Baptists, and Robertson's influence was limited primarily to charismatic Christians and a subset of evangelicals. Only a handful of Catholics, and even fewer conservative Jews, joined the movement. Some fundamentalists, including Bob Jones, Jr., distanced themselves from Christian Right leaders because they considered them too ecumenical, while many "moderates" in the Southern Baptist Convention criticized the Religious Right because they considered it too narrow-minded and exclusionary.

But if the Christian Right was never the "moral majority" that it claimed to be, it nevertheless represented an unprecedented development in conservative evangelicalism. For the first time, evangelical leaders openly welcomed Catholics, Jews, and other non-evangelicals into their organizations, and for the first time, they became leaders of a comprehensive political movement associated with a partisan cause. For the first time, they began to think that they could use their own political power to take the nation back from the "secular humanists." And for at least a short time, it appeared that they would be successful. Evangelicals exercised too much influence and power for politicians to ignore.

Evangelicals' Newfound Status

Evangelicals enjoyed a higher degree of wealth and social prestige in the late 1970s than they had at any other point in the twentieth century. In the early years of the fundamentalist movement, conservative Protestants had been socially marginalized because they were less educated, less wealthy, and less numerous than mainline Protestants. By the late 1970s, though, most mainline denominations had declined in membership, while evangelical churches grew. The Southern Baptist Convention added nearly 2 million new members between 1965 and 1975, and by the end of the 1970s, it was the largest Protestant denomination in America, with over 13 million members.[2]

When a 1976 Gallup poll found that nearly 50 million Americans, comprising one-third of the nation's adult population, had been "born again," evangelicals were jubilant. They were now the nation's largest religious demographic. SBC president James Sullivan exulted in 1976, "A world that had thought we were an ignorant, barefooted, one-gallused lot was jarred out of its seat when it found out that . . . our voluntary gifts in a year are approximately $1.5 billion, and that on an average Sunday our churches baptize about three times as many people as were baptized at Pentecost."[3]

Evangelicals made strides in other areas as well. In 1960, only 7 percent of evangelicals had received a college education, but by the mid-1970s, that figure had increased to 23 percent. Because of evangelicals' new demand for higher education, Christian colleges continued to grow, and conservative seminaries attracted a record number of new students even as enrollment at theologically liberal seminaries declined.[4]

By the 1970s, evangelicals were creating a host of cultural products that frequently proved more popular than secular offerings. *The Late, Great Planet Earth* (1970), by Hal Lindsey, an apocalyptic prediction of America's future based on a dispensationalist interpretation of biblical prophecy, sold more copies than any other nonfiction book of the decade, outpacing *All the President's Men*, *Roots*, and *The Joy of Sex*. In previous decades, fundamentalist apocalyptic speculation about the end-times had been confined to small religious presses, but after Lindsey's book appeared, nearly all Americans became familiar with such phrases as "the Antichrist" or "the Rapture." Christian bookstores also sold millions of copies of books by Francis Schaeffer, James Dobson, Tim and Beverly LaHaye, and Billy Graham. Conservative Christian teenagers who rejected the sexually suggestive lyrics of mainstream pop music created a thriving market for cleaner fare that glorified God with a contemporary beat. By 1977, approximately one thousand "Jesus rock" bands were performing in churches, outdoor concerts, and alcohol-free "Jesus nightclubs."[5]

By the end of the 1970s, conservative evangelicals controlled three national television networks, while sixty-six nationally syndicated religious broadcasters, as well as a host of local TV preachers, filled the airwaves with Christian messages. According to Arbitron ratings, 20 million Americans tuned in to watch televangelists, who varied in style from the calm, optimistic Robert Schuller to the shouting and weeping Jimmy Swaggart. Evangelicals had been preaching on radio and television shows for decades, but televangelism experienced dramatic growth in the 1970s, partly because of the 1960 FCC ruling that allowed stations to use paid religious programs to fulfill their public interest broadcast quotas. Evangelicals began purchasing an unprecedented number of time slots for their religious programs. They also found ways to solicit prodigious sums of money from their audiences. Relying on emotional appeals and direct mail pleas for donations, religious broadcasters far exceeded the fund-raising abilities of the nation's largest political action groups.[6]

Evangelicals even made a few high-profile converts. Charles Colson, who served time in prison for his role in the Watergate scandal, experienced a "born-again" conversion and became a prison ministry director and popular evangelical speaker. The former Black Panther leader Eldridge Cleaver likewise found God and produced a spiritual memoir entitled *Soul on Fire*. The ranks of the newly "born again" also included the singer Bob Dylan, who released an album with Christian lyrics in 1979. Even Larry Flynt, the publisher of the pornographic magazine *Hustler*, had a "born-again" experience after an encounter with Ruth Carter Stapleton, the president's evangelist sister, although in his case its effects lasted only a few months.[7]

Some evangelical churches grew so quickly that they became "megachurches," a new term for a congregation that had at least two thousand members. Before 1970, only sixteen white Protestant churches in the country fit this description, but by the end of the decade, that number had increased to fifty. Almost all of these megachurches were evangelical in their theology, and a large percentage were Baptist or charismatic. Most were located in the Sunbelt or the traditionally evangelical Midwest, and most were led by dynamic young pastors who filled services with contemporary praise songs and easily applicable, upbeat sermons. One of the most successful was Willow Creek, launched by the twenty-three-year-old Bill Hybels in the Chicago suburb of South Barrington, Illinois, in 1975. It started with 150 members and within fourteen years had been transformed into a 12,000-member congregation that became a model for megachurches around the country. After conducting a survey of unchurched people in his area, Hybels reached out to his target market of young suburban professionals by presenting the gospel through movies, slide shows, and rock music, and by offering marital counseling, family-oriented programs, and a church gymnasium. "This is the generation that grew up on television," Hybels explained. "You have to present religion to them in a creative and visual way. . . . We decided to defer to the customer except where it conflicted with Scripture."[8]

Jerry Falwell's Thomas Road Baptist Church grew from only 1,000 members to nearly 10,000 during the 1960s, and then increased to 16,000 by the end of the 1970s. During that time period, Falwell expanded his operations to include a Christian school, a college, a bus ministry, drug addiction recovery programs, a prisoner rehabilitation ministry, and a summer camp for children, in addition to his nationally syndicated radio and television programs. By 1980, his ministries were collecting $50 million a year, and his organization had a full-time staff of nearly 1,000 people.[9]

Tim LaHaye experienced similar success. By the end of the 1970s, LaHaye had transformed his Scott Memorial Baptist Church into three new large congregations in the San Diego suburbs, and his ministry included a Christian college, twelve Christian schools, an Institute for Creation Research to promote "creation science," and a national television program.[10]

In spite of all this, evangelicals felt that the federal government remained hostile to their interests. As their enterprises grew, evangelicals added a concern about federal regulation to their standard litany of complaints. In 1973, Jerry Falwell faced a court challenge from the Securities and Exchange Commission, which charged him with "fraud and deceit" in issuing church bonds. While he was cleared of deliberate wrongdoing—he admitted inadvertent error—the experience left him with a renewed antipathy toward federal regulatory power.[11]

In 1974, evangelicals across the nation became alarmed when two California professors who were annoyed with the proliferation of Christian radio and television programs urged the FCC to issue a temporary "freeze" on all broadcast licenses that came from "religious 'Bible,' Christian, and other sectarian schools, colleges, and institutes" until the agency completed an investigation of noncommercial radio and television stations. Religious broadcasters were outraged, and they asked their supporters to petition the FCC. They responded in droves, sending seven hundred thousand letters to the FCC in 1975. The FCC listened and declined to investigate, but many conservative Protestants remained wary of federal regulators. They emerged from the experience with a determination to become more politically active in order to defend their interests.[12]

Shortly after their dispute with the FCC, evangelicals came into conflict with the IRS, which announced in 1978 that it would attempt to enforce federal civil rights policies by requiring private schools to meet minority enrollment quotas in order to maintain their tax-exempt status. Administrators at the nation's five thousand Christian schools protested. They claimed that they did not discriminate, and some said that they had never denied an African American candidate's application for admission. But Christian schools had made no attempt to attract minority students, and the political and social conservatism that pervaded many Christian schools repelled the majority of African Americans. Rather than create new minority scholarships or encourage minority recruitment, Christian schools lobbied Congress to prevent the IRS from enforcing its new policy.[13]

Robert Billings, an Indiana Baptist school administrator who had launched Christian School Action in 1977 to protect the rights of Christian educators, encouraged evangelicals to deluge the IRS with letters of protest. Christians responded to Billings's call with 120,000 missives. Falwell, who enrolled only 5 African Americans at his 1,147-student Lynchburg Christian Academy, took time away from his anti-gay-rights campaign to speak out against the IRS's new directive. Evangelicals broadened their political coalition to include Catholic school administrators and even a few Orthodox Jews, who feared that the IRS directive would destroy their religious academies. The IRS gave in to the pressure and abandoned its plan to investigate private schools.[14]

The conservative evangelicals who waged this battle had no intention of leaving the political arena. Billings, who exuberantly declared that the IRS controversy had "done more to bring Christians together than any man since the Apostle Paul," converted his Christian School Action into a more comprehensive lobbying organization, the National Christian Action Coalition, and positioned himself as a self-described "liaison between Congress and the Christian community." Falwell founded the Moral Majority less than a year after the IRS controversy. Yet while the IRS fight was a seminal event in mobilizing Christian conservatives, it would not have had the same impact if it had not been preceded by a series of other evangelical campaigns against government policies, such as Anita Bryant's. As Billings admitted, evangelicals were already deeply antipathetic toward the federal government, and were on the verge of creating a national political movement. "The IRS ignited the dynamite [within the evangelical community] that had been lying around for years," he said.[15]

Christian Voice

Only a few months after their campaign against the IRS, evangelicals created the comprehensive, national political movement that the media labeled the "Religious Right" or "New Christian Right." The movement's first national organization was Christian Voice, which formed in January 1979.

Christian Voice was the brainchild of Robert Grant, a forty-two-year-old independent Baptist minister and Wheaton College graduate who had created the anti-gay-rights organization, American Christian Cause, to campaign for the Briggs initiative in 1978. After California voters rejected that measure, he invited several other "pro-family" organizations to join his under a new name, Christian Voice. The new organization would take on not only the gay rights movement, but also abortion, the ERA, and all of the other evils that evangelicals had been fighting. "If Christians unite, we can do anything," Grant declared. "We can pass any law or any amendment. And that is exactly what we intend to do."[16]

The associates that Grant recruited to Christian Voice were young, optimistic, and staunchly conservative. But even though Grant was the only one on the leadership staff who was older than thirty, his associates already had more political experience than he had. Gary Jarmin, who became the Voice's Washington lobbyist, was a Southern Baptist whose evangelical bona fides were somewhat suspect because he had been a member of Reverend Sun Myung Moon's Unification Church until 1974 and had not completely cut his ties to Moon's organization. Though some questioned Jarmin's commitment to evangelicalism, no one could impugn his conservative credentials. He had spent most of his career in political activism, first as secretary general of Moon's Freedom Leadership Foundation, and then as a staff member of the American Conservative Union. Fund-raising expert Colonel Doner had only recently become an evangelical Christian, but he had been raised as a committed conservative, and he claimed that by the time he was fourteen he had read over ten thousand pages of anticommunist literature. While many of his fellow students at the California State University at Fullerton were protesting the Vietnam War, Doner championed the Goldwaterite brand of Republican politics. He took a job as a paid political activist while still in his teens, and, like Jarmin, he worked for the American Conservative Union before coming to Christian Voice. With political conservatives of limited church experience handling his fund-raising and lobbying activities, Grant found a more theologically knowledgeable Christian, Richard Zone, a twenty-nine-year-old California minister who had participated in anti-gay-rights campaigns, to be the Voice's executive director. "It's time that Christians got together and lobbied like all the special interest groups," Zone said.[17]

Christian Voice grew quickly. Six months after its founding, the organization claimed one hundred thousand members. By October 1980, Christian Voice boasted that it had doubled its membership to two hundred thousand and that thirty-seven thousand ministers were on its mailing list. The organization attracted the support of Hal Lindsey, Pat Boone, Robert Billings, and Pat Robertson, as well as sixteen conservative members of Congress. Baptists and Pentecostals, particularly those who lived in the West, were more likely than other Christians to join the group, but since the Voice's leaders recognized that conservative Catholics were some of their best allies in the fight against abortion and gay rights, they welcomed three hundred priests into the organization.[18]

Grant's skill was not in creating new political programs; instead, his innovation lay in bringing together groups that had not previously been in cooperation. He introduced conservative congressmen to evangelical leaders and brought the pro-life, anti-gay-rights, and anti-ERA movements together in one organization. His organization's fund-raising letters targeted veterans of these campaigns by highlighting the issues that had initially brought them into politics. "How would you feel if tomorrow your child . . . was taught by a practicing homosexual?" one fund-raising letter asked. Jarmin was amazed at how easy it was to appeal to his constituency's fears and to use existing evangelical networks to spread his message. "The beauty of it is that we don't have to organize these voters," Jarmin told a reporter. "They already have their own television networks, publications, schools, meeting places and respected leaders who are sympathetic to our goals."[19]

Yet Grant's organization looked beyond single issues to candidates, saying that it wanted to replace liberal incumbents with "Christian statesmen." Christian Voice selected thirty-five congressional liberals for defeat in 1980, and issued a series of hard-hitting ads and fund-raising letters that publicized their liberal voting records. On the Sunday morning before the election, the organization dispatched two thousand volunteers to distribute congressional voting record scorecards outside of hundreds of churches. Christian Voice targeted six liberal Democratic senators—George McGovern (D-SD), Frank Church (D-ID), John Culver (D-IA), Alan Cranston (D-CA), Birch Bayh (D-IN), and Gaylord Nelson (D-WI)—as particularly deserving of defeat and, therefore, of excoriation. "John Culver is part of the crowd which made legal the killing of babies, made the streets safe for criminals and rapists and kicked God out of our schools," Colonel Doner said.[20]

To a casual observer, this may not have seemed unusual. But whereas earlier organizations had promoted the campaigns of a few evangelical candidates, Christian Voice engaged in a sweeping effort to oust liberals from office by supporting conservative challengers regardless of religion or personal morality. Liberalism, Grant said, was "inconsistent with Christianity," so he used his organization to promote conservative causes that went far beyond the range of issues that had energized evangelicals in the 1970s. When the organization released its "Moral Report Card" for members of Congress in late 1979, senators and congressmen could lose points not only for voting for gay rights, but also for supporting the Strategic Arms Limitation Treaty II (SALT II) or sanctions against the white supremacist government of Rhodesia, which Christian Voice considered a bulwark of anticommunism.[21]

Many Christians with politically liberal views were aghast that a group calling itself "Christian Voice" had declared that sanctions against the racist Rhodesian government were immoral or that voting to restrict nuclear weapons buildup was un-Christian. But these stances were consistent with evangelicals' long-standing fear of communism. Although they had temporarily shifted their focus from communism to sexual morality and secular humanism during the 1970s, conservative Protestants had never completely abandoned their concerns about Marxist subversion or a Soviet attack. They had worried about Nixon's policy of détente with the Soviet Union and his willingness to visit China, and they had expressed concern when the United States agreed to give up control of the Panama Canal. When Christian Voice revived traditional evangelical concerns about America's military strength vis-à-vis the Soviet Union and urged Christians to defend the United States as "the last stronghold of faith on the planet," the message resonated with conservative evangelicals. Christian Voice leaders warned evangelicals that arms limitation agreements with the Soviet Union presented a grave threat to the United States. "It's part of our attitude toward godless communism," Christian Voice administrator Sandra Ostbyu said in September 1979. "SALT compromises America in favor of Communists."[22]

The New Right

Christian Voice's appropriation of conservative political causes delighted a cadre of young political activists who dubbed themselves the "New Right." Distinguishing themselves from the "Old Right" of Senator Robert Taft's generation and the "Old Guard" or "country club" Republicans, New Right activists believed in an aggressively anticommunist foreign policy, tax cuts, and the promotion of "traditional values" through legislation. During their college years in the 1960s, most of the New Right activists, including Paul Weyrich, Richard Viguerie, and Howard Phillips, had been active in Young Republicans, Young Americans for Freedom, or Barry Goldwater's presidential campaign, and they had then pursued careers in Republican Party politics. But after President Richard Nixon displayed an unexpected willingness to expand government bureaucracy and social welfare spending, they abandoned Republican Party organizations and formed independent right-wing political action groups. By adopting the moniker "New Right," they proclaimed that they were no longer conventional Republicans and were, in the words of Weyrich, "radical—committed to sweeping changes and not to preserving the status quo."[23]

New Right activists combined the laissez-faire economic conservatism of Goldwater with the antielitist, blue-collar cultural conservatism of George Wallace, Richard Nixon, and the "silent majority." Some of the most prominent New Right activists came from the traditionally Democratic working-class Catholic families that Republican strategists had sought to attract through cultural politics. Weyrich acquired his lifelong antipathy to abortion and homosexuality from his devoutly Catholic working-class

German immigrant parents in Wisconsin. As an adult, he became so conservative in his faith that he joined an Eastern Rite Catholic church in order to escape the reforms of Vatican II. Viguerie was a southern Catholic whose father had been a construction worker. In his youth, Viguerie had admired antiestablishment populist conservatives such as Senator Joseph McCarthy and General Douglas MacArthur.[24]

Viguerie started out as a Goldwater Republican, but by the mid-1970s he had lost faith in the GOP. When President Gerald Ford selected former New York governor Nelson Rockefeller, a quintessential moderate "country club" Republican, as his vice president, Viguerie was outraged. "As a conservative," Viguerie wrote, "I could hardly have been more upset if Ford had selected Teddy Kennedy." Abandoning the Republican Party in favor of working-class populism, Viguerie supported George Wallace's 1976 Democratic primary campaign. "All the Republican party needs is a decent burial," Viguerie said.[25]

Most of the other New Right leaders likewise showed little affinity for the GOP after their hero, Ronald Reagan, lost his campaign against Gerald Ford for the Republican presidential nomination. In a 1978 Texas congressional race, Weyrich supported conservative Democrat Kent Hance's successful campaign against Republican George W. Bush, a Yale-educated scion of a blue-blooded Republican family. Howard Phillips, who had been a Massachusetts state Republican Party leader in the 1960s and had headed the Office of Economic Opportunity in the Nixon administration, became so frustrated with Republican senator Edward Brooke's moderately liberal voting record that he joined the Democratic Party and ran in the Massachusetts senatorial primaries in hopes of competing against him. Phillips's opposition to "forced busing, abortion, and racial quotas" may have appealed to some Catholic ethnics in the working-class suburbs of Boston, but it did not win over enough of the state's Democrats.[26] He realized that he could never feel comfortable in the party of Hubert Humphrey, George McGovern, and Jimmy Carter. Having renounced both parties, he and his allies in the New Right formed independent conservative political action groups to promote their favorite conservative causes outside the party structures.

Independent political action committees (PACs) enjoyed an unprecedented degree of power in the late 1970s. Campaign finance reform legislation, passed in the wake of Watergate, limited the amount that individuals could contribute to political candidates, but imposed less restrictive spending limits on PACs. Conservative PACs were well positioned to take advantage of this legislative change, because they had already been raising money for the previous decade. The leading figure in conservative fund-raising was Richard

Viguerie, who had started his direct-mail advertising company in 1965 with a mailing list from Barry Goldwater's presidential campaign.[27]

In this task Viguerie had the help of Terry Dolan, a former Young Republican who founded the National Conservative Political Action Committee (NCPAC) in 1975. For the 1978 election season NCPAC raised $3 million and for 1980 over $7 million, far surpassing the country's liberal PACs. As a closeted gay man with libertarian views, Dolan had little interest in advancing the moral causes that appealed to social conservatives, but as a Goldwater conservative, he wanted to do whatever he could to oust liberals from office, even if that required issuing alarmist warnings about abortion and gay rights. "The shriller you are, the better it is [sic] to raise money," he said.[28]

If Christian Voice patterned its fund-raising techniques on the work of Viguerie and Dolan, its political strategy mirrored that of Weyrich, who founded the Heritage Foundation in 1973 with financing from Colorado beer mogul Joseph Coors. In 1974, Weyrich created the Committee for the Survival of a Free Congress (CFSFC) to aid the campaigns of conservative congressional candidates' campaigns. It rated members of Congress on a 100-point scale, using a standard of conservatism that was so stringent that even Jesse Helms could score no higher than a 90.[29]

As New Right political operatives looked for controversial issues to highlight in their campaigns against congressional liberals, they turned with increasing frequency to the subject of abortion. Weyrich and other Catholics in the New Right were strongly pro-life, and they understood the abortion issue's potential appeal to politically liberal pro-life activists who had shown little interest in the New Right's other causes. "Whether they want to or not, right-to-lifers find they have to work with New Right activists, simply because no one else cares about protecting the unborn," Weyrich said. In the 1978 midterm elections, Weyrich's CFSFC, as well as NCPAC and the Viguerie Company, supported several pro-life candidates. Viguerie recognized that many of the traditionally Democratic Catholics who voted for conservative candidates solely because of abortion could later be persuaded to support the entire New Right agenda. "The abortion issue is the door through which many people come into conservative politics, but they don't stop there," he said. "Their convictions against abortion are like the first in a series of falling dominoes."[30]

The conservative Catholics in the New Right recognized that evangelicals shared many of their concerns, and they tried to figure out ways to bring born-again Protestants into their movement. "The next real major area of growth for the conservative ideology and (political) philosophy is among evangelical people," Viguerie told *Sojourners* magazine in the spring of 1976. As a Catholic who supplemented his religion with the reincarnation theories of Edgar Cayce, Viguerie might not have shared the theological beliefs of evangelicals, but he could articulate their grievances against the Carter administration. "What was Jimmy Carter's response to his biggest and most important single group of supporters?" Viguerie asked evangelicals with his typical rhetorical flourish. "Not only did the Carter administration ignore the born-again Christians, it actively and aggressively sought to hurt the Christian movement in America."[31]

From the beginning of the New Right movement, activists—especially Weyrich—offered aid to conservative evangelicals' moral campaigns. Weyrich shared evangelicals' opposition to abortion and gay rights—indeed, he had been campaigning against abortion longer than they had—and he also championed their view of parental rights in opposition to educational bureaucrats. His association with evangelical activists had begun as early as the fall of 1974, when his Heritage Foundation supported Alice Moore's textbook campaign in Kanawha County, West Virginia. In 1976, CSFC supported Robert Billings's unsuccessful campaign for Congress, and in early 1977, Weyrich encouraged Billings to come to Washington to create Christian School Action. In late 1979, Weyrich's associate Connie Marshner helped draft the Family Protection Act, a sweeping piece of "pro-family" legislation, and handed it to Senator Paul Laxalt (R-NV), who introduced the bill on the Senate floor but soon backed away from it and withdrew his sponsorship. Marshner's proposed legislation, which did not pass, addressed most of the major concerns of the emerging Christian Right by protecting voluntary school prayer, abolishing the "marriage tax," prohibiting the federal government from regulating church-run institutions, denying funds to any educational program that "promoted" homosexuality, and requiring parental notification for medical treatment of venereal disease.[32]

Weyrich became a welcome guest at conservative evangelical conferences, and his devotion to the pro-life agenda exceeded that of many Christian Right leaders. Recognizing that evangelicals could be his closest allies in his fight to protect the family, he helped Billings transform his Christian School Action into the more politically comprehensive National Christian Action Coalition (NCAC). In an imitation of New Right tactics, NCAC compiled a "Family Issues Voting Index" in 1980 to let conservative Christians know how members of Congress stood on the key issues of concern to the Christian Right. Weyrich also cultivated a relationship with Christian Voice, whose legislative consultant, David Troxler, was one of his associates.[33]

Organizations such as NCAC and Christian Voice introduced New Right fund-raising techniques to the conservative evangelical community and promoted the same causes that interested the New Right, but neither organization was able to effect the massive Christian voter mobilization that was necessary for conservative evangelicals to become a significant pressure group. Most of the millions of Americans who regularly watched religious television shared the New Right's views on gay rights and abortion, but large numbers of them were Democrats, and some never bothered to vote. The New Right activists wanted to turn these apolitical social conservatives into conservative Republican activists, but neither Weyrich, a Midwestern Eastern Rite Catholic, nor Phillips, a New England Jew, had the ability to appeal to southern born-again Christians. Both of them received a lucky break when Ed McAteer, a Southern Baptist layman, joined Phillips's Conservative Caucus and declared his interest in recruiting evangelicals to the New Right. His first target was Jerry Falwell.

Jerry Falwell and the Moral Majority

Falwell was a natural choice for New Right activists looking for a preacher capable of attracting large numbers of conservative Christians to a political movement. He had once been a provincially minded, segregationist pastor, but those days were now firmly in the past. A nationally known televangelist whose weekly *Old-Time Gospel Hour* program appeared on 373 stations across the country—more stations, he boasted, than carried Johnny Carson's *Tonight Show*—Falwell was a leading figure in conservative evangelical circles, and his church was one of the largest in the nation. By the end of the 1970s, he was a college president and the author of several Christian books. He had a private jet to take him on the two hundred fifty thousand miles he logged each year on speaking tours. He was also a fund-raising genius who used direct mail and on-air appeals to collect more money each year than the Democratic National Committee. *Esquire* suggested in October 1978 that he could become the "next Billy Graham."[34]

As Falwell's status had risen, he had become increasingly interested in national politics. In 1976, the same year in which he endorsed Gerald Ford for president and publicly rebuked Jimmy Carter for his *Playboy* interview, he decided to mix conservative politics with patriotic fervor by taking his Lynchburg Baptist College choir to the steps of the nation's state capitols for the bicentennial "I Love America" celebration. At each event, the choir, neatly attired in floor-length dresses or suits and ties, sang a medley of popular patriotic songs, and Falwell delivered a brief, encouraging message to the gathered crowd. To a casual observer, Falwell's rallies may have seemed no more partisan than a Fourth of July concert, but at each rally, the preacher offered a hint of a political agenda when he told audiences that God was calling America to collective repentance in order to receive the blessings of forgiveness. Falwell's rallies attracted the support of several New Right politicians who recognized the similarity between Falwell's message and their own. By the time that Weyrich and McAteer contacted him, Falwell was a veteran of campaigns against gay rights in Florida and California. In the fall of 1978, he spent thousands of dollars organizing a campaign to defeat a referendum that would have made racetrack gambling legal in his home state of Virginia. When the collective effort of six thousand churches succeeded, Falwell took heart. "I see the church getting very involved in moral issues in the next few years," he said.[35]

In 1978, Falwell took evangelicals' local, single-issue moral campaigns to a national audience. In May of that year, he devoted several *Old-Time Gospel Hour* broadcasts to the three moral issues—pornography, abortion, and homosexuality—that he considered "the worst symptoms of our inner moral decay." Hoping to arouse conservative evangelicals' ire and motivate them to become politically active, he launched a "Clean Up America" campaign by sending his supporters 1 million questionnaires focusing on these issues. "Do you approve of known practicing homosexuals teaching in public schools?" he asked in the questionnaire. "Do you approve of the present laws legalizing abortion-on-demand? . . . Do you approve of the laws of our land permitting the open display of pornographic materials on newsstands, TV, and in movies?" To no one's surprise, the people on Falwell's mailing list shared their favorite preacher's moral views: 94 percent of the respondents endorsed his position on all three issues.[36]

Falwell followed this effort with a book, *How You Can Help Clean Up America*, in which he gave instructions for launching local, single-issue moral campaigns. He encouraged his readers to launch boycotts against local stores that sold pornography, or to put anti-gay-rights initiatives on local ballots. Falwell was convinced that a city-by-city, grassroots campaign could turn back the tide of cultural liberalism in the United States. He dreamed of the day when a series of local victories across the nation would give conservative evangelicals the political influence they needed to "go to San Francisco and challenge the homosexual capital of America."[37]

Although Falwell's experience in grassroots campaigns seemingly made him an ideal recruit for the New Right, as a minister, he did not want to appear too blatantly partisan. It was no secret that he was a political conservative—he had, after all, endorsed President Gerald Ford from the pulpit in 1976—but like other fundamentalists and conservative evangelicals, he thought that it was unseemly for a pastor to participate directly in a political campaign. Billy Graham had tried to hide his partisan activity from public view, and his reputation had suffered after his close relationship with Nixon was revealed. Falwell did not want to sacrifice his ministerial career for a political cause. In 1965, he had preached a sermon against ministerial participation in politics. And as late as the fall of 1978, he continued to insist that he would "stay totally on spiritual issues," such as abortion and homosexuality, while avoiding any New Right cause that was merely "political," such as the Panama Canal Treaty. "I don't talk politics," he told *Esquire* in October 1978.[38]

Falwell was also reluctant to cooperate with allies outside of his own religious circle, which made it unlikely that he could create a viable political coalition. He still called himself a "fundamentalist," rather than an "evangelical." His theological views were closer to those of Bob Jones, Jr., or John R. Rice, both of whom he knew personally, than to those of Billy Graham or *Christianity Today*. "I believed that 'being yoked with unbelievers' for any cause was off limits," Falwell later recalled. "I didn't even get along very well with other kinds of Baptists, let alone with Methodists, Presbyterians, or Catholics." He disdained many of the best-known televangelists, saying that "the healer types, the Elmer Gantry types, are religious phonies who are raping America." Falwell was uneasy just being around those he considered less devout. As late as 1978, Falwell's secretary advised a female reporter who requested an interview with the pastor to wear a dress during their interview in order to avoid offending the preacher's sense of propriety.[39]

Falwell relinquished his scruples about associating with nonfundamentalists only after receiving a phone call from Francis Schaeffer, who had seen his television programs on abortion and other moral issues. Schaeffer encouraged Falwell to take his fight against "secular humanism" into the political arena and assured him that winning the fight against immorality was more important than maintaining rigid standards of separation from religious people who were in doctrinal error. "Dr. Schaeffer shattered that world of isolation for me," Falwell later recalled. "He was the one who pushed me into the arena and told me to put on the gloves."[40]

Falwell's willingness to allow nonfundamentalists into his political coalition earned him sharp rebukes from several fundamentalist leaders. Bob Jones, Jr., called Falwell "the most dangerous man in America today as far as Biblical Christianity is concerned." His son, Bob Jones III, was even harsher. Because the Moral Majority was open to Catholics, the younger Jones said, it was "a movement that holds more potential for hastening the church of Antichrist and building the ecumenical church than anything to come down the pike in a long time." Likewise, Carl McIntire said that by engaging in such ecumenism, the Moral Majority founder had committed the "mistake of separating his moral standards from the Bible and the Word of God."[41]

Most of these fundamentalists were quickly losing whatever political influence they had once enjoyed, so Falwell found it easy to brush off their criticism, but he occasionally expressed his personal discomfort with the interdenominational alliances that he thought he had to make in order to win a political victory. "The media had better understand that in another context we would be shedding blood [over doctrinal differences]," Falwell said in June 1979 at a rally that attracted Protestants, Catholics, and Jews. "But our commitment to the family has brought those of us of differing religious views and backgrounds together to fight a just cause . . . to fight for the family."[42]

Schaeffer helped convince Falwell to drop his scruples about allying with nonfundamentalists, but it was up to Ed McAteer to get the pastor to overcome his reluctance to join a partisan cause. McAteer was ideally suited for the task of mobilizing evangelical preachers. In his twenty-five years as a sales representative for Colgate Palmolive, he had acquired the skills of persuasion that he needed to market New Right ideology to the nation's leading evangelical pastors and televangelists. As a devout evangelical, lay missionary, and member of the board of the Wycliffe Bible Translators, he knew almost all of the leading televangelists.[43]

McAteer set to work on the task in January 1979, calling Falwell on a regular basis and, after establishing a relationship, arranging for Falwell to meet with him and Howard Phillips in Lynchburg. Falwell became so enthralled with the New Right's political plans that a one-hour meeting stretched into a nine-hour marathon. At the next meeting, Weyrich and Phillips, along with Robert Billings and Richard Viguerie, impressed upon Falwell the importance of using electoral politics to further the moral causes that he had been promoting through his television ministry. Weyrich told Falwell that there was a "moral majority" of Americans who would vote for conservative causes if Falwell could reach them with the New Right message.[44]

The Baptist preacher needed little persuasion. Instead of merely relying on local ballot initiatives and community boycotts, which he now believed were insufficient to bring the country back to morality, Falwell would commit himself to a massive effort to register Christian voters in the hope of capturing Congress and the White House. In June 1979, he took the first step by forming the Moral Majority, a political organization that would allow him to pursue partisan activities that would have been off-limits for his tax-exempt ministry. Falwell was now no longer merely a pastor; he was a professional lobbyist and political operative.

Falwell was convinced that Christians had the power to take control of the national government, but with 45 percent of evangelicals still not registered to vote, they had not yet been able to exercise that power. So he recruited pastors to launch voter registration drives in their churches. "If there is one person in this room not registered, repent of it," he told one gathering. "It's a sin." Calling his earlier sermon against ministerial involvement in politics "false prophecy," he now said that a pastor's mission was to get people "saved, baptized, and registered." And pastors should not hesitate to "endorse candidates, right there in church on Sunday morning."[45]

Falwell not only endorsed conservative candidates, but also provided them with campaign money. In September 1979, he created the Moral Majority PAC, whose purpose was to raise money for congressional candidates, just as Weyrich's CFSFC had done. The new PAC raised $10,000 in its first month of existence—not much, but enough to contribute funds to the campaigns of six conservative Republican challengers, including Charles Grassley, who was preparing for a campaign against liberal Democratic Senator John Culver in Iowa, and Frank Wolf, who was vying for a congressional seat from Virginia's tenth district.[46]

To any critics who objected to Falwell's politicization of the ministry, he responded by arguing that the government's "liberal" policies had compelled him to become politically active. "It is not the religious conservatives in this country who have politicized the gospel," he said. "It is the liberal in the church and in the government who has turned the basic moral values that were the foundation of this country into political issues." With the country's moral foundations allegedly under "liberal" attack, Falwell had no choice but to defend the nation.[47]

Like Christian Voice, Moral Majority was able to use the tried-and-true moral campaign issues of the 1970s to build a political coalition. Most of Moral Majority's board members and directors were veterans of evangelicals' recent single-issue, grassroots campaigns. Likewise, many of the organization's earliest recruits had initially become politically active because of these issues. Falwell capitalized on their sense that the nation was experiencing a rapid moral decline. In one of Moral Majority's earliest fund-raising appeals, Falwell wrote, "Homosexual teachers have invaded the classrooms, and the pulpits of our churches. . . . Smut peddlers sell their pornographic books—under the protection of the U.S. Constitution! And X-rated movies are allowed in almost every community because there is no legal definition of obscenity. . . . Believe it or not, we are the first civilized nation in history to legalize abortion—in the late months of pregnancy! Murder!"[48]

Tim LaHaye, a charter board member of Moral Majority, contributed to Falwell's cause by publishing *The Battle for the Mind*. LaHaye argued that the majority of Americans were moral, patriotic people who had, by their negligence, allowed a coterie of humanists and their allies—who numbered no more than 14 million—to take control of the nation's government and news media. (LaHaye's description of "humanists" closely paralleled the charges against "communist subversives" that he would have heard at the John Birch Society meetings he attended in the 1960s). Humanists "are more interested in world socialism than in America," LaHaye wrote, and had a "running romance with big government." Opponents of humanism, on the other hand, believed that "the less government, the more freedom—and vice versa."[49]

By connecting humanism with political liberalism, LaHaye strongly implied that readers who wanted to vote for righteousness would have to cast their ballots for conservative Republicans. To further drive that point home, LaHaye's book included a checklist of "preliminary questions for candidates to determine their positions on morals," which, not surprisingly, focused on pornography, the ERA, and gay rights. But simply voting for the right candidates was not enough; LaHaye also urged Christians to "volunteer to help in the campaign of pro-moral candidates." Churches should conduct voter registration drives on special "Christian Citizenship Sundays." "It may be too late for the Christians in Sweden to oust the humanists from office," he wrote, "but it certainly is not too late in America and Canada."[50]

Falwell echoed LaHaye's views on federal power. He said that Americans should "get rid of" the Occupational Health and Safety Administration, which currently held the nation's businesses in regulatory "shackles." On tax policy, he was just as conservative as the most fervent New Right ideologue. "I don't think a guy who makes a lot of money should pay more taxes than a guy who makes a little," he said. Falwell's strong opposition to communism impelled him to oppose any measure that would weaken America's military or limit free enterprise. If SALT II were ratified, he warned, "one day the Russians may pick up the telephone and call Washington, D.C., and dictate the terms of our surrender to them."[51]

Falwell believed strongly in American exceptionalism. The United States played a special role in the Lord's plan for world history—not least by defending against communism—and if it was in decline, the solution was to return to the God who had blessed America in former times. "The problem of the nation, the real problem is a moral one," he said. "The economic problems, the energy crisis, our international embarrassments are all simply symptoms of the fact that God is angry with us as a nation." The only hope lay in campaigning for a political agenda that would rescue the country from destruction. Falwell was just the man for the job. "I have a divine mandate to go right into the halls of Congress and fight for laws that will save America," he said.[52]

Falwell's message resonated with evangelicals. Watergate, the Vietnam War, stagflation, and the energy crisis had produced what the president termed a national "crisis of confidence"—or, as the pundits phrased it, a "malaise."[53] Evangelicals who, like other Americans, struggled to make their declining incomes meet their escalating living expenses found it easy to believe Falwell's claim that God was judging the United States for its unfaithfulness.

To his evangelical supporters, Falwell warned of God's imminent judgment, but to the broader public, he tempered his rhetoric in order to appear more mainstream than he actually was. In 1978, for example, he had campaigned to "remove all known practicing homosexuals from teaching positions in public schools." Two years later, he disavowed such views, saying, "We can certainly be for the civil rights of homosexuals without condoning their life style. . . . I have no objection to a homosexual teaching in the public classroom as long as that homosexual is not flaunting his life style or soliciting students." In his fund-raising letters, Falwell continued to take a hard-line position. "We are losing the war against homosexuals," he wrote. But in public, Falwell presented himself as a reasonable negotiator. "We're not religious fanatics who have in mind a Khomeini-type religious crusade to take over the government," he said in 1980. "We support the separation of church and state. . . . We want influence, not control."[54]

Despite such assurances, Falwell was never able to convince much of the public that he was not an extremist, and as a result, his ability to mobilize a "moral majority" was more limited than he had expected. He had hoped to be able to create a coalition of Catholics, Jews, and Protestants, but he found it difficult to sell his message to anyone except conservative Baptists. Only one of the pastors on the Moral Majority board was not a Baptist, and according to one estimate, Baptists accounted for 90 percent of the organization's members. Almost all of the Moral Majority state chairs were theologically conservative Baptist pastors, and more than half of them were members of Falwell's own denomination, the Baptist Bible Fellowship International. Even some Baptists refused to support him. Many of the most conservative fundamentalist Baptists shunned the Moral Majority leader because of his willingness to work with nonfundamentalists, while some members of the Southern Baptist Convention considered Falwell too extreme because he had refused to bring his church into the SBC. Although 43 percent of Southern Baptist pastors expressed general agreement with Falwell's moral and political views, only 3 percent joined the Moral Majority.[55]

Nor did many of the nation's leading televangelists support Falwell's organization. While Jim Bakker and Pat Robertson made no secret of their conservative political views, their charismatic faith alienated them from Falwell, who did not believe in faith-healing and tongues-speaking. New Right activists had hoped that Falwell would harness the power of religious broadcasting for political conservatism, but the two most popular televangelists, Oral Roberts and Rex Humbard, refused to discuss politics on their television programs and privately supported Carter. "If I backed a Republican for President, what about all the Democrats in my audience?" Humbard asked.[56]

Falwell's audience of 1.5 million comprised only a small fraction of the 20 million Americans who regularly watched religious television, and even they were reluctant to join the Moral Majority. The *Moral Majority Report* had a mailing list of only 482,000 in November 1980, and the number of active participants within the organization was far smaller.[57]

Yet despite its small constituency, the Moral Majority did more than any other organization to launch the Christian Right. Falwell used a small cadre of energized pastors in suburban megachurches in the Sunbelt to mobilize their congregations on behalf of political causes and vote congressional liberals out of office. While Christian television viewers, a group that included a disproportionately high number of elderly southern women, proved difficult to mobilize, Falwell found a ready audience among suburban pastors of his own generation. In Alabama, Moral Majority members in Birmingham's white, middle-class suburbs brought an unexpectedly high number of new voters to the polls for a Republican congressional primary. They made the difference as the staunchly conservative candidate, Albert Lee Smith, upset eight-term incumbent John Buchanan. In Oklahoma, Moral Majority members engaged in a successful door-to-door campaign to help Don Nickles defeat Senator Andrew Coats, whom they accused of being soft on pornography. In Alaska, Moral Majority members wrested control of the state GOP from the party regulars, and in the South, where the organization received its highest level of support, some Moral Majority leaders began building fledgling Republican Party chapters in counties where only token Republican organizations had existed.[58]

If the Moral Majority did not succeed in its goal of registering 4 million new voters, it most likely registered at least 2 million with the help of Christian Voice and the Religious Roundtable. While most Moral Majority members had, like Falwell, been Republican sympathizers for years, the group did bring some new voters to the polls, and it made a few Republican converts among traditionally Democratic southern evangelical voters. One survey showed that more than 20 percent of Moral Majority supporters who cast their ballots for Reagan in 1980 had voted for Carter in 1976.[59]

More important, Falwell gave the Christian Right a national voice that it would not otherwise have had. Falwell's masterful use of publicity gained him access to corridors of power that other Christian Right activists had never dreamed of entering. He regularly inflated the number of his sup- porters in a successful attempt to increase his influence, telling the press on several occasions that the *Old-Time Gospel Hour* had 25 million weekly viewers, rather than the 1.5 million that Arbitron ratings suggested his program attracted.[60] He did not represent a majority of voters, and his own organization may have been smaller and less religiously diverse than he would have liked. But he was good at promoting his cause, and by the end of the summer of 1980, Republican Party leaders were treating him like an influential lobbyist and the leader of an important swing constituency, rather than as the small-town Baptist preacher that he had been only a few years earlier.

Pat Robertson and Washington for Jesus

While the media focused on Falwell, out of the spotlight Pat Robertson orga- nized a more religiously diverse coalition of charismatics, Pentecostals, Southern Baptists, and other evangelicals who wanted to recapture Washington for righteousness and take political power in the name of the Lord. Politics was not a new vocation for Robertson, the son of the late Senator A. Willis Robertson (D-VA). "Constituents," he enjoyed telling people, was the third word that he had learned as a child. Upon reaching adulthood, Robertson showed signs of following in his father's political footsteps. He attended his first Democratic National Convention in 1952 at the age of twenty-two, and four years later, after graduating from Yale Law School, he served as president of the Stevenson for President Committee on Staten Island. Although he showed more interest in partying than in his studies, and failed the New York bar exam, Robertson, a Golden Gloves boxer and Marine Corps lieutenant, seemed to be a highly intelligent, personable, and successful son of senatorial privilege. His colleagues thought he might become a prosperous businessman or run for office, both of which he later did. But in the short term, Robertson followed a path that differed drastically from what his law school classmates had expected.[61]

In 1956, shortly after graduating from law school, Robertson experienced a "born-again" conversion. He poured his liquor down the drain, gave away almost all of his money and possessions, and moved into a decrepit boardinghouse in the slums of the Bedford-Stuyvesant neighborhood in Brooklyn in order to minister to the African American urban poor. Soon he began speaking in "tongues." He earned an M.Div. at a New York evangelical seminary, became an ordained Southern Baptist minister, and in 1961 launched the nation's first Christian television network from a station in Portsmouth, Virginia. Robertson proved to be a master of network broadcasting, and he found a ready market for religious programming, which he began transmitting over cable as soon as that technology became available. By 1980, his television network, CBN, included 150 affiliate stations. In his religious fervor, he temporarily forgot his earlier interest in politics. When his father requested his help during a close fight for reelection in 1966, Robertson refused to get involved, saying that God had forbidden him from aiding any political candidate. Willis Robertson lost narrowly.[62]

Ten years later, when Jimmy Carter ran for president, Robertson supported his candidacy because he believed that a born-again Christian would promote the interests of evangelicals. Robertson gave the Democratic candidate favorable press coverage on *The 700 Club*, and, unlike many other Southern Baptists, he graciously overlooked the governor's interview with *Playboy*. Immediately after the November election, Robertson sent Carter a list of hundreds of evangelicals he believed were qualified for government positions. To his chagrin, the president-elect ignored the list and did not appoint any evangelicals to prominent public positions. Robertson felt betrayed.[63]

Robertson became more active in conservative politics during Carter's administration. He invited New Right politicians such as Senator Roger Jepsen and Representative Larry McDonald (D-GA) to appear on *The 700 Club*. He also mobilized evangelical support for the unsuccessful candidacy of a fellow charismatic Christian, G. Conoly Phillips, the most conservative candidate in the Virginia Democratic Senate primary in 1978. As Robertson became more disillusioned with the Democrats who were in power in Washington, his prophetic expositions of national political events took a decidedly pessimistic turn. Two years before the Iranian hostage crisis, Robertson correctly predicted that a foreign country would take Americans captive. But some of his other predictions proved to be less accurate. When it became obvious that a worldwide economic depression and food shortage, a Soviet war against Israel, and an imminent Armageddon had failed to occur on Robertson's projected schedule, he turned away from prophetic speculation.[64]

Despite his disappointment with Carter, Robertson was convinced that evangelicals belonged in politics. In October 1979, he wrote an article that outlined his goals for a "Christian action plan for the 1980s." The restoration of school prayer headed his list. "President Roosevelt did not hesitate to use power to force the Supreme Court to acquiesce to New Deal legislation," Robertson wrote. *"Christians should not hesitate to use the lawful power at their disposal to secure reversal of onerous Supreme Court decisions."*[65]

Conservative Protestants had been divided on the school prayer issue in the 1960s, and by the 1970s, they had largely forgotten about it. But after launching a campaign against "secular humanism," some evangelicals came to believe that *Engel v. Vitale* had been a pivotal moment in the nation's moral decline. A constitutional amendment to restore school prayer, they decided, would help to reverse the nation's secular turn. In January 1980, Robertson joined with other leading evangelicals, including the newly elected conservative president of the Southern Baptist Convention, to organize the Coalition for the First Amendment, an organization whose primary purpose was to pass a school prayer constitutional amendment. The cause quickly received support from many evangelical leaders, including Falwell (and his Moral Majority) and Bill Bright. A Gallup poll in 1980 showed that 81 percent of evangelicals supported legislation to return classroom prayer to public schools.[66]

Robertson had the support of many prominent evangelical pastors, but he was not content with a movement of ministers; instead, he wanted to create a grassroots movement of lay Christians who would move from their church pews to the gates of power in Washington. In April 1980, he planned to bring 1 million evangelicals to the Washington Mall to "reclaim Washington for Jesus."

The "Washington for Jesus" (WFJ) rally was the idea of Robertson's friend John Gimenez, a Harlem-born, charismatic pastor in Virginia who thought that the prayer meeting might attract one hundred thousand Christians. But after Robertson joined the planning committee, plans for the event became far more grandiose. Robertson's Christian television network received nearly $50 million in donations each year, and he thought that he could use his resources to organize the largest march on Washington in the nation's history and save the nation through prayer. The conference organizers set up 380 offices throughout the country and spent approximately $1 million. Robertson also injected current political concerns into the prayer vigil. Abortion, homosexuality, and federal deficit spending plagued the country, a preliminary WFJ planning paper said, and Christians needed to pray for God to remove these sins from the nation. In a symbolic gesture of their intention to bring America back to the alleged ideals of its founders, Robertson and the WFJ committee scheduled the rally for the anniversary of the first English settlers' arrival at Jamestown.[67]

The march attracted only two hundred thousand Christians, and it failed to set a record for the largest demonstration in Washington's history. Nevertheless, the organizers considered their rally a success. Falwell was still too suspicious of charismatics to cooperate with Robertson, and Billy Graham decided not to interrupt his schedule to come to the rally, but most of the other prominent evangelical leaders in America converged on the capital. Campus Crusade founder Bill Bright and SBC president Adrian Rogers attended, as did Jim Bakker and other popular televangelists. As Robertson stood on the dais and surveyed the throng of Christians who had gathered to pray on the Mall, he realized that evangelicals had the numbers to effect change in Washington. "You have seen the great silent majority," he told the crowd.[68]

The rally's organizers claimed that "Washington for Jesus" was not political, but conservative themes pervaded the event. African American evangelicals convinced Robertson to withdraw an advertisement for the rally that encouraged Christians to entreat God's forgiveness for the sins of abortion, homosexuality, and the national debt, but some of the rally's speakers alluded to these evils in their addresses. More significantly, their rhetoric fostered the idea of America as a Christian nation that had fallen from grace and urgently needed to be redeemed. "America has one last chance," Jim Bakker, who had spent the previous year denouncing Jimmy Carter on *The PTL Club*, told the crowd. "God help us to put the Bible back in our schools and our public life, and may we truly be one nation under God."[69]

James Robison and the Religious Roundtable

Few televangelists at the rally trumpeted the national call to repentance more loudly than James Robison, a friend of Robertson and the chair of the Coalition for the First Amendment. Robison was a newcomer to politics in 1980, and his ministry was still in its infancy. But he was strongly convinced that a conservative political revolution was needed to protect Christians from the hostile actions of political liberals.

A thirty-six-year-old Southern Baptist preacher who had spent most of his life in Texas, Robison did not yet enjoy the national reputation of Falwell or Robertson, but he more than made up for it in charisma. Texas conservative billionaire H. L. Hunt called Robison "the most effective communicator I have ever heard." By the late 1970s, Christian television stations throughout the South carried the young preacher's sermons, and nearly half a million viewers tuned in each week to catch his hard-hitting denunciations of sin. Robison, the son of an impoverished, unmarried woman who had raised her child in a decrepit trailer, openly flaunted his humble origins and lack of formal education. He thrived on straight-shooting diatribes of moral ills, which he cast in the most scathing terms he could imagine. The Texas preacher's audience relished his comparison of homosexuals to rapists, bank robbers, and murderers, but such rhetoric made Robison's station managers uneasy. In 1979, when Robison proclaimed that homosexuals routinely recruited and murdered young boys, and that the recent assassinations of San Francisco mayor George Moscone and his openly gay city supervisor Harvey Milk constituted a judgment of God against homosexuals, Robison's Dallas station, WFAA-TV, decided that it had had enough, and it cancelled his program.[70]

Robison had eschewed politics for most of his life, but now he decided that he needed to become politically active in order to protect his "right to preach." He hired a lawyer to convince the FCC to require that WFAA reinstate his show, and he appealed to other evangelicals for help. In June 1979, a rally of support for Robison in Dallas attracted eleven thousand, one of whom was Jerry Falwell, who called the Texas televangelist "the prophet of God for our day." "When it comes to preaching the Bible, we will not back up, we will die for our right to preach," Falwell said.[71]

The station returned the show to the air, but Robison was not ready to quit the political scene. He worried about the state of a society in which a television station could cancel his program because they were worried about offending homosexuals. "If I cannot preach the Bible, then America is in serious trouble," he said. He considered it particularly galling that WFAA cited the FCC's Fairness Doctrine in the station's complaints about his program. "The bureaucracy and the government restrictions began to choke me and silence me from preaching the whole counsel of God," Robison told *Christianity Today*. He began arguing that Christians needed to make their voices heard in the halls of Congress. "I'm tired of hearing about radicals, perverts, liberals, leftists and Communists coming out of the closet," Robison said. "It's time for God's people to come out of the closet and the churches to influence positive changes in America."[72]

Robison addressed the antiabortion March for Life in Washington, DC, and joined Falwell's Moral Majority. In 1980, he released *Wake Up America, We're All Hostages*, a doom-and-gloom documentary that warned Christians that the country was in dire straits. With commentary from Christian Right leaders such as Falwell and Robertson, as well as conservative politicians such as Jesse Helms and Philip Crane, Robison's prime-time special had a strongly conservative tone. Robison continued to profess nonpartisanship, saying that it would be "a crime against this country and a crime against God to sell yourself to a party line or a candidate." But that stance became increasingly difficult to sustain when he asked his audience to pray for Republican candidate Ronald Reagan, while criticizing President Jimmy Carter for "walking in the counsel of the ungodly."[73]

When Ed McAteer noticed Robison's newfound interest in politics, he recruited the Southern Baptist televangelist to serve as the executive director of a new Christian Right organization, the Religious Roundtable. McAteer hoped that the Roundtable would have an ecumenical appeal that the Moral Majority had never attained. Robison, who got along well with both Falwell and Robertson, was an ideal choice for the director of an organization that sought to attract both charismatics and noncharismatic evangelicals. Indeed, the Roundtable's executive board read like a "who's who" of the Christian Right: it included Falwell, Robertson, and the conservative leaders of the Southern Baptist Convention. In addition to conservative Protestants, McAteer invited Jews and Catholics, as well as a few black conservatives, to join his organization's advisory board.[74]

By the summer of 1980, the evangelical unity that had seemed impossible to imagine only two years earlier had become a reality. Fundamentalists, charismatics, and evangelicals were working together in a political coalition to take the nation back for the cause of Christ. McAteer, Falwell, Robertson, and Robison differed in theology and personal background, but they and other evangelicals were united in the belief that the federal government was hostile to conservative Christians, that the government had fostered the cause of "secular humanism," and that only a conservative political revolution could restore the country to morality. They merely needed a presidential candidate to help them take power.

The Carter Administration's Attempt to Appease Evangelicals

By 1979, the White House realized it was in trouble. Carter received low public approval ratings from nearly all demographic groups, but because he was a Southern Baptist from Georgia, many of his supporters had expected him to retain his appeal among southern evangelicals. Instead, "born-again" preachers had become some of his harshest critics. Recognizing that the president needed help on the religious front, Reverend Robert Maddox, pastor of the First Baptist Church in Calhoun, Georgia (which the president's son Jack Carter attended), volunteered to become the White House's religious liaison. Maddox seemed to be an ideal candidate for the job. He had both the regional accent and the evangelical beliefs that Carter's campaign team hoped would appeal to the televangelists who had made the president a target. But Maddox underestimated the depth of evangelicals' anger toward Carter and the degree to which conservative evangelicals had allowed the culture wars to dominate their political and theological thinking. He assumed that evangelicals' defection from the Democratic Party was temporary and would be reversed as soon as the president's harshest evangelical critics were assuaged. But Maddox quickly discovered that conservative evangelicals' view of politics as a battleground between secular humanists and true believers left them little room to compromise with the White House.[75]

In January 1980, Maddox invited a few of Carter's most outspoken Christian opponents—including Falwell, Robertson, Robison, and Tim LaHaye—to join the president at the White House for a southern-style breakfast and present him with their toughest questions. Falwell asked the president about abortion. LaHaye expressed his concerns about the White House Conference on Families. Robert Dugan, president of the National Association of Evangelicals (NAE), asked about school prayer. Carter did not change his positions on these issues, but his willingness to listen to his critics may have improved his standing with a few televangelists. Jim Bakker told reporters that the president had presented himself as "a warm, decent man confessing his faith in Christ." But several others, including Falwell, refused to be appeased. The Moral Majority leader renewed his attacks on Carter within half an hour of his White House meeting.[76]

Carter found it difficult to mollify his evangelical critics because he could not compromise on his positions. He did not want to antagonize liberals in his party who already considered him too conservative and were thinking about supporting Senator Edward Kennedy's primary challenge. And he did not want to do anything that would violate his deeply held belief in church-state separation.

Having realized their voting power, conservative evangelicals were equally unwilling to compromise. By the time Christian Right leaders met with Carter at the White House, they were already searching for an alternative candidate they could support. When Ed McAteer arranged for Ronald Reagan to address the Religious Roundtable in August 1980, it seemed that the Christian Right had finally found its man.

NINE | Reagan

W HEN RONALD REAGAN CAME TO Dallas in August 1980 to speak to the fifteen thousand religious leaders who had gathered at the Religious Roundtable's National Affairs Briefing, Christian Right leaders viewed it as the beginning of a long-term alliance. The crowd that heard Reagan's address—a group that included Jerry Falwell, Pat Robertson, Ed McAteer, James Robison, and the president of the Southern Baptist Convention—had never before seen a presidential nominee adopt their cause with such enthusiasm. "I know you can't endorse me," Reagan told them. "But I want you to know that I endorse you and what you are doing."[1]

Conservative evangelicals could hardly believe their good fortune. Richard Nixon, Gerald Ford, and Jimmy Carter had at times tried to appeal to evangelicals, but no one had equaled Reagan in speaking out against abortion, the sexual revolution, communism, and moral decay, and in proclaiming a new moral vision for the nation as a "shining city upon a hill." Echoing the message of the Christian Right, Reagan told the National Affairs Briefing that "over the last two or three decades the Federal Government seems to have forgotten both 'that old-time religion' and that old time Constitution." But evangelicals, he believed, could change the direction of the nation and restore its traditional values.[2]

Electing Reagan, Christian Right leaders realized, was the key to accomplishing their goals. They expected his administration to roll back abortion rights, curb the gay rights movement, restore prayer in schools, and lead the nation back to morality. Abandoning their pretense of nonpartisanship, they became enthusiastic champions of the Republican ticket. "This movement will put Ronald Reagan in office," Ed McAteer confidently predicted. When Reagan won, evangelicals believed that it was the beginning of a new era of Christian revival. It was, Falwell said, "the greatest day for the cause of conservatism and morality in my adult life."[3]

Supporting Reagan in 1980

Conservative evangelicals began making overtures to Republican presidential contenders as early as the spring of 1979. In previous elections, evangelicals had not shown much interest in presidential primaries or positioned themselves to influence the selection of a party nominee, but the leaders of the newly emerging Christian Right were determined to transform their movement into an influential voting bloc within the GOP. Falwell invited Illinois congressman Phil Crane, a staunchly conservative ideologue who was a long-shot candidate for the nomination, to speak at Liberty Baptist College in early 1979. "You are the kind of man that we need in the White House," Falwell told him. Later that year, he and other evangelicals traveled to Texas to meet with former governor John Connally. But when it appeared that Ronald Reagan was the most viable conservative candidate, evangelicals threw their support behind him.[4]

Reagan had to make a few amends with evangelicals. As governor, he had signed a bill legalizing therapeutic abortion, and in 1978, he had opposed an anti-gay-rights referendum, a stance that had temporarily alienated him from Falwell. His church attendance was sporadic. He was also divorced. "Reagan was not the best Christian who ever walked the face of the earth," Christian Voice executive director Richard Zone conceded. "But we really didn't have a choice."[5]

Evangelicals were willing to forgive Reagan for these occasional lapses because he supported some of their moral causes and had long championed a civil religion that appealed to them. In 1964, Reagan had endorsed a campaign to return prayer to public schools. In 1967, as a newly elected governor of California, he had promised pastors at a prayer breakfast that "trusting in God for guidance will be an integral part of my administration." While campaigning for the Republican presidential nomination in 1976, he had told a California evangelical radio talk show host that he approved of efforts to promote personal morality through legislation and that he himself was a devout Christian who had "had an experience that could be described as 'born again.'"[6]

Reagan also shared evangelicals' religiously inspired antipathy to communism. America, he believed, was a divinely chosen nation in a battle for freedom. When he heard Pat Boone proclaim in 1962 that it would be better for his daughters to be "blown to Heaven in a nuclear war than to live in slavery under Communism," he felt such great admiration for the sentiment that he continued to quote the line for decades. In rhetoric that would have been familiar to evangelicals who had grown up believing in the "Christian America" of Billy Graham and the anticommunist radio preachers, Reagan borrowed a line from a Puritan forebear and referred to his country as a "shining city upon a hill," a radiant refuge of liberty that a "Divine Providence" had created for "all those people in the world who yearn to breathe freely." America's current situation looked bleak, and some of its leaders had lost sight of the nation's purpose, but he offered the hope of redemption. "Let's make America great again," a Reagan campaign slogan proclaimed.[7]

Reagan's campaign team realized the importance of winning evangelical votes, because they knew that the support of white, born-again Protestants would be the key to defeating Carter in the South. With the White House, Senate, and House of Representatives under Democratic control, Republicans were happy to receive support from any group that offered it. As one Republican senator said, "When you're as distinct a minority as we are, you welcome anything short of the National Order of Child Molesters." But whereas some Republicans disparaged the party's evangelical supporters as a necessary evil to be tolerated, others, including Reagan's campaign aide Lyn Nofziger, realized that the born-again Christians were a "natural constituency" for the GOP, because they shared many of Reagan's political views. "I was always convinced that there were a lot more pluses in the fundamentalists than there were minuses," Nofziger recalled in a 1986 interview.[8]

Reagan began making overtures to right-to-life organizations before the New Hampshire primary. In January 1980, shortly before the South Carolina primary, he spoke at Bob Jones University. In August, his campaign hired Moral Majority executive director Robert Billings as its religious liaison.[9]

At the Republican National Convention in Detroit, Reagan delegates adopted a platform endorsing evangelicals' favorite causes. The party retained the staunchly antiabortion platform plank that it had adopted in 1976, and added new language that promised "the appointment of judges at all levels of the judiciary who respect traditional family values and the sanctity of innocent human life." Reversing the position that the party had taken at every convention since 1940, the GOP refused to endorse the ERA, and instead expressed its opposition to "any move which would give the federal government more power over families." In a direct bid for conservative evangelical votes, the party platform called for the protection of private Christian academies and promised to "halt the unconstitutional regulatory vendetta launched by Mr. Carter's IRS Commissioner against independent schools." When the platform was unveiled, Falwell was in the convention hall, ready to celebrate what he called a "dream platform" that "could easily be the constitution of a fundamentalist Baptist Church."[10]

Falwell had less success trying to influence Reagan's choice of vice presidential nominee. A few hours before Reagan announced his selection, Falwell visited Reagan's hotel suite at the convention in Detroit and tried to persuade the Republicans that they needed to put another staunch conservative, such as Jesse Helms, on the ticket. George H. W. Bush, a favored candidate for the number-two position, alienated many religious conservatives with his moderate stance on abortion. But when Reagan ignored the Christian Right's advice and selected Bush, Falwell asked Reagan's running mate whether he supported the entire Republican Party platform, including its antiabortion statements. When Bush replied that he did, Falwell decided that he could support him.[11]

Reagan's endorsement of religious conservatives at the National Affairs Briefing shortly after the convention helped him with evangelicals, but it hardly bolstered his standing among moderates and liberals. The rally included a fulmination from James Robison against "the radicals and the perverts . . . coming out of the closet," but the greatest political damage for the Republicans may have come from some controversial musings that Southern Baptist Convention president Bailey Smith made about the Jewish religion. "It is interesting at great political rallies how you have a Protestant to pray, a Catholic to pray, and then you have a Jew to pray," Smith said. "With all due respect to those dear people, my friends, God Almighty does not hear the prayer of a Jew. . . . How in the world can God hear the prayer of a man who says that Jesus Christ is not the Messiah? It's blasphemous." Smith's comment proved to be such a political lightning rod that it prompted Pat Robertson to resign from the Religious Roundtable, which thereafter experienced a sharp decline in size and influence. Some Christian Right leaders worried that Smith's negative assessment of Jewish prayers could discredit not only the Roundtable, but also their entire political movement. Falwell attempted to do damage control by arguing that God hears the prayers of all "redeemed" Jews, which was what Smith had meant when he said that prayers must be offered in the name of Jesus to be acceptable.[12] But the explanation did little to assure people of the Christian Right's tolerance. As the fallout over Smith's remark showed, it was difficult for the Christian Right to build a broadly ecumenical political coalition as long as the movement's leaders continued to hold exclusivist religious beliefs.

Several journalists seized on Smith's statement and pressed Reagan for a clarification of his views. Reagan, who had no interest in getting involved in an evangelical controversy over which religious groups received answers to their prayers, assured the press that "since both the Christian and Judaic religions are based on the same God, the God of Moses, I'm quite sure those prayers are heard." Then, as a conciliatory gesture to the Christian Right, he added, "But then, I guess everyone can make his own interpretation of the Bible, and many individuals have been making different interpretations for a long time."[13]

While Reagan distanced himself from the Christian Right's theology, he endorsed the movement's attempt to bring religion into politics. Answering constitutional objections from the movement's critics, Reagan explained that Christian perspectives had a place in government. "The First Amendment was written not to protect the people and their laws from religious values, but to protect those values from government tyranny," he said.[14]

Reagan continued to strengthen his ties with the Christian Right during the last two months of his campaign. He endorsed the teaching of creationism in public schools, saying that evolution was "theory only." At the beginning of October, he visited a convention of the National Religious Broadcasters Association and told the assembled crowd that while he "remained absolutely opposed to a state-mandated prayer" in a public school classroom, he did favor voluntary, student-led prayer. "I don't think that we should ever have expelled God from the classroom," he said. Reagan then spoke at Falwell's Liberty Baptist College in Lynchburg, Virginia, inaugurating a tradition among Republican presidential candidates of making obligatory campaign stops at conservative evangelical and fundamentalist schools.[15]

By that point, it was obvious that the Christian Right had lost any claim that the movement ever had to political nonpartisanship. Some Christian Right organizers went so far as to coordinate their efforts with the Reagan campaign team, so that evangelical preachers who spoke on conservative themes could time their remarks to produce the greatest possible benefits for the Republican Party. Several, including Beverly LaHaye, joined the Reagan campaign as "family policy" advisers.[16]

As Reagan developed closer ties with the Christian Right, the Carter White House gave up its attempt to recover the support that it had lost among religious conservatives, and instead began to use Reagan's association with Falwell as a means of discrediting the Republican candidate. In September, Patricia Harris, the secretary of health and human services, compared Falwell to the Islamic fundamentalists who had taken control of Iran the previous year. "I am beginning to fear that we could have an Ayatollah

Khomeini in this country," she said. "He will not have a beard, but he will have a television program." President Carter lost patience with his co-religionists in the Christian Right. The Moral Majority and other Christian Right organizations propagated a "narrow definition of what a Christian is and also what an acceptable politician is, and I don't want to see that happen," the president said in early October.[17]

Carter had some reason to hope that Reagan's association with the Christian Right would alienate moderate voters in both parties. By late 1980, many Christians, including a number of leading Baptists, had decided that the Religious Right was badly misguided. Jimmy Allen, a former Southern Baptist Convention president, frequently voiced his objection to the Moral Majority, and James Dunn, the head of the moderately liberal Baptist Joint Council of Political Affairs, made no secret of his disdain for Christian Right leaders. "We've got a bunch of TV preachers who want to establish a theocracy in America, and each one of them wants to be Theo," Dunn told the press. Even some Republicans within the Reagan camp were alarmed at the Christian Right's growing influence. "This marriage of religion and politics is the most dangerous thing, the creepiest thing I've ever seen," one Reagan aide said.[18]

But the majority of voters in 1980 did not react against the Christian Right. Instead, they gave the movement legitimacy by voting for the conservative Republican candidates that Falwell and his allies supported. Forty of the forty-three House and Senate candidates who received the support of state Moral Majority chapters won election. Several of the most prominent targets of Christian Voice and other Christian Right organizations, including Senators George McGovern (D-SD), Birch Bayh (D-IN), and Frank Church (D-ID), were defeated, and a new group of conservative senators and representatives, including Senator Dan Quayle (R-IN), Representative Don Nickles (R-OK), and Representative Paula Hawkins (R-FL), were swept into office. Most important, in the Christian Right's view, Ronald Reagan defeated Jimmy Carter in a landslide electoral victory that put every southern state except Georgia in the Republican column. When Carter conceded the election even before the polls on the West Coast had closed, he received little sympathy from the born-again Christians who had eagerly supported his presidential candidacy four years earlier. "The people that put Jimmy in, put Jimmy out," James Robison said. "He ignored these people—the conservatives and conservative Christians who put him in—and they abandoned him." The Christian Right rejoiced at the "beginning of a new era of conservatism in America," as the Christian Voice's Gary Jarmin phrased it.[19]

The defeated members of Congress who had borne the brunt of Christian Voice's negative advertising blamed their losses on the Religious Right. "They beat my brains out with Christian love," Representative John Buchanan complained. Senator Birch Bayh predicted that the Christian Right would continue to be a potent threat to liberal politicians. "These hate groups have now tasted blood," Bayh said. "Step out of line one time, and they'll chop your head off."[20]

In actuality, Carter's unpopularity probably would have allowed Reagan to win regardless of whether or not Falwell and the Moral Majority supported him. In any case, most voters who cast their ballots for the Republicans had little regard for Falwell. A survey taken during the fall of 1980 showed that only 6 percent of whites "felt close" to the Moral Majority and other Christian Right organizations.[21]

But even if the Christian Right could not take credit for putting Reagan into office, it could claim at least partial responsibility for turning conservative evangelicals into a Republican voting bloc that party strategists could not afford to ignore. Sixty-seven percent of white evangelical voters cast their ballots for Reagan in 1980, compared to only 62 percent of white non-evangelicals. This was a shift from four years earlier, when Carter had won 49 percent of the evangelical vote—and 56 percent of the white Baptist vote—in an election in which he had received 50 percent of the total popular vote.[22] Evangelicals had been moving into the Republican Party for the previous three decades, but the GOP could not invariably count on their vote, and sometimes squabbles between fundamentalists and evangelicals had derailed any chances that the two groups had for partisan unity. After 1980, fundamentalists and evangelicals would be united in supporting Republican presidential candidates; no Democrat since has won a majority of white evangelical and fundamentalist support in a presidential race. Much of this partisan transformation was due to the work of Falwell, Robertson, and McAteer, as well as other Christian Right leaders and the new conservative leaders of the Southern Baptist Convention. Capitalizing on conservative evangelicals' unease with the social changes taking place in America, Falwell and his allies succeeded in channeling this anxiety about the nation's moral condition into a partisan movement.

Christian Right leaders' success in energizing a voting constituency for Reagan emboldened them to dream of a long-lasting political influence in the new administration. Years later, Moral Majority vice president Ed Dobson described the feelings that he and other conservative evangelicals had immediately after Reagan's victory. "We were somebody," Dobson said, adding that he felt that "we mattered, that we cared, that we were making a difference, that all of the years in the backwoods of the culture were over. We had come home, and the home was the White House."[23]

To capitalize on their newfound influence, Tim LaHaye, along with Paul Weyrich and Richard Viguerie, organized the Council for National Policy (CNP) in May 1981. In contrast to earlier Christian Right organizations, which had focused on mobilizing voters and lobbying Congress, the CNP was designed to be a policy-making think tank where Christian Right activists and administration officials could discuss areas of common concern. Its members included nearly all of the major Christian Right leaders and their allies, such as Jerry Falwell, Pat Robertson, Ed McAteer, Phyllis Schlafly, H. Edward Rowe, and Robert Billings, along with New Right activists Paul Weyrich, Richard Viguerie, and Howard Phillips. But the group also included a few Reagan aides and conservative congressmen. Morton Blackwell, the administration's religious liaison, was a member, as was Secretary of the Interior James Watt. Oil magnate Nelson Bunker Hunt and Amway president Richard DeVos, reliable sources of Christian Right funding, sat on the executive board. With a membership that included conservative PAC director Jack Abramoff and numerous congressional and executive office staff members, the organization was able to draw on the expertise of Washington's most influential Republican lobbyists. This would be an organization where Attorney General Edwin Meese could drop by to give a lecture titled "The Reagan Administration's Agenda," and where OMB director David Stockman and Ambassador Jeanne Kirkpatrick would also be invited speakers.[24] Evangelicals had spent the previous two years creating an ecumenical political coalition of social conservatives from all denominations. Now the government was part of the coalition as well.

The Reagan Administration's First Year

As he took the oath of office, Ronald Reagan's left hand rested on a King James Bible opened to one of the Christian Right's favorite verses—2 Chronicles 7:14, in which God tells his people that if they "pray, and seek my face, and turn from their wicked ways; then will I . . . forgive their sin, and will heal their land." Only one of Reagan's predecessors had turned to that verse at his swearing-in—Dwight Eisenhower. Reagan was letting evangelicals know that an era of civil religion had returned. "We are a nation under God," Reagan declared in his inaugural address.[25]

But evangelicals quickly discovered that Reagan's actions did not always live up to his soaring oratory. While Reagan gave Christian Right activists warm endorsements whenever he met with them, they were merely one interest group among many that he had to appease, and he showed only limited interest in making their causes a legislative priority.

Immediately after Reagan's election, some of the free-market advocates, business-oriented Republicans, and moderates in his coalition began distancing themselves from the Christian Right. They expected that tax cuts and defense spending, rather than moral concerns, would dominate the president's agenda. Less than a month after the election, Vice President George Bush scoffed at Paul Weyrich's insistence that he strengthen his opposition to abortion and proclaim his support for school prayer. "I am not intimidated by those who suggest I better hew the line," Bush said. "Hell with them."[26]

Reagan avoided such contempt, but he knew when it was best to ignore the Religious Right's demands. He selected only one evangelical—Secretary of the Interior James Watt—for his Cabinet. Reagan's choice of the outspoken abortion opponent C. Everett Koop for surgeon general was a plum for the Christian Right, but for the most part, the president confined Christian conservatives to marginal positions in the Department of Health and Human Services and the Department of Education—which he hoped to abolish. Christian conservatives appreciated the opportunity that these low-ranking positions gave them to set policies affecting Christian schools or to suggest minor restrictions on abortion, but they were frustrated to realize that they had been denied all of the key appointments in the administration.[27]

During Reagan's first year in office, a vacancy on the Supreme Court offered conservatives a chance to suggest potential nominees for the position. Religious Roundtable executive director H. Edward Rowe urged the president to appoint Phyllis Schlafly. Instead, Reagan nominated Sandra Day O'Connor, an Arizona judge with a record of supporting abortion rights. Falwell called the choice a "disaster" that would offend "good Christians." Immediately, Republicans tried to distance themselves from the Moral Majority leader. No senators opposed O'Connor's nomination, and some GOP conservatives delivered a stinging rebuke to Falwell for upbraiding the president. "I think that every good Christian ought to kick Falwell right in the ass," Senator Barry Goldwater told the press.[28] The division between the Baptist televangelist and the aging libertarian conservative symbolized the tension between two distinct wings of the GOP.

Falwell quickly decided that it was best not to sacrifice his influence with the president by opposing a popular Supreme Court nominee. After a call from Reagan, the Moral Majority leader fell into line, refusing to take a stand on the nomination. Although he had objections to O'Connor's position on abortion, he no longer criticized Reagan for the appointment. "I am very, very happy with this President," Falwell told the press in September 1981, as the Senate debated O'Connor's confirmation. Reagan, he said, was "the greatest President we've had in my lifetime and history may say the greatest President ever."[29]

Many other Christian Right leaders took Falwell's position and decided to support the president, despite the lack of substantive gains for their cause during Reagan's first year in office. They consoled themselves with the thought that perhaps they exercised influence over the administration in other ways that could not be tangibly measured. "There are a lot of good people being put into positions, not at the Cabinet level but behind the scenes—the kind of people who love our ways," Robert Billings told the National Association of Religious Broadcasters in January 1981.[30] Billings was correct. Reagan's religious liaison to Protestants, Morton Blackwell, used his position to give Christian Right leaders regular access to the president, and Gary Bauer, an undersecretary of education and domestic policy adviser, promoted conservative evangelicals' social causes. Yet even though there were more "born-again" Christians serving in the Reagan administration than at any other time in recent memory, they did not exercise much influence in policy making.

Republican leaders in the Senate gave the Christian Right early warning that its social concerns would have to give way to the more urgent task of fixing the economy. Senate majority leader Howard Baker (R-TN) declared that the Senate would concentrate on enacting the president's economic plan and would defer action on all social and moral legislative items until 1982. Ed McAteer protested that decision. Senate Republicans needed to realize that the "number one priority is to stop murdering babies," he said.[31]

In the first few weeks after Reagan's election, Falwell had expressed his hope that Congress would pass the Family Protection Act and a constitutional amendment prohibiting abortion. But in response to Baker's announcement, Falwell said that he would not expect Reagan to turn his agenda to moral issues until early 1982. The Moral Majority promised to "lay off overt politics for a year or so."[32]

For the next few months, the Moral Majority lobbied for the president's spending cuts. But by the fall, a few members of the Moral Majority began to wonder when the White House would reciprocate with the socially conservative legislation to which they believed they were entitled. "If we clean up the economy, but are still allowing the slaughter of one and one-half million babies a year, I will not be able to say that we are better off at all," Moral Majority vice president Cal Thomas told White House Chief of Staff James

Baker in October 1981. But despite his frustration, Thomas was careful to point out that he was still strongly supporting the president.[33]

Other Christian Right activists, particularly fundamentalists who were more conservative than Falwell, were more pointed in their criticism of the president. When Reagan backed away from his pledge to defend Bob Jones University against the IRS's attempts to rescind the college's tax exemption because of its alleged violation of federal civil rights statutes, Bob Jones III denounced the president as a "traitor to God's people." By 1982, Jones had decided that "we couldn't do any worse at the hands of the liberals," and he therefore suggested that "it might be good for us to stay away from the polls and let their ship sink."[34]

The New Right leaders who had recruited Falwell for their cause in 1979 likewise adopted a pessimistic view of the Reagan Revolution. "I knew conservatives would get the short end of the stick," Richard Viguerie grumbled. "I just didn't know the stick would be this short." Less than two weeks after Reagan's inauguration, Weyrich warned Republican Party operatives that they could not take the New Right's support for granted and that social conservatives would not be content if they found that Reagan's support for their cause was merely rhetorical. "We didn't get out there in the year of our Lord 1980 for symbolism," he proclaimed.[35]

Weyrich could not understand why the Moral Majority continued to give public support to a president who had not acted on their agenda. He was aghast that the Moral Majority was willing to allow conservative economic and defense issues to take its focus away from the social concerns that had initially energized evangelicals in the late 1970s. "The religious right was sweet-talked in 1981," Weyrich said at the end of Reagan's first term in office.[36]

But Moral Majority leaders viewed themselves as sophisticated political analysts who had shrewdly acquired political influence in Washington by refusing to criticize the Reagan administration. "We've been around the national scene and involved in politics for four to five years ourselves and we can find our way around town," Moral Majority vice president Ron Godwin said in 1984. "We understand the need to maintain open communications and access with the Administration rather than engaging in vitriolic attacks."[37]

The Moral Majority's choice gave them a strategic advantage over other religious groups. Catholic bishops, by contrast, undermined their influence in the administration by protesting Reagan's cuts in social services and his nuclear arms buildup. Mainline Protestant leaders objected to an even broader range of administration policies. But Falwell supported all of Reagan's initiatives, and as a result, he endeared himself to the White House. In 1982, the

Reagan administration's religious liaison estimated that "the President has had more contacts with Jerry than with any other religious leader" in the nation.[38] This was good news for the Baptist televangelist, who never passed up a chance for publicity.

The Crises of the Moral Majority

Falwell's alliance with Reagan was both strategic and fortuitous, because his connection with the White House enabled his organization to survive the crises that engulfed it in the early 1980s. Falwell discovered that it was more difficult to be the public face of a "moral majority" than he had expected, and his crusade against political liberalism and secularism quickly made him a target of ridicule. Immediately after the 1980 election, several new organizations, including television producer Norman Lear's People for the American Way, mobilized to stop the Moral Majority's bid for power. The American Civil Liberties Union launched a national advertising campaign against the Christian Right with the slogan "If the Moral Majority has its way, you'd better start praying." Rabbi Alexander Schindler accused the Christian Right of contributing to anti-Semitism, and others said that Falwell's agenda was opposed to the interests of African Americans. These charges were especially damaging, because many middle-class white evangelicals wanted to avoid any organization accused of bigotry. Although many evangelicals supported Reagan and the Republican Party, some of them disliked the negative tone of Falwell's campaigns and his willingness to link the gospel to a narrow set of political issues at a time when overt partisanship in the pulpit was still controversial. The Lynchburg pastor quickly became a pariah in many circles, even in the Bible Belt. Sixty-two percent of people in Falwell's home state disapproved of him, a worse rating than any other public figure received. "The only person I could imagine getting a bigger negative would be Ayatollah Khomeini but we don't put him on our polls," political analyst Larry Sabato said.[39]

Falwell also faced opposition from some of his fellow televangelists, who realized by early 1981 that his controversial political activities could be a liability for their brand of Christianity. Rex Humbard declared in early 1981 that Jesus "would never get into politics" and that evangelists who spoke out on political issues in lieu of preaching the gospel had misguided priorities. Even Billy Graham, whose public friendship with Richard Nixon had brought him into close alliance with several Republican leaders, cautioned Falwell to keep his distance from conservative political causes. "The hard right has no interest in religion except to manipulate it," Graham said in February 1981.[40]

In public, Falwell and his allies shrugged off these criticisms. "They must think we are doing something or they wouldn't take time and money to fight us," James Robison said. But privately, Falwell resented attacks on his organization, and he tried to defend himself against the charges that others leveled at him. Citing the Moral Majority's pro-Israeli foreign policy stances as proof of his love for the Jewish people, Falwell said, "Those who spread the myth that we are anti-Semitic don't know what they are talking about." Falwell also made an effort to reach out to African Americans by speaking at a black pastors' ministerial meeting on Chicago's South Side and enlisting the support of E. V. Hill, an African American pastor in Los Angeles, though by Falwell's own admission, only a "couple of hundred" of Moral Majority's four hundred thousand members were black pastors.[41]

Falwell's troubles mounted when local Moral Majority chapters deviated from his wishes and embarrassed the movement. When voter registration had been Moral Majority's primary objective, it had been easy to keep state organizations in line, but after the election, some of the state chapters, which had been formed hastily with minimal training or oversight, began to shift their focus. The Maryland Moral Majority attracted national ridicule when it launched a campaign against "anatomically correct" gingerbread figures that a local bakery was selling. The cookies had not been very popular, but protests caused sales to skyrocket. When Falwell heard that the Maryland Moral Majority had become a laughingstock, he rescinded the state chapter's charter. In California, the leader of the Santa Clara chapter created a more ominous controversy when he called for the death penalty against homosexuals, which Falwell quickly declared was "out of the question." Even in Falwell's home state, Reverend Tom Williams attempted to censor offensive books under the auspices of the Moral Majority without securing Falwell's approval.[42]

The Moral Majority was so decentralized that Falwell could not rein in recalcitrant leaders. Most of his troubles came from fundamentalists who misunderstood his political strategy. In early 1982, several months after the Moral Majority had instituted a national training program for its leaders, an Idaho chapter offended several state political candidates by mailing them a survey that included questions about their drinking habits and their personal salvation. To Falwell and the national Moral Majority leaders, who were trying to further their influence in Washington and effect national political change, voting records mattered far more than personal morality. "We don't think drinking habits and marital status would necessarily predict how a person would vote on a pornography bill," said Michael Farris, head of the Washington state Moral Majority chapter.[43]

Moral Majority's internal crises made it imperative for Falwell to regain credibility with his followers by securing substantive legislative results. Moral Majority leaders began pressuring the Reagan administration to act on their agenda. They had not lost faith in the president, whom they still believed was on their side, but they criticized moderate Republicans in the administration for keeping social issues off the legislative agenda. "Time is running out and our people are running out of patience," Cal Thomas wrote in the spring of 1982. If the Reagan administration did not begin working for antiabortion legislation, he warned, social conservatives might decide to stay home for the November midterm elections.[44]

Within a few weeks of Thomas's warning, Reagan announced his support for two constitutional amendment proposals—one to restore classroom prayer in public schools and the other to prohibit abortion. Falwell became an enthusiastic champion of both. He attended a candle-lighting ceremony at the White House to support the school prayer amendment, and lobbied for its passage. As he stood in the State Room with the president, Falwell was confident that at last the Moral Majority would realize its agenda and that moral order and civil religion would return to the nation. "The question is not if we're going to win, it's only when," Falwell declared. "The majority of the people of this country are with us."[45]

The Reagan Administration's Alliance with the Southern Baptist Convention

The Reagan administration welcomed Falwell's support, but conservative strategists such as Ed McAteer realized that the Moral Majority represented only a small contingent of conservative Protestants. If the administration wanted to solidify its relationship with evangelicals, it would need the support of the nation's largest Protestant denomination, the Southern Baptist Convention. Facilitating alliances between religious leaders and Republican activists had become something of a specialty for McAteer. As an active Southern Baptist layman, he decided that it was time to enlist the SBC in support of Reagan's political agenda, starting with the school prayer amendment. Many, though not all, of the SBC's executive leaders had had Republican leanings for more than a decade, and the SBC had shifted even more sharply to the right after conservatives took control of the denomination in

1979. By 1982, the SBC had already endorsed Reagan's conservative positions on abortion and the ERA. But school prayer was a different matter, because many pastors in the denomination had long opposed school prayer amendments and defended the separation of church and state.

Although the conservatives who exercised executive control of the denomination supported Reagan's school prayer measure, the denomination's moderates, who were still a sizable minority, opposed it. In 1980, the moderates had used their voting power to defeat a resolution proposal that would have endorsed a school prayer amendment. McAteer was undeterred. The 1982 convention was conveniently scheduled to take place only a few weeks after Reagan unveiled his proposed amendment. McAteer, with a politician's sense of timing, intended to produce the show of support from the nation's largest Protestant denomination at the precise moment when it would be needed to give the president's amendment a needed boost in Congress.

McAteer arranged to have his own pastor, former SBC president Adrian Rogers, appear with President Reagan in the Rose Garden at the official announcement of the president's prayer amendment. Rogers no longer held a leadership position in the denomination, but his presence at the ceremony would send a clear message to Southern Baptists that might alleviate their misgivings about breaking with their denomination's traditional opposition to such measures. To McAteer's disappointment, a flight delay deprived him of the photo opportunity that he wanted. Undaunted, McAteer pressed ahead, ensuring that the resolutions committee was filled with school prayer supporters. By the time he arrived in New Orleans for the convention, he was confident enough in his control of the resolutions process to promise the White House that the SBC would endorse the Reagan administration's school prayer amendment.

McAteer knew that Southern Baptists could be induced to support school prayer if they were convinced that the amendment would protect religious liberty rather than constrict it. The pastors that McAteer brought to the convention appealed to evangelicals' fear of secular humanism. When Christian children were forbidden to pray aloud in their classrooms, their right to worship God was denied in order to accommodate the wishes of atheists. As one McAteer ally, Wichita Baptist pastor Morris Chapman, explained, "The atheists, humanists and secularists are against prayer in schools, and that's not the company we need to be keeping." Morris's arguments persuaded the delegates, who approved McAteer's school prayer resolution by a 3–1 margin. Stan Hastey, a reporter for the *Baptist Press* and a member of the Baptist Joint Committee on Public Affairs, blamed McAteer, whom he accurately described as "a mover and shaker in the New Right," for "hav[ing] for the first time put the SBC on record in support of extremist political causes."[46]

As if to seal the alliance between the Southern Baptist Convention and the Reagan administration, the 1982 convention closed with an address by Vice President George Bush. In a striking departure from past statements, Bush extended a warm welcome to religious leaders who wanted to influence conservative politics. "The famous wall of separation between church and state is there to keep the state from interfering with the churches, not to keep the churches or individual religious leaders or ordinary church members from participating in our politics," Bush said.[47]

Bush's appearance at the Southern Baptist Convention helped to win over Christian Right leaders. In April 1983, the vice president gave an address at Falwell's Liberty Baptist College, where he lauded the Moral Majority founder's "ministry, his influence for good." Falwell, in turn, promised to start "working in a nonpartisan way" for Reagan's reelection, which he said was "no longer in question—it's guaranteed." The Moral Majority leader had become one of Bush's staunchest supporters. In a hint that his political commitment to the vice president and his family might even extend well beyond the mid-1980s, he announced, "God has a plan for the Bushes in our country."[48]

For two years after Bush spoke to the SBC, the Convention's leaders campaigned for the president's school prayer amendment and gave the administration strong support. Other Religious Right organizations also joined the campaign. Pat Robertson organized a letter-writing effort on its behalf, while Jerry Falwell highlighted the issue in his fund-raising appeals. The NAE testified before the Senate judiciary committee in support of the amendment, and Christian Voice likewise lobbied for its passage.[49]

Reagan's efforts on school prayer won him the long-standing gratitude of conservative evangelicals and endeared them to the Republican Party. By the summer of 1982, the Christian Right coalition had broadened to include the independent Baptists affiliated with Falwell, charismatic Christians associated with Robertson, a broad array of moderate evangelicals who were members of the NAE, and the Southern Baptist Convention. McAteer's success in enlisting the SBC in support of Reagan's agenda brought long-term benefits for the GOP. After 1982, Southern Baptist Convention leaders never again supported a Democrat for president.

Adjusting to Failure

The Religious Right's excitement turned to disappointment when evangelicals realized that congressional Democrats, and some Republicans, had no intention of banning abortion or reinstating prayer in public schools. In

March 1984, after two years of protracted negotiations between Congress and the president, the school prayer amendment fell eleven votes short of passage in the Senate. The antiabortion amendment did not even get that far. The Reagan administration could never get the Senate to introduce the amendment that pro-lifers preferred—which would have banned abortion nationwide—so it settled for an amendment proposed by Senator Orrin Hatch (R-UT) that would have overturned *Roe v. Wade* and left the issue to the states. When that measure fell eighteen votes short of passage in a Republican Senate, it sent a clear message to the White House that the antiabortion movement did not have much congressional support. Reagan continued to promise pro-life leaders that he would "not rest . . . until a human life amendment becomes part of our Constitution," but given the failure of Republican senators to support the antiabortion cause, there was little that Reagan could do to give the Christian Right what it wanted.[50]

Perhaps the Reagan administration could have lobbied harder for socially conservative legislation, but the Christian Right's biggest obstacle to achieving its goals was not White House lethargy. Nor was it congressional intransigence. Rather, it was a lack of public support. A majority of American voters approved of Reagan, but that did not mean that they shared the Religious Right's vision of a Christian moral order. They appreciated the progress that women's rights and religious pluralism had made during the previous two decades, and they did not want to see those gains eroded. Public opinion polls showed that a majority of Americans wanted abortion to remain legal. Politicians knew that Falwell was unpopular, and his endorsement was "the kiss of death" for many Republican candidates in swing districts. They had no incentive to acquiesce to his lobbying. Evangelicals won a few minor victories during Reagan's first term, such as the "Mexico City policy," which restricted federal funding for international abortion service providers, and the Equal Access Law, which gave student religious groups the right to hold meetings on public school property. Religious conservatives cheered when Reagan proclaimed 1983 the "Year of the Bible." But the Christian Right's major goals remained elusive.[51]

In the absence of substantive gains on abortion and school prayer, the Christian Right looked to foreign policy for signs of the Reagan administration's loyalty to their ideals. Conservative evangelicals had lauded Reagan's strong denunciations of communism during the campaign, and they were delighted when he embarked on a program of nuclear arms buildup. Reagan needed the Christian Right's support on this issue, because nearly all of the nation's other religious leaders, including Catholic clerics who had supported him on abortion, condemned his attempt to escalate the arms race. While liberal religious leaders and their secular allies called for a nuclear freeze, Falwell launched an "anti-freeze" campaign. Evangelicals were more likely than non-evangelicals to support a nuclear arms buildup, because they were more likely to believe that the Soviet Union had a nuclear advantage over the United States. Falwell, for instance, erroneously believed that the Soviet Union's nuclear arsenal was twice as large as America's. Fighting the "freez-eniks" was, for him, a matter of life and death. "I for one refuse to sit back and wait for the Soviets to enslave us or to destroy us in a rain of nuclear warheads," Falwell said.[52]

Realizing that evangelicals might be the only religious group that would endorse his policy, Reagan made a concerted effort to use them as publicists. He brought Falwell to the White House for a private conversation that lasted more than an hour, and then asked National Security Council aides to give him a briefing on nuclear policy. But Christian Right leaders were so eager to support the president's policies that they did not require official encouragement from the White House. Pat Robertson aired a documentary called *Afghanistan: Under the Iron Claw* on his television network. Billing itself as an in-depth look at "what may well be the Soviets' boldest attempt yet toward gaining total world domination," the documentary offered strong emotional support for the president's nuclear arms buildup. Falwell took out advertisements in major newspapers across the nation opposing a nuclear freeze, and urged members of the Moral Majority to lobby Congress on the issue. When the president unveiled his Strategic Defense Initiative, popularly known as "Star Wars," Falwell was equally supportive of the pres-ident on that matter. In keeping with his new priorities, he told his sup-porters that the nuclear freeze, rather than abortion, school prayer, or the economy, would be the most prominent political issue in the presidential election of 1984.[53]

One of the most prominent evangelical organizations supporting the president on the nuclear freeze issue was the NAE, which claimed a member-ship of more than 10 million. Already, the National Council of Churches and some Catholic clerics had spoken out against Reagan's nuclear policies. Evan-gelicals were inclined to support Reagan on the issue, NAE president Robert Dugan said, but many were beginning to drift into the pro-freeze camp. "Some well known evangelical voices," Dugan told the president, in what may have been a reference to Billy Graham, "are attempting to draw evangel-icals into support of a nuclear freeze. Your persuasive voice would have a marked impact upon the evangelical community." Noting that the NAE was solidly behind the president, he added, "You would seldom have a more friendly and appreciative audience." The administration evidently agreed.

Not only did White House staff schedule the president to speak at the NAE, but White House speechwriter Tony Dolan also met with Dugan and sent him drafts of the president's speech to make sure that they would meet with his approval.[54]

Reagan offered one of the most overtly religious speeches of his presidency. After discussing the religious origins of America's tradition of freedom, he told the evangelicals in the audience about his own faith, belief in the power of prayer, and opposition to "modern-day secularism." He received standing ovations when he endorsed school prayer and antiabortion legislation. "There's a great spiritual awakening in America, a renewal of the traditional values that have been the bedrock of America's goodness and greatness," he declared. Then he turned his attention to the nuclear freeze. He inveighed against the Soviets with the fervor of an evangelical revivalist. "There is sin and evil in the world," he declared, "and we're enjoined by Scripture and the Lord Jesus to oppose it with all our might." The Soviet Union was an "evil empire," he said, and the fight against communism was a "struggle against right and wrong and good and evil." Reagan's call to meet the nation's "test of moral will and faith" brought the evangelical pastors to their feet. They would stand with Reagan in his call to arms, knowing that they were engaged in a righteous cause. Reagan might not have been able to give the Christian Right the moral legislation that it wanted, but the Christian Right would give Reagan the endorsement he needed.[55]

The Election of 1984

Evangelicals gave Reagan and the Republican Party even stronger support in 1984 than they had in 1980. The Moral Majority registered 2.5 million new conservative voters in 1984, and other Christian Right groups registered at least another million, almost all of whom could be counted on to support the president's reelection. Falwell encouraged churches to hold a "God and Country" Sunday two days before Election Day, and called for voters to engage in a twenty-four-hour fast, accompanied with "deep prayer that God will send a spiritual awakening to America."[56]

Four years earlier, Christian Right leaders had supported a few conservative Democrats in congressional elections even while campaigning for Reagan, but by 1984, they had dropped all pretense of bipartisanship. The Democrats, Falwell charged, "have attempted to relegate Judeo-Christian values to the trash heap of ancient and outmoded ideas." Shortly before the Democratic National Convention in San Francisco, Falwell traveled to the city to lead a "Family Forum," where Phyllis Schlafly and Republican whip Newt Gingrich were guest speakers. Both Schlafly and Gingrich lambasted the Democrats as the party of social liberals, but neither of them could top Falwell's description of the Democrats as "soulmates of San Francisco's Wild Kingdom." A month later, Falwell traveled to Dallas to give a benediction at the Republican National Convention, and urged his supporters to vote for the GOP. "As it now stands, the Democratic party is basically controlled by the radical ideas of a dangerous minority—homosexuals, militant feminists, socialists, freezeniks, and others of the ilk," he said.[57]

Tim LaHaye contributed to Reagan's reelection campaign by launching a new organization to mobilize voters, the American Coalition for Traditional Values (ACTV). Under LaHaye's leadership, ACTV enlisted thirty-five thousand churches in a campaign to register more than 1 million new voters. Evangelical pastors who joined ACTV passed out voter registration forms during church services so that congregants could fill them out in their pews and drop them in the collection basket. LaHaye left no doubt about how he expected newly mobilized Christians to vote in the upcoming presidential election. "This President has done more to advance traditional moral values and to return our nation to those values than any President in my lifetime," LaHaye said of Reagan in August 1984.[58]

For LaHaye, Reagan's reelection was merely an initial step toward gaining political power for Christian conservatives. He began recruiting pastors to find "thousands of qualified Christians to run for public office" in order to reverse the late-twentieth-century trend of secularization that had produced legalized abortion and gay rights legislation. "Do you think it is reasonable for every Bible-believing church to recruit . . . one person during the next decade to run for public office and win? If we did, we would have more 'born-again' Christians running for office than there are offices to hold!" LaHaye told evangelicals. In a sign that LaHaye equated "Bible-believing" Christian values with conservative politics, he invited Jesse Helms, Newt Gingrich, and Representative Robert Dornan (R-CA) to speak alongside Paul Weyrich, Jerry Falwell, and Pat Robertson at a 1985 ACTV conference entitled "How to Win an Election."[59]

Eighty percent of evangelicals who went to the polls in 1984 cast their ballots for Reagan. This was the highest level of evangelical support for a Republican candidate since Nixon's reelection campaign of 1972, but what was even more striking was the degree to which evangelicals had become loyal to the entire Republican Party, not simply to the president. As late as 1980, only 29 percent of Southern Baptist pastors were registered Republicans, despite their general willingness to support Republican presidential candidates. But by 1984, 66 percent of Southern Baptist pastors were Republicans at a time when only 42 percent of white non-evangelical southerners were members of the GOP. White evangelicals had been voting Republican in presidential elections for decades, but until the 1980s, many of them had continued to register as Democrats, just as Billy Graham did. That phenomenon changed in 1984, when for the first time, more white evangelicals who frequently attended church identified as Republicans than as Democrats. For the next twenty years, the number of Republican evangelicals would steadily increase: by 2004, more than three times as many churchgoing white evangelicals would identify as Republicans than as Democrats. In the South and Midwest, the Republican Party became heavily dependent on the votes of evangelicals, who were more likely than their non-evangelical counterparts to support the GOP, and as a result, the GOP continued to shift to the right on social issues. Northern moderate Republicans began to feel increasingly uncomfortable in their own party, and support for the GOP from mainline, non-evangelical Protestants declined, making the GOP even more heavily dependent on the votes of conservative evangelicals.[60]

Since the 1950s, evangelicals had been moderately influential in the party. But as thorough Republican partisans after the mid-1980s, evangelicals were poised to exercise much greater influence; they could now dictate the terms of the Republican party platform, exercise veto power over presidential and vice presidential nominees, and force candidates to spend more time talking about abortion, gay rights, and school prayer. After the election of 1984, the Christian Right was positioned to become the most significant special interest group within the GOP. When *Time* featured a cover photo of Jerry Falwell under the heading "Thunder on the Right" in 1985, Christian Right activists knew that they had finally earned a place at the table.[61]

A Heightened Concern about Abortion

Conservative evangelicals' newfound devotion to the GOP stemmed partly from their increased attention to abortion. In 1980, evangelicals had opposed abortion, but they generally viewed it as only one of many national sins, including the sexual revolution, homosexuality, feminism, and pornography. In the mid-1980s, evangelicals moved closer to the conservative Catholic position on the issue and began to view abortion as a unique evil, far worse than other national sins.

Evangelicals' heightened concern about abortion was largely due to the influence of Francis Schaeffer and his son Franky. "We have reached a place today which is violently opposed to what the Founding Fathers of this country and those in the thirteen individual states had in mind when they came together and formed the union," the elder Schaeffer wrote in his book *A Christian Manifesto* (1981). "At a certain point there is not only the right, but the duty, to disobey the state." If abolitionists had been justified in using such extreme tactics to end slavery, then Christians in the late twentieth century would surely be justified in doing the same thing to stop abortion. And if even civil disobedience was justified, churches should show no compunction about engaging in any political activity that might help them reach their goal of making abortion illegal and reintroducing Christian values to the nation's legal code. "Today the separation of church and state in America is used to silence the church," Schaeffer wrote, and Christians would be foolish to let "humanist" liberals keep them out of politics.[62]

Although Schaeffer cautioned against a too-close alliance with political conservatives, he apparently abandoned such caution when endorsing the Moral Majority. Privately, he told Falwell and other associates that he disagreed with the Moral Majority's opposition to SALT II and gun control, but publicly, he endorsed the organization's political program because he thought that Falwell's efforts offered evangelicals the best chance they had to ban abortion in America. He acknowledged that political conservatives were motivated by economic ideas that he did not necessarily endorse, but he nevertheless applauded the conservative Republican electoral gains in 1980 as a "unique window open in the United States" to reverse the gains of humanism. His friendship with Representative Jack Kemp (R-NY), a Catholic who was one of the leading champions of the pro-life cause in Congress, led to a closer alliance with the Republican Party. In 1982, Schaeffer spoke at the Mayflower Hotel in Washington, DC, to a select group of conservative Republican leaders. Most of Schaeffer's speech consisted of well-worn arguments about the inevitable progression from abortion to euthanasia and infanticide. But at the conclusion of his speech, Schaeffer endorsed the Republicans' opposition to a nuclear freeze. It was a new theme for Schaeffer, and although it did not directly contradict any of his earlier writings, it seemed a surprising shift for a person whose previous political pronouncements had focused on environmentalism, race relations, and, most of all, the preservation of human life at every stage. By 1982, Schaeffer had decided that the Republican Party and the Christian Right represented the only hope for stopping abortion in the United States, and he was willing to do whatever was necessary to support them.[63]

Conservative evangelical leaders were delighted at Schaeffer's endorsement of their cause. Falwell included a copy of Schaeffer's *Christian Manifesto* in every "God Bless America Survival Kit" that he mailed to sixty-two thousand contributors in 1982. He also invited Schaeffer to speak at Liberty Baptist College and broadcast one of his sermons on the *Old-Time Gospel Hour*. President Reagan also came to realize Schaeffer's importance. When the evangelical theologian died of cancer in May 1984, Reagan sent a note of condolence to Schaeffer's widow, Edith. Schaeffer "will long be remembered as one of the great Christian thinkers of our century," Reagan wrote.[64]

In July 1984, two months after Schaeffer's death, Moral Majority vice president Cal Thomas gave a radio address on abortion that called for immediate action. "When is this craziness going to stop?" Thomas asked his listeners. "When you get angry enough to stop it. Picketed an abortion clinic lately? Reached out to a girl in a crisis pregnancy situation?" For Thomas, the presidential election contest between Reagan and Mondale was primarily about abortion. "Supreme Court judges will probably be chosen by the next President," Thomas told his listeners. "Will they keep the abortion floodgates open or start to close them? It's up to you."[65]

Yet even these efforts were not enough for Franky Schaeffer. After his father's death, the thirty-two-year-old Franky, who was now a full-time evangelical speaker and filmmaker living in northeastern Massachusetts, took up the evangelical pro-life mantle and began issuing calls for militancy that were even stronger than his father's. In 1984, he published *Bad News for Modern Man: An Agenda for Christian Activism*, an antiabortion clarion call whose back cover featured a picture of the author marching in a pro-life demonstration. Schaeffer declared that it was time to "alert, radicalize, and activate" all who opposed abortion. "I am distraught over this, as well as distressed and, yes, *angry*—angry at those who are doing nothing about stemming this tide of inhumanity," Schaeffer wrote. "Those who are evangelical, and therefore should know better, have been particularly derelict."[66]

Conservative southern evangelicals welcomed the younger Schaeffer's message, and they trembled at his rebuke. Falwell's Liberty Baptist College brought the zealous young speaker to campus in 1982 to tell students that they had a duty to renounce their last remaining fundamentalist scruples about engaging the world and become more strident in their political activism. Schaeffer pointedly urged the Southern Baptist Convention, which invited him to speak at their 1984 Pastors' Conference, to "make abortion a priority." "The fact that you have not done it and know that you should means you will stand in judgment for not using your resources," Schaeffer said, in a rebuke worthy of a biblical prophet. Although it may not have been a direct response to Schaeffer's exhortation, the SBC's Christian Life Commission directed Southern Baptist congregations to protest *Roe* by celebrating their first annual "Human Life Sunday" in January 1986, and began making the antiabortion cause one of the denomination's foremost concerns. When the strongly pro-life Richard Land became head of the Christian Life Commission in 1988, the denomination gave even greater emphasis to its campaign against abortion.[67]

The White House responded to the Christian Right's growing interest in abortion by highlighting the president's pro-life position. In 1983, the White House released an article under the president's byline to the antiabortion journal *Human Life Review*. Shortly after the article appeared, a Nashville-based evangelical publisher requested permission to include it as the leading essay in a book titled *Abortion and the Conscience of a Nation*. The book would have Reagan's photo and byline on the cover and would highlight the administration's opposition to abortion by pairing the president's article with a similar essay by surgeon general C. Everett Koop. Reagan readily agreed to the arrangement, and the book appeared just in time for his reelection campaign in 1984. Evangelicals who cast their ballots for Reagan did so with the confidence that a second Reagan term would bring the country closer to the human life amendment that the Republican platform promised.[68]

Reagan's Second Term

The Christian Right did not get that amendment. Nor did it realize any of its other major objectives during Reagan's second term. Instead, the Moral Majority and other evangelical political organizations spent much of their time lobbying for the White House's objectives. After the Democrats regained control of the Senate in 1986, the Christian Right's chance of passing socially conservative legislation rapidly dissipated. The Christian Right continued to make news headlines by rallying voters on behalf of the president's initiatives, but it no longer had significant influence in Washington. In 1987, several Christian Right organizations, as well as the Public Affairs Committee of the Southern Baptist Convention, lobbied the Senate to confirm Judge Robert Bork, an abortion opponent, to the Supreme Court. This was the first time that any Southern Baptist Convention agency had endorsed a judicial nominee, and some Southern Baptists were dismayed that their denomination had embarked on a "radical departure from Baptist policy." Bork's nomination failed, but Christian Right leaders continued to campaign for the administration's objectives. In 1988, in the midst of the Iran-Contra scandal, Falwell created a legal defense fund on behalf of Lieutenant Colonel Oliver North, a Reagan aide who was facing charges in the affair.[69]

Other disappointments followed. Christian Right leaders were shocked when Reagan engaged in nuclear reduction talks with Soviet president Mikhail Gorbachev and agreed to the Intermediate-Range Nuclear Forces (INF) Treaty, which required the United States to remove some of its nuclear missiles from Western Europe. The treaty was a "trap designed to seriously weaken NATO," Falwell's *Liberty Report* said. Yet rather than blame the treaty on a president whom it admired, the Moral Majority criticized the Democratic Senate for ratifying it.[70]

A few months later, evangelicals faced an additional upset when former administration officials revealed that Nancy Reagan relied heavily on astrology. Conservative evangelicals viewed astrology as an occult practice associated with paganism, and they were angry that the First Lady, whom they had viewed as a Christian woman, was a practitioner. The president needed to "put a halt to horoscope reading in his house," Tim LaHaye declared.[71]

Falwell remained loyal to the president despite his disappointments with the administration. Reagan, he said in 1986, had been the "finest President since Lincoln." But the pastor also began to distance himself from politics, because he felt that his political commitments had taken a toll on his church, college, and television ministries, which were facing financial challenges. "From now on," Falwell said in November 1987, "my real platform is the pulpit, not politics."[72]

Reagan had given conservative evangelicals public visibility and rhetorical support, and for that reason he earned their lasting gratitude. But he had given them few legislative achievements. Abortion was still legal, and school prayer was not. Evangelicals who had been worried about gay rights and pornography in the late 1970s had just as much reason to be concerned in the late 1980s. Yet evangelicals felt that they could not abandon the Republican Party or their political activism. Reagan's verbal support for their causes had given them hope that victory was in sight. His presidency had also launched the political careers of a few evangelicals. White House policy adviser Gary Bauer and Secretary of the Interior Don Hodel would capitalize on their political experience to become leading Christian Right lobbyists.

By the end of Reagan's presidency, evangelicals were frustrated, but also more determined than ever to seek political power. In October 1987, one month before Falwell announced his retirement from political activity, Pat Robertson told the nation that he was entering politics, not merely to register voters and lobby Congress, but to run for president. If Reagan had been unable to give the Christian Right what it wanted, perhaps a conservative evangelical in the White House could.

P AT ROBERTSON'S BID FOR THE Republican presidential nomination in 1988 shocked the GOP establishment. Never before had the party's presidential aspirants had to run against someone who spoke in tongues and practiced faith-healing. Neil Bush, the son of the vice president, called Robertson's supporters "cockroaches issuing out from underneath the baseboard of the South," while the chair of Michigan's Republican Party compared them to "the bar scene out of *Star Wars*." But when Robertson tied Vice President George Bush for first place in an early contest in Michigan, and then celebrated by sending out a letter proclaiming, "THE CHRISTIANS HAVE WON! . . . What a victory for the Kingdom," Republicans' snide denigrations of evangelical voters turned to dismay at their political power. They realized that the Religious Right might be "a viable force and not the ghost or phantom that some people have imagined."[1]

The power that evangelicals thought they had grasped proved to be elusive. From the failure of Pat Robertson's campaign in 1988 to conservatives' inability to remove President Bill Clinton from office in 1999, Christian Right leaders experienced repeated setbacks. Yet even in the absence of legislative victories, they managed to secure a controlling interest in the Republican Party. Despite the reluctance of mainstream Republicans to give them a seat at the table, Christian Right activists such as Pat Robertson were determined to force their way into the party's leadership. Because they had the votes on their side, they could not be ignored.

Pat Robertson's Presidential Campaign

Pat Robertson seemed to be an ideal candidate to challenge the party's "country club" establishment on behalf of evangelicals. He was a wealthy business owner and a senator's son. He was telegenic and personable. Most important, he had avoided many of the controversies in which Falwell and the Moral Majority had become embroiled. After a brief involvement in the Christian Right in the late 1970s and early 1980s, he had retreated from the political scene and concentrated on building his media empire. Regent University, which he founded in 1978, expanded to include a graduate school, and his television network continued to add new markets until it became the third largest cable network in the United States. By the mid-1980s, Robertson's ministries operated on an annual budget of $230 million, $30 million of which he distributed to the needy through Operation Blessing. His daily 700 *Club* news talk show, which was carried on 190 television stations in addition to the CBN cable network, continued to attract guests that ranged in political ideology from Jesse Jackson to George Will. At the end of 1985, Nielsen ratings showed that 27 million Americans tuned in to a 700 *Club* broadcast at least once a month.[2]

Even as he publicly professed nonpartisanship, Robertson engaged in a variety of political efforts that largely escaped media scrutiny. He used his Freedom Council to lobby for the rights of Christians to assert their faith in the public sphere, and he employed three hundred lawyers to defend Christians in religious liberty cases throughout the country. While Falwell received criticism from the media for his public promotion of the school prayer amendment, the Freedom Council worked quietly with the Reagan administration to lobby for the amendment in Congress. Robertson also promoted the Reagan administration's agenda on his television show, and he used his financial resources for conservative causes, sending millions of dollars in aid to the anti-Marxist Nicaraguan contras and to several right-wing Central American governments. "Robertson understands politics . . . better than anyone else in the Religious Right," Paul Weyrich wrote in 1985.[3]

In March 1985, two *Saturday Evening Post* reporters interviewed Robertson and concluded that he might be interested in the White House. Reagan had been a good president, Robertson acknowledged, but he was not conservative enough. The president ostensibly favored fiscal responsibility, but the budget deficit was ballooning and social welfare programs were thriving. Robertson felt that the country needed a president who would "take a meat ax to the federal budget," address the "ticking time bomb" of Social Security, and "change the court's abortion policy" by appointing conservative justices to the nation's highest court. In typical fashion, though, Robertson shrugged off any suggestion that he run for office until he had received a sign from God.[4]

By the spring of 1986, Robertson had decided that the Lord was urging him to run, and he entered the race for the White House in earnest. He chose the Michigan Republican delegate selection process as one of his earliest targets. With his multimillion-dollar television ministry and the names of millions of potential donors at his disposal, Robertson easily outspent his Republican rivals and mobilized grassroots support by communicating with born-again Christians through a network of conservative charismatic churches. As a result, Robertson matched Bush's delegate count in Michigan. Robertson supporters won similar bids for party takeovers in Virginia and South Carolina. Now a potentially serious candidate, Robertson began touring the country to speak on political issues. As a master of the populist gesture, he told the press in the fall of 1986 that he would run for office only if he received 3 million petitions from supporters who pledged to "pray . . . work . . . [and] give" for his candidacy.[5]

A year later, Robertson announced that he had received the requisite number of petitions, and with dramatic flair, he invited reporters to view the petitions at a press conference that coincided with the two hundredth anniversary of the signing of the Constitution. He then made his official declaration of candidacy not in front of his Virginia mansion, but on the steps of the Bedford-Stuyvesant boardinghouse that he had left in 1960. In a sign that his campaign would adopt a decidedly populist tone, Robertson told voters that despite his upper-class background and personal wealth, he was a candidate who had once lived in the slums of New York and was therefore someone who "care[d] about people."[6]

Some conservative political commentators, including Paul Weyrich and Joseph Coors, thought that Robertson could defeat party heavyweights, such as George Bush and Bob Dole, by taking almost all of the Christian Right vote, while simultaneously appealing to non-evangelical Republicans with his personable image and affability. As a former Democrat who had waited until 1984 to join the Republican Party, Robertson retained a populist economic vision that some thought might appeal to blue-collar Reagan Democrats. His antiestablishment economic proposals included a constitutional amendment to cancel all private debts every fifty years.[7]

Robertson assumed that the Christian Right would be his base of support. In late 1985, before announcing his candidacy, he convened a meeting of the leading Christian Right activists in America. Some gave Robertson their endorsement, because they knew that he, far more than any previous presidential candidate, was one of their own. "For the first time in human history the possibility definitely exists that the hand that lays on that Bible to take the oath of the highest office in the land will be joined to a shoulder and a hand and a heart that's saved by the blood of Jesus and baptized in the Holy Spirit," Jimmy Swaggart told a Louisiana congregation.[8]

But many other evangelicals refused to support Robertson. Some did not want to tie their fortunes to a candidate they did not think could win. Others, especially those from a noncharismatic fundamentalist background, did not want a tongues-speaking miracle worker as their political representative. A poll of delegates to the National Association of Evangelicals' annual conference in March 1987 showed that only 13 percent of the evangelical pastors in attendance supported Robertson, while 34 percent favored Bob Dole, 23 percent endorsed Jack Kemp, and 21 percent supported George Bush. Ed McAteer briefly supported Kemp in 1986 before deciding to cast his lot with Bush. Tim and Beverly LaHaye volunteered their services for Kemp and became national cochairs of his campaign. The nation's most prominent Christian Right leader, Jerry Falwell, continued to support Bush.[9]

Without the backing of Falwell, the LaHayes, or most of the nation's Baptist pastors, Robertson had to attract his support primarily from charismatics. Two-thirds of Robertson's campaign donors described themselves as charismatic Christians, and 85 percent had previously made a contribution to *The 700 Club*. Charismatics had traditionally been the least politically active evangelicals, so most of Robertson's supporters were political neophytes. While over half of those who contributed to Bush and Dole's campaigns had made contributions to other presidential campaigns in the past, only 25 percent of Robertson's donors had done so. Ninety-six percent of his delegates had no prior experience at a political convention.[10]

At first, Robertson tried to broaden his appeal by presenting himself as a fiscal conservative and successful business owner. "I'm a lawyer, I'm a businessman, I'm a professional broadcaster, etc., and not a parish priest," Robertson told prospective voters in 1986. In 1987, he resigned his ordination from the Southern Baptist Convention and severed his ties with CBN in order to present himself as a serious contender for a secular political position. While he did not ignore the Christian Right's favorite issues in his campaign, he devoted more attention to economic and foreign policy concerns, mostly hewing to the Republican Party line, but also promising to enact conservative policies that Reagan had never been able to effect. While Reagan had presided over a nearly 300 percent increase in the national debt, Robertson advocated a balanced budget amendment, and he promised a "massive across-the-board review" of federal spending. He attacked social welfare programs as misguided and said that some government offices and programs, including Amtrak subsidies, the Department of Education, and the Small Business Administration, "should be eliminated outright." Instead of allowing an "Establishment monopoly" to continue in public education, he favored a voucher system to promote school choice. He wanted to privatize Social Security and promised to promote tax cuts. Robertson planned to take a tougher line against the Soviet Union than Reagan had in his last years in office, and he would refuse to negotiate with communists or terrorists.[11]

Robertson's efforts to project himself as a mainstream conservative Republican foundered as soon as tapes of his old 700 *Club* broadcasts were released. Some observers recalled that Robertson had frequently practiced faith-healing on television in the 1970s. Fifteen-year-old videotapes showed Robertson, clad in a white-striped sports coat, shouting into the camera, "We come against cancer now and declare it gone in the name of Jesus! Come *out* now! In Jesus's name, high blood pressure give way. . . . Bone spurs are being taken away right now by Jesus! Thank you, Jesus! Thank you, Jesus!"[12] The image hardly matched most Americans' concept of appropriate presidential behavior.

Robertson revised his show in the late 1970s to give more emphasis to news and political discussions, rather than miraculous healing, but these later programs also provided fodder for attacks on his credibility. In the late 1970s and early 1980s, he had devoted many of his broadcasts to predictions of an imminent nuclear Armageddon and a worldwide economic collapse. He also believed that he received revelation directly from God and that the Lord would answer his prayers for miracles. As recently as 1985, Robertson had commanded Hurricane Gloria to veer out to sea so that it would not hit his television broadcasting headquarters in Virginia, and had then cited his successful petition for that divine favor as a sign that he was a suitable candidate for president. "If I couldn't move a hurricane, I could hardly move a nation," he said.[13]

The shenanigans and sexual peccadilloes of other television preachers also hurt Robertson's candidacy. When the public learned that *PTL Club* host Jim Bakker had engaged in illegal financial activities and had had an extramarital affair, they also found out that Bakker had launched his career in television as an assistant to Robertson. There was no hint that Robertson was guilty of the type of sexual and financial improprieties that had plagued Bakker, and in fact, the two had long since separated. But those subtleties were lost on the public. Robertson faced a renewed round of troubles in early 1988, when a photographer caught Jimmy Swaggart, who had endorsed Robertson's presidential candidacy, taking a prostitute to his hotel room. Robertson was so convinced that the news about his fellow televangelist was going to hurt his campaign that he erroneously assumed that the Bush campaign staff had leaked the story to the press. But Robertson also had troubles of his own. When the media discovered that Robertson had possibly exaggerated his experiences in the Korean War, and that he inflated his graduate educational achievements and covered up his premarital sexual activities in the 1950s, many Americans began viewing the candidate as a lying televangelist whom they could not trust.[14]

Nor could Robertson shake off accusations that he wanted to establish a theocracy in America. In 1984, only two years before organizing his presidential campaign, Robertson had published a description of government that struck many in the press as dangerously intolerant and antidemocratic. "Government was instituted by God to bring His law to people and to carry out His will and purposes," Robertson had said. "Perfect government comes from God and is controlled by God. Short of that, the next best government is a limited democracy in which the people acknowledge rights given by God but voluntarily grant government limited power to do those things the people cannot do individually." In 1985, Robertson had said on his television program that people who did not come from the Christian or Jewish faith were not qualified to hold public office. Even after he launched his presidential campaign, he occasionally hinted, despite his frequent protestations to the contrary, that he wanted to make America a Christian nation by tearing down the "wall of separation" that had stood between church and state in America for nearly two centuries. "It's amazing that the Constitution of the United States says nothing about the separation of church and state," Robertson said in June 1986. "That phrase does appear, however, in the Soviet Constitution."[15]

Robertson insisted that he would follow the Constitution, but he cited Andrew Jackson in arguing that he had the right to interpret America's founding document himself, without acceding to the demands of the Supreme Court. Elected officials, he said, could "ignore a Supreme Court ruling if they so choose." *Roe v. Wade*, he said, had been "based on very faulty law," and he made no promise to enforce it.[16]

Some of Robertson's other statements also lent credence to the charge that he was an extremist. As fundamentalists, evangelicals, and right-wing activists had been arguing for decades, Robertson claimed that there was an international conspiracy to undermine American institutions and that Americans could not afford to negotiate with communists—or even cooperate with the

United Nations. Echoing a long-standing fundamentalist suspicion of the international organization, he charged that the UN was an "exercise in futility," a "sounding board for anti-American, anti-Western, and anti-Israel propaganda," and a "forum for anti-American espionage."[17]

Robertson also advocated fiscal policies that were at odds with mainstream conservatism. Throughout the 1980s, Jerry Falwell, as head of the Moral Majority, had championed the economic policies of the Reagan administration. But Robertson drew on an older strain of fundamentalist suspicion of the Eastern "banking elite" and preached a message of class-based populism. The United States should return to the gold standard, he said, and the president should restrict the role of the Federal Reserve. "I would place my duty to God and country far above the demands of the Eastern Liberal Establishment, the international banking community, or any other special interest," Robertson promised. Business conservatives shuddered. A survey of Republican campaign donors showed that one-third of contributors to Bush's campaign viewed Robertson more negatively than they did Democratic presidential aspirant Michael Dukakis, and nearly one-third gave higher ratings to Jesse Jackson than to Robertson.[18]

Robertson blamed the scorn he received on discrimination against evangelical Christians. In its last stages, his candidacy turned into a campaign for the rights of a group he now considered a persecuted minority. When the New York Times and other news publications continued to label Robertson with the pejorative term "televangelist" despite his wish to be described as a "religious broadcaster," Robertson claimed that he was a victim of religious discrimination. "It's like calling a black man a nasty word that begins with an 'N,'" Robertson said, in a comparison that other white evangelicals soon began echoing. Although Robertson's continual references to religious discrimination hardly helped his candidacy among the general populace, his campaign message sparked a new consciousness among conservative evangelicals who began speaking out against the discrimination that they felt they were receiving from the "liberal media."[19]

By the time the primary contests were held, Robertson knew that he could win only with overwhelming evangelical support, which he did not receive. His network of support in charismatic congregations was sufficient to enable him to take second place in Iowa's caucus, which gave his campaign enough momentum to survive an embarrassing fifth-place finish in New Hampshire's primary a week later. But he then placed third—behind Bush and Dole—in the South Carolina primary, carrying only 19 percent of the vote in a state that he had hoped to win. Super Tuesday was also a disappointment. Instead of voting for the "old-time religion," southern Republicans

(40 percent of whom, according to surveys, were fellow born-again Christians) repudiated Robertson and cast their ballots for Bush. Robertson received far more votes in the South than he did in the North, but he did not win a single southern primary.[20] While Robertson's campaign disintegrated, Bush emerged from Super Tuesday as the Republican Party's unofficial nominee.

Robertson had shown that he could do well in caucuses, where his tightly organized, highly motivated supporters could dominate the electoral process. But among the general populace, Robertson could not attract a majority of the voters, even among evangelicals. He won only 9 percent of the Republican vote nationwide.[21]

Robertson emerged from the campaign angry with evangelicals for not uniting behind him and upset with the media for not treating him as a serious politician. His candidacy had divided charismatic Christians from other evangelicals, and the unfavorable attention that he had received in the media caused the Christian Right to lose ground. The experience convinced Robertson that Christians faced widespread discrimination in American society. As other evangelicals came to share this viewpoint, they became increasingly militant in their political activism, believing that they would have to fight to gain any concessions from the GOP establishment.

Disillusionment with Bush

In the early stages of the presidential primaries, when Robertson had still been a credible threat to his candidacy, Republican front-runner George Bush had engaged in an aggressive outreach effort to woo Christian conservatives. His evangelical campaign adviser, Doug Wead, had identified the South's 215 largest evangelical churches and had appointed campaign liaisons to report on the political sympathies of each congregation and entice voters away from Robertson's coalition. Bush had hired Ed McAteer as his official paid liaison to religious conservatives, and he had relied on Jerry Falwell's endorsement to keep Moral Majority leaders from drifting too far into the Robertson camp.

But as soon as Robertson dropped out of the race, all this came to an end. He dropped McAteer from his campaign staff and stopped discussing religious issues. He was willing to meet with Christian Right leaders, but gave them no promises when they asked for his commitment to appoint a few evangelical Christians to the federal judiciary. Bush assumed that Christian conservatives were unlikely to support his liberal Democratic opponent,

Massachusetts governor Michael Dukakis, so he saw no reason to make a special effort to solicit their vote.[22]

As Bush had expected, the Christian Right took an immediate dislike to Dukakis. Falwell said that if the Massachusetts governor succeeded in his bid for the White House, he might become "the only person who could take from Jimmy Carter the dubious honor of being the worst president in U.S. history." But Falwell found it difficult to evince enthusiasm for Bush. If the Republican presidential nominee wanted to get "some fire in the bones of those supporters," Falwell told the press, he needed to pick a pro-life running mate.[23]

Although Senator Dan Quayle (R-IN) lacked national stature, Christian Right leaders were pleased when Bush awarded him the second position on the ticket. Quayle attracted late-night comedy jibes and widespread derision from many Americans, but social conservatives were impressed with his solidly "pro-family" voting record in the Senate. Because Quayle was a faithful member of a theologically conservative Presbyterian church and displayed a keen interest in biblical prophecy, *Eternity* magazine heralded him as a "man of faith who seeks to bring his personal religious views to bear on the issues confronting America." Bush's campaign also appealed to social conservatives by focusing on patriotism, the pledge of allegiance, and "law and order."[24]

On Election Day, evangelicals supported Bush just as strongly as they had supported Reagan four years earlier: 81 percent of white evangelical voters cast their ballots for the Bush-Quayle ticket. Despite this showing, many Christian Right leaders doubted that Bush would do much to advance their agenda. Yet they also felt that they had little choice but to support Bush. During the Reagan administration, they had cut any remaining ties that they had had to the Democrats.[25]

The Bush administration turned out to be even worse for their cause than they had expected. Bush opposed conservative evangelicals' call for funding restrictions for the National Endowment for the Arts, and he ignored their complaints when he invited gay rights activists to the White House. He selected several social liberals for his Cabinet, including a pro-choice doctor to head the Department of Health and Human Services. His first Supreme Court nominee, David Souter, proved to be a reliable vote for abortion rights. By 1991, Pat Robertson was so fed up with the administration that he suggested that the president might be "unknowingly and unwittingly carrying out the mission and mouthing the phrases of a tightly knit cabal whose goal is nothing more than a new world order for the human race under the domination of Lucifer and his followers."[26]

From Moral Majority to Militant Minority

Evangelicals' political frustration was exacerbated by the collapse of most of the major Christian Right organizations at the end of the 1980s. The Moral Majority entered a steep decline after 1985, when Falwell alienated not only African Americans but also several of his own supporters by calling Bishop Desmond Tutu a "phony" and defending the white apartheid South African government. The Moral Majority leader estimated that he had lost $1 million in potential contributions in 1985 as a result of his controversial statements. The next year, he offended some of his supporters again by endorsing Bush instead of Robertson or Kemp, causing his contributions to decline by another 25 percent.[27]

In November 1987, Falwell, who could see the handwriting on the wall, resigned as president of the Moral Majority and entrusted its leadership to Jerry Nims, a California-born millionaire entrepreneur who had been "born again" at a Campus Crusade for Christ rally in the late 1960s and had then studied under Francis Schaeffer in Switzerland. But Nims lacked Falwell's name recognition, and contributions continued to fall. In 1988 the Moral Majority was able to collect only $3.5 million, a mere pittance compared to the $11 million that it had raised in 1984.[28]

Other Christian Right ministries fared just as poorly. In late 1987, public disclosure of some anti-Catholic statements that Tim LaHaye had made in the 1970s alienated him from Catholic conservatives and forced him to resign as cochair of Jack Kemp's presidential campaign. At the same time, charges that his ACTV had accepted a contribution from an associate of Reverend Sun Myung Moon upset some of his conservative evangelical allies. Pat Robertson also experienced financial and political setbacks, because his 700 *Club* had lost a significant number of viewers after he had resigned temporarily from the program during his presidential campaign.[29]

With conservative evangelicals' leading political organizations facing dire financial straits, it came as little surprise that some observers were ready to administer the last rites to the Christian Right and close the books on a movement that had captured the media headlines for the previous eight years. Titles such as *The Rise and Fall of the Christian Right: Conservative Protestant Politics in America, 1979–1988* (1988) and *Fall from Grace: The Failed Crusade of the Christian Right* (1989) began appearing on academic bookshelves, while popular periodicals carried articles such as "Why 'Moral Majority,' a Force for a Decade, Ran Out of Steam." Many evangelical leaders shared the media's pessimistic outlook on the movement's future. Falwell associate

Martin Mawyer complained that the movement's modest achievements over the past eight years had been "far outweighed by our unfinished agenda."[30]

Consciously drawing parallels between their own experience and that of African Americans, evangelicals began claiming that they were victims of "religious persecution" and discrimination, just as Robertson had claimed in his presidential campaign. "We are the last minority," Jerry Falwell said in 1988. "You can no longer attack a man's color, but right today you can refer to fundamentalists as Bible-bangers."[31]

To combat this alleged governmental and societal oppression, conservative evangelicals began to look outside conventional electoral politics. Instead of allying themselves with Republican politicians, most of whom wanted nothing to do with a movement that was now seen as a political albatross, they began considering less orthodox political tactics, such as civil disobedience. Francis Schaeffer had first advocated this tactic in 1981, but most evangelicals, including Jerry Falwell, were reluctant to endorse it, despite their admiration for Schaeffer.[32] By the late 1980s, some of them had changed their minds, partly because of the encouragement of an unconventional evangelical leader—a twenty-eight-year-old used car salesman and part-time preacher from upstate New York named Randall Terry.

Terry was not a person who did anything halfway. As a worldly high school student in the late 1970s, he had thrown himself into the drug scene with abandon, and when he came to Christ as a nineteen-year-old, he immediately renounced his former habits, enrolled in New York's Elim Bible Institute, and prepared to become a missionary to Mexico. But his plans changed again when he saw a screening of Schaeffer's *Whatever Happened to the Human Race?* which moved him to tears. He decided to devote his life to stopping abortion, and founded a new pro-life organization, Operation Rescue, in November 1987. While most other pro-life organizations had focused their efforts on legislative lobbying and peaceful marches, the twenty-eight-year-old Terry began using nonviolent human force to temporarily shut down abortion clinics.[33]

A handful of Catholic activists had tried to obstruct the entrances to abortion clinics in St. Louis and other cities in the late 1970s and early 1980s, but none of them had ever tried to apply this tactic on a national scale. Each of Terry's "rescue" operations succeeded in shutting down an abortion clinic for only a few hours, but the disruptive tactics forced the police to deal with hundreds of pro-life demonstrators, and the large-scale arrests that ensued inevitably attracted national headlines and encouraged recruits to join Operation Rescue. The young antiabortion activist viewed his confrontational tactics as a welcome change from the Christian Right's legislative lobbying, which he considered a failure. "The church has played Mr. Nice Guy," Terry said. "We've said, 'Let's play within the system. Let's be nice. Let's not be confrontational.' And America has slid into the jaws of hell. The Christian community does not control the levers of power in any major institution in this country."[34]

After conducting his first protests in Cherry Hill, New Jersey, in late 1987, Terry quickly expanded his movement to other areas of the country. Like Martin Luther King, Jr., whom he considered his model for civil disobedience, Terry chose target cities on which activists converged in an attempt to overwhelm police forces and make it impossible for anyone to procure an abortion. Terry trained his recruits to let their bodies go limp when they were arrested, to refuse to give their names to police when asked, and to use other nonviolent tactics of resistance in order to take up as much of the police officers' time as possible. Thousands of young evangelicals enlisted in Terry's movement, and their efforts sometimes temporarily overwhelmed local police forces. By December 1988, Operation Rescue demonstrators had faced more than eight thousand arrests nationwide, and by April 1989, that number had doubled.[35]

Terry devoted his most sustained effort to Atlanta, the site of the 1988 Democratic National Convention. Operation Rescue's forces moved into the city in July, during the week of the convention, and began blockading abortion clinics, resulting in the arrests of 134 demonstrators. At the end of the convention, the Operation Rescue activists refused to leave. By October, the Atlanta police, who had at first tried to be gentle with the protestors, were growing increasingly frustrated with Terry's unwillingness to cooperate with authorities, and they began using more heavy-handed tactics against the demonstrators, including the application of "come-along" holds to the necks and jaws of protestors. By December, they had arrested more than twelve hundred demonstrators, including Terry. But many other demonstrators escaped arrest, because as Atlanta's chief of police told the press in October, "With the large number of protestors, we do not have enough officers to carry all of these people."[36]

Before Terry launched Operation Rescue, 90 percent of antiabortion demonstrators were Catholic, but by December 1988, a year after Terry's first nationally publicized protest, 60 percent of the activists were Protestant. Terry's hard-edged style and charismatic preaching offered an attractive alternative to the unsuccessful legislative lobbying on which antiabortion advocates had long relied. Many antiabortion activists were delighted to see Terry regularly featured on the network television news. When they went to jail, they took comfort in the thought that television images of police callously dragging young Operation Rescue protestors across the pavement were moving the public to sympathize with the pro-life cause.[37]

Despite Terry's radical style, he received endorsements from respected evangelical leaders, mainly because he seemed to be able to achieve results that had eluded the mainstream pro-life lobbyists. Charles Colson, the former Nixon aide turned prison minister, expressed his support for Operation Rescue. "If we have exhausted the political process, we have to engage in the act of civil disobedience," Colson said.[38]

Terry's movement became so popular among evangelicals that Falwell, a longtime opponent of civil disobedience, endorsed Operation Rescue by giving the organization a $10,000 donation in the summer of 1988. The pastor who had once preached against the civil rights movement of the 1960s told his supporters that he was "personally joining the civil rights movement for the unborn" and promised that he would make support for Operation Rescue his organization's "*number one* priority" in the upcoming year.[39]

The Christian Right's brief flirtation with civil disobedience ended almost as quickly as it began. Local injunctions against antiabortion protestors forced them to stay off abortion clinics' property or risk paying massive fines that would soon bankrupt them. In 1990, while serving a two-year jail sentence and after paying a $450,000 fine, Terry announced that he would close the national office of Operation Rescue and would shift his focus to assisting pro-life candidates in state legislative races. Federal judges had made it impossible for him to continue a costly campaign of civil disobedience. Despite Terry's statement, Operation Rescue volunteers continued their protests and clinic blockades, and when Terry was released from prison, he rejoined them. Yet his glory days were over. After some antiabortion activists discredited the movement by bombing abortion clinics and shooting abortion doctors, Operation Rescue's popularity among conservative evangelicals experienced a sharp decline. The final blow to Terry's brand of activism came in 1994, when Bill Clinton signed the Freedom of Access to Clinic Entrances Act.[40]

Some Christian Right activists who, like Terry, had become disillusioned with their lack of success joined Rousas John Rushdoony's Christian Reconstructionist movement. Rushdoony, an Orthodox Presbyterian with a doctorate in educational philosophy, called for a sweeping overhaul of society and a replacement of American constitutional measures with the revival of Old Testament law. The Chalcedon Foundation, which he founded in 1965, advocated the reinstitution of slavelike indentured servitude and a restoration of the death penalty for homosexuals, adulterers, and "Sabbath-breakers."

Gary North, a Reconstructionist with a Ph.D. in economic history from the University of California, Riverside, infused the Reconstructionist legal code of the Old Testament with laissez-faire economics. North's books argued that if the Mosaic law code of the Old Testament were revived, church tithes could replace the income tax, and private charity could replace the government's social programs. The federal government was largely unnecessary, North said. In his opinion, almost all policy making should occur at the local level, and the federal government's only function should be the protection of property rights.[41]

Rushdoony's claim of 20 million Reconstructionists was highly exaggerated, but he did influence a few prominent individuals in the Christian Right. Randall Terry never became a full-fledged Reconstructionist, but after the failure of Operation Rescue he became increasingly sympathetic to the idea of imposing divine law on the nation through some form of theocracy. At a banquet for Human Life International, a Catholic antiabortion group, Terry proclaimed, "We need to preach the law and we need to say unashamedly that our goal is a Christian nation. Either God has called us to extend His law over all the earth or He hasn't."[42]

Other former activists in the Christian Right became full converts to Reconstructionism. Colonel Doner, who had helped launch Christian Voice in 1979, exchanged conservative lobbying for Rushdoony's radical program because he had become frustrated with the Christian Right's lack of substantive legislative gains. "It was clear that other than guaranteeing the election of Ronald Reagan . . . who immediately surrounded himself with moderates, technocrats, liberals of all shapes and sizes, astrologers, effete social climbers and assorted half wits, we had accomplished very little of lasting value," Doner wrote in 1994. "As a mobilizer and strategist I had raised and expended over 20 *million* dollars (and only God knows how many man hours) . . . and for what?!?! What was the final payoff—George Bush?"[43]

Fringe movements such as Operation Rescue and Reconstructionism were no more successful in achieving substantive political results than the Moral Majority had been. But among the many Christian Right organizations that emerged in the late 1980s, one group did succeed in capturing Washington's attention: the Christian Coalition, which capitalized on evangelicals' feeling of disfranchisement while simultaneously delivering them substantial influence in the GOP. By the mid-1990s, the Christian Right was more powerful than ever, primarily due to the efforts of Christian Coalition founder Pat Robertson and his politically savvy associate Ralph Reed.

The Christian Coalition

The Christian Coalition was born of political disillusionment. Robertson had ended the election year of 1988 in a despondent mood. He had lost his bid for the White House, but rather than abandon politics, he decided to enter Washington through the back door by becoming a lobbyist. His campaign mailing list, he decided, would make an ideal base for a new Religious Right organization.

In January 1989, Robertson recruited Ralph Reed, a young Republican activist in Atlanta, Georgia, to be his partner. Reed, whom Robertson barely knew, may have seemed an unusual choice for the position. He had been a born-again Christian for only five years. He had supported Jack Kemp, rather than Robertson, in the 1988 Republican presidential primaries. As a twenty-seven-year-old Ph.D. student in the history department at Emory University, Reed assumed that after he completed his dissertation on nineteenth-century southern evangelical colleges, he would find a university teaching position.[44] But he was intrigued by Robertson's proposal to create a new Christian Right organization, and he soon decided to alter his career plans.

Reed's work as a Republican activist in the early 1980s foreshadowed the political stratagems that he later used as a leader of the Christian Coalition. As an undergraduate at the University of Georgia, Reed had served as president of the College Republicans, and he had quickly established a reputation as a "fire-eating Republican" who was, according to one of his campus associates, "on the far right of every issue." His columns in the student paper had lampooned Mohandas Gandhi as the "ninny of the 20th century" and had called abortion "black genocide" because of the high percentage of African Americans who resorted to the procedure. Reed made few converts through his brash newspaper columns, but that did not matter, because he knew how to gain power through more dubious means. He forced a split in the College Republicans by secretly engineering what one of his co-conspirators later conceded was a "dirty election" in which 150 students who had never been to a meeting agreed to join the organization and vote for Reed's chosen candidate in exchange for a free keg party. One of his classmates complained that Reed "was about winning at any cost," an attitude that earned him the campus nickname "tricky Ralph."[45]

While he was successful, Reed was also unhappy. He was intellectually brilliant and had won the University of Georgia's prize for the best senior essay in history, but he had few real friends or admirers. He drank to excess. Even one of his fellow College Republicans characterized Reed as a "hard-driving, chain-smoking, wheeling-dealing, dirty politician." When Reed moved to Washington to take a position at the National College Republicans—where he later became executive director—he discovered that the "pursuit of power" was "an empty and unsatisfying exercise without a moral compass." Then he found God. He visited a local evangelical church one Sunday morning in 1983 and had a "born-again" conversion experience. He gave up smoking and drinking, sent written apologies to some of the people he had hurt in the past, and announced to his former classmates that his life had changed.[46]

After his conversion, Reed made Christian Right causes the center of his political program. He founded Students for America, a Christianized version of the Young Americans for Freedom, in order to promote Jerry Falwell's brand of politics on college campuses across the nation. In 1985, he participated in civil disobedience at an abortion clinic and faced arrest for publicly reading the Bible inside a clinic waiting room. But although Reed Christianized his message, "he didn't change his views," one of his classmates recalled. "He just found out that God agreed with him."[47]

Reed and Robertson hoped that the Christian Coalition would fill the "tremendous vacuum" that the demise of the Moral Majority had left. Robertson served as the public face for the new organization, while Reed, the consummate political strategist, provided the organizational skills. By the end of 1990, the Coalition had fifty-seven thousand members and an annual budget of $2.8 million. Most of that money came in small donations from people who had supported Robertson's presidential campaign, but in a sign that the Christian Coalition's fortunes were closely allied with the GOP, Reed also secured a $64,000 contribution from the Republican Senatorial Committee. By January 1992, the organization claimed one-hundred fifty thousand members, organized into 210 local chapters.[48]

With its headquarters located in a nondescript warehouse in Tidewater, Virginia, far outside the Washington Beltway, the Christian Coalition intentionally avoided publicity. Reed hoped to avoid the public relations mistakes that had plagued Jerry Falwell. Instead of fanfare, he sought results, and to achieve them, he concentrated on grassroots organizing.[49]

The Christian Coalition capitalized on Christians' feelings that they were quickly becoming a "persecuted" minority. "You can't legitimately govern a country when you are being consistently and systematically ridiculed as hayseeds, boobs, bigots and snake oil salesmen," Reed told potential recruits. He pledged to focus on alleged anti-Christian governmental policies, including the National Endowment for the Arts' funding of controversial art. This appealed to many conservative evangelicals, who saw no reason why their tax dollars should fund art that mocked their religious beliefs. Tom Minnery, a

Focus on the Family staff member, wrote in 1990, "Place a crucifix in a jar of urine, pose it in a public gallery, and you get a federal subsidy. Place a figure of the Christ in a manger, pose it on a public lawn, and you get a federal lawsuit."[50]

Reed and Robertson promised to lead beleaguered Christians into the halls of power, a tantalizing prospect for evangelicals who had begun to doubt they would ever realize the promises of the Moral Majority. "I honestly believe that in my lifetime we will see a country once again governed by Christians . . . and Christian values," Reed said. But it would have to be a gradual process, and Christians would have to demonstrate patience as they learned the secrets of the political game from Reed, the Christian Coalition's master strategist. Reed thought that previous Christian Right organizations had "missed the boat in the 1980s" by focusing on national political offices while ignoring local political structures. Unlike Falwell, Reed realized that his supporters were only a small minority of the population, so he concentrated on bringing his supporters to the polls in city council and school board elections, where a small number of activists could easily change the course of an election. "We think the Lord is going to give us this nation back one precinct at a time, one neighborhood at a time, and one state at a time," Reed said in 1990. "We're not going to win it all at once with some kind of millennial rush at the White House."[51]

Reed first tested his new political strategy in San Diego in November 1990. On the Sunday before Election Day, Christian Coalition representatives visited the parking lots of the city's evangelical and Catholic churches and distributed flyers urging Christians to vote for a "pro-life, pro-family future" by casting their ballots for one of the city council and school board candidates that Reed's organization had endorsed. Two-thirds of the eighty-eight candidates that Reed had backed in San Diego won election. It was a stunning upset in a city that normally shunned right-wing candidates, and it was possible only because Reed, by his own admission, had surprised his opponents with "guerilla warfare" and a "stealth" attack.[52]

The next year, Reed and Robertson targeted their own neighborhood in Virginia Beach. The Christian Coalition distributed one hundred thousand voter guides there in November 1991 and conducted a telephone campaign to bring conservative voters to the polls. But rather than simply relying on church voter mobilization campaigns, Reed reached out to non-evangelical Republicans. Only 28 percent of Reed's targeted voters in Virginia Beach opposed abortion, but Reed persuaded them to vote for conservative evangelical candidates by focusing on other issues, such as crime and education, in his telephone survey and direct-mail advertising campaign. As a result,

Republicans won seven of the nine races in Virginia Beach, a result that surprised local political experts.[53]

Unlike Falwell, Robertson and Reed did not publicize their vote-getting efforts in advance; instead they preferred to strike before their opponents were aware of what they were doing. Having seen the opposition that some state Republican Party leaders had directed at Robertson's candidacy in 1988, Christian Coalition leaders felt it was best not to attract undue attention. "You should never mention the name Christian Coalition in Republican circles," one Christian Coalition manual advised. "I want to be invisible," Reed explained, in one of his frequent references to military tactics. "I do guerilla warfare. I paint my face and travel at night. You don't know it's over until you're in a body bag. You don't know until election night."[54]

Whereas earlier Christian Right leaders had encouraged pastors to conduct voter mobilization campaigns in their churches, Reed went beyond that by purchasing eleven thousand church directories from congregations in central Florida, and then comparing the names in those membership rosters with Republican voter registration lists in order to determine whom he needed to target with election information. Reed also knew that it was just as important for him to decrease Democratic voter turnout as it was to increase the turnout among Republicans. He did not want Democrats "to know there's an election going on," he said. "I'm serious," he added. "We don't want them to know."[55]

While Reed infused the Christian Right with a political sophistication that it had once lacked, Robertson rallied the faithful with tried-and-true rhetoric. "America is at a crossroads," Robertson proclaimed in January 1992, in a message that closely echoed the sermons that Falwell had preached twelve years earlier. "Either she returns to her Christian roots and then goes on to further greatness, or she will continue to legalize sodomy, slaughter innocent babies, destroy the minds of her children, squander her resources, and sink into oblivion. I believe that God has raised up the Christian Coalition to restore America to greatness."[56]

The Christian Coalition claimed to be nonpartisan, but it was more closely allied with the Republican Party than any previous Christian Right organization had been, and it exercised an unprecedented degree of influence in the party. The Coalition's 1991 Road to Victory conference featured several sessions on how to become a delegate to the Republican National Convention, while a session that instructed members how to become a delegate to the Democratic National Convention did not attract even a single participant. In his election efforts in Virginia Beach, Reed had refused to give out election information to voters who informed him that they were registered

Democrats who had voted for Michael Dukakis in 1988. Despite its protestations to the contrary, the organization was almost exclusively Republican. "It is impossible for a Christian to vote for a Democrat," one delegate to the Coalition's 1992 Road to Victory conference declared, to a round of applause.[57]

If evangelical Christians had become Republicans, the Republican Party had also become Christianized, and it was becoming increasingly difficult to tell the difference between the Christian Coalition's issue positions and the GOP platform. "We want . . . to see a working majority of the Republican Party in the hands of pro-family Christians by 1996," Robertson told his supporters at a Christian Coalition conference in September 1991. By the following summer, evangelicals were already well on their way to that goal: Christian Coalition members and their allies held over one-third of the seats on the Republican National Committee in the summer of 1992, and they comprised a majority in ten state Republican Party organizations.[58]

The Christian Coalition solidified its control in the Republican Party with a strategic decision to support George Bush over his conservative challenger, Patrick Buchanan, in the 1992 Republican presidential primaries. The choice was in some ways a surprising one for an organization founded by a man who had once challenged Bush for the presidential nomination and who had never liked him. Many evangelicals supported the candidacy of the strongly pro-life, culturally conservative Buchanan. A poll that Robertson conducted of his national television audience showed that 71 percent of his Republican viewers favored Buchanan, while only 29 percent supported the president. But when the Bush campaign appealed to the Christian Coalition for help, Reed seized the opportunity. Reed wanted to develop a long-term relationship between social conservatives and the GOP, and he reasoned that even if evangelicals disagreed with Bush on a few issues, it was important for them to work from within the party. "We went through one suicide mission in 1988," Reed said, in a reference to Robertson's unsuccessful presidential campaign. "And we won't do it again."[59]

As Bush moved to the right to regain the loyalty of disaffected evangelicals, conservative Christians' influence in the party increased, just as Reed had hoped. The "culture war"—a conflict depicted as God versus gays and feminists versus families—became the predominant theme of the Republican campaign. In February, Dan Quayle spoke at Bob Jones University, while Bush addressed the NAE the following month. In May, Quayle denounced the *Murphy Brown* show for promoting out-of-wedlock pregnancies, and in June, he defended his remarks before an enthusiastic audience at the Southern Baptist Convention. The Republicans' culture war rhetoric reached a crescendo at the party convention, which included a "God and Country" rally keynoted by Robertson. Yet the most polarizing remarks at the convention came not from the religious broadcasters but from Pat Buchanan, whose prime-time address characterized the presidential election as a "religious war" that conservatives had to win in order to preserve the country's moral values. "In that struggle for the soul of America, Clinton and Clinton are on one side, and George Bush is on our side," Buchanan said.[60]

The Democrats presented the first presidential ticket in history that featured two Southern Baptists—Bill Clinton and Al Gore. But Clinton and Gore's religious affiliation did not endear them to Christian Right activists. As pro-choice Democrats who supported gay rights, they represented the opposing side in the culture wars. Hillary Clinton's professional career and Bill Clinton's philandering and youthful experimentation with marijuana only confirmed conservative evangelicals' doubts about the Democratic ticket. "To vote for Bill Clinton is to sin against God," Randall Terry proclaimed in a flyer that he distributed to one hundred thousand socially conservative pastors shortly before the election.[61]

Bush received only 38 percent of the popular vote, but 63 percent of all evangelicals—and 70 percent of evangelicals who regularly attended church—voted for his reelection, while only 18 percent of churchgoing evangelicals voted for Clinton. This strong Republican loyalty at a time when other voters were deserting President Bush reflected a shift in evangelicals' party identification. By 1992, only 21 percent of churchgoing evangelicals were Democrats, a decline from 55 percent in 1960. Evangelicals had become too committed to the GOP to reject a Republican president even if they had reservations about him. And Republican presidential candidates had become too beholden to the evangelical vote to be able to ignore the demands of the Christian Right, because they could not count on the support of any other demographic group.[62]

After the election, Reed felt confident enough about his own position in the GOP to abandon his "stealth strategy" and campaign openly for conservative Republican candidates. By 1994, the Coalition controlled eighteen state Republican parties and exercised a strong influence in thirteen others. While pundits prognosticated about the Christian Right's ineffectiveness in the wake of Bill Clinton's victory, the Christian Coalition realized the fund-raising potential that conservative ire against Clinton presented. By early 1994, Reed's mailing list included 1.3 million people, most of whom had made at least a small contribution to his organization during the previous four months.[63]

When GOP victories in the 1994 midterm elections put both houses of Congress in Republican hands for the first time in four decades, the Christian Coalition initiated a $1 million campaign to promote House Speaker Newt Gingrich's (R-GA) "Contract with America." At the same time, Reed unveiled his "Contract with the American Family," which demanded congressional votes on antipornography measures, parental rights legislation, and other hallmarks of the social conservatives' agenda, some of which the House considered. As Reed's political influence increased, so did the Christian Coalition's revenues. By 1996, the organization collected $26 million annually, more than double the $11 million that Moral Majority had raised at the height of its influence in 1984.[64]

The Christian Coalition benefited from a national party polarization that had produced a large-scale shift of white southern conservatives into the Republican Party. For most of the late twentieth century, white southerners generally voted for Republican presidential candidates, but they could still find many conservative Democrats to support in congressional and gubernatorial elections. As a result, Republicans won only about a third of senatorial and gubernatorial elections in the South during the 1980s, and only 40 percent during the early 1990s. But after 1994, Republican fortunes changed in the South. By that point, most conservative southern Democratic politicians had joined the Republican Party, and Gingrich's "Contract with America" had transformed the Republican Congress into a national symbol of conservatism at the same time that popular right-wing radio talk show hosts such as Rush Limbaugh were lambasting the Democratic Party as a corrupt, liberal organization representing high taxes and a "socialist" agenda. White southerners who had long identified as Democrats felt comfortable switching to the Republican Party, while first-time voters in the South were far more likely than their parents to register as Republicans. From 1994 to 1997, Republicans won 73 percent of the region's senatorial and gubernatorial races.[65]

By dominating southern Republican Party chapters, the Christian Coalition ensured that the GOP would nominate socially conservative candidates in local races. During the early 1980s, fewer than half of Republican candidates in senatorial and gubernatorial races had been social conservatives, but in the mid-1990s, 74 percent of them were. Although some Republicans worried that the Christian Right's success in nominating strongly pro-life, anti-gay-rights candidates would alienate moderate voters and hurt the party in general elections, Christian conservatives did succeed in electing several socially conservative governors, including, in 1994, Fob James in Alabama and David Beasley in South Carolina, and in 1998, Mike Huckabee in Arkansas and Jeb Bush in Florida. They also elected many social conservatives to Congress.[66]

Reed's success made him a national sensation. In May 1995, *Time* said that the young Christian Coalition executive director was "master of a much more powerful and effective machine than is almost any presidential candidate." Reed seemed to concur with that assessment. In early 1995 he turned down an offer to become political director of Texas senator Phil Gramm's presidential campaign, because he realized that he had more influence over GOP policy as head of the Christian Coalition than he would have in Gramm's operation.[67]

Reed knew that his Coalition's success could not continue if it were based only on a narrow appeal to white, southern, born-again Christians who objected to abortion and gay rights, so he attempted to broaden his coalition to include people who had not traditionally allied with the Christian Right. He launched Catholic Alliance in order to reach out to Catholics who had traditionally been uneasy about cooperating with conservative evangelical Protestants. He also made a special effort to recruit African Americans for anti-gay-rights campaigns, educational issues, and other political causes that he thought would resonate with the African American church community. "I want the Christian Coalition to be the truly rainbow coalition," Reed told an interviewer in 1995. "I want it to bring Christians of all faith traditions, all denominations, and all races and colors together."[68]

Reed's attempt to broaden his coalition necessitated a compromise of the Christian Right's original agenda, which presented a dilemma for his organization. The Christian Right's fund-raising depended on Reed and Robertson's ability to direct social conservatives' anger against abortion and, increasingly, gay rights, which became Christian conservatives' chief target in the early 1990s. But Reed knew that the candidates who could win election in the emerging Republican Sunbelt were often economic rather than social conservatives and that if he wanted to preserve his influence in the GOP, he would have to support some of the South's pro-choice Republican politicians. Accordingly, the Christian Coalition endorsed the senatorial campaigns of Kay Bailey Hutchinson (R-TX) and Paul Coverdell (R-GA), both of whom supported abortion rights in at least some circumstances.[69]

Similarly, Reed made a tactical decision to campaign for Republican issues that had never been the primary focus of the traditional Christian Right agenda. In 1993, at a time when President Clinton was instituting his "don't ask, don't tell" policy to allow gays to serve in the military and was repealing restrictions on federal funding of abortion, Reed turned his attention to other issues and announced that his top legislative priority for the year would be a middle-class tax cut, which Newt Gingrich designated as the centerpiece of the House Republican budget proposal. In addition, Reed enlisted the Christian Coalition in a campaign against Clinton's health care proposal by sending out 30 million postcards outlining his opposition to the plan. Similarly, in 1994, the Christian Coalition did not object when Gingrich's "Contract with America," the document that provided a unified strategy for the Republicans who won a new majority in the House of Representatives that year, ignored abortion, gay rights, and school prayer. "The pro-family movement has limited its effectiveness by concentrating disproportionately on issues such as abortion and homosexuality," Reed wrote. "These are vital moral issues, and must remain an important part of the message. To win at the ballot box and in the court of public opinion, however, the pro-family movement must speak to the concerns of average voters in the areas of taxes, crime, government waste, health care, and financial security." Exit polls indicated that only 12 percent of voters allowed a presidential candidate's position on abortion to determine their voting choice, so to retain their influence, Christian conservatives would have to learn to talk about other issues.[70]

Many evangelicals repudiated Reed's strategy. The Christian Coalition had become the "mistress of the Republican Party," Randall Terry complained in 1994, and had betrayed "the sacred law of heaven for short-term political gain." Gary Bauer, president of the Family Research Council, spoke for many Christian conservatives when he warned Reed that his compromises with the Republican Party leadership would cost him the support of true believers. "Ralph is going to have to be really careful to not end up a leader without a following," Bauer warned.[71]

James Dobson's Focus on the Family

Reed received the most damaging criticism from James Dobson. Unlike most of the leaders of the Christian Right, Dobson was neither a pastor nor a political strategist. He had grown up in Oklahoma in the 1940s as the son of a Church of the Nazarene minister, but rather than follow his father into the ministry, he had decided to pursue psychology. After earning a Ph.D. at the University of Southern California, he became a professor of pediatrics in USC's School of Medicine and a researcher at the Los Angeles Children's Hospital.[72]

Dobson's conservative religious beliefs put him at odds with much of his profession. He opposed the era's permissive trends in child-rearing practices, and in 1970, he struck back with the parenting guide *Dare to Discipline*. Dobson encouraged parents to set clear guidelines with their children instead of capitulating to their whims, and to use corporal punishment when necessary. The book was an instant success; it sold over 2 million copies, and it launched Dobson's speaking career. During the next decade, he traveled across the nation to evangelical churches that wanted to hear his parenting insights, turned his lectures on parental discipline into a widely distributed film series, and produced several more best-selling books about family matters.[73]

Buoyed by this success, Dobson launched a national radio program, *Focus on the Family*, in 1977. He dispensed advice on a wide range of family concerns, including parenting, marital issues, divorce recovery, advice for singles, and caring for elderly parents, all of which he and his cohosts discussed from a Christian perspective. Dobson's books and radio shows found a ready audience, particularly among evangelical women who were delighted to discover a Christian psychologist who seemed to understand their problems. By 1991, when Dobson moved his organization from Pomona, California, to a forty-seven-acre campus in Colorado Springs, he employed nine hundred staff members and was receiving so much mail that the post office assigned Focus on the Family its own zip code. By 1995, *Focus on the Family* was the third most popular radio broadcast in America, right behind Rush Limbaugh and Paul Harvey. Dobson's mailing list had 3.5 million names, which far exceeded the size of Ralph Reed's.[74]

Throughout the late 1970s and 1980s, Dobson dabbled in politics without ever becoming a major figure in the Christian Right. The liberal tone of the national International Women's Year conference in 1977 turned him against the Carter administration. Carter "appointed the most radical feminists of the day to run the event," Dobson recalled years later. When Carter announced a White House Conference on Families in 1980, Dobson encouraged his supporters to lobby the executive director of the conference, James Guy Tucker, to give him a spot on the panel. After receiving eighty thousand letters from Dobson's supporters, Tucker invited him to join the proceedings. That gave Dobson an opportunity to meet with the president, but it did not endear him to his administration.[75]

Dobson had admired Ronald Reagan ever since the late 1960s, so when the former California governor became president, he was elated. During the Reagan administration, he served on the Attorney General's Commission on Pornography and contributed to a report that accused pornography of encouraging violence against women. He also lobbied for the president's agenda by encouraging his supporters to call the Capitol Hill switchboard in support of the school prayer amendment and the confirmation of Robert Bork to the Supreme Court. In 1985, he met with the president to discuss lobbying strategies for the Reagan administration's tax proposals, which he promoted on his radio program and in his capacity as cochair of Americans for Tax Reform. Domestic policy adviser Gary Bauer noted in a 1987 White House memo, "When Focus on the Family is asked by Reagan administration aides to lobby for an issue, they respond with convincing and informative media campaigns to bolster the President's proposals in the public eye and on the Hill." That same year, the White House held a dinner for Dobson to honor his service to the administration.[76]

Dobson created the Family Research Council (FRC) in 1983 in order to be able to engage in lobbying that Focus, as a tax-exempt, nonprofit organization, was legally prohibited from conducting. But unlike other Christian Right leaders, Dobson kept his political activities out of public view, which allowed him to maintain a nonpartisan public image throughout the 1980s. He concentrated on his radio show and best-selling books. Sensitive to any suggestion from his associates that he might be becoming too political, he allowed the FRC to founder until 1989, when he recruited Gary Bauer to head the organization.[77]

Bauer had grown up a Southern Baptist in a working-class family in the steel mill town of Newport, Kentucky, and had attended Georgetown University, where he was a classmate of Bill Clinton. After earning his law degree, he began doing political work for the Republican Party in Kentucky and then volunteered for Reagan's presidential campaign in 1980. He appeared to share the typical policy concerns of most other Reagan Republicans, such as tax cuts and deregulation. But when Reagan gave him an appointment in his administration, he surprised some of his colleagues by devoting more attention to social conservatism than to other policy issues. He interjected his moral beliefs into reports such as "The Family: Preserving America's Future" and became such a strong opponent of abortion that First Lady Nancy Reagan, along with Chief of Staff Donald Regan, asked him to tone it down. Bauer ignored their requests, which earned him the admiration of Dobson, who invited him to make several guest appearances on his radio show. When Dobson put him in charge of the FRC, he knew that Bauer would use his insider knowledge of Washington politics to defend social conservatives' interests.[78]

Bauer did not disappoint. Under his leadership, the FRC became a formidable lobbying force that eventually surpassed the Christian Coalition in influence. By the end of the decade, the FRC had a staff of 120 and a mailing list of nearly five hundred thousand.[79]

Publicly, Dobson continued to project an apolitical image and acted as though he was content to let Bauer take care of political lobbying, while he stuck to the family advising that had made him so successful. Surveys of pastors showed that Dobson was the second-most-admired evangelical leader after Billy Graham, and he was wary of compromising that influence by appearing to be too partisan.[80]

But Dobson escalated his political activities in the late 1980s and early 1990s. In 1988, he launched a new magazine, *Focus on the Family Citizen*, to inform evangelicals about political issues that affected them. Although Focus on the Family advertised the magazine as a nonpartisan, issues-oriented publication, its pages included a lot more political strategizing than Dobson wanted to admit. During its first two years of publication, the magazine criticized Michael Dukakis and applauded George Bush, and then published an article urging the new president to consider District Court Judge Kenneth Starr, who would later become well known as a special prosecutor of President Bill Clinton, for a Supreme Court appointment. The magazine supported Clarence Thomas's nomination to the Court, lauded the sentiments that Dan Quayle expressed in his "Murphy Brown" speech, and thanked President Bush for the efforts that he made to restrict abortion. Occasionally the magazine put in a favorable word for a socially conservative Democrat, but in general, the magazine supported the Republican Party's policies on social issues. President Bush appeared on Dobson's radio program in August 1992 in an attempt to rally Christian conservatives to his flagging campaign.[81]

Dobson's opposition to gay rights pushed him further into politics. In November 1989, Bauer predicted that same-sex marriage, which the California State Bar Association had recently endorsed, would be "a major battleground of the 1990's." Dobson took Bauer's warning seriously. In 1988, he devoted three episodes of his daily radio program to lobbying against the Civil Rights Restoration Act because he believed it would force religious organizations to hire homosexuals, but the five hundred thousand calls that Dobson's supporters placed to Capitol Hill switchboards were not sufficient to prevent the bill from becoming law. In 1992, Dobson campaigned for a Colorado state referendum that would amend the state constitution to prohibit antidiscrimination laws on behalf of homosexuals. Before Dobson began his campaign for the referendum, political analysts gave it little chance of gaining enough signatures to be put on the ballot, let alone passed into law, but Dobson's strong support of the measure changed public opinion on the issue, and Colorado citizens defied the pundits' predictions by passing the initiative by a 53 percent majority in November.[82]

Dobson did not have long to bask in his triumph. On the same day that Colorado citizens voted for Amendment 2, the nation elected Bill Clinton president. Dobson increasingly began to devote his broadcasts to discussions of political issues, followed by a plea for listeners to call their congressional representatives to register their views. In 1993, he mobilized a phone campaign to block Attorney General Janet Reno's proposal to loosen restrictions on child pornography, and in 1994, he convinced 1 million listeners to call the congressional switchboard to stop legislation that would have tightened regulations on home schooling. Republicans took notice of Dobson's growing influence. One month after the Republicans' takeover of Congress, Bob Dole, the new senate majority leader, appointed Dobson to a fifteen-member Commission on Child and Family Welfare. Dole and most of the other major Republican presidential contenders met with Dobson before the 1996 primaries to seek his blessing for their campaigns.[83]

But Dobson did not give endorsements. Unlike Reed, who was willing to back almost any leading Republican candidate in order to secure the Christian Right's long-term influence in the party, Dobson believed that he could force the party into compliance with his demands by refusing to back any candidate who was not a purist on abortion and gay rights. He was tired of seeing presidential candidates "double-talk, sidestep, obfuscate, and ignore the concerns that burn within our hearts," he told Republican National Committee chair Haley Barbour. Some evangelicals, he believed, would boycott the party if it were not sufficiently conservative on social issues, and that "could prove fatal in 1996" for the GOP presidential candidate. The Focus on the Family founder also turned his ire on the Christian Coalition, along with the Republican establishment, for allegedly betraying the pro-life cause by supporting a few pro-choice Republicans. "A struggle [is] under way for the soul of the party, [and] I am committed never again to cast a vote for a politician who would kill one innocent baby," he stated in March 1995. Later that year, he wrote to Reed, saying that in view of the Christian Coalition leader's "unfaithful[ness] to the principles we are duty-bound as Christians to defend," he and Bauer "had considered the need to distance ourselves from you and the Christian Coalition."[84]

When Dole received the party's nomination, Dobson began to worry about the Christian Right's future in the GOP. Twenty years earlier, Dole had helped to create the GOP's antiabortion platform statement, but by 1996 he had decided that the call for an antiabortion constitutional amendment was hurting the party's image among centrist voters. Dole talked with Reed about the possibility of moderating the party's antiabortion stance with a platform statement that would acknowledge the differences in Republicans' views on the issue, and initially the Christian Coalition leader was receptive to the proposal. But when Dobson and Bauer heard about Dole's idea, they once again warned the party that some evangelicals would "vote for a third-party candidate who doesn't have a chance, rather than a cast a vote for a candidate of either party who is not committed to the sanctity of life."[85]

Faced with pressure from Dobson and other conservative evangelicals, Reed abandoned his conciliatory approach and came to the Republican convention determined to hold the party to its traditional, strong antiabortion platform. He arrived in San Diego with 102 floor whips, 40 runners to bring him word of platform committee negotiations, and a state-of-the-art computer system to help him keep track of delegates' votes. With the help of Bauer and Phyllis Schlafly, Reed persuaded the Dole campaign that it could not afford to antagonize the Christian Right, and in the end, the language in the party platform remained intact. Dole also capitulated to his party's conservative base by selecting Jack Kemp, a pro-life Catholic, as his running mate. Some pro-choice Republicans complained that the Christian Right had deprived the party of the ability to reach centrist voters. "This is not Bob Dole's party, this is Ralph Reed's party," one of them griped.[86]

Although Dobson continued to distrust Dole, other Christian Right leaders, including Reed and Falwell, argued that the Christian Right had to be willing to support almost any Republican candidate in order to prevent Clinton's reelection. Clinton had been the Christian Right's bogeyman since the early days of his presidential candidacy, and Christian Right organizations had experienced a fund-raising bonanza by attacking his efforts to put gays in the military, his appointment of socially liberal Joycelyn Elders to be surgeon general, and his extension of federal funding for abortion. Conservative evangelicals also continued to believe that the president was personally corrupt. In 1994, Falwell used his *Old-Time Gospel Hour* to market an anti-Clinton video set that suggested that the president might be guilty of a long list of crimes, including money laundering, drug dealing, and murder. Across the nation, conservative Christian radio talk show hosts launched similar attacks on the president. "The worst thing [Clinton] has done might have been the appointment of Darth Vader Ginsburg to the Supreme Court," Randall Terry, who began a new career as a radio talk show host after the decline of Operation Rescue, told his listeners in February 1994. "It might have been the Sodomite agenda. But killing babies is more wicked before God."[87]

To mollify his critics, Clinton invited evangelical leaders to several White House breakfasts in early 1994 and agreed to a lengthy interview with *Christianity Today*. But when Falwell began marketing the *Clinton Chronicles* video set, the president reacted in anger. Clinton understood that the Christian Right had made "abortion and homosexuality the litmus test of whether you're a true Christian," but he resented the movement's refusal to respect his faith.[88]

Any hope that Clinton might have been able to win over some of his evangelical critics vanished after he vetoed a bill to ban "partial-birth abortion," a late-term abortion procedure in which a fetus is partially extracted from the uterus. The issue had widespread emotional appeal; even many members of Congress who were normally pro-choice supported the ban, as did more than 70 percent of the American public. When Clinton vetoed the bill on the grounds that it did not include an exception for late-term abortions that were necessary to preserve a woman's health, it confirmed conservative evangelicals' worst opinions of the president. "A nation which sanctions infanticide is no better than China, no better than Nazi Germany," Charles Colson said.[89]

James Dobson mobilized several hundred thousand of his listeners to call their senators and demand an override of the president's veto, while Ralph Reed arranged for his supporters to send 8 million postcards to the Senate urging the same thing. Even Billy Graham, who had not been outspoken on political issues for two decades, rebuked the president. When the Senate failed to override the president's veto, Reed promised that evangelicals would take revenge at the polls. "We're going to put partial-birth abortion on 45 million voter guides," he promised, adding that the issue would "boost evangelical and Catholic turnout."[90]

Despite social conservatives' fervor, Bob Dole lost the election to Clinton, carrying only 41 percent of the popular vote. A majority of evangelicals supported Dole, primarily because of their distrust of Clinton. Yet evangelical turnout was six percentage points lower than it had been in 1992, and Dole received far fewer votes from evangelicals than Bush had four years earlier. Clinton, on the other hand, carried 36 percent of the churchgoing, born-again vote, a surprisingly high percentage for someone who was so unpopular with Christian Right leaders. Was the Republican Party losing its hold on evangelical voters? Ralph Reed tried to put the best face on the situation by arguing, with some plausibility, that Republicans had been able to hold on to both houses of Congress primarily because evangelicals remained loyal to the party at the local and state level. "Conservative evangelicals were the fire wall that prevented a Bob Dole defeat from mushrooming into a meltdown all the way down the ballot," Reed told the press.[91]

Dobson cited Dole's defeat as a sign of what could happen if the Republican Party failed to show proper deference to the Christian Right. He told the press after the election that he had cast his ballot for the third-party Christian conservative Howard Phillips. In the late 1970s Phillips had been a disaffected Republican Jew and New Right activist, but since that time, he had converted to Christianity and had adopted Reconstructionist beliefs, calling for the implementation of a biblical legal code in America and capital punishment for abortion doctors.[92] Dobson did not necessarily embrace those positions, but he found Phillips's candidacy more acceptable than Dole's, and he used his vote to protest the GOP's lack of action on abortion.

When Reed resigned from the Christian Coalition in 1997 to become a Republican political strategist, Dobson became the nation's most prominent Christian Right leader. He used his position to make new demands on the Republican Party. In the spring of 1998, he threatened to leave the GOP, saying that in the sixteen months following the November 1996 election, Republicans had failed to deliver on socially conservative issues. "If they want our votes every two years and then say, 'Don't call me, I'll call you,' then I will take the next step," Dobson threatened. "If I go, I'll take as many people with me as possible."[93]

Congressional Republicans rushed to reassure Dobson and mute his criticism. House Majority Leader Dick Armey and Majority Whip Tom DeLay met privately with the *Focus on the Family* leader, as did twenty-five of the most socially conservative members of the House. Many of the congressmen were longtime admirers of Dobson who had listened to his radio program for years. At least one credited his decision to follow Christ to Dobson's influence. During the two-hour meeting, they appealed to Dobson, a friend and fellow Christian, urging him not to damage their party. One congressman's wife broke down in tears, saying that she did not want to see the revered family leader tear apart everything that Republicans had accomplished. Dobson was moved by what he saw. He cancelled interviews he had scheduled with the *New York Times* and the *Washington Post*, and decided to avoid firing any more shots at the Republican Party for a while.[94]

But Republican leaders realized that they could not placate Dobson merely with words, so they scheduled votes on issues of concern to the Christian Right. Partial-birth abortion came up for another vote in the Senate, and a school prayer amendment returned to the congressional agenda for the first time since the 1980s.[95] More important, congressional Republicans decided to make Dobson and his allies a permanent part of the legislative process. Many of the House Republicans, especially members of the freshman class of 1994, worshipped at conservative evangelical churches and opposed abortion and gay rights as strongly as Dobson did, but they thought that Dobson underestimated the obstacles that congressional conservatives faced on social issues. If they could bring Dobson into the legislative process, they thought, he would temper his rhetoric, but he would also use his influence to help them pass the antiabortion and "protection of marriage" bills that both he and they favored.

Acting on these concerns, House Majority Whip Tom DeLay created the Values Action Team (VAT), a coalition between conservative Republicans in Congress and leaders of the Christian Right, in May 1998. Each week, the VAT, led by the socially conservative freshman congressman Joseph Pitts (R-PA), brought together several dozen Christian Right leaders to coordinate a legislative strategy with conservative Republicans in the House. Congressional representatives, including DeLay, let the Christian Right leaders know which members of Congress they needed to target with their lobbying pressure in order to ensure the passage of socially conservative bills, and the Christian Right leaders in turn promised to mobilize their phone banks. They realized that passing constitutional amendments was unrealistic, so they focused on an incremental agenda that would gradually make abortions more difficult to obtain and slow the advance of gay rights. House Speaker Newt Gingrich, who met with the Christian Right leaders for three hours in May, agreed to bring the socially conservative legislation to a vote.[96]

In the summer of 1998, Republicans introduced bills to ban human cloning, prevent gay couples from adopting children, prohibit the District of Columbia from granting domestic partner benefits to employees, and cut off funding for the National Endowment for the Arts. Another bill would have made it illegal to bring an underage girl across state lines to obtain an abortion without her parents' consent. Most of this legislation did not pass, but House Republicans' willingness to bring the bills to a vote indicated the power of the Christian Right lobbyists.[97]

The formation of the VAT reflected a shift in the Christian Right from voter mobilization to legislative influence. Jerry Falwell had assisted the Republican Party by mobilizing conservative evangelical voters, and Ralph Reed had orchestrated a strategy for a Christian Right takeover of the GOP, but it was not until the late 1990s that conservative evangelicals began to have substantive influence in Congress. When Reed left the Christian Coalition, Pat Robertson replaced him with former Republican congressman Randy Tate, who had been one of Tom DeLay's deputy whips in the House.[98] Tate's appointment, combined with Dobson's effort to hold congressional Republicans accountable for their legislative record, signaled the Christian Right's interest in controlling the agenda in Congress, rather than merely in winning electoral victories.

The Christian Right decided to use its new legislative influence to remove the president. In June 1997, at a secret meeting of the Council for National Policy (CNP), Christian Right operatives discussed impeachment with the organization's congressional members, including DeLay. The CNP had long been opposed to Clinton and had helped to distribute the *Clinton*

Chronicles videos in 1994. By June 1997, the group thought it had enough evidence against the president to merit his forced removal from office, so it drew up a resolution of impeachment that Representative Bob Barr (R-GA) introduced in November of that year. At the time, no one had heard of Monica Lewinsky, but Barr and his conservative allies wanted to impeach Clinton on the charge that the president's reelection campaign had received illegal donations from Chinese sources. House Speaker Newt Gingrich was hesitant, but when evidence of the president's relationship with the White House intern surfaced, he and other Republicans in the House realized that they might have grounds for impeaching the president on charges of perjury and obstruction of justice.[99]

But the Christian Right was not in step with the American public on this issue, as the majority of Americans did not support Clinton's removal from office. In frustration, Christian Right leaders began to realize that perhaps their primary obstacle to imposing moral law on the nation was not the president, the Congress, the Democrats, or moderate Republicans. "What has alarmed me throughout this episode has been the willingness of my fellow citizens to rationalize the President's behavior even as they suspected, and later knew, he was lying," Dobson wrote in a mass mailing to his supporters in September 1998, a few weeks after President Clinton publicly admitted to personal error in his relationship with Lewinsky. "I am left to conclude that our greatest problem is not in the Oval Office. It is with the people of this land." "If there really were a 'moral majority' in the country," Paul Weyrich wrote in February 1999, "Clinton would have been driven from office a year ago."[100]

A few despairing evangelicals suggested that it might be time for the Christian Right to abandon its efforts. In 1999, two former vice presidents of the Moral Majority, Cal Thomas and Ed Dobson (no relation to James Dobson), repudiated political activism. Clinton's actions had "erased the little that the Moral Majority had been able to accomplish during its brief existence," they wrote, so what had been the use of investing millions of dollars in get-out-the-vote efforts and lobbying campaigns? Even worse, the Religious Right's political activities were alienating people from the Christian message. "When pastors become too deeply entangled with politics, they harm the gospel of Jesus," Dobson and Thomas wrote.[101]

But for other evangelicals, the failure to secure their agenda only increased their determination to continue the fight. They had forced the Republican establishment to begin treating them as serious political players. Congress was now largely amenable to their demands. If only they could recapture the White House, perhaps the moral agenda that had proved so elusive could be realized.

| Capturing the White House

"MY DEAR FRIEND," PAT ROBERTSON told Don Hodel in 1997, when he appointed him executive director of the Christian Coalition, "I want to hold out to you the possibility of selecting the next president of the United States."[1]

Four years later, when George W. Bush took office, it seemed that perhaps the Christian Right really did have such power. As conservative commentator George Will observed, the new president did not merely pander to the evangelicals; he promoted their causes with the conviction of a true believer. "Bush *is* the religious right," Will wrote.[2] Indeed, he combined nearly all of the qualities that evangelicals wanted in a president. He was a devout Christian who appointed more evangelicals to his Cabinet than any of his predecessors had. He pushed for conservative legislation on abortion, sex education, and other socially conservative causes. He prosecuted the war on terror with the zeal of a Cold Warrior, often employing religious rhetoric to promote his military aims. Christian Right leaders such as James Dobson and Richard Land enjoyed regular access to the White House. Bolstered by their association with the president, evangelicals turned out in force in 2004, ready to reelect Bush and prohibit gay marriage. Never had the Christian Right's power seemed to be so strong.

But if Bush's presidency demonstrated the power that the Christian Right exercised within the Republican Party, it also revealed the limits of its influence in the national culture. When evangelicals failed to achieve substantive legislative results, some pundits began talking about the "crackup" of the Christian Right. The nation's cultural drift to the left continued, especially on gay rights. Many younger evangelicals began denouncing the religious alliance with the Republican Party. Pundits prepared to write an obituary for the movement, saying that "the era of the Religious Right is over."[3]

Yet in November 2008, evangelicals once again proved to be the Republicans' most loyal demographic group. Was this merely the last gasp of a dying movement? Or was it a sign that the Christian Right was more enduring than pundits had expected?

The 2000 Presidential Election

By the time George W. Bush began signaling his interest in the Republican Party's presidential nomination in early 1999, the Christian Right had established itself in the party as a formidable force that no candidate—not even a popular Sunbelt governor who was the son of a former president—could afford to ignore. Bush initially tried to hold evangelicals at arm's length, believing that, as the front-runner, he had that luxury. But when his statement that "America is not ready to ban abortions" earned him a sharp rebuke from James Dobson, and when other presidential contenders, including the Christian Right's own Gary Bauer, began vying for the support of evangelicals, Bush realized that he needed to make a direct appeal to the Religious Right. In October 1999, he held a closed-door meeting with the Christian Right's Council for National Policy, and then moved sharply to the right on cultural issues. In November 1999, he told television correspondent Tim Russert that he would "probably not" meet with representatives from the Log Cabin Republicans, a group representing gay Republicans. The next month, in a debate between the Republican candidates in Iowa, he answered the question "What political philosopher or thinker do you most identify with?" by giving an evangelical testimony. "Christ, because he changed my heart," he responded.[4]

Unlike some of his opponents, Bush had had an authentic "born-again" experience that evangelicals understood. In his youth, he had been an irresponsible, tobacco-chewing, whiskey-drinking "good ol' boy." Like the prodigal son, he had squandered his opportunities and brought shame on his family's good name. As his drinking problem worsened, his marriage began to fall apart. But then Bush discovered Jesus. After saying the "sinner's prayer" with evangelist Arthur Blessit in 1984, and having a life-changing talk with Billy Graham in the summer of 1985, Bush started what he described as "a new walk where I would recommit my heart to Jesus Christ." He joined an evangelical Bible study group and quit drinking.[5]

Thirteen years later, Bush had another life-changing religious experience. At Highland Park Methodist Church in Dallas, Bush listened to his pastor preach a sermon on the contemporary relevance of God's call to Moses to lead the Israelites out of Egypt. Americans, the pastor said, were "starved for leaders who have ethical and moral courage." Soon thereafter, Bush summoned Texas televangelist James Robison to his office. "I've heard the call," Bush said. "I believe God wants me to run for president."[6]

Robison had played a critical role in mobilizing evangelicals for Ronald Reagan's campaign in 1980, but his flirtation with politics had been brief, and he had no thought of reentering the fray. But the televangelist could not resist the appeal of a politician who had such strong personal faith. "I feel like the destiny of the world has been touched today," Robison told his wife immediately after meeting with Bush. He began introducing the candidate to a national network of evangelical pastors in the spring of 1999. Shortly after Bush's conversation with Robison, about a dozen nationally known evangelical leaders met with the governor to discuss his political future.[7]

Thus, when Bush's race for the 2000 Republican presidential nomination narrowed to a contest with Senator John McCain (R-AZ), he was able to call on the Christian Right. After losing the New Hampshire primary to McCain by a humiliating nineteen points, Bush knew that he needed to win in South Carolina. He decided to make a trip to Bob Jones University.[8]

But Bush had miscalculated. Although the Texas governor had been "born again," he was not an expert in evangelicalism, and he failed to realize that most evangelicals viewed BJU as a symbol of a hard-line style of fundamentalism that they wanted to repudiate. Most evangelicals had abandoned anti-Catholicism, but Bob Jones University continued to view the Catholic Church as a "cult." Most Christian Right leaders had apologized for the movement's segregationist past and had welcomed African Americans into their churches and organizations, but BJU maintained a ban on interracial dating. The university had cut itself off from nearly all other conservative Protestants through its attacks on Billy Graham, Jerry Falwell, the NAE, and the Southern Baptist Convention. Richard Cizik, the NAE's vice president for governmental affairs, said that Bush's trip to BJU was "unfortunate," because "it tarred a lot of evangelicals with an old fundamentalist practice of racism." When Gary Bauer endorsed McCain three days before the South Carolina primary, it accentuated the tensions between Bush and a few of the social conservatives who he had assumed would be his strongest supporters.[9]

Bush's visit to Bob Jones threatened to expose decades-old divisions between fundamentalists and evangelicals. For the previous three decades, evangelicals and fundamentalists had cooperated, albeit sometimes uneasily, in a conservative Republican political coalition. Bush's visit to BJU threatened to divide that political coalition to the detriment of both the Christian Right and his own campaign. Eventually, he realized this. After weeks of relentless criticism in the press, he decided to make amends with Catholics—and also show moderate evangelicals that he was not as intolerant as his critics claimed—by writing a public letter of apology to John Cardinal O'Connor.[10]

Evangelicals forgave Bush for his misstep because of their fear of McCain. The Arizona senator had generally supported pro-life and other conservative legislation, but he incurred the suspicion of groups such as the Christian Coalition after he proposed a campaign finance reform bill to restrict the ability of special interest groups, including those that were part of the Christian Right, to run the issue-oriented ads that had been a staple of their election-year efforts. Christian Right leaders considered McCain's lack of interest in wooing conservative evangelical voters even more alarming. If McCain became president, they feared, evangelicals would have little influence in his administration.

Falwell went on the warpath against the senator. "I will certainly speak out when I see an overt display of hostility toward conservative people of faith, especially when it is emanating from the party that has historically welcomed and encouraged our participation," Falwell wrote in an e-mail to his supporters in mid-February. "And that is exactly what I see from the McCain campaign."[11]

Dobson entered the fray as well. Although he had once expressed skepticism about Bush's commitment to the pro-life cause, he was so dismayed when Bauer endorsed McCain that he released a statement to the press directly attacking the senator's record. McCain had committed adultery twenty years earlier, Dobson noted, and he had been involved in the Keating Five scandal of the late 1980s. He was also known to have a "violent temper." "Those red flags about Senator McCain's character," Dobson said, "are reminiscent of the man who now occupies the White House."[12]

The Christian Right's attacks on McCain, which came less than two days before the South Carolina primary, succeeded. McCain and Bush had been almost even in the polls a week before the primary, but when South Carolinians cast their ballots, they gave Bush a decisive victory. Bush received the support of more than two-thirds of South Carolina voters who identified with the Religious Right, a group that comprised more than 33 percent of the electorate. "Ralph Reed, Pat Robertson and Jerry Falwell are to be congratulated," John Weaver, McCain's campaign manager, told the press.[13]

McCain struck back by denouncing Robertson and Falwell as "agents of intolerance" comparable to "union bosses," Al Sharpton, and Louis Farrakhan. "We are the party of Ronald Reagan, not Pat Robertson," he said in a speech in Robertson and Falwell's home state of Virginia. The next day, he repeated the attack. Falwell and Robertson, he said, exerted an "evil influence" on the Republican Party.[14]

Many evangelicals were outraged. Although McCain had prefaced his remarks by lauding the achievements of evangelical leaders such as Charles Colson and James Dobson—a line that he had included only at the urging of Gary Bauer—many evangelicals felt the attack was aimed at them. Bauer called his words "unwarranted, ill-advised and divisive." Richard Cizik likewise argued that McCain had made a serious blunder, because even evangelicals who did not approve of Falwell or Robertson "felt tarnished" by the senator's criticisms. McCain "may have not only shot himself in the foot but in the head," Cizik said. McCain apologized for his remarks, but he could not reverse the damage.[15] After losing a string of state primaries, he dropped out of the race.

Bush, relying on Ralph Reed as a political consultant, continued to bolster his standing with the Christian Right. In April, he acceded to a request from the March for Jesus organization by proclaiming June 10 "Jesus Day" in Texas. He also continued to trumpet his plan for "compassionate conservatism." For Bush, this was a personal cause. He had been able to reform his own life only through faith, and he wanted to give other Americans the same opportunity. Thus, when Marvin Olasky, a Texas journalism professor and editor of the conservative Christian newsweekly *World*, approached Bush with the idea of a government partnership with religious organizations to provide charitable relief, the governor endorsed Olasky's plan.[16]

Bush's endorsement of charitable choice heightened his appeal among younger and more moderate evangelicals who might have objected to his visit to Bob Jones University. Many evangelical churches had become leading providers of needed social services in their communities. By the late 1990s, the nation's best-known evangelical leaders included not only pastors and evangelists, but also relief workers and social justice advocates such as Charles Colson. *Christianity Today* began regularly featuring articles on evangelical programs to help AIDS victims, fight poverty at home and abroad, and promote international debt relief.[17] Many evangelicals wanted to find a conservative presidential candidate who would promote these causes but who would allow churches, rather than the federal government, to take the lead. Bush, who made "compassionate conservatism" his campaign slogan, was their man.

Democratic presidential candidate Al Gore tried to counter Bush's appeal with his own evangelical strategy. "The Democratic Party is going to take back God this time," one of Gore's policy advisers promised in the spring of 1999. If any Democrat could recover the now solidly Republican evangelical vote, Gore seemed to be that candidate. He was a churchgoing Southern Baptist who had long thought deeply about religious faith and had briefly attended Vanderbilt Divinity School. As a Tennessee senator in the early 1980s, he had opposed abortion rights, and he had earned the respect of many conservative evangelicals. Even after Gore switched positions on abortion, some evangelicals still viewed him as an ally. At the beginning of his campaign, he announced his support for federal funding of faith-based initiatives, just as Bush had. He frequently spoke of his religious faith and quoted scripture in his speeches. And he assured Christians that he based his decisions on the question "What would Jesus do?"[18]

Gore expanded his outreach to religious voters by selecting as his running mate Senator Joseph Lieberman (D-CT), an Orthodox Jew whom the *Washington Times* called "the most visibly religious running mate on a modern presidential ticket." When Lieberman said that the First Amendment guaranteed freedom of religion but not "freedom from religion," he received plaudits from Jerry Falwell and Pat Robertson, as well as spokespersons for the NAE and the Southern Baptist Convention. "Religious conservatives like him a lot and they like Orthodox Jews," Robertson told the press in September 2000. "They like people who will stand up for their faith."[19]

But Gore could not overcome conservative evangelicals' belief that the Democrats were on the wrong side of the culture wars. His position on abortion and gay rights, two hot-button issues for the Christian Right, echoed the Democratic Party line that most evangelicals opposed. Many evangelicals viewed him as a symbol of the Clinton administration, which for them epitomized moral lapses and corruption. Bush won 74 percent of the evangelical vote, and 84 percent of the votes of white evangelicals who regularly attended church. In a close election in which Bush lost the popular vote by a narrow margin and received a slim margin of victory in the electoral college only after weeks of litigation and intervention by the Supreme Court, his strong appeal to the Religious Right was crucial to his success, because his efforts to reach out to other demographic groups largely failed. He lost 96 percent of African Americans to Gore, and 65 percent of secular Americans. The lesson for Bush adviser Karl Rove was clear: despite Bush's attempt to run a centrist campaign as a "compassionate conservative," most of his core support came from white religious voters who were energized by the "wedge issues" of abortion and gay rights. As Pat Robertson reminded the administration, "Without us, I do not believe that George Bush would be sitting in the White House." Four million registered evangelical voters had stayed home from the polls, Rove discovered, suggesting that perhaps Bush had not made a sufficient effort to mobilize his conservative Christian base. Rove resolved not to let that happen again. In 2004, Bush would run as the candidate of the Christian Right.[20]

The Bush Administration's Outreach to Christian Conservatives

Early in his term, Bush found evangelical outreach more challenging than he might have expected, mainly because he was reluctant to alienate moderates in his party by pushing the Christian Right's agenda. Evangelical leaders were disappointed when the new president appointed several moderate, pro-choice Republicans, including Colin Powell and Christine Todd Whitman, to key positions in his Cabinet. When Bush appointed an openly gay Republican to head the White House Office of National AIDS Policy, Dobson criticized the decision as "unwise," and Bauer noted that his "pessimism about the administration" was "growing." In March 2001, *Focus on the Family Citizen* asked, "Is there any reason to expect bold policy stances on family-values issues from someone who has peppered his speeches for two months with phrases like 'bipartisan consensus' and 'common ground' and who—let's face it—has never been considered conservative enough by many in the pro-family camp?"[21]

But conservative evangelicals said little during the first few months of the administration, partly because they were hesitant to criticize a Republican president, and partly because they were too disorganized to challenge the White House. At the beginning of Bush's presidency, the Christian Right was more decentralized than it had been at any point since 1979. The movement's long-standing political power brokers, such as Falwell and Robertson, no longer had much influence. The Christian Coalition's membership dropped from 2.8 million to 2.1 million in the two years after Ralph Reed left the organization, and its finances suffered. In 1999, Robertson wrote the organization a personal check for $1 million to keep it afloat. Without a Democratic president to demonize, the Christian Right found it difficult to raise money.[22]

James Dobson's Focus on the Family might have been able to replace the Christian Coalition as a political force, but as a nonprofit, nonpartisan organization, it had to limit its political activities. The organization was also plagued by a severe drop in fund-raising in the aftermath of two scandals that rocked the organization in the fall of 2000. Less than a month before the presidential election, the longtime cohost of Dobson's daily radio program resigned after admitting to an extramarital affair with another staff member. At the same time, the director of Dobson's ex-gay ministry was caught on camera at a gay bar.[23] As Dobson dealt with these blows to his organization's credibility, he had little time to go on the political offensive.

Gary Bauer's temporary departure from the Family Research Council in 2000 left the organization in a weakened state, and his subsequent failure to garner much support in his bid for the Republican presidential nomination diminished his lobbying ability on Capitol Hill. The Southern Baptist Convention's Richard Land and the NAE's Richard Cizik regularly met with public officials, and exercised some influence in Washington, but their positions did not give them the ability to mobilize voters in the way that Jerry Falwell and Ralph Reed had. There was a power vacuum in the Christian Right at the very moment that it should have been poised to take the lead in Washington policy making. "Religious Right Loses Its Political Potency," proclaimed one headline.[24]

Yet the president's own evangelical sympathies and desire to build evangelical support for 2004 ensured that the Christian Right's causes would not be forgotten. Bush's Cabinet and White House staff selections made his administration the most overtly evangelical in American history. He appointed John Ashcroft, a Pentecostal who had strong support among the Christian Right, as his attorney general. Condoleezza Rice, who served as national security advisor in Bush's first term and secretary of state in his second, gave talks about her faith at evangelical churches and occasionally led office prayer services. Bush's secretary of education, Rod Paige, lauded Christian schools. Bush's father had appointed a pro-choice doctor to be his secretary of health and human services, but the younger Bush made it a point to appoint a pro-life candidate to that position. Forty percent of Bush's White House staff participated in weekly White House Bible studies or prayer meetings. There were so many evangelicals in the administration that Jewish speechwriter David Frum reported some discomfort, noting that attendance at the weekly Bible studies felt, "if not compulsory, not quite uncompulsory, either."[25]

While Bush surrounded himself with evangelical policy advisers, everyone knew that the top evangelical in the White House was the president himself. He frequently discussed his faith and born-again conversion experience with other evangelicals, and he began every day with prayer and devotional Bible reading. Each day, he also read an excerpt from Oswald Chambers's book *My Utmost for His Highest*, a classic evangelical devotional guide. Observers often noted that Bush seemed most at ease when talking with evangelical groups, and he regularly participated in short, spontaneous prayers with the people he met with.[26]

In keeping with his campaign promise to promote a "culture of life," Bush ended the Clinton policy of funding international family-planning clinics that offered abortion services or provided abortion counseling. He signed into law the Partial-Birth Abortion Act (2003), the first federal measure to prohibit an abortion procedure. In a step toward recognizing fetuses as persons with legal rights, his administration enacted the Unborn Victims of Violence Act (2004), which mandated that anyone who caused injuries to a pregnant woman's fetus would be subject to additional penalties beyond those exacted for injuring the woman. He increased funding for abstinence-only sex education, and restricted it for embryonic stem cell research, stating that the federal government would not pay for research that would destroy human embryos.[27]

Yet on other issues, Bush faced the same problem that had bedeviled Reagan: he found that it was difficult to get his measures passed in the Senate, which was under Democratic control for nearly half of his first term. His plan for faith-based initiatives ran into unexpected obstacles. Within days of his inauguration, he issued an executive order establishing a White House Office of Faith-Based and Community Initiatives, and appointed a politically centrist Catholic, John DiIulio, to oversee its operations. The Republican-controlled House passed a bill to provide the federal aid for faith-based initiatives that the president had requested, but the measure languished in the Senate, which was skeptical about the constitutional implications of Bush's proposal. Bush eventually gave up on the legislative process and issued an executive order prohibiting government agencies from discriminating against religious organizations that applied for federal funding.[28]

But this limited measure disappointed the Christian Right. Several evangelical leaders distanced themselves from Bush's proposal as soon as they learned that under the White House plan, religious charities that proselytized could not receive federal funds. "If government provides funding to the thousands of faith-based institutions but, under a tortured definition of separation of church and state, demands in return that those institutions give up their unique religious activities, then not only the effectiveness of these institutions but possibly their very raison d'être may be lost," Pat Robertson wrote. Even Marvin Olasky, the person who had first given Bush the idea of funding religious charities, criticized the White House.[29]

By the summer of 2001, Bush's unwillingness to roll back gay rights and his failure to secure the Christian Right's major policy aims caused some conservative evangelicals to question whether he was fully committed to their cause. Though few Christian Right leaders were willing to challenge Bush publicly, some admitted to "privately shaking their heads at some of the developments within his administration."[30]

The terrorist attacks of September 11, 2001, not only transformed Bush into a wartime leader and gave him an instantaneous boost in his public approval ratings but also earned him the unquestioning loyalty of conservative evangelicals. Bush's war on terror helped to unify and revive a flagging Christian Right, and it cemented the movement's ties to the president. After September 2001, Bush became the de facto leader of the evangelical right.

Evangelicals looked to the president for leadership partly because some of the Christian Right's own leaders had failed to provide clear direction, having badly misjudged the national mood following the attacks of September 11. Two days after the attacks, Jerry Falwell and Pat Robertson stated on the 700 *Club* that the terrorist attacks were a judgment from God on the sexual sins, abortion, and secular humanism that they had been fighting for over two decades. "The abortionists have got to bear some burden for this because God will not be mocked," Falwell said on Robertson's 700 *Club* television program on September 13. "And when we destroy 40 million little innocent babies, we make God mad. I really believe that the pagans, and the abortionists, and the feminists, and the gays and the lesbians who are actively trying to make that an alternative lifestyle, the A.C.L.U., People for the American Way, all of them who have tried to secularize America, I point the finger in their face and say, 'You helped this happen.'"[31]

Falwell's statement reflected a long tradition of jeremiads in fundamentalist and evangelical circles, but many evangelicals repudiated his message. Instead of interpreting the attacks as a divine judgment, they considered them an "evil" assault that a righteous nation would need to avenge. Although Falwell apologized for his remarks, he and Robertson fell further out of favor.

The terrorist attacks, evangelicals quickly decided, signaled the beginning of a new, long-term war against Islamic terrorism akin to the struggle against the communist "evil empire" during the Cold War. Just as evangelicals of the 1950s had enthusiastically promoted the federal government's Cold War efforts, evangelicals of the early twenty-first century expected to be an integral part of America's War on Terror. "Religious terrorism is the communism of the 21st century," a *Christianity Today* cover story stated in late October. "Christians have a unique and vital role to play in the historical drama that is unfolding." Much to the consternation of religious pluralists, many evangelical leaders portrayed the terrorist attacks of 9/11 as a sign of Islam's allegedly violent or "evil" nature. Billy Graham's son Franklin, who had led a prayer at Bush's first inauguration, called Islam a "wicked" religion, a remark for which he refused to apologize even after repeated public criticism.[32]

Although the Bush administration occasionally tried to distance itself from some evangelicals' more extreme denunciations of Islam, it welcomed their view of the war on terror as a righteous struggle against "evil." "We will rid the world of the evil-doers," Bush promised America five days after the terrorist attacks on New York and Washington. "This is our calling," he declared, in language that reflected a Christian theology of divine election.[33]

Other presidents had employed the language of civil religion in moments of national crisis, but the relentless focus on "evil" and the talk of a divine "calling" for the nation more closely reflected Bush's evangelical beliefs than it did presidential tradition. With a speechwriting team that included devout evangelical Michael Gerson, Bush had no trouble finding a ready supply of Bible verses and evangelical catchphrases for his prepared addresses. His speeches began to include more overt references to divine approval of the nation's course of action. "Freedom and fear, justice and cruelty, have always been at war, and we know that God is not neutral between them," he told the nation in September 2001.[34]

Bush's evangelical supporters welcomed the suggestion that the president was guided by a sense of divine calling in his war on terror. "I think that God picked the right man at the right time for the right purpose," Christian broadcaster Janet Parshall said. The Bush administration encouraged such thinking. White House director of public liaison Tim Goeglein told Marvin Olasky's *World* magazine, "I think President Bush is God's man at this hour, and I say that with a great sense of humility."[35]

Evangelicals' view of politics as a spiritual battle between good and evil led them to support not only the military's actions in Afghanistan, but also President Bush's war in Iraq. Saddam Hussein ruled over a country that was the site of the ancient city of Babylon, which several biblical prophets had used as a metaphor for evil. While many mainline Protestant clerics condemned the war as unjust and un-Christian, prominent evangelicals argued that the Iraqi dictator was an agent of spiritual darkness. "Saddam's regime has been not only anti-democratic but Satanic in its treatment of human beings," *World* stated. Refusing to invade Iraq would thus be tantamount to appeasing the forces of evil. Three prominent evangelical leaders—Richard Land, Charles Colson, and Bill Bright—wrote the president a letter urging him to go to war against Saddam Hussein. "The United States must be a force for freedom and justice in the world," they stated.[36]

Though there were a few evangelicals on the left who dissented, the evangelical population as a whole was more supportive of the war than any other demographic group. Sixty-four percent of evangelicals—and 70 percent of those who self-identified with the "religious right"—favored the idea of invading Iraq in February 2003. In contrast, only 59 percent of the American public—and 49 percent of those who said that "religion was not very important" to them—supported the invasion. Evangelical support for the war increased to 79 percent in May 2003, and it remained high long after other Americans had given up hope for success in Iraq. As late as September 2007, more than three years after a majority of Americans had first expressed their disapproval of the Iraq war, the majority of evangelicals continued to believe that Bush had made the correct decision.[37]

Gay Marriage in 2004

Bush was mostly silent on gay rights during his first term. He opposed same-sex marriage, but endorsed civil unions and appointed gays to high office. His vice president, who had a gay daughter, was opposed to a constitutional amendment prohibiting same-sex marriage. Bush felt a natural affinity with evangelicals on many issues, but he did not share the movement's strong antipathy to homosexuality, so he took a more moderate stance than most leaders of the Christian Right.[38]

For a few years, conservative evangelicals were willing to tolerate Bush's vacillation, even though they complained about it in private. But by 2004, they decided to force the president's hand. They were acutely aware that court decisions and shifts in public opinion had caused them to lose ground rapidly in their fight to restrict gay rights. Evangelicals thought that only a constitutional amendment would be able to prevent same-sex unions from being recognized nationwide. In January 2004, James Dobson and Richard Land approached Karl Rove with an ultimatum: if Bush wanted strong support from the Christian Right in the election, he would have to endorse the Federal Marriage Amendment (FMA), a measure to make same-sex marriage unconstitutional.[39]

Rove, a cynical political strategist who was a lifelong agnostic, had no personal affinity for the Christian Right, but he had great respect for the power of the evangelical vote. Even though the president was not eager to become embroiled in the debate over the FMA, Rove wanted to find an issue that would energize the socially conservative voters he believed were the key to victory.

The Republican Party's willingness to acquiesce to the Christian Right on the FMA demonstrated the power that the movement—and James Dobson in particular—exercised in the GOP. The FMA had originated in the late 1990s but did not receive much publicity, even in conservative evangelical circles, until Dobson began speaking out in favor of it in 2002.[40]

Dobson approached the campaign for the FMA with the zeal of a convert. The amendment was not only a good idea, he argued; it was the linchpin of civilization. "The homosexual activist movement, which has achieved virtually every goal and objective it set out to accomplish more than 50 years ago, is poised to deliver a devastating and potentially fatal blow to the traditional family," Dobson told his supporters in September 2003. "Unless we act quickly, the family as we have known it for 5,000 years will be gone. With its demise will come chaos such as the world has never seen." Dobson was convinced that even in the worst circumstances, a faithful remnant of godly families would survive, but he predicted that for most Americans, traditional, lifelong, heterosexual marriage would become a relic of the past.[41]

Many Americans outside of conservative circles were puzzled by the argument that legalizing same-sex marriage would negatively affect heterosexual marriage, let alone abolish it. But Dobson viewed the gay rights lobby as a sinister force that wanted to "destroy marriage altogether." Homosexuals, he argued, had no interest in, or respect for, lifelong marital commitments, so after securing the right to same-sex marriage, they would soon grow tired of it and would quickly act to remove state recognition of all marriages. Without the public support for heterosexual marriage, few couples would commit themselves to a lifelong union, and an increasing number of children would grow up without the stability of a two-parent home. Dobson viewed the push for same-sex marriage as the natural product of all of the liberal social trends that he had opposed unsuccessfully for the previous thirty years. The FMA was his last chance to rescue the nation. "This effort to save the family is our D-Day, our Gettysburg, our Stalingrad," he wrote.[42]

As Dobson was preparing his campaign for the FMA, the Supreme Court struck down a state antisodomy law in *Lawrence and Garner v. Texas* (2003). The fact that the decision was grounded in the "right to privacy" that had been the basis for *Roe v. Wade* was not lost on evangelicals. They decided to preempt a gay-marriage *Roe* by amending the Constitution. The Defense of Marriage Act (DOMA), which President Clinton had signed into law in 1996, already gave states the right to deny recognition to gay unions licensed by other states, but social conservatives argued that the *Lawrence* decision showed how easy it would be for a future Court ruling to invalidate the DOMA and all state laws against gay marriage or civil unions. Within days of the Court ruling, Senate Majority Leader Bill Frist urged Congress to pass a constitutional amendment defining marriage as a covenant between a man and a woman, a bill that conservative Republicans had already introduced in the House the previous month. In June, Gary Bauer, James Dobson, Richard Land, and other evangelical leaders formed a new umbrella organization, the Arlington Group, whose main purpose was to unite various Christian Right organizations in lobbying for the FMA. The Southern Baptist Convention also joined the fray in June by passing a resolution opposing same-sex unions, and in August, Jerry Falwell, who since 2000 had been devoting more attention to his university than to politics, announced that he would begin a campaign for the FMA. Catholic clergy joined evangelicals in endorsing the amendment. Sensing the prevailing political winds, Republican National Committee chair Ed Gillespie told the press in September 2003 that the Republican Party platform of 2004 would likely contain a statement in favor of the FMA.[43]

Conservative evangelicals were shocked to see how quickly the tide of gay rights seemed to be advancing. In June, they had rallied against the *Lawrence* decision. In August, the Episcopal Church appointed its first openly gay bishop. And in November, the Massachusetts Supreme Judicial Court fulfilled evangelicals' worst fears by declaring that under state constitutional law, gays in Massachusetts had the same right to marriage that heterosexuals had. Gay couples in the state began applying for marriage licenses the following spring, and many gays from other states traveled to Massachusetts to have legally recognized weddings.

By the end of 2003, Christian Right activists had decided to make same-sex marriage their major issue in the upcoming presidential election. All the Democratic presidential contenders opposed the FMA. "This will be the issue for Evangelicals and many Catholics in the 2004 election," Richard Land said in November 2003. "At the presidential, senatorial, congressional and state legislative levels, every candidate will be asked, 'Will you vote to ratify a federal marriage amendment?'"[44]

But despite the demand from his base, Bush was reluctant to endorse the FMA. In December 2003, he told ABC News that even if he were to consider a federal marriage amendment, he would continue to view gay civil unions as an issue for state rather than federal policy. Gary Bauer reacted sharply. "What the president said is confusing, and some will find it hard to distinguish from Howard Dean," he said. Concerned Women for America president Sandy

Rios said that she foresaw social conservatives "staying home in droves" on Election Day if the president did not "show strength" on the issue of same-sex marriage.[45]

Land, Dobson, and other members of the Arlington Group made their move in the weeks leading up to the president's State of the Union address in January 2004. The president's speech would have to include a clear endorsement of the FMA, they told Rove. Mindful of the need to maintain the goodwill of such a vital constituency, Rove assured the group that the president was in favor of the amendment, and a few days later, Bush obliged. "Activist judges . . . have begun redefining marriage by court order, without regard for the will of the people and their elected representatives," Bush said. "If judges insist on forcing their arbitrary will upon the people, the only alternative left to the people would be the constitutional process. Our nation must defend the sanctity of marriage." Bush's speech alienated gay Republican organizations, which withdrew their support of his reelection bid. But Land and other Christian Right leaders did not think the president had gone far enough, and they renewed their pressure on Rove to get Bush to endorse the amendment directly. Rove promised that the president would do so as soon as he found an "appropriate moment." That moment came in February, when he announced his support for a constitutional amendment mandating that "marriage in the United States shall consist only of the union of a man and a woman." But at the same time, Bush said that he did not support attempts to prevent states from offering civil unions to gay couples, and some Republican officials, speaking to the press on condition of anonymity, reported that the president's advisers were divided on the wisdom of the amendment. The president refused to offer his own wording for the amendment, and he largely avoided discussing it on the campaign trail, except when speaking to evangelical audiences. With the American public evenly divided on the amendment, Bush did not view the FMA as a winning political issue.[46]

But the FMA was a godsend to the Religious Right, because it energized a movement whose fortunes had been flagging. For the previous three years, it had been difficult for Christian Right organizations to raise money. With an evangelical president and social conservatives such as Representative Tom DeLay and Senator Rick Santorum in the congressional leadership, no one could plausibly argue that secular liberals were poised to destroy the nation's values. The Massachusetts Supreme Judicial Court's decision to mandate same-sex unions changed all that. Evangelical leaders began to argue that unelected judges were forcing their liberal social views on the population. Donations to Christian Right organizations immediately increased. "I have never seen anything that has energized and provoked our grass roots like this issue," Land said, "including *Roe v. Wade*."[47]

After the FMA failed in July 2004, Christian Right activists in thirteen states introduced referenda to make same-sex marriage illegal in their states. One of those states was Ohio, which both the Kerry and Bush campaigns thought might determine the outcome of the presidential election. Megachurch pastors such as Rod Parsley mobilized voters on behalf of the referendum. By the end of September, Parsley had a list of one hundred thousand socially conservative voters in Ohio whom he planned to call on the night before the election in order to get them to the polls. Republicans knew that most of the voters who went to the polls to support the anti-gay-marriage initiative would probably vote for Bush, so the Bush campaign got behind the referendum. "George W. Bush shares your values," proclaimed one Bush campaign flyer distributed in Ohio. "Marriage. Life. Faith."[48]

Buoyed by support from the White House, the nation's evangelical leaders enlisted in the president's reelection campaign. California megachurch pastor Rick Warren, whose book *The Purpose-Driven Life* had sold 25 million copies since its release in 2002, sent a letter to 134,000 pastors, telling them that there were five "non-negotiable" issues that Christians should consider when selecting a candidate—abortion, same-sex marriage, stem cell research, human cloning, and euthanasia. Throughout the presidential campaign, veteran Christian Right organizers such as Land, Dobson, and Colson, as well as NAE president Ted Haggard, held weekly conference calls with Rove or Goeglein. When the Bush campaign team realized in the early summer how crucial evangelical support would be to the president's reelection, it asked evangelical congregations to send copies of church directories to the campaign so that it could target individual members for voter registration. By the end of the summer, Land and Dobson were regularly receiving calls from Ralph Reed, who had joined the Bush campaign as the Southeast regional coordinator, and Ken Mehlman, the campaign chair. The White House effort to reach out to evangelicals paid off. Dobson, who had never before officially endorsed a presidential candidate, did so for Bush in 2004. Land, in his role as head of the Southern Baptist Convention's Ethics and Religious Liberty Commission, organized an "I Vote Values" campaign to register Southern Baptists, the first voter registration campaign in the SBC's 139-year history. "We want to get them to vote their values and convictions over economic issues," Land said.[49]

Although the Convention's churches protected their tax-exempt status by refraining from an official endorsement of either candidate, few people had any doubt about the denomination's loyalties. Their 2004 annual gathering included a live telecast address from President Bush, who used the opportunity to highlight his support for pro-life initiatives, the FMA, faith-based initiatives, and the war on terrorism. The Bush campaign also paid for a "pastors' reception" at the SBC, which featured a seminar by Ralph Reed on how ministers could register their congregants to vote. In an even more blatant display of partisanship, the SBC's outgoing president, Jack Graham, hosted a Bush-Cheney reception at the 2004 Convention, although he tried to preserve the denomination's increasingly implausible claim to nonpartisanship by stating that he hosted the reception in his capacity as an individual citizen, not as president of the SBC.[50]

In 2000, the Democrats had lost the socially conservative religious vote, but Gore and Lieberman had at least made an effort to appeal to members of that constituency. John Kerry, the most secular presidential nominee since Michael Dukakis, largely ignored them. Kerry presented Sunday morning messages at several African American churches during his campaign, and he frequently referenced his Catholic faith when discussing social questions such as abortion, but he was uncomfortable talking about religion, and he made almost no effort to reach out to evangelical voters. One of his evangelical campaign aides was dismayed when he turned down an interview request from *Christianity Today*.[51]

Though Kerry had been a Catholic churchgoer throughout his life, his liberal stance on abortion brought him into conflict with bishops from his own church. In January, the archbishop of St. Louis refused to allow Kerry to take communion in his city because of his pro-choice stance. In the early summer, Cardinal Joseph Ratzinger, who would become Pope Benedict XVI the following year, sent a memo to American bishops instructing clergy to deny communion to Catholic politicians who were guilty of "consistently campaigning and voting for permissive abortion and euthanasia laws." Most bishops in the United States said that they would let individual Catholics, including pro-choice politicians such as Kerry, judge for themselves whether they could receive communion in good conscience. But at a time when evangelicals and conservative Catholics were becoming close allies on social issues, the rift between Kerry and the Catholic clergy damaged his credibility not only among Catholics but also among conservative Protestants.[52]

In November, 78 percent of evangelicals and 52 percent of Catholics voted for Bush. Rove realized his dream of mobilizing the "missing" evangelicals; the *Economist* estimated that the total number of evangelicals who voted for Bush increased by 3.5 million between 2000 and 2004.[53]

Bush needed those 3.5 million votes. Within hours of the election, it was apparent that the outcome of the race had depended on only 120,000 votes in Ohio—which Kerry had lost. Pundits quickly cited the gay marriage referendum as a reason that the Bush campaign was able to mobilize socially conservative voters in that state, and possibly in the eleven other states that passed similar initiatives. Some wondered whether Karl Rove was behind the ballot measures, though the White House insisted he was not. Regardless, Americans associated the Bush administration with social conservatism and opposition to same-sex marriage. Of the 22 percent of voters who told exit pollsters that "moral values" were the most important issue to them in the election, 79 percent cast their ballots for Bush. "Values voters" also helped the Republicans increase their majority in both houses of Congress.[54]

Christian conservative leaders were jubilant, because they believed that the moment had finally come when they could enact their long-delayed agenda. Rove promised Christian Right leaders that the president would "absolutely" work to prohibit same-sex marriage through a constitutional amendment. Christian Right activists also expected the president to appoint conservative judicial nominees to the Supreme Court, and they warned the Senate Judiciary Committee not to oppose the president's choices—a warning that Rove echoed.[55]

The Christian Right had had moments of triumph before, but not since 1980 had they been so confident about their prospects to change the direction of the nation and its government. Republicans controlled both houses of Congress and the White House and looked forward to potential vacancies on the Supreme Court.

Evangelicals were also well positioned for long-term influence over the nation's culture. By 2005, there were nearly fourteen thousand Christian radio stations in the United States, and 16 percent of American adults said that they tuned in to these stations daily. The *Left Behind* series of end-times novels that Tim LaHaye coauthored—in which Christians fought the Antichrist, depicted as a Romanian secretary general of the United Nations—had sold 60 million copies. After the commercial success of Mel Gibson's film *The Passion of the Christ* in 2003 and the rise in popularity of other conservative Christian films in the nation's theaters, some evangelicals began envisioning the possibility of capturing Hollywood, or at least creating a rival film industry.

The Christian Right was also training a new generation of political activists at Patrick Henry College, which the former Moral Majority state chapter president and home schooling advocate Michael Farris had founded in 1997 for a select group of home-schooled students who wanted to influence the nation's governmental affairs. By 2004, seven out of the one hundred White House interns were Patrick Henry College students, and the college had also placed interns in conservative Republican offices on Capitol Hill. "The most common thing I hear is parents telling me they want their kids to be on the Supreme Court," Farris said. "And if we put enough kids in the farm system, some may get to the major leagues."[56]

Bush's second term would mark the beginning of their long-term plan to transform America, Christian Right leaders thought. Even the movement's most hard-line fundamentalists were confident that Bush was one of their own, and they warned him to hold nothing back in his effort to return America to a conservative moral standard. "If you have any weaklings around you who do not share your biblical values, shed yourself of them," Bob Jones III wrote in a letter to the president immediately after the election. "Put your agenda on the front burner and let it boil." "Now comes the revolution," Richard Viguerie proclaimed. "If you don't implement a conservative agenda now, when do you?"[57]

The Campaign to Change the Supreme Court

Once again, the Christian Right would be disappointed. Their top priority, the FMA, came up for a vote in 2006, just before the midterm elections, and it failed. On abortion, abstinence-only sex education, and stem cell research, the Bush administration did little more than hold the line, and on other issues, it could not even maintain the status quo. In 2006, the FDA, under the threat of a lawsuit from the Center for Reproductive Rights, acted against the wishes of the Christian Right and the pro-life lobby by approving the "morning-after pill" for over-the-counter sale to women over the age of eighteen.[58]

But the failure of the Bush administration to pass even one socially conservative bill during the president's second term did not arouse immediate ire from the Christian Right, because conservative evangelical activists had turned their attention to the Supreme Court. Recognizing that their movement had failed to secure its long-term aims despite electing several Republican presidents and Congresses, Christian Right leaders blamed the nation's court system, and especially the Supreme Court. During the previous half-century, the Court had ruled against antipornography laws, school prayer, and abortion restrictions, and it had expanded gay rights. Perhaps the Christian Right had made a mistake in focusing so much of its attention on the nation's executive and legislative branches. Christian Right leaders expected several aging justices to retire from the Court during Bush's second term, and they hoped that they might be able to push the Court to the right. But they faced a potential hurdle: Democratic senators might filibuster the president's judicial nominees if he selected judges who met the Christian Right's standards. To prevent that from happening, they organized a campaign to support Republican Senate Majority Leader Bill Frist's call for a ban on filibusters of judicial nominees.

On April 24, 2005, the Family Research Council organized a telecast entitled "Justice Sunday: Stopping the Filibuster against People of Faith," which reached an estimated 61 million people in evangelical churches across the nation. Featuring messages from Charles Colson and James Dobson, the telecast gave viewers a clear sense that the future of the nation's moral climate depended on the Republican Senate's ability to confirm judicial nominees. Supreme Court justices, Dobson said, were "unelected and unaccountable and arrogant and imperious and determined to redesign the culture according to their own biases and values, and they're out of control. . . . This matter of judicial tyranny to people of faith . . . has to stop." For three decades, conservative evangelicals had been decrying the "liberal" Supreme Court, and at first glance, it might have seemed that Dobson's speech was yet another sermon in that well-established genre. But "Justice Sunday" went beyond that. As millions of evangelical worshippers watched Dobson's speech on the large-screen televisions at their churches, they saw the names, phone numbers, and photographs of the politicians that Dobson described as "six or eight very squishy Republicans" flash across their screens. Viewers learned that they needed to call Senators John McCain and Lisa Murkowksi (R-AK), among others, to urge them to support Frist's plan to change the Senate's rules on filibusters. Then Senator Frist himself appeared on the screen to give a six-minute address in support of Justice Sunday.[59] Control of the nation's court system had now become the Christian Right's Holy Grail, and conservative evangelical activists were prepared to mobilize millions of followers and work with the highest level of congressional leadership to ensure that their dream of transforming the nation's highest court became a reality. But they were disappointed when a last-minute compromise scuttled Frist's plan.

Christian Right leaders found another opportunity to castigate the nation's judiciary when a Florida court order allowed Michael Schiavo to remove a feeding tube from his wife, Terri Schiavo, who had been in a vegetative state for fifteen years. In the spring of 2005, Christian Right veterans such as Randall Terry and James Dobson called for legislators to intervene to save Schiavo's life, and they championed the efforts of Schiavo's parents, Robert and Mary Schindler, to keep their daughter alive despite her husband's claim that she would not have wanted to continue living in a vegetative state. Christian Right activists convinced Congress to pass emergency legislation authorizing the Schindlers to take their case to a federal court, and the president made a special trip to Washington from his Texas ranch to sign the bill. But when the federal court upheld the Florida judge's ruling authorizing the removal of Schiavo's feeding tube, there was nothing more that they could do, and she died within two weeks. For some Christian Right activists, the removal of Schiavo's feeding tube was a fulfillment of Francis Schaeffer's prediction that abortion would soon lead to euthanasia of the terminally ill or defenseless members of society. It was also yet another example, in the Christian Right's view, of the tyranny of the unelected judiciary.[60]

Three months later, Supreme Court Justice Sandra Day O'Connor announced her retirement. When President Bush nominated the conservative judge John Roberts to replace her, Christian Right leaders were delighted. Roberts had served in the Reagan administration's Justice Department and had once filed a brief for an antiabortion case. Although Roberts was coy about his personal views, social conservatives were happy to hear that he was a devout Catholic and that his wife was a member of Feminists for Life. Shortly before the Senate's confirmation hearings began, the Family Research Council organized Justice Sunday II in order to launch yet another attack on "activist judges" and voice its support for Roberts.[61] One month after Justice Sunday II, Chief Justice William Rehnquist died, and Bush, rather than looking for a new nominee to be chief justice, selected Roberts for the spot. As most observers expected, the Senate voted to confirm Roberts, whom even his ideological opponents lauded as a brilliant intellect.

The president's next judicial appointment—for O'Connor's seat—divided the president from many of his supporters and strained the White House's alliance with the Christian Right. Instead of appointing another conservative federal judge, as many on the right expected, Bush nominated his White House counsel, Harriet Miers. Leading conservatives such as William Kristol, George Will, Robert Bork, and David Frum quickly criticized Bush's choice, but the White House had a plan to bypass the conservative punditry by appealing to the Christian Right for support. In the days leading up to the president's announcement in early October 2005, Karl Rove repeatedly called Dobson and assured him that Miers was a devout member of a pro-life, non-denominational, evangelical church. Marvin Olasky, after receiving a call from a Texas judge alerting him to Miers's imminent nomination, called her pastor in Dallas and conducted a lengthy telephone interview. Although no one knew Miers's personal views on social issues, conservative evangelicals were convinced that her active membership at a theologically conservative evangelical church was sufficient evidence that she would be a reliable vote on the Court. "Our church is strong for life," Miers's pastor told Olasky. "We believe in the biblical approach to marriage." Olasky was persuaded. Miers seemed to have "an internal compass," he wrote, with a "needle pointed toward Christ."[62]

On the day that Bush nominated Miers, Rove called Richard Land to secure his support for the nominee, and he then arranged a conference call with the Arlington Group. With Dobson presiding over the meeting, two Texas judges vouched for Miers's social conservative bona fides. Miers would vote to overturn *Roe v. Wade* if she had the opportunity, they said. She would also be an ally of the Christian Right on same-sex marriage. Dobson returned to his radio studio to plug the president's nominee. "When you know some of the things that I know—that I probably shouldn't know—you will understand why I have said, with fear and trepidation, that I believe Harriet Miers will be a good justice," he told his listeners. Dobson's comment prompted Senator Arlen Specter to threaten to subpoena the Focus on the Family director to tell the Senate Judiciary Committee the confidential information about Miers that he refused to disclose to the public.[63]

But Dobson never had to testify before the Judiciary Committee, because Miers withdrew her nomination before confirmation hearings could begin. Rove's plan to secure Christian Right support for Miers backfired. As he gave assurances to the Christian Right, secular conservatives and Republican senators, along with many Democrats, stepped up their criticism of Miers, citing her lack of judicial experience as one reason she was unqualified for a seat on the nation's highest court. Several Christian Right activists also concluded that Miers was not the best person for the job. "She sounds to me like another swing vote, which is the last thing conservatives want," Gary Bauer said. As support for Miers eroded, the Bush administration relied on Dobson to shore up the Christian Right base in support of the nomination. The day after Dobson gave his broadcast in support of Miers, the White House arranged a conference call between Dobson, Land, Colson, and hundreds of conservatives across the country who questioned the president's selection. Dobson tried to reassure the conservative activists that Miers was the right choice for the job. But in the end, he, too, had doubts about her. When documents surfaced that suggested that Miers might have supported gay rights and abortion rights in the late 1980s and early 1990s, Dobson became concerned, and he was relieved when she withdrew her name from consideration. "Based on what we now know about Miss Miers, it appears that we would not have been able to support her candidacy," Dobson said. "Thankfully, that difficult evaluation is no longer necessary." Christian Right activists, including Dobson, breathed a sigh of relief when President Bush nominated Samuel Alito, a conservative judge with a record of opposing abortion rights, to replace O'Connor.[64]

Bush's attempt to use conservative evangelicals to promote Miers's nomination may have irreparably harmed his relationship with the Christian Right. Religious and secular conservatives had repeatedly stated that the one thing that they most wanted from a Republican president was a set of staunchly conservative judicial nominees. When Bush ignored the list of acceptable judicial choices that conservative activists had spent years carefully crafting, most leading conservatives were outraged. And when Bush divided the right by appealing to a few Christian Right activists to deflect the criticisms that his nominee was receiving from other conservatives, he compounded his problems with his base.

In the end, when Christian Right leaders realized that Miers might not have been as staunchly pro-life as they had been led to believe, they felt betrayed. They had spent valuable political capital in support of someone whom, it turned out, they could not trust. Gary Bauer considered the president's abuse of the Christian Right's confidence a fatal mistake. "The ramifications will be felt not just against him but against the Republican Party," he said.[65]

The End of the Christian Right—or a New Beginning?

The ill will that Bauer had foreseen between conservative evangelicals and the GOP became more apparent during Bush's last two years in office, when a series of scandals and political missteps shook both the Republican Party and the Christian Right, with disastrous consequences for both.

Political scandals destroyed the careers of several leaders who had been key allies of the Christian Right. Tom DeLay, who had played a critical role in forging an alliance between Christian Right leaders and conservative members of Congress, resigned in disgrace after he was indicted for wrongdoing in his connection with lobbyist Jack Abramoff. Ralph Reed also suffered because of his connection with Abramoff after e-mails emerged showing that he had accepted money from Abramoff's firm in order to organize conservative Christians against Native American casinos that were competing with gambling operations run by Abramoff's clients. Representative Randy "Duke" Cunningham (R-CA) and Representative Bob Ney (R-OH) resigned from the House because of bribery charges, while Representative Mark Foley (R-FL) left when it was discovered that he had sent sexually explicit messages to underage congressional pages.

Scandals also affected the top echelons of the Christian Right. In October 2006, Ted Haggard, the president of the NAE and a close ally of James Dobson, had to resign his leadership positions at his Colorado Springs megachurch and the NAE after admitting to paying a male prostitute for crystal methamphetamine and engaging in "sexual immorality." Because Haggard had been a prominent leader in the fight for state constitutional amendments to ban same-sex marriage and was president of one of the most prominent evangelical organizations, the revelation that he was leading a double life may have hurt the Christian Right even more than the televangelist scandals of the late 1980s had.[66]

Although 70 percent of evangelical voters cast their ballots for Republican candidates in the midterm elections of 2006, their support for Republicans was an indication of their distrust of the Democratic Party rather than their enthusiasm for the GOP. A poll taken in July 2006 revealed that only 47 percent of evangelicals viewed the Republican Party as "friendly to religion," compared to 55 percent who had held that position the previous year. They also began to distance themselves from the president, whose public opinion ratings dropped precipitously following Americans' disillusionment with his handling of the Iraq war and Hurricane Katrina. Young evangelical voters—those under the age of thirty—were the first to leave the president's coalition. In 2002, 87 percent of evangelicals under the age of thirty approved of Bush's job performance, but by August 2007, only 45 percent did. Some younger evangelicals who lost faith in Bush decided to abandon the Republican Party as well. By 2007, only 40 percent of young evangelicals identified themselves as Republicans, compared to 55 percent only two years earlier. While older evangelicals were slower to criticize the Republican Party than their younger counterparts were, they too began to lose patience with the president. "This has been an unholy alliance in which the evangelicals have given everything and gotten nothing in return," Richard Cizik complained in January 2008.[67]

Seizing an opportunity, Democratic gubernatorial and congressional candidates vied for the support of evangelical voters in the 2006 midterm elections. In Ohio, which both parties viewed as a bellwether state, Democratic candidate Ted Strickland, a Methodist minister, not only won the gubernatorial election by a wide margin, but also picked up 51 percent of the evangelical vote. Even though Strickland ran against the socially conservative Republican candidate Ken Blackwell, who had spearheaded the campaign for his state's referendum against same-sex marriage in 2004, he won the support of Christian conservatives by running campaign ads on Christian radio stations, citing Bible verses in support of social justice and claiming that "the example of Jesus" had inspired him to enter politics. Democrats who favored Strickland's strategy of appealing to "people of faith" were also encouraged by pro-life

Catholic Democrat Bob Casey's senatorial victory in Pennsylvania. Casey defeated Senator Rick Santorum, a close ally of the Christian Right, while highlighting his socially conservative stances and devout religious belief.[68]

After regaining control of both houses of Congress, Senate Democrats selected Harry Reid, a pro-life Mormon, to be their new majority leader. The new Speaker of the House, Nancy Pelosi, invited a Southern Baptist, Representative James Clyburn (D-SC), to organize the Faith Working Group to reach out to religious voters. Mara Vanderslice, an evangelical who had volunteered for the Kerry campaign only to have her advice ignored, launched Common Good Strategies to train candidates to reach evangelical and Catholic voters. Jim Wallis, who had been leading a beleaguered group of left-leaning evangelicals ever since the McGovern campaign of 1972, became one of the most sought-after evangelical speakers at Democratic strategy sessions. Many considered his best-selling book *God's Politics: Why the Right Gets It Wrong and the Left Doesn't Get It* (2005) a perceptive analysis of the reason why secular liberalism had never won presidential elections, and they took heart from his optimistic argument that political liberals could win evangelical votes if they anchored their proposals in the principles of the Bible.[69]

One rising star in the party—Senator Barack Obama—seemed to have an intuitive grasp of how to frame liberal policy proposals in the language of faith. An adult convert to Christianity and a committed member of an African American liberal Protestant church in Chicago, Obama had thought deeply about the relationship between religion and politics, and he was well versed in the Bible and Christian theological traditions. In June 2006, he gave a speech at a conference that Wallis had organized in which he told the story of his conversion, spoke of the value of the church in his life and the lives of others, and argued that Democrats could confront the radicalism of the Religious Right only if they welcomed the place of religion in political life.[70]

Democrats also began traveling to conservative evangelical venues that they had traditionally eschewed. In 2006, Democratic National Committee chair Howard Dean, who had once bragged about his infrequent church attendance and had said during his 2004 presidential campaign that "my religion doesn't inform my public policy," appeared on Pat Robertson's *700 Club*, where he argued that Democrats "have an enormous amount in common with the Christian community, and particularly with the evangelical Christian community." When popular evangelical author and pastor Joel Osteen moved his fifty-thousand-member congregation into the Houston Rockets' former stadium, Nancy Pelosi was on hand to attend the inaugural service, even though she was neither a Texan nor an evangelical. And when Rick

Warren held a "Summit on AIDS and the Church" at his twenty-two-thousand-member megachurch in Orange County, California, Barack Obama showed up to give a speech.[71]

Many conservative evangelicals criticized Warren for inviting Obama to address the congregation: they said it was inappropriate for a pro-choice politician to speak at an evangelical church. But Warren defended his decision, arguing that although he refused to compromise his pro-life convictions, he believed that conservative evangelicals could find common ground with liberal Democrats in the fight against AIDS. Warren had supported Bush in 2004, but his increasing involvement in the campaign against AIDS in Africa was moving him to the left. Other evangelicals who had supported Bush's reelection campaign also suggested that they might consider supporting a Democrat in 2008. Randy Brinson, the organizer of the pro-Bush "Redeem the Vote" campaign of 2004, began meeting with the Democratic Leadership Council in 2006.[72]

The failure of most of the nation's Christian Right leaders to focus on social justice issues put them at odds with a younger generation of evangelicals who wanted to make such causes a priority. Most of the power brokers in the Christian Right, including Jerry Falwell, Pat Robertson, James Dobson, and Richard Land, had formed their political thinking decades earlier, during the Cold War or the campaigns against the ERA and abortion. They approached politics with a siege mentality. The nation was under threat, they believed—if not from communism, then from Islamic-inspired terrorism. The family was in mortal danger, they thought—if not from feminism, then from gays or abortion. They had remained loyal to the Republican Party for the previous fifty years because the GOP shared their vision of a "Christian" nation resolutely defending itself against internal and external enemies.

But evangelicals who had been born after the Cold War and who were too young to remember a prefeminist era did not share this vision. They were more likely to take their religious cues from cultural icons such as Bono—the leader of the popular band U2, who spoke publicly about the link between his Christian faith and social justice—than from Robertson and Dobson. The "emerging church" movement among young evangelicals focused heavily on service to the poor, and even the nation's most conservative evangelical churches began organizing short-term mission trips for young people to build schools and churches in Belize or Uganda, clean up debris in New Orleans after Hurricane Katrina, or work with Habitat for Humanity in their own neighborhoods. Younger evangelicals had come to terms with the religious and cultural pluralism of their generation, and they viewed their religion not as a venue to protest against social trends, but as a means to show their culture the love of Christ through service. For a short time, the Bush campaign had held together an uneasy coalition of social-justice-oriented younger evangelicals and culture warriors of the older generation by portraying the Iraq War as both a new Cold War and a social-justice campaign to liberate oppressed people and promote democracy, and by talking about faith-based initiatives. But when the war turned sour and when the president failed to enact the Christian Right's agenda on other issues, the coalition that the GOP and Christian Right leaders had held together for so long threatened to break apart. In February 2008, Richard Cizik admitted that the votes of 40 percent of evangelicals were "up for grabs." The GOP was "no longer God's Own Party," he said.[73]

Cizik was not ready to defect to the Democratic camp himself, but on the issue of climate change, he was moving in that direction. In 2004, he convinced the NAE to make "creation care" a priority, and he increased his attention to environmental issues after Ted Haggard's downfall in late 2006. In 2007, in an apparent rebuke to the Bush administration, the NAE issued a declaration against torture. James Dobson rebuked Cizik. "If he cannot be trusted to articulate the views of American evangelicals on environmental issues, then we respectfully suggest that he be encouraged to resign his position with the NAE," Dobson said.[74]

But Cizik's moderately progressive stances on the environment may have better represented the views of a new generation of evangelicals than Dobson's staunch conservatism did. By the early twenty-first century, Dobson's followers consisted mainly of graying Baby Boomers. In 1988, the age of his average audience member had been thirty-three, but by 2002, it was forty-seven. And it was not only Dobson who failed to appeal to younger evangelicals. In 1985, more than 7 million viewers had watched *The 700 Club* each week, but twenty years later, the show's audience had shrunk to 828,000.[75]

When Jerry Falwell died in May 2007, many observers noted that his heyday had passed some years earlier and that younger evangelicals were eager to distance themselves from his polarizing brand of politics. Three months before his death, Falwell had sharply rebuked evangelicals who championed environmentalism, calling it "Satan's attempt to redirect the church's primary focus." But Falwell had lost touch with his movement: a poll released in October 2007 showed that 84 percent of evangelicals—a higher percentage than had ever voted Republican in any previous presidential election—favored legislation to stop global warming. In March 2008, even the president of the Southern Baptist Convention signed "A Southern Baptist Declaration on the Environment and Climate Change," which called on the denomination to make amends for its past lack of concern for the environment.

"We humbly take responsibility for the damage that we have done to God's cosmic revelation and pledge to take an unwavering stand to preserve and protect the creation over which we have been given responsibility by Almighty God Himself," the Southern Baptists stated.[76]

Faced with an apparent "evangelical crack-up," as a *New York Times Magazine* headline phrased it, the Republican Party's presidential hopefuls were uncertain whether any Christian Right leader or organization had the power to deliver evangelical votes. In the absence of a new evangelical leader with strong ties to the Republican Party, most of the candidates looked to the Christian Right's "old guard." John McCain, hoping to make amends for the insults in 2000, gave a commencement speech at Falwell's Liberty University in 2006. Rudy Giuliani, whose pro-choice, pro-gay-rights record was at least as objectionable to the Christian Right as anything in McCain's past, was so pleased to get Pat Robertson's endorsement that he traveled to Norfolk, Virginia, to receive it in person. The formerly pro-choice Mormon governor Mitt Romney tried to assure evangelicals that he was the true social conservative in the race, welcoming an endorsement from Bob Jones III. But endorsements from Christian Right leaders meant little, partly because they could not agree on a single candidate.[77]

One might have expected that Mike Huckabee, a former Arkansas governor, would have been the darling of the Christian Right. In 1980, when he was only twenty-four years old, he had been a public relations director for James Robison's ministry. He had then served as a Baptist pastor, televangelist, and president of the Arkansas Baptist Convention before leaving the ministry to enter politics in the 1990s. He had a consistent record of opposing abortion and gay rights. But Huckabee also embraced antipoverty and environmental initiatives, and as governor of Arkansas he had raised taxes several times. He preferred to talk about helping children rather than the Christian Right's favorite causes.[78]

Huckabee was popular with evangelicals in the pews, and he won handily in a Values Voter Debate Straw Poll held in Fort Lauderdale in the fall of 2007. A few evangelical leaders who had fallen afoul of the Christian Right also appreciated Huckabee's candidacy. Jim Wallis, who rarely had a good word for Republican candidates, lauded Huckabee's campaign message as a new brand of socially responsible evangelical politics. And Randy Brinson, who had been thinking about supporting a Democrat, threw his support to Huckabee in late 2007 and gave his candidacy a crucial boost by supplying him with the list of e-mail contacts from his Redeem the Vote campaign of 2004—a list that included the names of 414,000 young evangelicals in Iowa. That contact list may have been the key to Huckabee's first-place finish in the state's Republican caucuses, because 60 percent of Iowa Republican caucus-goers were evangelicals, and Huckabee won more than two-thirds of their votes.[79] Huckabee went on to win primaries in Alabama, Arkansas, Georgia, Louisiana, and Tennessee, as well as caucuses in Kansas and West Virginia, all of which had sizable evangelical constituencies.

But the established leaders of the Christian Right never warmed to his candidacy—another sign that they had lost touch with evangelicals in the pews. Gary Bauer complained that the former Arkansas governor was not sufficiently supportive of the war in Iraq, and he wondered whether he would be too conciliatory toward Iran. Others expressed skepticism about a candidate who had attracted strong opposition from the anti-tax Club for Growth—which Huckabee had dubbed the "Club for Greed"—and Rush Limbaugh, among others.[80]

But Christian Right leaders faced a dilemma in opposing Huckabee, because they also had a strong dislike for McCain. Some evangelicals could not forgive the man who had repeatedly insulted them and had rarely supported their causes. The senator had committed the cardinal sin of voting against the FMA in both 2004 and 2006, which, in Dobson's view, made him anathema. McCain, Dobson stated, "is not a conservative, and in fact, has gone out of his way to stick his thumb in the eyes of those who are." He therefore would not vote for him "under any circumstances."[81]

The two Democratic presidential front-runners, Hillary Clinton and Barack Obama, were delighted to see this infighting, and they made an unprecedented effort to solicit the evangelical vote. Both candidates made campaign stops at predominantly white evangelical churches, a first for Democratic presidential candidates. In April 2008, they held a Sunday evening "Compassion Forum" at Messiah College, a Pennsylvania evangelical school, where evangelical leaders including Wallis, Cizik, and the president of the Southern Baptist Convention gathered to ask the candidates about their faith. "Should it be God's plan to have me in the White House, I look forward to our collaboration," the Illinois senator said to Cizik while complimenting the NAE leader on his "creation care" program.[82]

After Obama won the nomination, both he and McCain continued to reach out to evangelicals, believing that, for the first time in years, social conservatives might be a swing constituency. Evangelical leaders welcomed the attention. In August, Rick Warren brought Obama and McCain together for the Saddleback Civil Forum on the Presidency, a two-hour session that gave the candidates a chance to answer questions about their personal faith, abortion, same-sex marriage, and other issues of concern to evangelical voters.

Warren tried to maintain an image of impartiality, saying, "Both of these guys are my friends."[83]

With Obama's encouragement, the Democratic Party adopted a platform advocating policies that would "reduce the need for abortions." Obama also selected a white evangelical minister, Florida megachurch pastor Joel Hunter, to lead the benediction at the party's convention. Some pro-lifers, including Warren, derided the party's moderate softening of its pro-choice stance as mere "window-dressing," but Wallis called it a "step in the right direction." For many evangelicals, Obama's willingness to listen to their concerns made them reticent to speak out against his candidacy.[84]

Recognizing that he had not yet won the loyalty of the Christian Right, McCain made a bid for their support by selecting Alaska governor Sarah Palin, a strongly pro-life evangelical Christian, as his running mate. He would have preferred to select Joe Lieberman for the role, but his campaign aides warned him that the choice of the pro-choice, pro-gay-rights senator from Connecticut would anger the Christian Right and doom his candidacy. They convinced him to follow the advice of Richard Land, who recommended Palin as a vice presidential nominee.[85]

Palin, the first woman to earn a place on a Republican presidential ticket, was also the most overtly evangelical candidate ever to run for vice president. She supported the teaching of "intelligent design" in public schools, opposed abortion under any circumstance except to save a mother's life, and staunchly defended marriage as an exclusively heterosexual institution. Her background was similar to that of many socially conservative evangelicals. She had spent most of her life in rural or suburban areas and had obtained her education at small state colleges. She was a mother of five children, including a young son with Down syndrome. Her home congregation, the thousand-member Wasilla Bible Church, was a rapidly growing evangelical enterprise whose exuberant worship services and family-focused messages were nearly identical to those of the suburban evangelical megachurches that most Christian Right activists attended. Even her personal struggles seemed to appeal to evangelicals. When conservative Christians learned that Palin's seventeen-year-old, unmarried daughter was pregnant, they did not condemn the Alaska governor, as some media analysts had expected, but instead lauded her for encouraging her daughter not to have an abortion.[86]

Palin's place on the ticket won over most of the evangelicals who had been skeptical about McCain. Never before had they seen a national ticket that included a conservative evangelical Christian whose policy positions were so closely in line with the Christian Right. James Dobson announced that despite his vowing never to support McCain, he would vote for the Republican ticket. Shortly after McCain picked Palin, his approval rating among white evangelical voters rose from 61 to 71 percent. McCain's vice presidential selection was a "grand slam home run," Gary Bauer declared.[87]

On Election Day, conservative evangelicals rallied to McCain. Although he received only 46 percent of the popular vote, McCain won the votes of 73 percent of white evangelicals and more than 80 percent of white evangelicals who attended church weekly. Even younger evangelicals gave the McCain-Palin ticket strong support. Obama received the support of 66 percent of voters under the age of thirty, but only 32 percent of evangelical voters in that age group. Evangelical turnout was also higher than many had expected: 23 percent of all voters were white evangelicals, an increase of 3 percentage points from 2004. Obama did make modest gains among evangelicals, winning 26 percent of their vote compared to the 21 percent that Kerry had received in 2004. Nevertheless, evangelicals' importance to the Republican coalition was increasing. Whereas 36 percent of Bush's supporters in 2004 had been evangelicals, 38.5 percent of McCain's were.[88] In a year of evangelical disillusionment with the GOP and a concerted effort by the Democrats to narrow the "God gap," most evangelicals remained loyal to the GOP, ensuring their continued dominance in the party.

The Future of the Christian Right

If evangelical voting behavior in the 2008 election provided evidence that the Christian Right would endure despite premature journalistic predictions of its demise, it also suggested that the movement's political approach would change. Mike Huckabee's success in appealing to evangelicals with a platform that combined compassion with opposition to abortion, and younger evangelicals' distaste for the old-style culture warriors in the movement, suggested that the confrontational style of Falwell, Robertson, and Dobson was fading away. Survey data indicated that most megachurch pastors disliked the politics of the Christian Right, even though they and their congregants continued to vote Republican and oppose same-sex marriage and abortion. Polls showed that evangelicals under thirty were just as strongly opposed to abortion as older evangelicals were. More than two-thirds of younger evangelicals opposed same-sex marriage, but they disliked overt gay-bashing. They believed in the "sanctity of marriage" and the idea that "life begins at conception," but as Rick Warren told Fox News, they also cared about poverty, sex trafficking, and AIDS, because "Jesus' agenda is far bigger than one or two issues."[89]

The fifty-four-year-old Warren, whom *Time* declared "America's most powerful religious leader," epitomized a new generation of evangelical activism and provided a glimpse of the possible future direction for the Christian Right. Combining theological conservatism and an endorsement of some of the Christian Right's traditional political positions with a new interest in the environment, poverty, and bipartisan dialogue, Warren promoted a brand of evangelicalism that appealed to many Baby Boomers and their children. He reached out to candidates of both parties, addressing the Clinton Global Initiative on poverty while at the same time speaking out against abortion and campaigning for a California ballot initiative prohibiting same-sex marriage. Journalists who interviewed Warren invariably described the goateed, Hawaiian-shirt-wearing pastor as "affable," "gregarious," and "charming." By 2009, his *Purpose-Driven Life* had become the best-selling hardcover book in American publishing history.[90]

Warren insisted that he wanted to practice a less confrontational brand of politics than previous Christian Right leaders had adopted, but his conservative stances on same-sex marriage and abortion created a firestorm in liberal circles immediately after Obama invited him to lead a prayer at the inauguration. When gay rights supporters learned that Warren had not only campaigned against same-sex marriage in California but had also compared gay marriage to incest and pedophilia, they picketed outside his church. The Obama transition team was deluged with angry letters. The pastor who had built his reputation on creating a less divisive brand of politics found himself branded as a politically polarizing figure.[91]

The controversy showed that while the heyday of Falwell, Robertson, Reed, and Dobson had passed, the culture wars were far from over. The debate that began in the 1920s continues in the early twenty-first century. For decades, evangelicals used the Republican Party to try to enforce a code of morality that would provide a religiously based structure for society. Their attempts mostly failed, because the majority of Americans were unwilling to abandon the values of pluralism, tolerance, and egalitarianism. But evangelicals were not ready to leave the public sphere and retreat to their churches, nor were they willing to give up their convictions. Despite what pundits predicted, evangelicals have not called off the culture wars; they have merely changed strategies. At the beginning of the Obama administration, the Christian Right is still many millions strong, and well positioned to continue exerting its influence in national life. Conservative Christian leaders still have faith that, with the help of God and the Republican Party, they can restore a Christian moral order to the nation.

Abbreviations

AHC	American Heritage Center, University of Wyoming, Laramie, WY
AJC	*Atlanta Journal-Constitution*
BBT	*Baptist Bible Tribune*
BG	*Boston Globe*
BGCA	Billy Graham Center Archives, Wheaton, IL
BJU	Fundamentalism File, J. S. Mack Library, Bob Jones University, Greenville, SC
BJUA	Bob Jones University Archives, Greenville, SC
CB	*Christian Beacon*
CCW	*Christian Crusade Weekly*
CD	*Conservative Digest*
CSM	*Christian Science Monitor*
CT	*Christianity Today*
EPL	Dwight D. Eisenhower Presidential Library, Abilene, KS
FFC	*Focus on the Family Citizen*
GFL	Gerald R. Ford Presidential Library, Ann Arbor, MI
JC	*Journal-Champion,* Lynchburg, VA
JCL	Jimmy Carter Library, Atlanta, GA
LAT	*Los Angeles Times*
LBJL	Lyndon Baines Johnson Library, Austin, TX
LUA	Liberty University Archives, Lynchburg, VA
MMR	*Moral Majority Report*
NPL	Nixon Presidential Library, Yorba Linda, CA
NYT	*New York Times*
PFAW	People for the American Way, Washington, DC
PRA	Political Research Associates, Somerville, MA

RRPL	Ronald Reagan Presidential Library, Simi Valley, CA
RTD	*Richmond Times-Dispatch*
SBHLA	Southern Baptist Historical Library and Archives
SFC	*San Francisco Chronicle*
SWL	*Sword of the Lord*
UEA	*United Evangelical Action*
USN	*U.S. News and World Report*
WSJ	*Wall Street Journal*
WP	*Washington Post*
WT	*Washington Times*

Introduction

1. Kathy Sawyer and Robert G. Kaiser, "Evangelicals Flock to GOP Standard Feeling They Have Friend in Reagan," *WP*, 16 July 1980.

2. William E. Leuchtenburg, *The Perils of Prosperity, 1914–1932*, 2nd ed. (Chicago: University of Chicago Press, 1993), 224. Historical narratives that locate the Christian Right's origins in the culture wars of the 1970s include William Martin, *With God on Our Side: The Rise of the Religious Right in America* (New York: Broadway Books, 1996); Kenneth J. Heineman, *God Is a Conservative: Religion, Politics, and Morality in Christian America* (New York: New York University Press, 1998); and Ruth Murray Brown, *For a "Christian America": A History of the Religious Right* (Amherst, NY: Prometheus Books, 2002). Numerous political science studies adopt a similar interpretation. For examples, see Robert C. Liebman and Robert Wuthnow, ed., *The New Christian Right: Mobilization and Legitimation* (Hawthorne, NY: Aldine, 1983); Matthew C. Moen, *The Transformation of the Christian Right* (Tuscaloosa: University of Alabama Press, 1992); John C. Green et al., *Religion and the Culture Wars: Dispatches from the Front* (Lanham, MD: Rowman & Littlefield, 1996); and Duane M. Oldfield, *The Right and the Righteous: The Christian Right Confronts the Republican Party* (Lanham, MD: Rowman & Littlefield, 1996). For a concise summary of this view, see Kenneth D. Wald and Allison Calhoun-Brown, *Religion and Politics in the United States*, 5th ed. (Lanham, MD: Rowman & Littlefield, 2007), 210–217. Clyde Wilcox's *God's Warriors: The Christian Right in Twentieth-Century America* (Baltimore: Johns Hopkins University Press, 1992) and *Onward Christian Soldiers? The Religious Right in American Politics* (Boulder, CO: Westview Press, 1996) are unusual among political science studies in comparing early-twentieth-century fundamentalist political movements with the recent activities of the Christian Right, though Wilcox sees more contrasts than continuities between the contemporary Christian Right and early-twentieth-century fundamentalist campaigns, and agrees with other political scientists in locating the origins of the modern Christian Right in the culture wars of the 1970s. For interpretations of the Religious Right's origins that emphasize race and the 1978 IRS ruling, see Thomas F. Edsall and Mary D. Edsall, *Chain Reaction: The Impact of Race, Rights, and Taxes on American Politics*

(New York: Norton, 1992); Dan T. Carter, *From George Wallace to Newt Gingrich: Race in the Conservative Counterrevolution, 1963–1994* (Baton Rouge: Louisiana State University Press, 1996); Joseph Crespino, *In Search of Another Country: Mississippi and the Conservative Counterrevolution* (Princeton, NJ: Princeton University Press, 2007); and Joseph Crespino, "Civil Rights and the Religious Right," in *Rightward Bound: Making America Conservative in the 1970s*, ed. Bruce J. Schulman and Julian E. Zelizer (Cambridge, MA: Harvard University Press, 2008), 90–105. For a study that challenges this conventional narrative and traces modern evangelical political mobilization to the Cold War of the 1950s and 1960s, see Kevin M. Kruse, "Beyond the Southern Cross: The National Origins of the Religious Right," in *The Myth of Southern Exceptionalism*, ed. Matthew D. Lassiter and Joseph Crespino (New York: Oxford University Press, 2010), 286–307.

3. This argument parallels the approach of Allan J. Lichtman's *White Protestant Nation: The Rise of the American Conservative Movement* (New York: Atlantic Press Monthly, 2008), which argues that modern American conservatism has its roots in evangelical-inspired moral campaigns of the 1920s. But whereas Lichtman portrays nearly all manifestations of the American conservative movement as a quest to create a "white Protestant nation"—an interpretation that may be too broad—this book restricts its analysis to white conservative Protestants and examines the moral order they sought to create.

4. For studies that emphasize anticommunism in prompting conservative evangelical political mobilization, see Lisa McGirr, *Suburban Warriors: The Origins of the New American Right* (Princeton, NJ: Princeton University Press, 2001); and Angela M. Lahr, *Millennial Dreams and Apocalyptic Nightmares: The Cold War Origins of Political Evangelicalism* (New York: Oxford University Press, 2007).

5. For conservative Catholic politics in the 1970s, see Patrick Allitt, *Catholic Intellectuals and Conservative Politics in America, 1950–1985* (Ithaca, NY: Cornell University Press, 1993); Donald T. Critchlow, *Phyllis Schlafly and Grassroots Conservatism: A Woman's Crusade* (Princeton, NJ: Princeton University Press, 2005); Mary Jo Weaver and R. Scott Appleby, eds., *Being Right: Conservative Catholics in America* (Bloomington: Indiana University Press, 1995); William R. Prendergast, *The Catholic Voter in American Politics: The Passing of the Democratic Monolith* (Washington, DC: Georgetown University Press, 1999); and George J. Marlin, *The American Catholic Voter: 200 Years of Political Impact*, 2nd ed. (South Bend, IN: St. Augustine's Press, 2006).

6. For Richard Nixon's role in the culture wars, see Rick Perlstein, *Nixonland: The Rise of a President and the Fracturing of America* (New York: Scribner, 2008); Robert Mason, *Richard Nixon and the Quest for a New Majority* (Chapel Hill: University of North Carolina Press, 2004); and Bruce J. Schulman, *The Seventies: The Great Shift in American Culture, Society, and Politics* (New York: Free Press, 2001), 23–52.

7. E. J. Dionne, Jr., *Souled Out: Reclaiming Faith and Politics after the Religious Right* (Princeton, NJ: Princeton University Press, 2008), 54. For studies exploring the relationship between the growth of the Sunbelt and the rise of the Christian Right, see Darren Dochuk, "Evangelicalism Becomes Southern,

Politics Becomes Evangelical: From FDR to Reagan," in *Religion and American Politics: From the Colonial Period to the Present*, ed. Mark A. Noll and Luke E. Harlow, 2nd ed. (New York: Oxford University Press, 2007), 297–325; John G. Turner, *Bill Bright and Campus Crusade for Christ: The Renewal of Evangelicalism in Postwar America* (Chapel Hill: University of North Carolina Press, 2008); Bethany Moreton, *To Serve God and Wal-Mart: The Making of Christian Free Enterprise* (Cambridge, MA: Harvard University Press, 2009); and Steven P. Miller, *Billy Graham and the Rise of the Republican South* (Philadelphia: University of Pennsylvania Press, 2009).

8. For the secularization of the Democratic Party, see Mark Stricherz, *Why the Democrats Are Blue: How Secular Liberals Hijacked the People's Party* (New York: Encounter Books, 2007); Amy Sullivan, *The Party Faithful: How and Why Democrats Are Closing the God Gap* (New York: Scribner, 2008); and Bruce Miroff, *The Liberals' Moment: The McGovern Insurgency and the Identity Crisis of the Democratic Party* (Lawrence: University Press of Kansas, 2007).

9. For analyses of Republicans' attempts to win Christian Right voters—some of which may exaggerate the degree to which GOP strategists were responsible for the introduction of the culture wars to American politics—see Bruce Nesmith, *The New Republican Coalition: The Reagan Campaigns and White Evangelicals* (New York: Peter Lang, 1994); E. J. Dionne, Jr., *Why Americans Hate Politics*, 2nd ed. (New York: Simon & Schuster, 2004); and Thomas Frank, *What's the Matter with Kansas? How Conservatives Won the Heart of America* (New York: Metropolitan Books, 2004).

10. For predictions of the Christian Right's demise, see Dionne, *Souled Out*, 4; and David D. Kirkpatrick, "The Evangelical Crackup," *NYT Magazine*, 28 October 2007.

Chapter 1

1. "Drys Assail Smith; Wets Hit Wheeler," *NYT*, 23 June 1924; Daniel Lynn Turner, "Fundamentalism, the Arts, and Personal Refinement: A Study of the Ideals of Bob Jones, Sr., and Bob Jones, Jr." (Ed.D. diss., University of Illinois at Urbana-Champaign, 1988), 223; "Bryan Flings Dry Gauntlet at Governor Smith's Feet," *NYT*, 10 June 1923.

2. Joel A. Carpenter, *Revive Us Again: The Reawakening of American Fundamentalism* (New York: Oxford University Press, 1997), 141–160; William Ward Ayer, "Evangelical Christianity Endangered by Its Fragmentized Condition," in *Evangelical Action! A Report of the National Association of Evangelicals for United Action*, ed. Executive Committee of the National Association of Evangelicals (Boston: United Action Press, 1942), 45–46, facsimile reprinted in *A New Evangelical Coalition: Early Documents of the National Association of Evangelicals*, ed. Joel A. Carpenter (New York: Garland, 1988).

3. Mark A. Noll, *America's God: From Jonathan Edwards to Abraham Lincoln* (New York: Oxford University Press, 2002), 170, 197.

4. For a history of the fundamentalist movement, see George Marsden, *Fundamentalism and American Culture*, 2nd ed. (New York: Oxford University Press, 2006). Studies of fundamentalist leaders in the 1920s include Ralph

G. Giordano, *Satan in the Dance Hall: Rev. John Roach Straton, Social Dancing, and Morality in 1920s New York City* (Lanham, MD: Scarecrow Press, 2008); Barry Hankins, *God's Rascal: J. Frank Norris and the Beginnings of Southern Fundamentalism* (Lexington: University Press of Kentucky, 1996); William V. Trollinger, Jr., *God's Empire: William Bell Riley and Midwestern Fundamentalism* (Madison: University of Wisconsin Press, 1991); and Mark Summer Still, "'Fighting Bob' Shuler: Fundamentalist and Reformer" (Ph.D. diss., Claremont Graduate School, 1988). For analyses of cultural conflict in the 1920s, see William E. Leuchtenburg, *The Perils of Prosperity, 1914–1932*, 2nd ed. (Chicago: University of Chicago Press, 1993); and Matthew Avery Sutton, *Aimee Semple McPherson and the Resurrection of Christian America* (Cambridge, MA: Harvard University Press, 2007).

5. Kenneth K. Bailey, *Southern White Protestantism in the Twentieth Century* (New York: Harper & Row, 1964), 45–106; Still, "'Fighting Bob' Shuler," 465.

6. Joseph L. Larsen, "What Makes the United States Great and What Detracts from Her Greatness," *Moody Monthly*, July 1929, 526.

7. Robert Hill, "The Home, the Key to the Situation," *Moody Monthly*, November 1928, 104. For a study of fundamentalists' views of gender roles, see Margaret Lamberts Bendroth, *Fundamentalism and Gender, 1875 to the Present* (New Haven, CT: Yale University Press, 1993); and Betty A. DeBerg, *Ungodly Women: Gender and the First Wave of American Fundamentalism* (Minneapolis: Fortress Press, 1990).

8. "Text of W. J. Bryan's Speech That Aroused a Great Storm," *NYT*, 3 July 1924; Willard H. Smith, "William Jennings Bryan and the Social Gospel," *Journal of American History* 53 (1966): 41, 59. For a detailed study of Bryan's political and religious beliefs, see Michael Kazin, *A Godly Hero: The Life of William Jennings Bryan* (New York: Knopf, 2006).

9. Annual of the Alabama Baptist Convention, 1933, 26; *Moody Monthly*, July 1933, 481–482; John R. Rice, "Vote Beer Out Nov. 6!" *SWL*, 2 November 1934, 1; *SWL*, 9 November 1934; Wayne Flynt, "Religion for the Blues: Evangelicalism, Poor Whites, and the Great Depression," *Journal of Southern History* 71 (2005): 28–38; Bailey, *Southern White Protestantism*, 114–125.

10. See, for example, George McCready Price, "World Civilization Nearing Its Climax," *Moody Monthly*, July 1933, 483–484.

11. Paul Boyer, *When Time Shall Be No More: Prophecy Belief in Modern American Culture* (Cambridge, MA: Harvard University Press, 1992), 90–230; Timothy P. Weber, *Living in the Shadow of the Second Coming: American Premillennialism, 1875–1982* (Chicago: University of Chicago Press, 1987), 179–180.

12. David M. Kennedy, *Freedom from Fear: The American People in Depression and War, 1929–1945* (New York: Oxford University Press, 1999), 619–649, 856–858.

13. Boyer, *When Time Shall Be No More*, 106; Mark Ward, Sr., "Chronology of Religious Broadcasting," *National Religious Broadcasters Directory of Religious Media* (1994), 26–46; Mark Ward, Sr., *Air of Salvation: The Story of Christian Broadcasting* (Grand Rapids, MI: Baker Books, 1994), 17–21; Tona J. Hangen, *Redeeming the Dial: Radio, Religion, and Popular Culture in America* (Chapel Hill: University of North Carolina Press, 2002), 80–141.

14. Harold J. Ockenga, "Christ for America," *United We Stand: A Report of the Constitutional Convention of the National Association of Evangelicals, May 3–6, 1943* (n.p., 1943), 11, 13, facsimile reprinted in Carpenter, *New Evangelical Coalition*.

15. James DeForest Murch, *Cooperation without Compromise: A History of the National Association of Evangelicals* (Grand Rapids, MI: William B. Eerdmans, 1956), 60–61, 137–138; Harold Lindsell, *Park Street Prophet: A Life of Harold John Ockenga* (Wheaton, IL: Van Kampen Press, 1951), 84.

16. Sara Diamond, *Not by Politics Alone: The Enduring Influence of the Christian Right* (New York: Guilford Press, 1998), 23–24; Peter G. Horsfield, *Religious Television: The American Experience* (New York: Longman, 1984).

17. John W. Bradbury, "Cooperation among Evangelicals," *United We Stand: A Report of the Constitutional Convention of the National Association of Evangelicals, May 3–6, 1943* (n.p., 1943), 20–21, facsimile reprinted in Carpenter, *New Evangelical Coalition*; *UEA*, 1 July 1951, 6; *UEA*, 1 June 1954, 13; A. Ray Cartlidge, "The Inside Story of the 'Battle of Champaign,'" *UEA*, 15 October 1945, 4; Louis Gasper, *The Fundamentalist Movement* (The Hague: Mouton, 1963), 146.

18. George W. Robnett, "Our Schools in Danger of Centralized and Subversive Controls," *UEA*, 1 October 1945, 6.

19. A. Ray Cartlidge, 'The Inside Story of the 'Battle of Champaign,'" *UEA*, 15 October 1945, 3–7.

20. Marsden, *Fundamentalism and American Culture*, 209; Joseph T. Larsen, "America's Sin Is Forgetting God," *Moody Monthly*, July 1933, 486; Boyer, *When Time Shall Be No More*, 157.

21. Sara Diamond, *Roads to Dominion: Right-Wing Movements and Political Power in the United States* (New York: Guilford Press, 1995), 101; Church League of America, *What Is the Church League of America?* (Wheaton, IL: Church League of America, [1959?]), 2–3, PRA.

22. *UEA*, February 1943, 2; Gasper, *Fundamentalist Movement*, 52–54; Murch, *Cooperation without Compromise*, 151–152, 161.

23. Russell T. Hitt, "The Christian Trend in Congress," *Christian Life*, May 1951, 15; Lisa Getter, "Showing Faith in Discretion," *LAT*, 27 September 2002; Jeff Sharlet, *The Family: The Secret Fundamentalism at the Heart of American Power* (New York: HarperCollins, 2008), 87–124, 183–204; Lee Edwards, *Missionary for Freedom: The Life and Times of Walter Judd* (New York: Paragon House, 1990); Stephen J. Whitfield, *The Culture of the Cold War*, 2nd ed. (Baltimore: Johns Hopkins University Press, 1996), 87.

24. Wesley and Beverly Allinsmith, "Religious Affiliation and Politico-Economic Attitude: A Study of Eight Major U.S. Religious Groups," *Public Opinion Quarterly* 12 (1948): 385; Lyman Kellstedt et al., "Faith Transformed: Religion and American Politics from FDR to George W. Bush," in *Religion and American Politics: From the Colonial Period to the Present*, ed. Mark A. Noll and Luke E. Harlow, 2nd ed. (New York: Oxford University Press, 2007), 272; James T. Patterson, *Grand Expectations: The United States, 1945–1974* (New York: Oxford University Press, 1996), 165–242; Harry S. Truman, Inaugural

Address, 20 January 1949, www.trumanlibrary.org/whistlestop/50yr_archive/inagural20jan1949.htm.

25. *Christian Life*, June 1951, 39; John C. Pollack, *A Foreign Devil in China: The Story of L. Nelson Bell, an American Surgeon in China* (Minneapolis: Worldwide Publications, 1971); "Behind the Iron Curtain," *Christian Life*, October 1951, 36; "More Communist Treachery," *Christian Life*, October 1951, 54.

26. Roy L. Laurin, "Are 'Reds' Hiding in Our Churches?" *UEA*, 1 December 1953, 10; Richard M. Fried, *Nightmare in Red: The McCarthy Era in Perspective* (New York: Oxford University Press, 1990), 22.

27. Billy Graham, "We Need Revival!" and "Prepare to Meet Thy God!" in *Revival in Our Time: The Story of the Billy Graham Evangelistic Campaigns* (Wheaton, IL: Van Kampen Press, 1950), 72–73, 122–123. For biographical information on Graham's early life, see William Martin, *A Prophet with Honor: The Billy Graham Story* (New York: William Morrow, 1991), 55–172.

28. For information on Youth for Christ and the changes in evangelicalism in the early 1940s, see Carpenter, *Revive Us Again*, 151–176.

29. For Graham's Los Angeles crusade, see Martin, *Prophet with Honor*, 112–120. Information on the culture of the Cold War and Graham's appropriation of Cold War imagery comes from Patterson, *Grand Expectations*, 165–205, 238–239, and Whitfield, *Culture of the Cold War*, 77–82.

30. William G. McLoughlin, *Billy Graham: Revivalist in a Secular Age* (New York: Ronald Press, 1960), 50; "Billy Graham Revival Shakes South Carolina," *SWL*, 7 April 1950, 5.

31. Billy Graham, "Our Teenage Problem," *Hour of Decision*, 1955, BGCA; Billy Graham, "The Home," *Hour of Decision*, 1956, BGCA.

32. "Smut Held Cause of Delinquency," *NYT*, 1 June 1955; "U.S. Court Upsets Ban on 'Playboy,'" *NYT*, 31 October 1958; Billy Graham, "Christ's Answer to the World," Sermon, Charlotte, NC, 21 September 1958, BGCA, www.wheaton.edu/bgc/archives/docs/bg-charlotte/0921.html.

33. "The New Evangelist," *Time*, 25 October 1954, 54; Timothy Alan Crippen, "'Born Again' Politics: The Persistence of Revival Traditions" (Ph.D. diss., University of Texas–Austin, 1982), 93.

34. McLoughlin, *Billy Graham*, 94, 108–114; Billy Graham to Dwight Eisenhower, 3 December 1951, folder 1-12, collection 74, BGCA (original in EPL; Eisenhower to Graham, 8 November 1951, folder 1-12, collection 74, BGCA (original in EPL); "Evangelist Has Word for Taft," 18 October 1951, unidentified news clipping, folder 1-12, collection 74, BGCA (original in EPL).

35. Martin, *Prophet with Honor*, 148–149; McLoughlin, *Billy Graham*, 115, 117–118.

36. Gary Scott Smith, *Faith and the Presidency: From George Washington to George W. Bush* (New York: Oxford University Press, 2006), 222; McLoughlin, *Billy Graham*, 151.

37. William R. Conklin, "Eisenhower Says Farewell to Columbia University," *NYT*, 17 January 1953; Whitfield, *Culture of the Cold War*, 88; Murch, *Cooperation*

without Compromise, 150–151. For a discussion of "civil religion"—a political religion that links the purposes of God with those of the state—see Robert Bellah, "Civil Religion in America," *Daedalus* 96 (1967): 1–21.

38. Whitfield, *Culture of the Cold War*, 89, 90; Clayton Knowles, "Big Issue in D.C.: The Oath of Allegiance," *NYT*, 23 May 1954; "'In God We Trust,' Label Slated for All U.S. Money," *NYT*, 8 June 1955; "'In God We Trust' Voted as Official Motto of the U.S.," *NYT*, 24 July 1956.

39. Graham to Eisenhower, 8 February 1954, folder 1-12, collection 74, BGCA; Graham to Eisenhower, 2 December 1957, folder 1-12, collection 74, BGCA; Graham to Eisenhower, 18 November 1959, folder 1-12, collection 74, BGCA (originals in EPL).

40. Smith, *Faith and the Presidency*, 221–258; Jean White, "Ike Stresses Free Religion at Mosque Rites," *WP*, 29 June 1957; Michelle Mart, *Eye on Israel: How America Came to View the Jewish State as an Ally* (Albany: State University of New York Press, 2006), 106; Sydney E. Ahlstrom, *A Religious History of the American People* (New Haven, CT: Yale University Press, 1972), 954. For examples of Eisenhower's endorsement of religious faith as a foundation for American democracy, see W. H. Lawrence, "Eisenhower Cites Price of Freedom," *NYT*, 16 May 1953; and "President Voices Liking for 'Militant Chaplains,'" *NYT*, 26 May 1953.

41. Graham to Eisenhower, 24 August 1956, folder 1-12, collection 74, BGCA (original in EPL); Eisenhower to Leonard W. Hall, 3 September 1956, folder 1-12, collection 74, BGCA (original in EPL).

42. Kellstedt et al., "Faith Transformed," 272; "Ministers Favor Eisenhower 8 to 1," *CT*, 29 October 1956, 28; "How Will America Vote?" *CT*, 24 October 1960, 25.

43. Graham to Eisenhower, 10 May 1954, folder 1-12, collection 74, BGCA (original in EPL).

44. Nixon to Ambassador Raymond A. Hare, 23 April 1959, microfilm reel 1, collection 74, BGCA (original in NPL); Graham to Nixon, 17 November 1959, microfilm reel 1, collection 74, BGCA (original in NPL); Nancy Gibbs and Michael Duffy, *The Preacher and the Presidents: Billy Graham in the White House* (New York: Center Street, 2007), 63.

45. Steven P. Miller, *Billy Graham and the Rise of the Republican South* (Philadelphia: University of Pennsylvania Press, 2009), 40-63; Martin, *Prophet with Honor*, 170–172; *CT*, 29 October 1956, 38; Edward Lee Moore, "Billy Graham and Martin Luther King, Jr.: An Inquiry into White and Black Revivalistic Traditions" (Ph.D. diss., Vanderbilt University, 1979), 454.

46. George Dugan, "Arkansas Events Disturb Graham," *NYT*, 25 September 1957; Martin, *Prophet with Honor*, 245.

47. UPI, "Billy Graham Protests," *NYT*, 28 November 1960. See Mary Dudziak, *Cold War Civil Rights: Race and the Image of American Democracy* (Princeton, NJ: Princeton University Press, 2000), for an analysis of the Cold War's effect on liberal white Americans' reception of the civil rights movement.

48. Graham to Eisenhower, 4 June 1956, folder 1-12, collection 74, BGCA (original in EPL).

49. Ibid.

50. Ibid.

51. Joel L. Alvis, Jr., *Religion and Race: Southern Presbyterians, 1946–1983* (Tuscaloosa: University of Alabama Press, 1994), 108–110; Mark Newman, *Getting Right with God: Southern Baptists and Desegregation, 1945–1995* (Tuscaloosa: University of Alabama Press, 2001), 20–27; L. Nelson Bell, "Christian Race Relations Must Be Natural, Not Forced," *Southern Presbyterian Journal*, 17 August 1955, 3; *Southern Presbyterian Journal*, 22 June 1955 and 11 April 1956; W. A. Criswell, "Segregation in Society," sermon, Columbia, SC, 22 February 1956, in *The Social Conscience of W. A. Criswell*, ed. James E. Towns (Dallas: Crescendo Publications, 1977), 226–234. For white southern pastors' response to *Brown*, see David L. Chappell, *A Stone of Hope: Prophetic Religion and the Death of Jim Crow* (Chapel Hill: University of North Carolina Press, 2004), 105–130.

52. *UEA*, 1 July 1951, 6; "The Church and the Race Problem," *CT*, 18 March 1957, 20–22; E. Earl Ellis, "Segregation and the Kingdom of God," *CT*, 18 March 1957, 6–9; *Christian Life*, November 1951, 37.

53. "100,000 Jam Stadium to Hear Billy Graham," *New York Journal-American*, 21 July 1957, www.wheaton.edu/bgc/archives/exhibits/NYC57/13sample114-2.htm.

Chapter 2

1. Jerry Falwell, "Segregation or Integration—Which?" Sermon preached at Thomas Road Baptist Church, and reprinted in *Word of Life*, October 1958.

2. Bob Jones, Jr., Transcript of chapel talk, 8 February 1965, "Bob Jones University" folder, G. Archer Weniger Files, BJU; Mark Taylor Dalhouse, *An Island in the Lake of Fire: Bob Jones University, Fundamentalism, and the Separatist Movement* (Athens: University of Georgia Press, 1996), 81–82; William Martin, *A Prophet with Honor: The Billy Graham Story* (New York: William Morrow, 1991), 216–224.

3. Howard Edgar Moore, "The Emergence of Moderate Fundamentalism: John R. Rice and 'The Sword of the Lord'" (Ph.D. diss., George Washington University, 1990), 61, 103; Barry Hankins, *God's Rascal: J. Frank Norris and the Beginnings of Southern Fundamentalism* (Lexington: University Press of Kentucky, 1996), 50–64.

4. *SWL*, 2 November 1934 and 9 November 1934; Moore, "Emergence of Moderate Fundamentalism," 74–192.

5. Moore, "Emergence of Moderate Fundamentalism," 147, 191, 256; Martin, *Prophet with Honor*, 220–222; Warren L. Vinz, "*Sword of the Lord*, 1934–," in *The Conservative Press in Twentieth-Century America*, ed. Ronald Lora and William Henry Longton (Westport, CT: Greenwood Press, 1999), 132.

6. John R. Rice, "Who for President?" *SWL*, 24 September 1948, 6.

7. *SWL*, 15 August 1952, 12; Moore, "Emergence of Moderate Fundamentalism," 165, 351, 364.

8. Randall Balmer, *Encyclopedia of Evangelicalism*, 2nd ed. (Waco, TX: Baylor University Press, 2004), s.v. "Robert R. 'Bob' Jones, Jr.," 370; Daniel Lynn Turner, "Fundamentalism, the Arts, and Personal Refinement: A Study of the Ideals of Bob Jones, Sr., and Bob Jones, Jr." (Ed.D. diss., University of Illinois at Urbana-Champaign, 1988); 181, 199–200, 223; Bob Jones, Sr., *Things I Have Learned: Chapel Talks at Bob Jones University* (New York: Loizeaux Brothers, 1944), 67–68; Moore, "Emergence of Moderate Fundamentalism," 534.

9. Dalhouse, *Island in the Lake of Fire*, 72, 105.

10. Undated, unidentified newspaper clipping [1951], "Special Events" folder, BJUA; "World Outlook Meet at Bob Jones U.," *Charlotte News*, 12 December 1950.

11. "BJU Students Favor Ike in 'Convention,'" *Greenville News*, 20 October 1952.

12. Thomas Langford, "States Rights Is Advocated as Bulwark," *Greenville (SC) Piedmont*, 14 December 1950; "BJU Session Opens Dec. 14," *Greenville (SC) Piedmont*, 23 November 1951; "BJU for Strom, Asks McNamara to Resign," *Greenville (SC) Piedmont*, 28 September 1961; Public Relations Scheduling Form Number 6, List of Speakers at Bob Jones University Americanism Conference, February 1962, "Americanism Releases, Feb. 5–10, 1962" folder, BJUA.

13. Lawrence L. Lucas, "A Study of Carl McIntire, Leading Fundamentalist Minister and Conservative Political Spokesman" (M.A. thesis, Glassboro State College, 1971), 16–44; George M. Marsden, *Reforming Fundamentalism: Fuller Seminary and the New Evangelicalism* (Grand Rapids, MI: William B. Eerdmans, 1987), 41–44.

14. Carl McIntire, *The Rise of the Tyrant: Controlled Economy versus Private Enterprise* (Collingswood, NJ: Christian Beacon Press, 1945), xi, 25, 250; *CB*, 5 May 1949, 4, 5.

15. Louis Gasper, *The Fundamentalist Movement* (The Hague: Mouton, 1963), 66–67; Erling Jorstad, *The Politics of Doomsday: Fundamentalists of the Far Right* (Nashville: Abingdon, 1970), 48, 51; *CB*, 8 May 1952, 1, 4; 7 May 1953, 1, 8; Brooks R. Walker, *The Christian Fright Peddlers* (Garden City, NY: Doubleday, 1964), 39.

16. Reese Cleghorn, *Radicalism Southern Style: A Commentary on Regional Extremism of the Right* (Atlanta: Southern Regional Council, 1968), 19; *CB*, 19 May 1960, 2; 15 September 1960; "Bob Jones University—Honorary Degrees," [1999], "Compiled Lists" folder, BJUA.

17. Walker, *Christian Fright Peddlers*, 84.

18. Transcript of interview with Billy James Hargis conducted for *With God on Our Side*, television documentary, 1996, tape 244, transcript pp. 3–4, 6 (used with permission from William Martin); Fernando Penabaz, *Crusading Preacher from the West* (Tulsa, OK: Christian Crusade, 1965), 62–63; Pete Martin, "I Call on Billy James Hargis, Part I," *Christian Herald*, February 1967, 78; Peter T. Beckman, Jr., "The Right Wing and the Christian Faith" (Ph.D. diss., University of Chicago Divinity School, 1969), 161–163.

19. Walker, *Christian Fright Peddlers*, 88–89; Jim Ernest Hunter, Jr., "A Gathering of Sects: Revivalistic Pluralism in Tulsa, Oklahoma, 1945–1985" (Ph.D. diss., Southern Baptist Theological Seminary, 1986), 177.

20. Penabaz, *Crusading Preacher from the West*, 150–151, 159; "Gospel According to Billy," *Newsweek*, 24 August 1964, 77; Billy James Hargis obituary, *Time*, 17 December 2004; Donald Janson, "Big Gain Claimed for the Far Right," *NYT*, 10 August 1964.

21. *Christian Echoes*, February 1951, 5; Billy James Hargis to Bob Jones, Jr., 22 June 1961, BJU.

22. *Christian Echoes*, September 1950, 6–7; Billy James Hargis, "How Troubled the Waters!" Radio Sermon, 18 March 1951, published in *Christian Echoes*, April 1951, 3; Hargis, *Communist America—Must It Be?* (Tulsa, OK: Christian Crusade, 1960), 28–29, 77.

23. Hargis, *Communist America*, 31.

24. John Harold Redekop, *The American Far Right: A Case Study of Billy James Hargis and Christian Crusade* (Grand Rapids, MI: William B. Eerdmans, 1968), 17; Hargis interview, tape 244, transcript pp. 4–6; tape 247, transcript pp. 34–35; Billy James Hargis, *The Total Revolution* (Tulsa, OK: Christian Crusade, 1972), 25; Mark Newman, *Getting Right with God: Southern Baptists and Desegregation, 1945–1995* (Tuscaloosa: University of Alabama Press, 2001), 64–108; Martin, "I Call on Billy James Hargis, Part I," 19.

25. Billy James Hargis, "A Communist World: Must It Be?" *Christian Crusade*, October 1964, 34, 44; Hargis, *Communist America*, 175; Billy James Hargis, Transcript of Independence Day Radio Broadcast, 4 July 1961, "Billy James Hargis" folder, W. O. H. Garman Files, BJU.

26. Billy James Hargis, *The United Nations: Destroying America by Degrees* (Tulsa, OK: Christian Crusade, [1961]), "Billy James Hargis" folder, Garman Files, BJU; Billy James Hargis, *What Can You Do to Save Our Country?* (Tulsa, OK: Christian Crusade, n.d. [1961?]), "Billy James Hargis" folder, Garman Files, BJU.

27. Frances FitzGerald, *Cities on a Hill: A Journey through Contemporary American Cultures* (New York: Simon & Schuster, 1986), 144–148; Jerry Falwell, *Strength for the Journey: An Autobiography* (New York: Simon & Schuster, 1987), 1–120.

28. Clifton Potter and Dorothy Potter, *Lynchburg: A City Set on Seven Hills* (Charleston, SC: Arcadia, 2004), 105, 134–137; Darrell Laurant, *A City unto Itself: Lynchburg, Virginia in the 20th Century* (Lynchburg, VA: self-published, 1997), 94–110; FitzGerald, *Cities on a Hill*, 132–133.

29. FitzGerald, *Cities on a Hill*, 148–149.

30. Carl Abbott, *The New Urban America: Growth and Politics in Sunbelt Cities*, 2nd ed. (Chapel Hill: University of North Carolina Press, 1987), 17; Jeffrey K. Hadden and Charles E. Swann, *Prime-Time Preachers: The Rising Power of Televangelism* (Reading, MA: Addison-Wesley, 1981), 25–29, 106–107. For a study of the political and social culture of the southern evangelicals who started thriving churches in the metropolitan areas to which they moved in the 1940s and 1950s, see Darren Dochuk, "'They Locked God outside the

Iron Curtain': The Politics of Anticommunism and the Ascendancy of Plain-Folk Evangelicalism in the Postwar West," in *The Political Culture of the New West*, ed. Jeff Roche (Lawrence: University Press of Kansas, 2008), 97–131.

31. Ruth McClellan, *An Incredible Journey: Thomas Road Baptist Church and Fifty Years of Miracles* (Lynchburg, VA: Liberty University, 2006), 88, 98; Sean Wilentz, "The Trials of Televangelism," *Dissent*, Winter 1990, 42.

32. Mary Murphy, "The Next Billy Graham," *Esquire*, 10 October 1978, 29; McClellan, *Incredible Journey*, 39–57, 92–157; Jerry Falwell and Elmer L. Towns, *Church Aflame* (Nashville: Impact Books, 1971), 13–20, 139–155; *Word of Life*, 10 September 1970, September and November 1971, TRBC 4-8, LUA.

33. Jerry Falwell, "Outlines on Eschatology," [1961], "Falwell Sermons—1963" folder, FAL 5-3, LUA; Jerry Falwell and Elmer Towns, *Capturing a Town for Christ* (Old Tappan, NJ: Fleming H. Revell, 1973), 12–48, 75–85; *Word of Life*, October 1971, TRBC 4-8, LUA; Jerry Falwell, "New Revolution Needed in America," Transcript of *Old Time Gospel Hour* broadcast, 16 January 1977, OTGH 224, FM 3-5, LUA.

34. Falwell, "Segregation or Integration—Which?" For an analysis of segregationists' use of anticommunism, see George Lewis, *The White South and the Red Menace: Segregationists, Anticommunism, and Massive Resistance, 1945–1965* (Gainesville: University Press of Florida, 2004).

35. Matthew D. Lassiter and Andrew B. Lewis, "Massive Resistance Revisited: Virginia's White Moderates and the Byrd Organization," in *The Moderates' Dilemma: Massive Resistance to School Desegregation in Virginia*, ed. Matthew D. Lassiter and Andrew B. Lewis (Charlottesville: University Press of Virginia, 1998), 7; James H. Hershman, Jr., "Massive Resistance Meets Its Match: The Emergence of a Pro-Public School Majority," in Lassiter and Lewis, *Moderates' Dilemma*, 113; James Murdock, "New Defenders Group Will Open Campaign at Mass Meet April 1," *Lynchburg (VA) Daily Advance*, 24 March 1959; James Murdock, "Perrow Report Called 'Futile' by Supt. Story," *Lynchburg (VA) Daily Advance*, 2 April 1959.

36. Ernest Q. Campbell and Thomas F. Pettigrew, *Christians in Racial Crisis: A Study of Little Rock's Ministry* (Washington, DC: Public Affairs, 1959), 41–42, 137–170; "Christian Summit Conference to Feature Nine Dynamic Speakers!" *Christian Crusade*, July 1960, 4–5.

37. Billy James Hargis, "Integration by Force Is Not a Christian Crusade!" *Christian Echoes*, October 1956, 5.

38. John R. Rice, "Segregation or No?" *SWL*, 2 July 1954, 8.

39. Noel Smith, "The 'Insight' King Brought McCall," *BBT*, 26 May 1961, 4; "Rev. M. L. King Confesses to Apostasy," *Blu-Print*, 2 October 1962.

40. *Bob Jones University News*, 5 September 1963.

Chapter 3

1. W. H. Lawrence, "Nixon Forecasts Reuther Control if Kennedy Wins," *NYT*, 4 November 1960; "Transcript of Nixon's News Conference on His Campaign Plans and Election Issues," *NYT*, 30 July 1960.

2. Will Herberg, *Protestant, Catholic, Jew: An Essay in American Religious Sociology* (Garden City, NY: Doubleday, 1955). On the ecumenicalism of the 1950s, see Robert Wuthnow, *The Restructuring of American Religion: Society and Faith since World War II* (Princeton, NJ: Princeton University Press, 1988); Mark Silk, *Spiritual Politics: Religion and America since World War II* (New York: Simon & Schuster, 1988); and Patrick Allitt, *Religion in America since 1945: A History* (New York: Columbia University Press, 2003).

3. Richard E. Morgan, *The Politics of Religious Conflict: Church and State in America* (New York: Pegasus, 1968), 52–53; "Two Protestants Find '60 Queries Proper," *NYT*, 26 April 1960; Sara Diamond, *Roads to Dominion: Right-Wing Movements and Political Power in the United States* (New York: Guilford Press, 1995), 104.

4 ."Test of Religion," *Time*, 26 September 1960, 21.

5. "Worldview," *UEA*, October 1960, 27–28; Peter Braestrup, "Protestant Unit Wary on Kennedy," *NYT*, 8 September 1960; Lowell Streiker and Gerald S. Strober, *Religion and the New Majority: Billy Graham, Middle America and the Politics of the Seventies* (New York: Association Press, 1972), 60; "Political Anxieties as Party Conventions Approach," *CT*, 4 July 1960, 21–22; "Should Americans Elect a Roman Catholic President?" *CT*, 26 October 1959, 66–67.

6. "Dr. Bob Jones Jr. Will Not Vote for Senator Kennedy," *BBT*, 21 October 1960.

7. Richard T. Hughes, *Reviving the Ancient Faith: The Story of Churches of Christ in America* (Grand Rapids, MI: William B. Eerdmans, 1996), 264–265; AP, "A Catholic President Opposed," *NYT*, 5 August 1960; AP, "Religious Issue Raised," *NYT*, 3 September 1960.

8. John Wicklein, "Baptists Question Vote for Catholic," *NYT*, 21 May 1960; Southern Baptist Convention, Resolution on Christian Citizenship, May 1960, www.sbc.net/resolutions/amResolution.asp?ID=936; John Wicklein, "Anti-Catholic Groups Cooperate Closely in Mail Campaign to Defeat Kennedy," *NYT*, 17 October 1960; AP, "Kennedy Is Attacked," *NYT*, 4 July 1960.

9. Billy Graham to Richard Nixon, 17 November 1959, microfilm reel 1, collection 74, BGCA (original in NPL); "Baptists Call Church Issue in Presidency," *Chicago Tribune*, 21 May 1960.

10. Billy Graham to Richard Nixon: 17 November 1959, 27 May 1960, 29 August 1960, 17 October 1960, and 23 August 1960, microfilm reel 1, collection 74, BGCA (originals in NPL).

11. Billy Graham to Richard Nixon, 1 September 1960 and 22 August 1960, microfilm reel 1, collection 74, BGCA (original in NPL).

12. Richard Nixon to Billy Graham, 4 June 1960 and 29 August 1960, microfilm reel 1, collection 74, BGCA (original in NPL); Graham to Nixon, 21 June 1960, microfilm reel 1, collection 74, BGCA (original in NPL).

13. Billy Graham, LTE, *Time*, 19 September 1960; William Martin, *A Prophet with Honor: The Billy Graham Story* (New York: William Morrow, 1991), 278–280; Graham to Nixon, 24 September 1960 and 1 September 1960, microfilm reel 1, collection 74, BGCA (originals in NPL).

14. Billy Graham to Richard Nixon, 27 May 1960, 22 August 1960, and 23 August 1960, microfilm reel 1, collection 74, BGCA (originals in NPL).

15. Shaun A. Casey, *The Making of a Catholic President: Kennedy vs. Nixon, 1960* (New York: Oxford University Press, 2009), 123–125, 132.

16. Casey, *Making of a Catholic President*, 93–122; Martin, *Prophet with Honor*, 269–283.

17. John Wicklein, "Study Finds Bigotry Heavy in 1960 Campaign," *NYT*, 18 February 1962; George H. Gallup, *The Gallup Poll: Public Opinion, 1935–1971* (New York: Random House, 1972), 1693.

18. G. Archer Weniger, *Blu-Print*, 22 November 1960, 6 December 1960, 17 January 1961; "Bob Jones Asserts: Billy Could Have Swung Vote," *Spartanburg Herald*, 25 November 1960.

19. Billy Graham to Richard Nixon, 12 June 1961, microfilm reel 1, collection 74, BGCA (original in NPL).

20. L. Nelson Bell to Richard Nixon, 11 November 1960, folder 39-15, collection 318, BGCA.

21. George L. Ford, "A Protestant Strategy for the Sixties," *UEA*, December 1960, 5; Douglas Stave, "Should Christians Go into Politics?" *Moody Monthly*, November 1960, 97–101; Don Gill, "Capital Commentary," *UEA*, December 1960, 4 (emphasis in original).

22. "Cuba Handling Called 'Stupid,'" *Greenville News*, 3 May 1961; "'Stupid' Kennedy Assailed," *Greenville Piedmont*, 2 May 1961.

23. Carl McIntire, *Muzzling the Military*, 1961, box 3, folder 17, Carl McIntire Collection, Bentley Historical Library, University of Michigan, Ann Arbor (BHL); "Hargis Hits Socialistic Legislation," *Columbia (SC) State*, 7 February 1962; "BJU for Strom, Asks McNamara to Resign," *Greenville Piedmont*, 28 September 1961. For a detailed analysis of the Edwin Walker case, see Jonathan M. Schoenwald, *A Time for Choosing: The Rise of Modern American Conservatism* (New York: Oxford University Press, 2001), 101–123.

24. Richard Reeves, *President Kennedy: Profile of Power* (New York: Simon & Schuster, 1993), 245; Carl McIntire, *The State Department and the Word of God*, November 1961, folder 17, box 3, McIntire Collection, BHL; Billy James Hargis, *The Stirring Fourth of July Radio Broadcast of Billy James Hargis over a Nationwide Network on Independence Day 1961* (Tulsa, OK: Christian Crusade, [1961]), "Billy James Hargis" folder, W. O. H. Garman Files, J. S. Mack Library, Bob Jones University, Greenville, SC.

25. Bob Jones, Sr., to Strom Thurmond, 15 August 1960, "Political Affairs 8-1-1 (Presidential Election), Folder I; June 28-August 20, 1960" folder, box 25, Subject Correspondence 1960, Strom Thurmond Papers, Mss 100, Special Collections, Clemson University Libraries, Clemson, SC; Bob Jones, Sr., to Strom Thurmond, 23 January 1963, "Civil Rights 3 (Race Relations & Integration), Folder I; January 7–February 28, 1963" folder, box 4, Subject Correspondence 1963, Thurmond Papers; McIntire, *Muzzling the Military*; "Senator Strom Thurmond Speaks," *Bob Jones University Bulletin: Voice of the Alumni*, November 1961.

26. Donald Janson, "Rightists Called to Unity Meeting," *NYT*, 2 February 1962; Donald Janson, "Vote Push Urged for U.S. Rightists," *NYT*, 31 January 1962.

27. For information on Fulbright's campaign in 1962, see Randall Bennett Woods, *Fulbright: A Biography* (Cambridge: Cambridge University Press, 1995), 296–300.

28. Cited in John Harold Redekop, *The American Far Right: A Case Study of Billy James Hargis and Christian Crusade* (Grand Rapids, MI: William B. Eerdmans, 1968), 38, 43.

29. For conservatism in the early 1960s, see Mary C. Brennan, *Turning Right in the Sixties: The Conservative Capture of the GOP* (Chapel Hill: University of North Carolina Press, 1995); Donald T. Critchlow, *The Conservative Ascendancy: How the GOP Right Made Political History* (Cambridge, MA: Harvard University Press, 2007), 6–76; Lisa McGirr, *Suburban Warriors: The Origins of the New American Right* (Princeton, NJ: Princeton University Press, 2001); Gregory L. Schneider, *Cadres for Conservatism: Young Americans for Freedom and the Rise of the Contemporary Right* (New York: New York University Press, 1999); and Schoenwald, *Time for Choosing.*

30. Donald Janson, "Right-Wing Leaders Shape Secret Fraternity," *NYT,* 16 September 1961; Bill Becker, "Rightist Attack Flares on Coast," *NYT,* 8 April 1963; "Democracy Assailed," *NYT,* 18 September 1961; "Rightist Merger? Major Groups Will Attempt to Form a Federation," *NYT,* 21 January 1962; Rick Perlstein, *Before the Storm: Barry Goldwater and the Unmaking of the American Consensus* (New York: Hill and Wang, 2001), 104–110, 215; Schoenwald, *A Time for Choosing,* 77–99; Richard Grid Powers, *Not without Honor: The History of American Anticommunism* (New Haven, CT: Yale University Press, 1995), 286–318.

31. Billy James Hargis to Bob Jones, Jr., 16 April 1968, BJU.

32. Public Relations Scheduling Form #4, "Americanism Conference—BJU Conservative Position, Etc.," 27–28 January 1962, BJUA.

33. "Americanism Releases, Feb. 5–10, 1962" folder, BJUA; "BJU to Present Political Issues," *Greenville Piedmont,* 29 January 1962; Gil Rowland, "Get Rid of U.N., Free Cuba, Rivers Demands Here," *Greenville News,* 10 February 1962.

34. Gregory L. Schneider, *The Conservative Century: From Reaction to Revolution* (Lanham, MD: Rowman & Littlefield, 2009), 79; Peter T. Beckman, "The Right Wing and the Christian Faith" (Ph.D. diss., University of Chicago Divinity School, 1968), 169-197; UPI, "Graham Praises JFK School Stand," *Oakland (CA) Tribune,* 17 May 1961; Charles Grutzner, "Anti-Red Crusade Rallies at Garden," *NYT,* 29 June 1962.

35. John Wicklein, "Christian Group Aims at Politics," *NYT,* 1 February 1962; Diamond, *Roads to Dominion,* 105.

36. Wicklein, "Christian Group"; Diamond, *Roads to Dominion,* 105.

37. Bruce J. Dierenfield, *The Battle over School Prayer: How Engel v. Vitale Changed America* (Lawrence: University Press of Kansas, 2007); Gallup, *Gallup Poll,* 1779.

38. Anthony Lewis, "Both Houses Get Bills to Lift Ban on School Prayer," *NYT,* 27 June 1962; "What's Being Said about Court's Ruling," *USN,* 9 July 1962, 44; UPI, "Goldwater Hits Court Decision," *WP,* 1 July 1962; "President Urges Court Be Backed on Prayer Issue," *NYT,* 28 June 1962.

39. Alexander Burnham, "Churchmen Voice Shock at Ruling," *NYT*, 26 June 1962; "Spellman Scores Ruling on Prayer," *NYT*, 3 August 1962.

40. "Supreme Court Prayer Ban: Where Will It Lead?" *CT*, 20 July 1962, 25–26; "Repercussions of Supreme Court Prayer Ruling," *CT*, 3 August 1962, 25; "Should We Support the Bible-Reading Amendment?" *Eternity*, May 1964, 4–6, 12; Michael Jay Sider-Rose, "Between Heaven and Earth: Moody Bible Institute and the Politics of the Moderate Christian Right, 1945–1985" (Ph.D. diss., University of Pittsburgh, 2000), 40; Carl McIntire, "Supreme Court on School Prayer," *CB*, 13 September 1962, 1, 8.

41. "School Prayer Declared Unconstitutional," *Alabama Baptist*, 5 July 1962, 3.

42. "America Needs God No More?" *UEA*, August 1962, 18; Executive Committee of the National Association of Evangelicals, "What Did the Supreme Court Really Say?" *UEA*, September 1962, 7, 20; "The Editor at Random," *UEA*, October 1962, 5; *BBT*, 9 March 1973, reprint of editorial originally published in *BBT*, 3 August 1962; Sam Morris, "Supreme Court and Prayer in the Public Schools," *BBT*, 10 August 1962, 2–3.

43. Don Gill, "Capital Commentary," *UEA*, August 1963, 2–3.

44. "America Needs God No More?" 18.

45. *CB*, 27 August 1964, 8; *Christian Crusade*, November 1963, 4–5, and September 1964, 8; Billy James Hargis, "America—Let's Get Back to God!" *Christian Crusade*, August 1963, 26.

46. Donald H. Gill, "Will the Bible Get Back into School?" *Eternity*, May 1964, 9; "Church and State: A Tide Reversed," *Time*, 19 June 1964, 65; "New Uproar over School Prayers," *USN*, 4 May 1964, 12.

47. "Goldwater Endorses School Prayers," *Christian Century*, 21 October 1964, 1292; *CB*, 27 August 1964, 8; Erling Jorstad, *The Politics of Doomsday: Fundamentalists of the Far Right* (Nashville: Abingdon Press, 1970), 117; Earl Black and Merle Black, *The Rise of Southern Republicans* (Cambridge, MA: Harvard University Press, 2002), 93–94.

48. Southern Baptist Convention, Resolution on Religious Liberty, June 1964, www.sbc.net/resolutions/amResolution.asp?ID=940; Press Release from Protestant Ministers for School Prayer and Bible Reading, Collingswood, NJ, 2 August 1966, "Bible Reading and Religion in Public Schools" folder, Gilbert Stenholm Files, BJU; "The Supreme Court Upholds the Constitution," *Alabama Baptist*, 27 June 1963, 3.

49. Barry Hankins, "Principle, Perception, and Position: Why Southern Baptist Conservatives Differ from Moderates on Church-State Issues," *Journal of Church and State* 40 (1998): 359; "Religious Amendment Defeated by Religious Leaders," *Christian Century*, 24 November 1971, 1375; "Prayer Comeback Bid Hasn't Got a Prayer," *CT*, 4 May 1979, 48–49; "Repercussions of Supreme Court Prayer Ruling," *CT*, 3 August 1962, 25.

50. "Prayer in the Schools—It's Thriving Despite Court Rulings," *USN*, 11 December 1972, 47–48.

51. "The Meaning of the Supreme Court Decision," *CT*, 5 July 1963, 30; Ronald C. Doll, "Prayer, the Bible, and the Schools," *CT*, 8 May 1964, 13–15; "What about the Becker Amendment?" *CT*, 19 June 1964, 20–22; Russell

T. Hitt, "We *Can* Teach the Bible in the Schools," *Eternity*, April 1965, 16–17; "America Needs God No More?" *UEA*, August 1963, 18; Carl F. H. Henry, "Religion in the Schools," *CT*, 1 February 1974, 24–25.

Chapter 4

1. Nancy Gibbs and Michael Duffy, *The Preacher and the Presidents: Billy Graham in the White House* (New York: Center Street, 2007), 133.
2. Richard Reeves, *President Kennedy: Profile of Power* (New York: Simon & Schuster, 1993), 522.
3. Noel Smith, "Mob Rule Is Not a Civil Right," *BBT*, 28 June 1963, 5. For white southerners' view of civil rights, see Joseph Crespino, *In Search of Another Country: Mississippi and the Conservative Counterrevolution* (Princeton, NJ: Princeton University Press, 2007); and Jason Sokol, *There Goes My Everything: White Southerners in the Age of Civil Rights, 1945–1975* (New York: Vintage, 2007).
4. Smith, "Mob Rule Is Not a Civil Right," 6.
5. Minutes of the Annual Meeting of the Board of Trustees, 1 June 1965, "Personal 10-1-2 (Bob Jones University); March 16–July 2, 1965" folder, box 19, Subject Correspondence, 1965, Strom Thurmond Papers, Special Collections, Clemson University, Clemson, SC; "Two Southern Evangelists Stop Here to Beat the Drums for Goldwater," Unidentified, undated newspaper clipping [Virginia, 1964], "Politics—Republican—Goldwater" folder, Gilbert Stenholm Files, BJU.
6. Robert McHugh, "Wallace Receives Praise, Honorary Degree from BJU," *Greenville (SC) State*, 28 May 1964; *Christian Crusade*, July 1964.
7. Arnold Forster and Benjamin R. Epstein, *Danger on the Right* (New York: Random House, 1964); Brooks R. Walker, *The Christian Fright Peddlers* (Garden City, NY: Doubleday, 1964); H. A. Overstreet and Bonaro Overstreet, *The Strange Tactics of Extremism* (New York: Norton, 1964); Richard Hofstadter, "Pseudo-Conservatism Revisited," in *The Radical Right*, ed. Daniel Bell (Garden City, NY: Doubleday, 1963), 103.
8. For an account of Goldwater's campaign, see Rick Perlstein, *Before the Storm: Barry Goldwater and the Unmaking of the American Consensus* (New York: Hill and Wang, 2001). For conservatism and the Republican Party, see Jonathan M. Schoenwald, *A Time for Choosing: The Rise of Modern American Conservatism* (New York: Oxford University Press, 2002); and Donald T. Critchlow, *The Conservative Ascendancy: How the GOP Right Made Political History* (Cambridge, MA: Harvard University Press, 2007).
9. "The Rockefeller Marriage," *SWL*, 26 July 1963, 3; G. Archer Weniger, *Blu-Print*, 11 February 1964.
10. Gayle White, "Evangelical Power Couple," *AJC*, 7 July 2001; Rob Boston, "If Best-Selling End Times Author Tim LaHaye Has His Way, Church-State Separation Will Be Left Behind," *Church and State*, February 2002, 9. For grassroots conservatism in southern California in the late 1950s and early 1960s, see Lisa McGirr, *Suburban Warriors: The Origins of the New American Right* (Princeton, NJ: Princeton University Press, 2001).

11. Tim F. LaHaye, Mass Mailing, 27 May 1964, "Rockefeller, Nelson" folder, G. Archer Weniger Files, BJU.

12. Erling Jorstad, *The Politics of Doomsday: Fundamentalists of the Far Right* (Nashville: Abingdon Press, 1970), 118–119.

13. Donald Janson, "Hargis Group to Back Goldwater Despite Some Members' Attacks," *NYT*, 7 August 1964; Donald Janson, "Rightist Pledges to Aid Goldwater," *NYT*, 8 August 1964; Billy James Hargis, "Crusader's Journal," *Christian Crusade*, November 1964, 10.

14. "Two Southern Evangelists Stop Here to Beat the Drums for Goldwater"; Larry L. King, "Bob Jones University: The Buckle on the Bible Belt," *Harper's*, June 1966, 51, 53.

15. "Church Deplores Goldwater Views," *NYT*, 19 September 1964; "McCracken Warns Apathy Can Lead to Dictatorship," *NYT*, 20 July 1964; Paul L. Montgomery, "Protestant Unit Backs President," *NYT*, 21 September 1964. For liberal ministerial involvement in politics in the early 1960s, see Michael D. Friedland, *Lift Up Your Voice Like a Trumpet: White Clergy and the Civil Rights and Antiwar Movements, 1954–1973* (Chapel Hill: University of North Carolina Press, 1998).

16. Clergymen for Social and Political Conservatism, "A Declaration of Political Faith," n.d. [1964], "Patriotism" folder, Weniger Files, BJU; "Putting God on the Ballot," *CT*, 6 November 1964, 29. See also "The Church and Political Pronouncements," *CT*, 28 August 1964, 29–30.

17. Charles Mohr, "Goldwater Hits U.S. Moral 'Rot,'" *NYT*, 11 October 1964.

18. James Reston, "Washington: Barry Goldwater Examples of Morality," *NYT*, 23 October 1964; Sara Diamond, *Spiritual Warfare: The Politics of the Christian Right* (Boston: South End Press, 1989), 49–50; "Dr. Bob Jones Jr. Raps President in Address Here," unidentified newspaper clipping, n.d. [1965], "Politics—National" folder, BJUA.

19. Mark Newman, *Getting Right with God: Southern Baptists and Desegregation, 1945–1995* (Tuscaloosa: University of Alabama Press, 2001), 30; George W. Long, "One Nation, Under God," *CT*, 3 July 1964, 14–16; Donald A. Kruse, "Evangelicals in Government," *CT*, 28 August 1964, 16.

20. Max Goldberg, North American Newspaper Alliance, Transcript of Interview with Billy Graham, Denver, CO, 25 September 1965, folder 3-6, collection 74, BGCA (original in LBJL); Steven P. Miller, *Billy Graham and the Rise of the Republican South* (Philadelphia: University of Pennsylvania Press, 2009), 89–96.

21. Billy Graham to Lyndon Johnson, 6 July 1964, and Graham to Johnson, 27 August 1964, folder 3-6, collection 74, BGCA (originals in LBJL); Gibbs and Duffy, *The Preacher and the Presidents*, 129–132.

22. William Martin, *A Prophet with Honor: The Billy Graham Story* (New York: William Morrow, 1991), 302; *CT*, 6 November 1964, 47.

23. "A Question of Values," *CT*, 20 November 1964, 44; Jack Stillman, "Billy Says Church Too Much in Politics," *Greenville (SC) News*, 6 November 1964.

24. Friedland, *Lift Up Your Voice Like a Trumpet*, 140–236.

25. Richard V. Pierard, *The Unequal Yoke: Evangelical Christianity and Political Conservatism* (Philadelphia: Lippincott, 1970), 151–152; G. Archer Weniger, "Dr. Bob Jones, Jr. on Vietnam Issue," *Blu-Print*, 5 March 1968; Mark Taylor Dalhouse, *An Island in the Lake of Fire: Bob Jones University, Fundamentalism, and the Separatist Movement* (Athens: University of Georgia Press, 1996), 106.

26. Michael Jay Sider-Rose, "Between Heaven and Earth: Moody Bible Institute and the Politics of the Moderate Christian Right, 1945–1985" (Ph.D. diss., University of Pittsburgh, 2000), 187; "The W.C.C. and Viet Nam," *CT*, 4 March 1966, 31; *CT*, 4 March 1966; L. Nelson Bell to Lyndon Johnson, 2 April 1965, folder 3-6, collection 74, BGCA (original in LBJL).

27. Graham to Eisenhower, 10 May 1954, folder 1-12, collection 74, BCGA (original in EPL); Max Goldberg, North American Newspaper Alliance, Transcript of Interview with Billy Graham, Denver, CO, 25 September 1965, folder 3-6, collection 74, BGCA (original in LBJL); Transcript of TV Broadcast, "Billy Graham on Vietnam" [February 1967], folder 3-6, collection 74, BGCA (original in LBJL); Friedland, *Lift Up Your Voice Like a Trumpet*, 156–157.

28. Billy Graham to Lyndon Johnson, 11 July 1965, folder 3-6, collection 74, BGCA (originals in LBJL).

29. Diane Stepp, "Nixon Touted Here by Billy Graham," *Atlanta Constitution*, 30 December 1967; James Rowe to Lyndon Johnson, 31 July 1968, folder 3-6, collection 74, BGCA (original in LBJL).

30. Allen J. Matusow, *The Unraveling of America: A History of Liberalism in the 1960s* (New York: Harper & Row, 1984), 275–307, 329, 362–363.

31. G. Archer Weniger, *Blu-Print*: 19 May 1964, 9 February 1965, 30 March 1965, and 15 June 1965; *BBT*: 21 February 1964 and 5 January 1973; *SWL*: 12 January 1968, 2; 26 January 1968, 6; and 28 June 1968, 7.

32. Tapes of Billy Graham's *Hour of Decision* broadcast, collection 191, BGCA: "A Nation Rocked by Crime," 20 November 1966; "Victory over Despair," 11 December 1966; "Hope in Days of Evil," 22 January 1967; "Students in Revolt," 5 February 1967; "Conquering Teenage Rebellion," 9 April 1967; "Obsession with Sex," 14 May 1967; "The Shadow of Narcotics Addiction," 18 June 1967; "Flames of Revolution," 25 June 1967; "Rioting, Looting, and Crime," 30 July 1967; "America Is in Trouble," 6 August 1967; "Can America Survive?" 10 March 1968.

33. Beth Bailey, *Sex in the Heartland* (Cambridge, MA: Harvard University Press, 1999), 75–145, 175–218.

34. David Allyn, *Make Love, Not War: The Sexual Revolution, An Unfettered History* (Boston: Little and Brown, 2000), 60–70; Paul S. Boyer, *Purity in Print: Book Censorship in America from the Gilded Age to the Computer Age*, 2nd ed. (Madison: University of Wisconsin Press, 2002), 276–288; Merv Rosell, "What Is This Thing Called Sex?" *SWL*, 23 April 1954, 1; "California: The Men from CLEAN," *Newsweek*, 5 September 1966, 23; William Wingfield, "The Politics of Smut: California's Dirty Book Caper," *Nation*, 18 April 1966, 457–458; McGirr, *Suburban Warriors*, 226–227.

35. Jeffrey P. Moran, *Teaching Sex: The Shaping of Adolescence in the Twentieth Century* (Cambridge, MA: Harvard University Press, 2000), 165–173. For analyses of the controversy over sex education, see Janice M. Irvine, *Talk about Sex: The Battles over Sex Education in the United States* (Berkeley: University of California Press, 2002); and Kristin Luker, *When Sex Goes to School: Warring Views on Sex—and Sex Education—since the 1960s* (New York: Norton, 2006).

36. William Martin, *With God on Our Side: The Rise of the Religious Right in America* (New York: Broadway Books, 1996), 101–113; Douglas Robinson, "Sex Education Battles Splitting Many Communities across U.S.," *NYT*, 14 September 1969; Fred M. Hechinger, "Storm over the Teaching of Sex," *NYT*, 7 September 1969.

37. Robinson, "Sex Education Battles"; McGirr, *Suburban Warriors*, 221–222.

38. Martin, *With God on Our Side*, 108; Gordon V. Drake, *Is the School House the Proper Place to Teach Raw Sex?* (Tulsa, OK: Christian Crusade, 1968); Gordon V. Drake, "The NEA and Sex Education," *Christian Crusade*, July 1968, 7–8; John H. Fenton, "At Conservative Rally, the Tone Is Moral," *NYT*, 7 July 1969.

39. Resolution of the American Council of Christian Churches of California, December 1969, "Sex Instruction" folder, Weniger Files, BJU; *SWL*, 12 January 1968, 2; "El Paso Preachers Fight Sex Education in Schools—and Win," *Western Voice*, 3 April 1969.

40. Joseph Fletcher, *Situation Ethics: The New Morality* (Philadelphia: Westminster Press, 1966); Press Release from the American Council of Christian Churches, April 1967 (MS 76.15, HH 148, box 1B, Hall-Hoag Collection, John Hay Library, Brown University, Providence, RI).

41. James C. Hefley, *Textbooks on Trial* (Wheaton, IL: Victor Books, 1976), 13–26, 52–61, 115–118; Martin, *With God on Our Side*, 120–121; Educational Research Analysts, "Meet Mel and Norma," www.textbookreviews.org/about.htm; Gary North, "Mel Gabler, RIP," www.lewrockwell.com/north/north332.html; Dena Kleiman, "Influential Couple Scrutinizes Books for 'Anti-Americanism,'" *NYT*, 14 July 1981.

42. Susan D. Rose, *Keeping Them Out of the Hands of Satan: Evangelical Schooling in America* (New York: Routledge, 1988), 34–35; Kenneth A. Briggs, "Fundamentalist Schools Fight Controls," *NYT*, 26 January 1979.

43. Jerry Falwell, *Strength for the Journey: An Autobiography* (New York: Simon & Schuster, 1987), 298; Martin, *With God on Our Side*, 70; "Christian Academy Taking Applications," *Lynchburg News*, 8 April 1967; Jerry Falwell, "Will Your Children Live under Communism?" [1967], folder 1B, FAL 5-3, LUA. The extent to which racial attitudes contributed to the formation of Christian schools is a subject of continuing scholarly examination. No study of Christian schools attributed their growth solely to racist motivations, and all studies conceded that at least some churches had formed private schools partly to avoid busing or integration, but scholars were divided in their assessment of the degree to which the Christian school movement was a product of racism. David Nevin and Robert E. Bills's *The Schools That*

Fear Built: Segregationist Academies in the South (Washington, DC: Acropolis Books, 1976) recognized the distinction between Christian schools and segregationist academies, but argued that white parents' desire to avoid busing or school integration contributed to the growth of Christian schools in the South, even if the fundamentalist schools differed in some ways from the older "segregation academies." On the other hand, Virginia Davis Nordin and William Lloyd Turner's "More Than Segregation Academies: The Growing Protestant Fundamentalist Schools" (*Phi Delta Kappan*, February 1980, 391–394), and Peter Sherry, "Christian Schools versus the I.R.S." (*Public Interest* [Fall 1980]: 18–41), cited several studies of the late 1970s that showed that religious and moral, rather than racist, reasons accounted for most of Christian schools' growth. Yet Paul F. Parsons's *Inside America's Christian Schools* (Macon, GA: Mercer University Press, 1987) pointed out that although almost all Christian schools were officially nondiscriminatory, and although a few did enroll a sizable percentage of blacks, the student body at most Christian schools was still almost entirely white in the mid-1980s.

44. Falwell, *Strength for the Journey*, 294–299. For evidence that Falwell may have been slower to abandon his racist views than he suggested in retrospect, see Martin, *With God on Our Side*, 69–72.

45. Jerry Falwell, "Ministers and Marches," March 1965, in Perry Deane Young, *God's Bullies: Native Reflections on Preachers and Politics* (New York: Holt, Rinehart & Winston, 1982), 311, 313.

46. Carl McIntire, "What Is the Gospel of Jesus Christ?" [1965], box 3, folder 24, Carl McIntire Collection, Bentley Historical Library, University of Michigan, Ann Arbor.

47. John R. Rice, "Moral Principles in National Politics," *SWL*, 24 July 1964, 7; Falwell, *Strength for the Journey*, 299; Martin, *With God on Our Side*, 58.

48. John R. Rice, "Martin Luther King Is Dead," *SWL*, 26 April 1968, 9; Bill J. Leonard, "A Theology for Racism: Southern Fundamentalists and the Civil Rights Movement," *Baptist History and Heritage* 33 (Winter 1999): 63.

49. Billy Graham, "Rioting or Righteousness," *Hour of Decision* Tract, 1967, BGCA; Goldberg, Transcript of Interview with Billy Graham, Denver, CO, 25 September 1965; Religious News Service, "Graham to Candidates: Americans Want Change in U.S. Moral Direction," *Western Voice*, 7 November 1968, 3; Miller, *Billy Graham and the Rise of the Republican South*, 89–131.

50. James T. Patterson, *Grand Expectations: The United States, 1945–1974* (New York: Oxford University Press, 1996), 649; McGirr, *Suburban Warriors*, 188–209; Steven F. Hayward, *The Age of Reagan: The Fall of the Old Liberal Order, 1964–1980* (New York: Three Rivers Press, 2001), 95–102.

51. Robert Mason, *Richard Nixon and the Quest for a New Majority* (Chapel Hill: University of North Carolina Press, 2004), 20.

Chapter 5

1. Richard M. Nixon, "What Has Happened in America?" *Reader's Digest*, October 1967, 49–54.

2. Ibid., 50, 53.

3. Nancy Gibbs and Michael Duffy, *The Preacher and the Presidents: Billy Graham in the White House* (New York: Center Street, 2007), 158–160; Richard Nixon, *The Memoirs of Richard Nixon* (New York: Grosset & Dunlap, 1978), 292–293.

4. Billy Graham, *Just As I Am: The Autobiography of Billy Graham* (San Francisco: HarperCollins, 1997), 444–445; Gibbs and Duffy, *The Preacher and the Presidents*, 159–171.

5. Diane Stepp, "Nixon Touted Here by Billy Graham," *Atlanta Constitution*, 30 December 1967; Gibbs and Duffy, *The Preacher and the Presidents*, 161, 162, 170.

6. Louis Cassels, "Protestant Factions Join in Gun-Curb Drive," *WP*, 15 June 1968; T. W. Wilson, "America Facing God's Judgment," *Hour of Decision* tract (1970), BGCA; Gibbs and Duffy, *The Preacher and the Presidents*, 163–164.

7. Dan T. Carter, *The Politics of Rage: George Wallace, the Origins of the New Conservatism, and the Transformation of American Politics*, 2nd ed. (Baton Rouge: Louisiana State University Press, 2000), 366; Wallace Henley, "The Clergy on George Wallace," *CT*, 25 October 1968, 36–37; Anthony M. Orum, "Religion and the Rise of the Radical White: The Case of Southern Wallace Support in 1968," *Social Science Quarterly* 51 (1970): 676; Billy James Hargis to Richard Nixon, "EX TR 48-1, Knoxville, Tenn. to Speak at Billy Graham's 'Crusade,' Univ. of Tenn., 5/28/70" folder, box 38, TR, White House Central Files (WHCF), NPL; John R. Rice, *SWL*, 26 January 1968, 6.

8. "Fundamentalists: Dr. McIntire's Magic Touch," *Time*, 14 November 1969, 81; Michael Jay Sider-Rose, "Between Heaven and Earth: Moody Bible Institute and the Politics of the Moderate Christian Right, 1945–1985" (Ph.D. diss., University of Pittsburgh, 2000), 87–100; W. A. Criswell, "Church of the Open Door," Sermon, First Baptist Church, Dallas, TX, 9 June 1968, in *The Social Conscience of W. A. Criswell*, ed. James E. Towns (Dallas: Crescendo Publications, 1977), 162–171; Wallace Henley, "The Clergy on George Wallace," *CT*, 25 October 1968, 36–37.

9. "Dave Leip's Atlas of U.S. Presidential Elections," County Results for 1968 Presidential Election, http://uselectionatlas.org/.

10. Carl Abbott, *The New Urban America: Growth and Politics in Sunbelt Cities*, 2nd ed. (Chapel Hill: University of North Carolina Press, 1987); Bruce J. Schulman, *From Cotton Belt to Sunbelt: Federal Policy, Economic Development, and the Transformation of the South, 1938–1980* (New York: Oxford University Press, 1991), 135–173.

11. Dean M. Kelley, *Why Conservative Churches Are Growing: A Study in Sociology of Religion* (New York: Harper & Row, 1972); Scott L. Thumma, "The Shape of Things to Come: Megachurches, Emerging Churches, and Other New Religious Structures," in *Faith in America: Changes, Challenges, New Directions*, ed. Charles H. Lippy (Westport, CT: Greenwood, 2006), 185–206;

Elmer Towns, "*Christian Life*'s Annual 100 Largest Sunday Schools," *Christian Life*, September 1971, 28–33.

12. White House memo from David Parker to Dwight L. Chapin, 2 November 1971, "RM2-1 Religious Service in the White House, 9/1/71–9/30/71" folder, box 15, Subject Files—Religious Matters, WHCF, NPL; White House memo from K. R. Cole, Jr., to Charles Colson, 23 February 1970, folder 3-7, collection 74, BGCA (original in NPL). On Nixon's religious beliefs, see Stephen E. Ambrose, *Nixon: The Education of a Politician, 1913–1962* (New York: Simon & Schuster, 1988), 57–58; and Anthony Summers, *The Arrogance of Power: The Secret World of Richard Nixon* (New York: Viking, 2000), 11–13.

13. White House memo from Lucy Winchester to Dwight Chapin, 9 July 1970, folder 3-7, collection 74, BGCA (original in NPL).

14. White House memo from Constance Stuart to George Bell, 23 July 1970, folder 3-7, collection 74, BGCA (original in NPL); White House memo from George Bell to Connie Stuart, 17 June 1970, "Southern Baptist Convention" folder, box 113, Charles Colson files, White House Staff Files (WHSF), NPL.

15. "Nixon's Support among Baptists Increases," *Baptist Courier*, September 1970; White House memo from Charles W. Colson to Jim Keogh, 26 May 1970, "Southern Baptist Convention" folder, box 113, Charles Colson files, WHSF, NPL; Fred Rhodes to Richard Nixon, 3 August 1970, "RM 3-3 Protestant [69/70]" folder, box 20, Subject Files—Religious Matters, WHCF, NPL.

16. White House memo from Bud Wilkinson to Dwight Chapin, 22 January 1969, "RM2-1 Religious Service in the White House, begin 3-31-69" folder, box 6, Subject Files—Religious Matters, WHCF, NPL; Charles B. Wilkinson to Billy Graham, 24 January 1969, folder 3-7, collection 74, BGCA (original in NPL); Billy Graham to Richard Nixon, 25 January 1969, folder 3-7, collection 74, BGCA (original in NPL); Joseph R. Wood to Richard Nixon, 17 February 1970, "RM2-1 Religious Service in the White House, 3-1-70 / 3-31-70" folder, box 13, Subject Files—Religious Matters, WHCF, NPL.

17. Billy Graham to Dwight Chapin, 18 June 1970, folder 3-7, collection 74, BGCA (original in NPL); White House memo from Lawrence Higby to H. R. Haldeman, 14 June 1972, "Lawrence Higby—June 1972" folder, box 98, H. R. Haldeman Files, WHSF, NPL; William Martin, *A Prophet with Honor: The Billy Graham Story* (New York: William Morrow, 1991), 370–371; Billy Graham, Press Release, "Statement to Define Dr. Billy Graham's Position Regarding the Recent Conduct of the Vietnam War," 5 January 1973, folder 3-7, collection 74, BGCA (original in NPL); Nixon, *Memoirs*, 440–443.

18. White House memo from H. R. Haldeman to Henry Kissinger, 11 November 1971, "Henry Kissinger, November 1971" folder, box 86, H. R. Haldeman Files, WHSF, NPL.

19. *CCW*, 22 June 1971, 1; *CCW*, 8 August 1971, 1; Hargis, "The Suicide of a Nation—Ours!" *CCW*, 17 October 1971; Julian Williams, "The Kissinger Influence on U.S. Foreign Policy," *CCW*, 30 January 1972, 7; L. Nelson Bell, Remarks on President Richard Nixon's Trip to China, 13 February 1972, audio tape, T39, collection 45, BGCA; Bell, Remarks on President

Richard Nixon's Trip to China, [1972], audio tape, T40, collection 45, BGCA; White House memos from Lawrence Higby to H.R. Haldeman, 17 and 29 March 1972, "Lawrence Higby, March 1972" folder, box 93, H.R. Haldeman files, WHSF, NPL.

20. Billy Graham to Leonard Garment, 16 May 1970, "Religious Matters, 1-69 / 12-70" folder, box 1, Subject Files—Religious Matters; WHCF, NPL; Petition from Senior Citizens Group (Dahlonega, GA) to Richard Nixon, 11 February 1969, and Mrs. W. Ray Mings (Campbellsville, KY) to Nixon, 3 February 1969, "Religious Matters, begin 2-28-69" folder, box 1, Subject Files—Religious Matters, WHCF, NPL; Billy James Hargis to Richard Nixon, 14 July 1970, "EX TR 48-1, Knoxville, Tenn. to speak at Billy Graham's 'Crusade,' Univ. of Tenn., 5/28/70" folder, box 38, TR, WHCF, NPL; Ken Adrian (Wichita, KS) to Richard Nixon, 27 January 1969, "RM 2-1 Religious Service in the White House, begin 2-5-69" folder, box 7, WHCF, Subject Files—Religious Matters, NPL.

21. H. R. Haldeman, Handwritten notes on meeting with Billy Graham, 2 February 1972, "Haldeman Notes, Jan.–March 1972 [1 Jan. 1972 to 18 Feb. 1972], Part 1" folder, box 45, WHSF, H. R. Haldeman Files, NPL; "Open Letter to John Mitchell," *Baptist Messenger*, 2 March 1972, 2; Carl E. Bates to William Covington, Jr., 10 March 1972, folder 1, Carl E. Bates Papers, SBHLA; Tape recording of White House conversations between Richard Nixon and H. R. Haldeman, 14 March 1972 and 22 March 1972, Oval 685-3 and EOB 324-22, NPL; Lee Porter to Dwight L. Chapin, 7 April 1972, "[Ex] UT 1-3 Telephone 1/1/71" folder, box 19, UT, WHCF, NPL.

22. White House memo from Lucy Winchester to Alexander Butterfield, 3 August 1971, folder 3-7, collection 74, BGCA (original in NPL); White House memo from Charles Colson to Jonathan Moore, 30 May 1972, "May 1972" folder, box 131, Charles Colson Files, WHSF, NPL.

23. "Lay Leader of Southern Baptists," *NYT*, 7 June 1972; Jo G. Pritchard III, "Owen Cooper (1908–1986): Business Leader and Humanitarian," *Mississippi History Now* (online publication of the Mississippi Historical Society), mshistory.k12.ms.us/articles/239/owen-cooper-1908-1986-business-leader-and-humanitarian; "Mississippian Is Re-elected by Southern Baptists," *NYT*, 13 June 1973.

24. Tape recording of meeting between Richard Nixon, John Ehrlichman, Alexander Haig, Caspar Weinberger, and George Shultz, 19 October 1971, EOB 292-11; Tape recording of telephone conversation between Richard Nixon and Charles Colson, 20 October 1971, WHT 11-163; Tape recording of meeting between Richard Nixon, Billy Graham, and evangelical leaders, Oval Office, 10 August 1971, Oval 560-3; Tape recording of meeting between Richard Nixon and Russell Kirk, Oval Office, 4 April 1972, Oval 702-9, NPL.

25. Kevin P. Phillips, *The Emerging Republican Majority* (New Rochelle, NY: Arlington House, 1969); Richard M. Scammon and Ben J. Wattenberg, *The Real Majority* (New York: Coward-McCann, 1970); Robert Mason, *Richard Nixon and the Quest for a New Majority* (Chapel Hill: University of North Carolina Press, 2004), 92–94, 151–156.

26. Richard Nixon to H. R. Haldeman, 30 November 1970, folder 3-7, collection 74, BGCA (original in NPL).

27. White House memo from George Strachan to H. R. Haldeman, 10 February 1972; George Strachan, Talking Papers for Billy Graham, 11 April 1972, 16 May 1972, 27 June 1972, 20 September 1972, 25 October 1972, folder 3-7, collection 74, BGCA (originals in NPL); Martin, *Prophet with Honor*, 398.

28. Billy Graham to Richard Nixon, 4 August 1972, online document, NPL, National Archives, www.nixon.archives.gov/virtuallibrary/documents/donated/080472_graham.pdf; Steven P. Miller, *Billy Graham and the Rise of the Republican South* (Philadelphia: University of Pennsylvania Press, 2009), 153.

29. "On Befriending Presidents," *CT*, 17 March 1972, 26.

30. Thomas J. Brazaitis, "Graham Spins His Spiritual Magic at Stadium," *Cleveland Plain Dealer*, 15 July 1972.

31. Columbus Salley and Ronald Behm, *Your God Is Too White* (Downers Grove, IL: Intervarsity Press, 1970); Ronald J. Sider, *Rich Christians in an Age of Hunger: A Biblical Study* (Downers Grove, IL: Intervarsity Press, 1977); "The Evangelical Vote," *Newsweek*, 30 October 1972, 93; Evangelicals for McGovern, direct mail, 20 September 1972, folder 1-4, collection 37, BGCA.

32. Evangelicals for McGovern, direct mail, 20 September 1972.

33. Excerpts from George McGovern's Address, Wheaton College, 11 October 1972, folder 1-4, collection 37, BGCA.

34. "Evangelical Vote," 93.

35. Randall Balmer, *Thy Kingdom Come: How the Religious Right Distorts the Faith and Threatens America* (New York: Basic Books, 2006), xxv; John Dart, "Billy Graham Values Seen Key to Election," *LAT*, 22 July 1972.

36. David A. Noebel, "The Emerging Evangelical 'Left,'" *CCW*, 24 December 1972, 8.

37. Harold J. Ockenga, "McGovern vs. Nixon," *Hamilton-Wenham (MA) Chronicle*, 2 November 1972; Lyman Kellstedt et al., "Faith Transformed: Religion and American Politics from FDR to George W. Bush," in *Religion and American Politics: From the Colonial Period to the Present*, ed. Mark A. Noll and Luke E. Harlow, 2nd ed. (New York: Oxford University Press, 2007), 272–273.

38. *CT*, 22 December 1972, 39; *Eternity*, January 1973, 7.

39. RNS, "Graham Says Nixon Not in Watergate," *Baptist Standard*, 16 February 1973, 18; Tape recording of phone conversation between Richard Nixon and Billy Graham, 11 April 1973, AOGP 44-143, cassette E-257, NPL; Billy Graham, "Watergate: What We Can Do about It," 6 May 1973, *Hour of Decision* broadcast, T1217, collection 191, BGCA.

40. Martin, *Prophet with Honor*, 398–399.

41. Gibbs and Duffy, *The Preacher and the Presidents*, 157; Mark O. Hatfield, *Between a Rock and a Hard Place* (Waco, TX: Word Books, 1976), 90–91.

42. Billy Graham, Address to Prayer Congress, 1976, audio tape, T4, collection 176, BGCA.

43. Cal Thomas and Ed Dobson, *Blinded by Might: Can the Religious Right Save America?* (Grand Rapids, MI: Zondervan, 1999), 38.

1. For information on evangelical women's activism against the ERA in Texas, see Kent L. Tedin, "Religious Preference and Pro / Anti Activism on the ERA Issue," *Pacific Sociological Review* 21 (1978): 59–60; David W. Brady and Kent L. Tedin, "Ladies in Pink: Religion and Political Ideology in the Anti-ERA Movement," *Social Science Quarterly* 56 (1976): 564–575; Donald T. Critchlow, *Phyllis Schlafly and Grassroots Conservatism: A Woman's Crusade* (Princeton, NJ: Princeton University Press, 2005), 220–224.

2. Nancy Gibbs and Michael Duffy, *The Preacher and the Presidents: Billy Graham in the White House* (New York: Center Street, 2007), 233–234, 239–240; "The Sins of Billy James," *Time*, 16 February 1976; "Dr. McIntire's Magic Touch," *Time*, 14 November 1969.

3. George A. Akerlof and Janet L. Yellen, "An Analysis of Out-of-Wedlock Births in the United States," *Brookings Policy Brief,* August 1996, www.brookings .edu/papers/1996/08childrenfamilies_akerlof.aspx; Steven Mintz and Susan Kellogg, *Domestic Revolutions: A Social History of American Family Life* (New York: Free Press, 1988), 203-210. For analyses of changing views of sexual behavior in the late 1960s, see David Allyn, *Make Love Not War: The Sexual Revolution: An Unfettered History* (New York: Routledge, 2001); and Beth Bailey, *Sex in the Heartland* (Cambridge, MA: Harvard University Press, 1999). For Americans' anxiety about the family in the 1970s, see Natasha Zaretsky, *No Direction Home: The American Family and the Fear of National Decline, 1968-1980* (Chapel Hill: University of North Carolina Press, 2007).

4. Thomas J. Brazaitis, "Dr. Graham Marvels at Turnout," *Cleveland Plain Dealer*, 17 July 1972; George E. Plagenz, "Billy Seeks Full House," *Cleveland Plain Dealer*, 17 July 1972.

5. For an account of the women's rights movement in the 1960s and 1970s, see Flora Davis, *Moving the Mountain: The Women's Movement in America since 1960*, 2nd ed. (Urbana: University of Illinois Press, 1999).

6. Jane J. Mansbridge, *Why We Lost the ERA* (Chicago: University of Chicago Press, 1986), 1–15.

7. Ibid., 13, 104. For a survey of the changes in American popular culture's portrayal of gender roles in the 1970s, see Bruce J. Schulman, *The Seventies: The Great Shift in American Culture, Society, and Politics* (New York: Free Press, 2001), 159–189.

8. John Roach Straton, *The Menace of Immorality in Church and State* (New York: George H. Doran, 1920), 82, 115; John R. Rice, *The Home: Courtship, Marriage, and Children* (Wheaton, IL: Sword of the Lord, 1945); William Martin, *A Prophet with Honor: The Billy Graham Story* (New York: William Morrow, 1991), 159; Brazaitis, "Dr. Graham Marvels at Turnout."

9. Gerald S. Pope, "Beware the Equal Rights Amendment," in Julian E. Williams et al., *Women's Lib: One Way Street to Bondage* (Tulsa, OK: Christian Crusade, 1972), 11; Maxine Secrest, "Confidential to Christian Women," *CCW*, 26 March 1972, 6; Charles V. Secrest, "Difference Is not Revolution," in Williams et al., *Women's Lib*, 22.

10. Donald T. Critchlow, *Phyllis Schlafly and Grassroots Conservatism: A Woman's Crusade* (Princeton, NJ: Princeton University Press, 2005); Ruth Murray Brown, *For a "Christian America": A History of the Religious Right* (Amherst, NY: Prometheus Books, 2002), 47–49; Carol Felsenthal, *The Sweetheart of the Silent Majority: The Biography of Phyllis Schlafly* (Garden City, NY: Doubleday, 1981), 54–162, 171–178; Phyllis Schlafly, *A Choice Not an Echo* (Alton, IL: Pere Marquette Press, 1964).

11. Felsenthal, *Sweetheart of the Silent Majority*, 240.

12. Brown, *For a "Christian America,"* 53; Felsenthal, *Sweetheart of the Silent Majority*, 235–239, 274, 298–299.

13. Phyllis Schlafly, "The Right to Be a Woman," *Phyllis Schlafly Report*, November 1972.

14. Beverly LaHaye, *The Spirit-Controlled Woman* (Eugene, OR: Harvest House, 1976), 71; Anita Bryant, *Bless This House* (Old Tappan, NJ: Fleming H. Revell, 1972); Helen B. Andelin, *Fascinating Womanhood* (Santa Barbara, CA: Pacific Press, 1965; 2nd ed., New York: Bantam Books, 1974); Elisabeth Elliot, *Let Me Be a Woman: Notes on Womanhood for Valerie* (Wheaton, IL: Tyndale House, 1976); Marabel Morgan, *The Total Woman* (Old Tappan, NJ: Fleming H. Revell, 1973), 80; "Editors' Choice," *NYT*, 27 April 1975.

15. Brown, *For a "Christian America,"* 49, 52, 57; Brady and Tedin, "Ladies in Pink," 573.

16. Brown, *For a "Christian America,"* 63–76; Jerry Falwell, *Listen, America!* (Garden City, NY: Doubleday, 1980), 152; Rosemary Thomson, "Jerry Falwell: 'Let's Love America,'" *Christian Life*, September 1980, 37.

17. Catherine E. Rymph, *Republican Women: Feminism and Conservatism from Suffrage through the Rise of the New Right* (Chapel Hill: University of North Carolina Press, 2006), 205; Joseph Lelyveld, "Normally Proper G.O.P. Women Come Out Fighting over E.R.A.," *NYT*, 17 August 1976.

18. "Abortion Inquiries Flooding Colorado," *NYT*, 27 April 1967; Sydney H. Schanberg, "Javits Calls on Legislature to Pass Abortion Reform," *NYT*, 20 February 1967; "Reagan Reluctantly Signs Bill Easing Abortions," *NYT*, 16 June 1967; Lee Edwards, *Goldwater: The Man Who Made a Revolution* (Washington, DC: Regnery, 1995), 420–421.

19. Kristin Luker, *Abortion and the Politics of Motherhood* (Berkeley: University of California Press, 1984), 14–15, 45–62; Rice, *Home*, 156. For information on abortion in the United States during the 1950s, see David J. Garrow, *Liberty and Sexuality: The Right to Privacy and the Making of* Roe v. Wade, 2nd ed. (Berkeley: University of California Press, 1998), 275–283; and Frederick S. Jaffe, Barbara L. Lindheim, and Philip R. Lee, *Abortion Politics: Private Morality and Public Policy* (New York: McGraw-Hill, 1981), 22. For news coverage of abortion during the 1950s, see "One Doctor's Choice," *Time*, 12 March 1956; "The Death of a Girl," *Time*, 26 September 1955; "The Ethics of Abortion," *Time*, 15 July 1957; and "Abortion in the U.S.," *Time*, 2 June 1958.

20. Luker, *Abortion and the Politics of Motherhood*, 76–85.

21. Garrow, *Liberty and Sexuality*, 285–290; Rosemary Nossiff, *Before Roe: Abortion Policy in the States* (Philadelphia: Temple University Press, 2001), 130.

22. Nossiff, *Before Roe*, 130; Jim Risen and Judy L. Thomas, *Wrath of Angels: The American Abortion War* (New York: Basic Books, 1998), 11–16.

23. Luker, *Abortion and the Politics of Motherhood*, 12–13, 59; UPI, "Vatican Bitter at Decision," *San Francisco Examiner*, 4 August 1962; "Abortion Bill Killed—Catholic Pressure," *SFC*, 4 June 1965; "Bishops Fight Changes in State Abortion Law," *SFC*, 8 December 1966; Lou Cannon, *Governor Reagan: His Rise to Power* (New York: Public Affairs, 2003), 209–213.

24. "Right to Life League: Abortion Foes Open Campaign Here," *SFC*, 20 April 1967; Roy Faulstick, "The Case against Abortion," *Lutheran News*, 20 March 1967, 6. For the politics of birth control, see Donald T. Critchlow, *Intended Consequences: Birth Control, Abortion, and the Federal Government in Modern America* (New York: Oxford University Press, 1999).

25. Martin, *Prophet with Honor*, 159; S. I. McMillen, "Abortion: Is It Moral?" *Christian Life*, September 1967, 52.

26. "A Protestant Affirmation on the Control of Human Reproduction," *CT*, 8 November 1968, 18–19; Robert D. Visscher, "Therapeutic Abortion: Blessing or Murder?" *CT*, 27 September 1968, 6–8. See also Nancy Hardesty, "Should Anyone Who Wants an Abortion Have One?" *Eternity*, June 1967, 32–34.

27. Risen and Thomas, *Wrath of Angels*, 15–16; Carl F. H. Henry, "Is Life Ever Cheap?" *Eternity*, February 1971, 20–21; "The War on the Womb," *CT*, 5 June 1970, 24–25; Don Bell, "The Healer Has Become the Murderer," *Christian News*, 19 October 1970, 6; "Christians Observe Black Monday, January 22, 1973, Protest Murder of Unborn Infants," *Christian News*, 20 January 1975, 1.

28. Paul L. Sadler, "The Abortion Issue within the Southern Baptist Convention, 1969–1988" (Ph.D. diss., Baylor University, 1991), 11–17, 25–26; "House in Carolina Backs Bill Easing Curbs on Abortion," *NYT*, 6 May 1967; Eva R. Rubin, *Abortion, Politics, and the Courts: Roe v. Wade and its Aftermath* (Westport, Conn., 1987), 27.

29. Southern Baptist Convention, Resolution on Abortion, June 1971, www .sbc.net/resolutions/amResolution.asp?ID=13; Sadler, "The Abortion Issue within the Southern Baptist Convention," 33; Edward Gardner to Carl E. Bates, 14 March 1972, folder 2, Carl E. Bates Papers, SBHLA; Carl E. Bates to Wade M. Jackson, 21 June 1971, folder 3, Bates Papers, SBHLA.

30. "And Now, a Nation of Mass Murder," *BBT*, 22 September 1967, 6.

31. John R. Rice, "The Murder of the Helpless Unborn," *SWL*, 22 October 1971.

32. "Effect of Ruling on States' Laws," *NYT*, 23 January 1973; Garrow, *Liberty and Sexuality*, 324–325, 544–547; Nossiff, *Before Roe*, 106–122; Risen and Thomas, *Wrath of Angels*, 20; Jaffe, Lindheim, and Lee, *Abortion Politics*, 73.

33. "Effect of Ruling."

34. *CCW*, 5 May 1973, 13 May 1973, and 5 May 1974; David A. Noebel, *Slaughter of the Innocent* (Tulsa, OK: American Christian College, 1973); Noebel, "America: Home of Abortion, Infanticide, and Euthanasia?" *CCW*, 7 October 1973, 3; "Murder of Babies: It's a Major Issue in New York," *BBT*, 9 February 1973;

"Does a Woman Have a Right to Murder?" *Blu-Print*, 6 January 1976; "The Sacrifice of Human Life Goes On," *Blu-Print*, 20 April 1976.

35. Phil Strickland, "Changes Needed in Texas Abortion Bill," *Baptist Standard*, 31 March 1971, 3; Religious News Service (RNS), "The Supreme Court's Decision on Abortion: Dr. Criswell Says He Agrees with It," *BBT*, 16 February 1973, 1.

36. T. A. Patterson, "The Abortion Question," *Baptist Standard*, 22 May 1973, 7; Southern Baptist Convention, Resolution on Abortion and Sanctity of Human Life, June 1974, www.sbc.net/resolutions/amResolution .asp?ID=14.

37. Foy Valentine to Rev. C. H. McClure, 21 December 1970, folder 8-3, "Abortion, 1970–1972," Christian Life Commission Files, SBHLA; Barry Hankins, *Uneasy in Babylon: Southern Baptist Conservatives and American Culture* (Tuscaloosa: University of Alabama Press, 2002), 171–172; Religious Coalition for Abortion Rights, "A Call to Concern," 1977, AR 658, Southern Baptists for Life Collection, SBHLA; "Christian Life Commission Fails to Appoint Successor to Foy Valentine," *Southern Baptists for Life Report*, October 1986; Foy Valentine to Adrian Rogers, 21 November 1977, "Abortion— Correspondence, 1977–1987" folder, Christian Life Commission Files, SBHLA.

38. Robert Holbrook, "Court Ruling Forces Issue," *Baptist Standard*, 16 May 1973, 13; Baptist Press, "Pastor Sends 15,000 Letters Urging SBC Abortion Action," *Alabama Baptist*, 3 June 1976, 9; "Baptists for Life," *Southern Baptist Journal*, May 1974, 12.

39. "Abortion Change Loses," *Baptist Standard*, 23 June 1976, 9; Southern Baptist Convention, Resolution on Abortion, June 1976, www.sbc.net /resolutions/amResolution.asp?ID=15.

40. Louis Moore, "This Baptist Is Fighting Abortion," *Houston Chronicle*, 6 April 1974; "Leaders Conflict on Anti-Abortion Stand," *Baptist Standard*, 20 March 1974, 9; Sadler, "The Abortion Issue within the Southern Baptist Convention," 190; AP, "Southern Baptists, Catholics Allied on Abortions," *Denver Post*, 10 June 1977.

41. Floyd Robertson, "Now That Abortion Is Legal," *UEA*, Summer 1973, 11; "Abortion and the Court," *CT*, 16 February 1973, 32–33.

42. RNS, "Aids 'Defense of Life,'" *Baptist Standard*, 3 September 1975, 4; RNS, "Protestants v. Abortion," *Catholic Voice*, 18 August 1975, 7; "Anti-Abortion: Not Parochial," *CT*, 8 August 1975, 22; Anthony J. Lauinger, "Focus: Mildred F. Jefferson, M.D.," *National Right to Life News*, January 1977, 3; Patrick Riley, "Pro-Life Leader Marjory Mecklenburg Joins Ford-Dole Campaign Committee," *National Catholic Register*, 10 October 1976; Connie Paige, *The Right to Lifers: Who They Are, How They Operate, Where They Get Their Money* (New York: Summit Books, 1983), 81–82.

43. John G. Turner, *Bill Bright and Campus Crusade for Christ: The Renewal of Evangelicalism in Postwar America* (Chapel Hill: University of North Carolina Press, 2008); "'Tomorrow the World,'" *Time*, 3 January 1977, 78.

44. "'Tomorrow the World,'" 78; "Yoking Politics and Proclamation—Can It Be Done?" *CT*, 24 September 1976, 20.

45. Rus Walton, *One Nation under God* (Old Tappan, NJ: Fleming H. Revell, 1975), 36–37, 200–265; Jim Wallis and Wes Michaelson, "The Plan to Save America," *Sojourners*, April 1976, 4; "Yoking Politics and Proclamation," 21; *In the Spirit of '76: The Citizen's Guide to Politics* (Washington, DC: Third Century, 1975).

46. "Yoking Politics and Proclamation," 22; Wallis and Michaelson, "The Plan to Save America," 6–7.

47. Wallis and Michaelson, "The Plan to Save America," 4, 6.

48. Kenneth L. Woodward, "Politics from the Pulpit," *Newsweek*, 6 September 1976, 49.

49. Woodward, "Politics from the Pulpit," 49; "'Tomorrow the World.'"

50. James T. Paterson, *Restless Giant: The United States from Watergate to Bush v. Gore* (New York: Oxford University Press, 2005), 93; UPI, "Betty Ford Would Accept 'an Affair' by Daughter," *NYT*, 11 August 1975; Catherine E. Rymph, *Republican Women: Feminism and Conservatism from Suffrage through the Rise of the New Right* (Chapel Hill: University of North Carolina Press, 2006), 205, 222–225.

51. Viola B. Phillips, "Dr. Bob Jones Views Carter as Phony," *Anderson (IN) Herald*, 26 September 1976.

52. Adam Clymer, *Drawing the Line at the Big Ditch: The Panama Canal Treaties and the Rise of the Right* (Lawrence: University Press of Kansas, 2008), 19–39; "Reagan Will Sign Two Antismut Bills," *NYT*, 22 June 1969; Douglas Robinson, "Sex Education Battles Splitting Many Communities across U.S.," *NYT*, 14 September 1969; Lawrence E. Davies, "Reagan Promises to Rid Campuses of 'Anarchists,'" *NYT*, 8 January 1969; Cannon, *Governor Reagan*, 285–286, 417–428; William A. Link, *Righteous Warrior: Jesse Helms and the Rise of Modern Conservatism* (New York: St. Martin's Press, 2008), 156.

53. Tim Miller and Tonda Rush, "God and the GOP in Kansas City," *CT*, 10 September 1976, 59; Daniel L. Turner, *Standing without Apology: The History of Bob Jones University* (Greenville, SC: Bob Jones University Press, 1997), 304–305; Survey of Republican Party delegates conducted by Thomas Roback, "Stenholm—Political Activity" folder, Gilbert Stenholm Files, BJU. See Oran P. Smith, *The Rise of Baptist Republicanism* (New York: New York University Press, 1997), for an analysis of Bob Jones University administrators' political activity in 1976.

54. "Reagan on God and Morality," *CT*, 2 July 1976, 39–40.

55. William Martin, *With God on Our Side: The Rise of the Religious Right in America* (New York: Broadway Books, 1996), 148–154; Myra MacPherson, "Evangelicals Seen Cooling on Carter," *WP*, 27 September 1976.

56. MacPherson, "Evangelicals Seen Cooling"; Woodward, "Born Again! The Year of the Evangelicals," *Newsweek*, 25 October 1976.

57. Howard Norton and Bob Slosser, *The Miracle of Jimmy Carter* (Plainfield, NJ: Logos International, 1976); *CT*, 16 July 1976, 43.

58. MacPherson, "Evangelicals Seen Cooling"; AP, "Carter Fields Some Biblical Questions," *San Francisco Chronicle*, 25 October 1976; *Plains Baptist Challenger* (Lubbock, TX), September 1976, "James Earl Carter" folder, G. Archer Weniger Files, BJU; Ron Boehme with Rus Walton, *What about Jimmy Carter?* (Washington, DC: Third Century Publishers, 1976).

59. Robert Scheer, Interview with Jimmy Carter, November 1976, in *The Playboy Interview*, ed. G. Barry Colson (New York: Wideview Books, 1981), 488.

60. AP, "A Baptist Leader Backs Ford," *San Francisco Chronicle*, 11 October 1976; MacPherson, "Evangelicals Seen Cooling."

61. *Voices of Victory* (Greenville, SC), 25 June 1976, "James Earl Carter" folder, Weniger Files, BJU; "Carter—The Southern Baptist Candidate," *Plains Baptist Challenger* (Lubbock, TX), June 1976, 1–4; A. J. Matt, Jr., "Carter in the Gutter," *Christian News*, 4 October 1976, 3; Jim Merriner, "17 Ministers Blast Carter," *Atlanta Constitution*, 12 October 1976.

62. "BJU President Comments on Jimmy Carter's Interview in *Playboy* Magazine," Bob Jones University Press Release [1976], "James Earl Carter" folder, Weniger Papers, BJU; Merriner, "17 Ministers Blast Carter."

63. *Word of Life*, 6 November 1969, TRBC 4-8, LUA; "Falwell Omits Tape, Offers Rebuttal Time," *BBT*, 29 October 1976, 4.

64. "Falwell Omits Tape, Offers Rebuttal Time," 1, 4; Martin, *With God on Our Side*, 197.

65. Rita E. Hauser to Rogers C. B. Morton, 3 May 1976, "Voter Groups—General" folder, President Ford Committee Records, 1975–1976, box B10, GFL; "Southern Baptists: Platform for Presidents," *CT*, 16 July 1976, 48; Transcript of President Gerald R. Ford's Address to the Southern Baptist Convention, 15 June 1976, "Religion" folder, A. James Reichley Files, box 5, GFL.

66. Harry M. Covert, Jr., to Bill Nicholson, 8 June 1976, "6-21-76—Thomas Rd. Baptist Church" folder, Paul Theis and Robert Orben Files, box 61, GFL; "HCD" to Bill Nicholson, [June 1976], and transcript of Gerald Ford's videotaped speech for use at Thomas Rd. Baptist Church in Lynchburg, VA, 21 June 1976, "6-21-76—Thomas Rd. Baptist Church" folder, Paul Theis and Robert Orben Files, box 61, GFL.

67. "Election '76: Indifference Is No Virtue," *CT*, 22 October 1976, 38; Kenneth A. Briggs, "Ford Makes Appeal to Evangelical Groups," *NYT*, 10 October 1976; AP, "Baptist Leader Backs Ford."

68. *Religious Broadcasting*, November 1976, 10; Joseph Lelyveld, "President's Latest TV Commercials Portray Him as Father Figure Who Inspires Quiet Confidence," *NYT*, 29 September 1976.

69. James Reston, "Nixon and Muskie on Abortion," *NYT*, 7 April 1971; "Nixon Abortion Statement," *NYT*, 4 April 1971; Tanya Melich, *The Republican War against Women: An Insider's Report from Behind the Lines* (New York: Bantam Books, 1998), 53.

70. Richard Steele, "The Right to Life Candidate," *Newsweek*, 9 February 1976, 23.

71. Martin Tolchin, "Rally Demands Ban on Abortion," *NYT*, 23 January 1976; Ralph Stanley to George Van Cleve, 22 July 1976, "Republican Party Platform—Issue Papers (5)" folder, box 29, Michael Raoul-Duval Files, GFL.

72. "Ford Asks States' Rule on Abortion," *Minneapolis Star*, 4 February 1976; AP, "Ford Abortion Stand Draws Criticism," *NYT*, 5 February 1976.

73. Mark Stricherz, *Why the Democrats Are Blue: How Secular Liberals Hijacked the People's Party* (New York: Encounter Books, 2007), 161–223; Al McConagha, "Abortion Issue Is Nagging Carter's Campaign," *Minneapolis Tribune*, 12 September 1976; Andrew Mollison, "Do Catholics Cut Carter Chances?" *Atlanta Constitution*, 13 July 1976; Willmar Thorkelson, "Religion Issue Enters Presidential Campaign," *Minneapolis Star*, 17 July 1976.

74. George Van Cleve to Michael Duval, 23 July 1976, "Republican Party Platform—Issue Papers (5)," box 29, Raoul-Duval Files, GFL; Alice Hartle, "GOP to Focus on Abortion," *National Right to Life News*, September 1976; Melich, *The Republican War against Women*, 63–64; Republican Party Platform of 1976, www.presidency.ucsb.edu/showplatforms.php?platindex=R1976.

75. Timothy A. Byrnes, *Catholic Bishops in American Politics* (Princeton, NJ: Princeton University Press, 1991), 72–77; Gerald R. Ford to Joseph L. Bernardin, 10 September 1976, "Material Not to Be Released to the Press—Catholic Bishops, 9-10-76" folder, box 40, Ronald H. Nessen Files, GFL; John Fialka, "Not Endorsement, Bishop Says," *Washington Star*, 17 September 1976; "Pat Boone Statement," [n.d.], box 45, American Citizens Concerned for Life Records, GFL.

76. Americans Against Abortion, Press Release [September 1976], "ACCL Political File: '76 Presidential Campaign—NRL Project" folder, box 46, Americans Concerned for Life Records, GFL.

77. Lyman Kellstedt et al., "Faith Transformed: Religion and American Politics from FDR to George W. Bush," in *Religion and American Politics: From the Colonial Period to the Present*, ed. Mark A. Noll and Luke E. Harlow (New York: Oxford University Press, 2007), 273; Sara Diamond, *Roads to Dominion: Right-Wing Movements and Political Power in the United States* (New York: Guilford Press, 1995), 173; Transcript of Cal Skaggs's interview with Pat Robertson, conducted for the television documentary *With God on Our Side,* 6 February 1996, 25–26 (used with permission from William Martin).

Chapter 7

1. Kenneth A. Briggs, "Capital Church Wants Carters to Feel at Home," *NYT*, 30 January 1977.

2. *CB*, 11 November 1976, 1.

3. John Steinbacher, *The Child Seducers* (n.p.: Educator Publications, 1971), 7–10; *BBT*, 21 February 1975, 2.

4. William Martin, *With God on Our Side: The Rise of the Religious Right in America* (New York: Broadway Books, 1996), 122–127; Ben A. Franklin, "3 Held in Dispute over Textbooks," *NYT*, 19 September 1974; James C. Hefley, *Textbooks on Trial* (Wheaton, IL: Victor Books, 1976), 160.

5. Martin, *With God on Our Side*, 122–127, 135–136; Hefley, *Textbooks on Trial*, 160; Franklin, "3 Held in Dispute over Textbooks"; UPI, "11 Coal Mines Shut as Textbook Dispute Stirs West Virginia," *NYT*, 9 October 1974;

Melissa M. Deckman, *School Board Battles: The Christian Right in Local Politics* (Washington, DC: Georgetown University Press, 2004), 15.

6. Memo from Connaught Coyne Marshner to Heritage Foundation staff, "Re: West Virginia Press Conference," 22 November 1974, "Memos from Connaught 'Connie' Marshner, 1974–1975" folder, box 19, Paul M. Weyrich Papers, AHC; Heritage Foundation, "Here Is a Summary of What Heritage Foundation Has Done with Your Contributions," n.d. [Spring 1975], "Memos from Connaught 'Connie' Marshner, 1974–1975" folder, box 19, Weyrich Papers, AHC; Memo from Connaught Marshner to Heritage Foundation staff, "Re: West Virginia Hearings, January 13–15," 14 February 1975, "Memos from Connaught 'Connie' Marshner, 1974–1975" folder, box 19, Weyrich Papers, AHC.

7. Speech written by Connaught Marshner for Rep. Phil Crane, n.d. [late 1974], "Speeches created by Connaught Marshner, 1973–1974" folder, box 82, Weyrich Papers, AHC; Connaught Coyne Marshner, *Blackboard Tyranny* (New Rochelle, NY: Arlington House, 1978).

8. Onalee McGraw, *Secular Humanism and the Schools: The Issue Whose Time Has Come* (Washington, DC: Heritage Foundation, 1976), 8, 20.

9. Marshner, *Blackboard Tyranny*, 89–226.

10. Paul Houston and Gaylord Shaw, "Helms Thinks Reagan Will Support Him in Floor Fight for Conservative Planks," *LAT*, 15 August 1976; Republican Party Platform of 1976, www.presidency.ucsb.edu/ws/index.php?pid=25843.

11. Daymon Johnson, "Reformed Fundamentalism in America: The Lordship of Christ, the Transformation of Culture, and Other Calvinist Components of the Christian Right" (Ph.D. diss., Florida State University, 1994), 100–110; Michael S. Hamilton, "The Dissatisfaction of Francis Schaeffer," *CT*, 3 March 1997, 22–26. For a biography of Schaeffer, see Barry Hankins, *Francis Schaeffer and the Shaping of Evangelical America* (Grand Rapids, MI: William B. Eerdmans, 2008).

12. Johnson, "Reformed Fundamentalism," 114.

13. Hamilton, "The Dissatisfaction of Francis Schaeffer," 27.

14. Francis A. Schaeffer, *Pollution and the Death of Man: The Christian View of Ecology* (Wheaton, IL: Tyndale House, 1970); Francis A. Schaeffer, "Race and Economics," *CT*, 4 January 1974, 18–19; Hamilton, "The Dissatisfaction of Francis Schaeffer," 27, 29.

15. Johnson, "Reformed Fundamentalism," 105; Billy James Hargis, "Comments on 'The Church at the End of the 20th Century,'" *CCW*, 3 October 1971, 5.

16. Francis A. Schaeffer, *Death in the City* (Downers Grove, IL: Intervarsity Press, 1969), 71.

17. Francis A. Schaeffer, *The Great Evangelical Disaster* (1984), 11, as cited in Johnson, "Reformed Fundamentalism," 115.

18. Francis A. Schaeffer, *How Should We Then Live? The Rise and Decline of Western Thought and Culture* (Westchester, IL: Crossway Books, 1976), 223.

19. Schaeffer, *How Should We Then Live?* 256.

20. Frank Schaeffer, *Crazy for God: How I Grew Up as One of the Elect, Helped Found the Religious Right, and Lived to Take All (or Almost All) of It Back* (New York: Carroll & Graf, 2007), 253–263.

21. Nancy Gibbs and Michael Duffy, *The Preacher and the Presidents: Billy Graham in the White House* (New York: Center Street, 2007), 233–236, 249; Marjorie Hunter, "Ford's Wife Undergoes Breast Cancer Surgery," *NYT*, 29 September 1974; Garry Wills, "'Born Again' Politics," *NYT*, 1 August 1976; William Gildea, "And Now the White House Has . . . Another Reverend Billy," *WP*, 29 January 1975 (ellipses in original).

22. Schaeffer, *Crazy for God*, 2, 270; Frank Schaeffer, "I Should Be Supporting Allen; Instead, I'm Leaving the Party," *Dallas Morning News*, 1 November 2006; Hankins, *Francis Schaeffer and the Shaping of Evangelical America*, 201.

23. David Outlaw, "The Impact of Francis Schaeffer on Selected American Evangelical Thinkers" (Ph.D. diss., Mid-America Baptist Theological Seminary, 2001), 125.

24. H. Edward Rowe, *Save America!* (Old Tappan, NJ: Fleming H. Revell, 1976), 12, 18–21.

25. Ibid., 29, 38, 43.

26. Ibid., 128, 134, 149–151.

27. AP, "Abzug Reported Due to Manage Women's Year," *WP*, 20 March 1977; Dick Dabney, "God's Own Network," *Harper's*, August 1980, 38.

28. Ruth Murray Brown, *For a "Christian America": A History of the Religious Right* (Amherst, NY: Prometheus Books, 2002), 106.

29. Jennifer Dunning, "At State Women's Conference, a New Constituency Speaks," *NYT*, 15 July 1977; Brown, *For a "Christian America,"* 109–110; "What's Next for U.S. Women," *Time*, 5 December 1977; Rosemary Thomson, *Withstanding Humanism's Challenge to Families: Anatomy of a White House Conference* (Morton, IL: Traditional Publications, 1981), i–ii.

30. Brown, *For a "Christian America,"* 111–114, 117–120; Judy Klemesrud, "Equal Rights Plan and Abortion Are Opposed by 15,000 at Rally," *NYT*, 20 November 1977.

31. Carol Felsenthal, *The Sweetheart of the Silent Majority: The Biography of Phyllis Schlafly* (Garden City, NY: Doubleday, 1981), 279.

32. Terence Smith, "Carter, in Angry Exchange, Ousts Bella Abzug from Women's Unit," *NYT*, 13 January 1979; "Carter Urges Extension for Rights Amendment," *NYT*, 13 July 1978; Marjorie Hunter, "New Voice for Women in the White House," *NYT*, 6 November 1978.

33. Holly G. Miller, "Concerned Women for America: Soft Voices with Clout," *Saturday Evening Post*, October 1985, 70; Beverly LaHaye, *I Am a Woman by God's Design* (Old Tappan, NJ: Fleming H. Revell, 1980), 134; John Rees, "Christian Leader Beverly LaHaye: An Exclusive Interview with the Pro-Family President of the 500,000-Member Concerned Women for America," *Review of the News*, 8 May 1985, 31–38.

34. Brown, *For a "Christian America,"* 142–152.

35. Intercessors for America newsletter, 1 July 1980 and 1 September 1980, MS 76.15, HH 394, box 4B, Hall-Hoag Collection, John Hay Library, Brown University, Providence, RI.

36. John D'Emilio, *Sexual Politics, Sexual Communities: The Making of a Homosexual Minority in the United States, 1940–1970* (Chicago: University of

Chicago Press, 1983), 57–125, 132–133, 137–138; David Allyn, *Make Love, Not War: The Sexual Revolution, an Unfettered History* (Boston: Little and Brown, 2000), 115; Noel Smith, "As in the Days of Sodom," *BBT*, 26 February 1965, 1–2.

37. D'Emilio, *Sexual Politics, Sexual Communities*, 231–233; Leila J. Rupp, *A Desired Past: A Short History of Same-Sex Love in America* (Chicago: University of Chicago Press, 1999), 178; Dudley Clendinen and Adam Nagourney, *Out for Good: The Struggle to Build a Gay Rights Movement in America* (New York: Simon & Schuster, 1999), 215–216, 240.

38. Fred Fejes, *Gay Rights and Moral Panic: The Origins of America's Debate on Homosexuality* (New York: Palgrave Macmillan, 2008), 85; Bob Maddox to Kenneth Bowden, 2 September 1980, "Gay Issues" folder, box 105, Robert L. Maddox Papers, Public Outreach, JCL; Clendinen and Nagourney, *Out for Good*, 272–273; William Willoughby, "Gay Issue to Plague Carter's Campaign?" *National Courier*, 17 September 1976, 2.

39. Letha Scanzoni, "Gay Confrontation," *CT*, 12 March 1976, 54; Fejes, *Gay Rights and Moral Panic*, 54, 73; Southern Baptist Convention, Resolution on Homosexuality, June 1976, www.sbc.net/resolutions/amResolution.asp?ID=606.

40. Adon Taft, "Anita on Crusade," *Christian Life*, June 1977, 16–17, 59–61; Perry Deane Young, *God's Bullies: Native Reflections on Preachers and Politics* (New York: Holt, Rinehart, and Winston, 1982), 39–41; Anita Bryant, *Bless This House* (Old Tappan, NJ: Fleming H. Revell, 1972), 43–50, 72.

41. Anita Bryant, *The Anita Bryant Story: The Survival of Our Nation's Families and the Threat of Militant Homosexuality* (Old Tappan, NJ: Fleming H. Revell, 1977), 15–16, 52, 114–116; "Bias against Homosexuals Is Outlawed in Miami," *NYT*, 19 January 1977.

42. B. Drummond Ayres, Jr., "Miami Debate over Rights of Homosexuals Directs Wide Attention to a National Issue," *NYT*, 10 May 1977; Bryant, *Anita Bryant Story*, 85.

43. Clendinen and Nagourney, *Out for Good*, 293–300; B. Drummond Ayres, Jr., "Miami Acts Tuesday on Homosexual Law," *NYT*, 5 June 1977; Ayres, "Miami Debate."

44. Bryant, *Anita Bryant Story*, 41–43; Young, *God's Bullies*, 37; Fejes, *Gay Rights and Moral Panic*, 122, 134; Ayers, "Miami Acts Tuesday on Homosexual Law."

45. "Carter Aide 'Impressed' by Parley with Homosexuals Alleging Bias," *NYT*, 16 February 1977; AP, "Carter Says Plans of Government Should Keep Families Together," *NYT*, 19 June 1977.

46. "Gay Rights Showdown in Miami," *Time*, 13 June 1977; "The Unmaking of an Amendment," *Time*, 25 April 1977, 89, 122; Ayres, "Miami Debate"; Bryant, *Anita Bryant Story*, 43, 122; Fejes, *Gay Rights and Moral Panic*, 134.

47. "Thousands Backing Homosexuals March Uptown to Columbus Circle," *NYT*, 9 June 1977; AP, "Orange Juice Boycott," *NYT*, 9 June 1977; "Enough! Enough! Enough!" *Time*, 20 June 1977; Ayres, "Miami Votes 2 to 1."

48. "Entertainer Weeps after Walkout," *NYT*, 10 June 1977; Southern Baptist Convention, Resolution on Homosexuality, June 1977, www.sbc.net/resolutions; "We Love You, Anita," *Baptist Standard*, 1 June 1977, 6; Norman Jameson, "Bryant Asked to Accept SBC Vice-Presidency," *Baptist Standard*, 31 May 1978, 3; "The Anita Enigma," *Baptist Standard*, 21 June 1978, 6.

49. "Controversy Has Its Price," *CT*, 18 March 1977, 30 (emphasis in original); G. Archer Weniger, *Blu-Print*, 31 May 1977 and 14 June 1977; Carl McIntire, "Finding a New Name: The Homosexuals," sermon, [1977], folder 3, box 1, Carl McIntire Collection, Bentley Historical Library, University of Michigan, Ann Arbor; *CT*, 23 March 1979, 53.

50. Anita Bryant, Direct Mail for Protect America's Children, n.d. [1977–1980], "Anita Bryant" folder, Gilbert Stenholm Files, BJU.

51. Taft, "Anita on Crusade"; Bryant, *Anita Bryant Story*, 62; Helen Farmley, "Anita Bryant Calls Marriage Troubled One from the Start," Religious News Service, 30 May 1980, "James Robison" folder, G. Archer Weniger Files, BJU; Cliff Jahr, "Anita Bryant's Startling Reversals," *Ladies' Home Journal*, December 1980, 68.

52. Young, *God's Bullies*, 37; Bryant, *Anita Bryant Story*, 122; Barry Hankins, *Uneasy in Babylon: Southern Baptist Conservatives and American Culture* (Tuscaloosa: University of Alabama Press, 2002), 66–67; Jerry Falwell, *How You Can Help Clean Up America* (Lynchburg, VA: Liberty, 1978), 6–14.

53. Advertisement for California Save Our Children, *Long Beach Telegram*, 25 September 1977, "Briggs Initiative 6" folder, PRA; Bob Harris, "Batema: No to Gays," *JC*, 29 September 1978, 1; Clendinen and Nagourney, *Out for Good*, 365–366, 377–384.

54. Falwell, *How You Can Help Clean Up America*, 23, 27, 31, 72; Harris, "Batema: No to Gays," 1; Michael D. Lopez, "Evangelist Helps Raise a Hope, a Prayer and Money for Prop. 6," *San Diego Union*, 31 October 1978.

55. Tim LaHaye, *The Unhappy Gays: What Everyone Should Know about Homosexuality* (Wheaton, IL: Tyndale House, 1978), 176–177, 197.

56. Lisa McGirr, *Suburban Warriors: The Origins of the New American Right* (Princeton, NJ: Princeton University Press, 2001), 258; Alan Crawford, *Thunder on the Right: The "New Right" and the Politics of Resentment* (New York: Pantheon, 1980), 314; Lopez, "Evangelist Helps Raise a Hope."

57. Dinesh D'Souza, *Falwell: Before the Millennium: A Critical Biography* (Chicago: Regnery Gateway, 1984), 111–112; McGirr, *Suburban Warriors*, 259; "Is Morality All Right?" *CT*, 2 November 1979, 76–77.

58. Religious News Service, "Fundamentalists Told Carter Is Neutral on Homosexuality," 26 March 1980, Weniger Files, BJU; Patrick J. Buchanan, "Carter's Pact with Gay Liberation," *Christian News*, 21 July 1980, 15.

59. Sarah Weddington to H. Darrel Darby, 4 August 1980, "Abortion Letters" folder, box 103, Robert L. Maddox Papers, Public Outreach, JCL; "High Marks on His Early Exams," *Time*, 4 April 1977.

60. Clayton Fritchey, "A Costly Ban on Abortion," *WP*, 25 September 1976; Laura Foreman, "President Defends Court's Action Curbing Federal Aid for Abortion," *NYT*, 13 July 1977; "The Supreme Court Ignites a Fiery Abortion Debate," *Time*, 4 July 1977.

61. Ward Sinclair, "Anti-Abortion Activists Help Scuttle Clark in Iowa," *WP*, 9 November 1978; Crawford, *Thunder on the Right*, 36, 273; Sara Diamond, *Roads to Dominion: Right-Wing Movements and Political Power in the United States* (New York: Guilford Press, 1995), 170.

62. "Abortion Change Loses," *Baptist Standard*, 23 June 1976, 9; Frank Schaeffer, *Crazy for God*, 271–273; Francis A. Schaeffer and C. Everett Koop, *Whatever Happened to the Human Race?* (Old Tappan, NJ: Fleming H. Revell, 1979), 50–63, 81–85, 195–198.

63. Jim Risen and Judy L. Thomas, *Wrath of Angels: The American Abortion War* (New York: Basic Books, 1998), 125.

64. Outlaw, "The Impact of Francis Schaeffer on Selected American Evangelical Thinkers," 125; Edith Schaeffer, *Dear Family: The L'Abri Family Letters, 1961–1986* (New York: Harper & Row, 1989), 313–314; Risen and Thomas, *Wrath of Angels*, 142–143, 232.

65. Jerry Falwell, *Strength for the Journey: An Autobiography* (New York: Simon & Schuster, 1987), 335; Falwell, *How You Can Help Clean Up America*, 9, 59, 65; Jerry Falwell, "Strengthening Families in the Nation," Transcript of speech, Atlanta, 1982, "Speeches, 1982" folder, FAL 5-1, LUA.

66. Falwell, *How You Can Help Clean Up America*, 60–61.

67. Schaeffer, *Crazy for God*, 299–300.

68. Hankins, *Uneasy in Babylon*, 17. For studies of the conflict between moderates and conservatives in the SBC, see Hankins, *Uneasy in Babylon*; Nancy Tatom Ammerman, *Baptist Battles: Social Change and Religious Conflict in the Southern Baptist Convention* (Piscataway, NJ: Rutgers University Press, 1990); and David T. Morgan, *The New Crusades, the New Holy Land: Conflict in the Southern Baptist Convention, 1969–1991* (Tuscaloosa: University of Alabama Press, 1996).

69. Hankins, *Uneasy in Babylon*, 36–37.

70. George Vecsey, "Baptist Leader Keyed to Bible," *NYT*, 14 June 1979; George Vecsey, "Southern Baptists Divided over Bible," *NYT*, 10 June 1979; Hankins, *Uneasy in Babylon*, 5–10, 43.

71. Hankins, *Uneasy in Babylon*, 1–13, 41–106; Southern Baptist Convention, Resolutions, 1980, www.sbc.net/resolutions.

72. Tim LaHaye, "The Questions?" *MMR*, 6 June 1980, 10.

Chapter 8

1. "Mobilizing the Moral Majority," *CD*, August 1979, 14.

2. Dean M. Kelley, *Why Conservative Churches Are Growing: A Study in Sociology of Religion*, 2nd ed. (San Francisco: Harper & Row, 1977); Roger Finke and Rodney Stark, *The Churching of America, 1776–1990: Winners and Losers in Our Religious Economy* (New Brunswick, NJ: Rutgers University Press, 1992), 148–149, 248–249; Walter B. Shurden, "Southern Baptist Convention," in

Encyclopedia of Religion in the South, ed. Samuel S. Hill (Macon, GA: Mercer University Press, 1984), 720–722.

3. Kenneth L. Woodward, "Born Again!" *Newsweek*, 25 October 1976, 68, 70.

4. Jeffrey K. Hadden and Anson Shupe, *Televangelism: Power and Politics on God's Frontier* (New York: Henry Holt, 1988), 83; Ronald B. Flowers, *Religion in Strange Times: The 1960s and 1970s* (Macon, GA: Mercer University Press, 1984), 43.

5. Hal Lindsey, *The Late, Great Planet Earth* (Grand Rapids, MI: Zondervan, 1970); Ray Walters, "Ten Years of Best Sellers," *NYT*, 30 December 1979; "Religious Best Sellers," *NYT*, 12 March 1978; Eileen Luhr, *Witnessing Suburbia: Conservatives and Christian Youth Culture* (Berkeley: University of California Press, 2009), 23–27, 53; Wayne King, "'Jesus Rock' Now a New Musical Industry," *NYT*, 10 June 1977.

6. Jeffrey K. Hadden and Charles E. Swann, *Prime-Time Preachers: The Rising Power of Televangelism* (Reading, MA: Addison-Wesley, 1981), 29–40, 55, 109; Hadden and Shupe, *Televangelism*, 51–52. The three Christian networks were Pat Robertson's Christian Broadcasting Network (CBN), Paul Crouch's Trinity Broadcasting Network (TBN), and Jim and Tammy Bakker's PTL.

7. Charles Colson, *Born Again* (Old Tappan, NJ: Fleming H. Revell, 1976); Eldridge Cleaver, *Soul on Fire* (Waco, TX: Word Books, 1978); *CT*, 5 October 1979, 60; George Vecsey, "Self-Styled Pornographer Says He Has Changed, but Not into a Traditional Christian," *NYT*, 2 February 1978.

8. Scott Thumma and Dave Travis, *Beyond Megachurch Myths: What We Can Learn from America's Largest Churches* (San Francisco: Jossey-Bass, 2007), 7; Scott L. Thumma, "The Shape of Things to Come: Megachurches, Emerging Churches, and Other New Religious Structures," in *Faith in America: Changes, Challenges, New Directions*, ed. Charles H. Lippy (Westport, CT: Praeger, 2006), 1: 195–197; Lynne and Bill Hybels, *Rediscovering Church: The Story and Vision of Willow Creek Community Church* (Grand Rapids, MI: Zondervan, 1995); Barbara Dolan, "Full House at Willow Creek," *Time*, 6 March 1989.

9. Gerald Strober and Ruth Tomczak, *Jerry Falwell: Aflame for God* (Nashville: Thomas Nelson, 1979), 31–34; *Christian Life*, September 1971, 28; Jerry Falwell and Elmer Towns, *Church Aflame* (Nashville: Impact Books, 1971), 13–20, 139–155; Robert Wuthnow, *The Restructuring of American Religion: Society and Faith since World War II* (Princeton, NJ: Princeton University Press, 1988), 197; Jerry Falwell, Chapel Talk, 30 January 1980, "Falwell Sermons—1980" folder, FAL 5-3, LUA.

10. Robert Dreyfuss, "Reverend Doomsday," *Rolling Stone*, 28 January 2004.

11. Frank Fenton, "Thomas Rd. Church Cleared of Fraud, Deceit Charges," *Lynchburg News & Advance*, 10 August 1973; Jerry Falwell, *Strength for the Journey: An Autobiography* (New York: Simon & Schuster, 1987), 326–333.

12. Matthew C. Moen, *The Christian Right and Congress* (Tuscaloosa: University of Alabama Press, 1989), 24–25.

13. A. O. Sulzberger, Jr., "Private Academies Protest Tax Plan," *NYT*, 11 December 1978; Joseph Crespino, "Civil Rights and the Religious Right," in *Rightward Bound: Making America Conservative in the 1970s*, ed. Bruce J. Schulman and Julian E. Zelizer (Cambridge, MA: Harvard University Press, 2008), 100–102.

14. Hadden and Swann, *Prime-Time Preachers*, 135; Sulzberger, "Private Academies Protest Tax Plan"; "Politicizing the Word," *Time*, 1 October 1979, 68; William Martin, *With God on Our Side: The Rise of the Religious Right in America* (New York: Broadway Books, 1996), 172–173.

15. Thomas Byrne Edsall and Mary D. Edsall, *Chain Reaction: The Impact of Race, Rights, and Taxes on American Politics* (New York: Norton, 1991), 133; Robert C. Liebman, "Mobilizing the Moral Majority," in *The New Christian Right: Mobilization and Legitimation*, ed. Robert C. Liebman and Robert Wuthnow (Hawthorne, NY: Aldine, 1983), 60; Alan Crawford, *Thunder on the Right: The "New Right" and the Politics of Resentment* (New York: Pantheon Books, 1980), 161; George J. Church, "Politics from the Pulpit," *Time*, 13 October 1980, 35.

16. Edward E. Plowman, "Is Morality All Right?" *CT*, 2 November 1979, 77; Tom Morganthau, "The Religion Lobby," *Newsweek*, 16 July 1979, 37.

17. Morganthau, "Religion Lobby," 37; Plowman, "Is Morality All Right?" 76; Perry Deane Young, *God's Bullies: Native Reflections on Preachers and Politics* (New York: Holt, Rinehart and Winston, 1982), 97, 101; "Preachers in Politics," *USN*, 24 September 1979, 40; Robert Digitale, "A Christian in Transition: Leader of Religious Right Lobbies Less, Reflects More," *Santa Rosa (CA) Press Democrat*, 18 December 1988; Colonel V. Doner, *The Samaritan Strategy: A New Agenda for Christian Activism* (Brentwood, TN: Wolgemuth and Hyatt, 1988), xiii; Robert Lindsey, "Fundamentalist Christian Unity in Politics Sought," *NYT*, 20 September 1979.

18. Morton Mintz, "Evangelical Group Plans Nov. 2 Political Appeal at Churches," *WP*, 5 October 1980; James L. Guth, "The New Christian Right," in Liebman and Wuthnow, *New Christian Right*, 31–32; Morganthau, "Religion Lobby," 37.

19. "A Christian Political Lobby," *SFC*, 15 June 1979; Crawford, *Thunder on the Right*, 146–147; "Preachers in Politics," 38.

20. Erling Jorstad, *The Politics of Moralism: The New Christian Right in American Life* (Minneapolis: Augsburg, 1981), 86–87; Mintz, "Evangelical Group Plans Nov. 2 Political Appeal"; Church, "Politics from the Pulpit," 35.

21. L. J. Davis, "Conservatism in America," *Harper's*, October 1980, 25; "Preachers in Politics," 38.

22. Robert Zwier and Richard Smith, "Christian Politics and the New Right," *Christian Century*, 8 October 1980, 940; "Preachers in Politics," 39; "Stacking Sandbags against a Conservative Flood," *CT*, 2 November 1979, 76; Russell Chandler, "Conservative Religious Group Prepares for Political Crusade," *San Jose Mercury News*, 18 August 1979; Lindsey, "Fundamentalist Christian Unity."

23. Crawford, *Thunder on the Right*, 269. For information on the New Right of the late 1970s, see Crawford, *Thunder on the Right*; "The New Right: A Special Report," *CD*, June 1979, 9–17; Richard Viguerie, *The New Right: We're Ready to Lead* (Falls Church, VA: Viguerie Company, 1981); Robert W. Whitaker, ed., *The New Right Papers* (New York: St. Martin's Press, 1982); and Alf Tomas Tonnessen, *How Two Political Entrepreneurs Helped Create the American Conservative Movement, 1973–1981: The Ideas of Richard Viguerie and Paul Weyrich* (New York: Edwin Mellen, 2009).

24. Kathleen Tyman, "Paul Weyrich: A Conservative Force," *CD*, August 1984, 27; Viguerie, *The New Right*, 27–28.

25. Gregory L. Schneider, *The Conservative Century: From Reaction to Revolution* (Lanham, MD: Rowman & Littlefield, 2009), 127; Viguerie, *The New Right*, 36; William B. Hixton, Jr., *Search for the American Right Wing: An Analysis of the Social Science Record, 1955–1987* (Princeton, NJ: Princeton University Press, 1992), 213.

26. Paul Weyrich, "Blue Collar or Blue Blood? The New Right Compared with the Old Right," in *The New Right Papers*, ed. Robert W. Whitaker (New York: St. Martin's Press, 1982), 61; "Conservative Phillips Goes After Ed Brooke," *CD*, July 1978, 18–19.

27. Anthony Corrado et al., eds., *Campaign Finance Reform: A Sourcebook* (Washington, DC: Brookings Institution, 1997), chapter 5, www.brook.edu/gs/cf/sourcebk/chap5.htm; Young, *God's Bullies*, 84–88; Viguerie, *The New Right*, 32–36.

28. "Terry Dolan: Conservative Point Man," *CD*, January 1979, 26–27; Margaret Ann Latus, "Ideological PACs and Political Action," in Liebman and Wuthnow, *New Christian Right*, 78–79; Surina Khan, "Gay Conservatives: Pulling the Movement to the Right," *Public Eye*, Spring 1996; Crawford, *Thunder on the Right*, 272.

29. Richard Starnes, "Right-Wing Voice Avoids 'Lunatic' Label," *Knoxville News-Sentinel*, 7 November 1977; Tyman, "Paul Weyrich," 26–27.

30. Sara Diamond, "Trench Tactics on the Anti-Abortion Front," *Z Magazine*, December 1992, 38–41; Weyrich, "Blue Collar or Blue Blood?" 60; Crawford, *Thunder on the Right*, 273; James Ridgeway, "The Prolife Juggernaut," *Voice*, 16 July 1985, 28–29.

31. Jim Wallis and Wes Michaelson, "The Plan to Save America," *Sojourners*, April 1976, 11; Davis, "Conservatism in America," 22–24; Viguerie, *The New Right*, 124.

32. Martin, *With God on Our Side*, 135; Paul Weyrich to Terry Dolan, 2 September 1976, "Correspondence—September 1976" folder, box 1, Paul M. Weyrich Papers, AHC; Paul A. Fisher, "The Wanderer Asks Paul Weyrich about the New Right," *Wanderer*, 18 December 1980; Paul Weyrich to Mary Hunt, 28 March 1977, "Correspondence—March 1977" folder, box 2, Weyrich Papers; Connaught Coyne Marshner, Briefing Book on the Family Protection Act, 24 September 1979, "Family Protection Act—Briefing Book, 1979" folder, box 37, Weyrich Papers; John D. Beckett to Connie Marshner, 12 October 1979, "Correspondence—Connaught 'Connie' Marshner, 1979"

folder, box 83, Weyrich Papers; Margot Hornblower, "'Pro-Family Push': Political Minefield," *WP*, 25 July 1980; Steven V. Roberts, "Reagan's 'First Friend,'" *NYT*, 21 March 1982; Plowman, "Is Morality All Right?" 76.

33. Jerome L. Himmelstein, "The New Right," in Liebman and Wuthnow, *The New Christian Right*, 26; Moen, *Christian Right and Congress*, 71; Davis, "Conservatism in America," 24.

34. Dudley Clendinen, "Rev. Falwell Inspires Evangelical Vote," *NYT*, 20 August 1980; Bruce Nesmith, *The New Republican Coalition: The Reagan Campaigns and White Evangelicals* (New York: Peter Lang, 1994), 27; Falwell, *Strength for the Journey*, 379; "Politicizing the Word," 62; Robert Wuthnow, *The Restructuring of American Religion: Society and Faith since World War II* (Princeton, NJ: Princeton University Press, 1988), 197; Anthony Gierzynski, *Money Rules: Financing Elections in America* (Boulder, CO: Westview Press, 2000), 72; Mary Murphy, "The Next Billy Graham," *Esquire*, 10 October 1978, 26. For the growth of Falwell's enterprises, see Dirk Smillie, *Falwell Inc.: Inside a Religious, Political, Educational, and Business Empire* (New York: St. Martin's Press, 2008).

35. Falwell, *Strength for the Journey*, 358; Megan Rosenfeld, "The Evangelist and His Empire: Cleaning Up America with Jerry Falwell," *WP*, 28 April 1979; Jon Hall, "Falwell Credited with Voter Influence outside Virginia," *JC*, December 1978, 5.

36. Jerry Falwell, *How You Can Help Clean Up America* (Lynchburg, VA: Liberty, 1978), 9–10, 28.

37. Ibid., 14, 31–32.

38. Murphy, "Next Billy Graham," 32.

39. Falwell, *Strength for the Journey*, 360; Murphy, "Next Billy Graham," 29.

40. Falwell, *Strength for the Journey*, 361–362; Craig Unger, *The Fall of the House of Bush* (New York: Scribner, 2007), 69.

41. Bob Jones, Jr., to Jerry Falwell, 29 July 1980, "Jerry Falwell" folder, G. Archer Weniger Files, BJU; Bob Jones III, "The Moral Majority," *Faith for the Family*, September 1980, 27; Carl McIntire, "Christians Should Stand Up for Morality," *CB*, 11 December 1980, 3.

42. Edward E. Plowman, "Is Morality All Right?" *CT*, 2 November 1979.

43. "Roundtable's President Ed McAteer Is Music Man of Religious Right," *CD*, January 1981, 3; Thomas Lindberg, Jonathan Lindberg, and Daniel E. Johnson, *The Power of One: The Ed McAteer Story* (published by the authors, 2004), 60, 65, 87–93.

44. Lindberg, Lindberg, and Johnson, *The Power of One*, 95–96; Martin, *With God on Our Side*, 199–200; Paul M. Weyrich to Elmer L. Towns, 4 March 1979, "Correspondence—March 1979" folder, box 3, Weyrich Papers, AHC; Howard Phillips to Jerry Falwell, 27 February 1979, "Christians in Politics" folder, box 15, Weyrich Papers, AHC.

45. Church, "Politics from the Pulpit," 32; "Politicizing the Word," 68; William Martin, *With God on Our Side: The Rise of the Religious Right in America* (New York: Broadway Books, 1996), 70; Lisa Myers, "Falwell Strives for Role as Political Kingmaker," *Washington Star*, 3 July 1980; Vecsey,

"Militant Television Preachers Try to Weld Fundamentalist Christians' Political Power."

46. Maxwell Glen, "The Electronic Ministers Listen to the Gospel according to the Candidates," *National Journal*, 22 December 1979, 2144; "All on the Family," *Boston Phoenix*, 15 July 1980.

47. Jerry Falwell, "The Maligned Moral Majority," *Newsweek*, 21 September 1981, 17.

48. Liebman, "Mobilizing the Moral Majority," 58–69; Jerry Falwell, Moral Majority Direct Mailing, [1979], "Moral Majority" folder, Weniger Files, BJU.

49. Tim LaHaye, *The Battle for the Mind* (Old Tappan, NJ: Fleming H. Revell, 1980), 38, 72, 77, 181–185.

50. Ibid., 219, 229–230.

51. Jim Auchmutey, "The Gospel according to Falwell," *AJC*, 23 August 1980; Jerry Falwell, Moral Majority Direct Mailing, [1979], "Moral Majority" folder, Weniger Files, BJU.

52. William J. Petersen and Stephen Board, "Where Is Jerry Falwell Going?" *Eternity*, July–August 1980, 19.

53. Peter G. Bourne, *Jimmy Carter: A Comprehensive Biography from Plains to Post-Presidency* (New York: Scribner, 1997), 376, 445–446.

54. Jerry Falwell, Direct Mail for Clean Up America campaign, 28 April 1978, "Jerry Falwell" folder, Weniger Files, BJU; Megan Rosenfeld, "The New Moral America and the War of the Religicos," *WP*, 24 August 1980; Martin, *With God on Our Side*, 205; Janice M. Irvine, *Talk about Sex: The Battles over Sex Education in the United States* (Berkeley: University of California Press, 2002), 173; Allan J. Mayer, "A Tide of Born-Again Politics," *Newsweek*, 15 September 1980, 36.

55. Loch Johnson and Charles S. Bullock III, "The New Religious Right and the 1980 Congressional Elections," in *Do Elections Matter?* ed. Benjamin Ginsberg and Alan Stone (Armonk, NY: M. E. Sharpe, 1986), 149; Liebman, "Mobilizing the Moral Majority," 61–66; Kenneth A. Briggs, "Moral Majority Spawns Backlash in the Bible Belt," *AJC*, 4 April 1981; James L. Guth, "Southern Baptists and the New Right," in *Religion in American Politics*, ed. Charles W. Dunn (Washington, DC: Congressional Quarterly, 1989), 178.

56. White House memo from Bob Maddox to Rosalynn Carter, n.d. [early 1980], "Memos" folder, box 107, Robert Maddox Papers, Public Outreach Papers, JCL; Guth, "New Christian Right," 41.

57. Hadden and Swann, *Prime-Time Preachers*, 50–51, 165.

58. Liebman, "Mobilizing the Moral Majority," 58–69; Wayne Flynt, *Alabama Baptists: Southern Baptists in the Heart of Dixie* (Tuscaloosa: University of Alabama Press, 1998), 590; Don Campbell, "New Right Could Be Long-Term Trouble for Democrats," *Reno Gazette*, 20 March 1981; Wallace Turner, "Group of Evangelical Protestants Takes Over the G.O.P. in Alaska," *NYT*, 9 June 1980; Guth, "New Christian Right," 36–37.

59. Seymour M. Lipset and Earl Raab, "The Election and the Evangelicals," *Commentary*, March 1981, 25–31; Clyde Wilcox, *God's Warriors: The*

Christian Right in Twentieth-Century America (Baltimore: Johns Hopkins University Press, 1992), 117.

60. Hadden and Swann, *Prime-Time Preachers*, 47.

61. Kirk Kidwell, "Marion Gordon 'Pat' Robertson: The Lawyer-Turned-Businessman-Turned-Evangelist Wants to Be President," *New American*, 29 February 1988, 44; Daniel J. Nicholas, "Pat Robertson: Leading a Moral Reformation," *Religious Broadcasting*, February 1986, 68; Cory SerVaas and Maynard Good Stoddard, "CBN's Pat Robertson: White House Next?" *Saturday Evening Post*, March 1985, 55–56; John J. Fialka and Ellen Hume, "Pulpit and Politics: TV Preacher, Possibly Eyeing the Presidency, Is Polishing His Image," *WSJ*, 17 October 1985. For information on Robertson's early life, see David Edwin Harrell, Jr., *Pat Robertson: A Personal, Religious, and Political Portrait* (San Francisco: Harper & Row, 1987); and David John Marley, *Pat Robertson: An American Life* (Lanham, MD: Rowman & Littlefield, 2007).

62. Pat Robertson, with Jamie Buckingham, *Shout It from the Housetops* (Plainfield, NJ: Logos International, 1972), 8–79, 179; SerVaas and Stoddard, "CBN's Pat Robertson," 56, 106; Richard N. Ostling, "Evangelical Publishing and Broadcasting," in *Evangelicalism and Modern America*, ed. George M. Marsden (Grand Rapids, MI: William B. Eerdmans, 1984), 52; Ben A. Franklin, "200,000 March and Pray at Christian Rally in Capital," *NYT*, 30 April 1980.

63. Dudley Clendinen and Adam Nagourney, *Out for Good: The Struggle to Build a Gay Rights Movement in America* (New York: Simon & Schuster, 1999), 283.

64. Religious News Service, "TV Evangelist Resigns Roundtable Membership," 1 October 1980, "Moral Majority" folder, Weniger Files, BJU; Alan Abramowitz, John McGlennon, and Ronald Rapoport, *Party Activists in Virginia: A Study of the Delegates to the 1978 Senatorial Nominating Conventions* (Charlottesville: Institute of Government at the University of Virginia, 1981), 20–21, 63; Hubert Morken, *Pat Robertson: Where He Stands* (Old Tappan, NJ: Fleming H. Revell, 1988), 218–219; *Pat Robertson's Perspective*, December 1980; Kenneth L. Woodward, "This Way to Armageddon," *Newsweek*, 5 July 1982, 79.

65. Pat Robertson, "A Christian Action Plan for the 1980s," in *Tactics of Christian Resistance*, ed. Gary North (Tyler, TX: Geneva Divinity School Press, 1983), 310–311 (emphasis in original). Article originally published in October 1979.

66. Stan Hastey, "Adrian Rogers Supports School Prayer Legislation," *Religious Herald*, 14 February 1980, 3; James Davison Hunter, *American Evangelicalism: Conservative Religion and the Quandary of Modernity* (New Brunswick, NJ: Rutgers University Press, 1983), 105.

67. Wuthnow, *Restructuring of American Religion*, 197; Edward E. Plowman, "Washington for Jesus: Revival Fervor and Political Disclaimers," *CT*, 23 May 1980, 46–47; AP, "Religious Rally on Mall in the Capital Draws Support and Criticism," *NYT*, 27 April 1980.

68. Franklin, "200,000 March and Pray"; Plowman, "Washington for Jesus," 46–47.

69. Franklin, "200,000 March and Pray."

70. William Martin, "God's Angry Man," *Texas Monthly*, April 1981, 152, 154, 223; Hadden and Swann, *Prime-Time Preachers*, 52.

71. Martin, "God's Angry Man," 223; *Arlington's Family Center Life*, 21 October 1979, "Baptist Bible Fellowship" folder, Weniger Files, BJU; Elmer Towns, "Falwell Vows: Never Give Up Right to Preach the Bible on the Air," *JC*, 15 June 1979, 8.

72. "Evangelist James Robison to Battle Legality of Cancelling Dallas TV Program over Preaching against Homosexuality," *JC*, 6 April 1979, 6; John Maust, "Evangelist James Robison: Making Waves—and a Name," *CT*, 21 March 1980, 50; James Robison, "Commit To: Biblical Principles—Not Political Promises," *Life's Answer*, October 1980, 2.

73. Maust, "Evangelist James Robison," 50; Martin, "God's Angry Man," 157, 227; Steve Haner, "Broadcasters' Parley Was a Council of War," Religious News Service, 9 October 1980, "Jerry Falwell" folder, Weniger Files, BJU.

74. Guth, "New Christian Right," 33; "The Roundtable: Is There Not a Cause?" [Religious Roundtable, 1980?], "Religious Roundtable" folder, box 15, Sara Diamond Collection on the U.S. Right, Bancroft Library, University of California at Berkeley; "Roundtable's President Ed McAteer Is Music Man of Religious Right," *CD*, January 1981, 4.

75. Robert Maddox, *Preacher at the White House* (Nashville: Broadman Press, 1984); Transcript of Exit Interview with Robert Maddox, 8 December 1980, JCL.

76. White House memo from Bob Maddox, "Question and Answer Session with Evangelical Leaders," [January 1980], "Memos—Bob Maddox Weekly Reports" folder, box 107, Maddox Papers, Public Outreach, JCL; George Vecsey, "Carter Sways Some Evangelicals in 2-Day Blitz to Regain Support," *NYT*, 28 January 1980; Transcript of exit interview with Robert Maddox.

Chapter 9

1. Howell Raines, "Reagan Backs Evangelicals in Their Political Activities," *NYT*, 23 August 1980.

2. Ibid.; Ronald Reagan, Address to the Roundtable National Affairs Briefing, Dallas, TX, 22 August 1980, "Family Policy Advisory Board, 1980–1981" folder, box 36, Paul M. Weyrich Papers, AHC.

3. James Mann, "Preachers in Politics: Decisive Force in '80?" *USN*, 15 September 1980, 24; Kenneth A. Briggs, "Dispute on Religion Raised by Campaign," *NYT*, 9 November 1980.

4. "Dr. Falwell, South Koreans Discuss 'Perils,'" *JC*, 9 February 1979, 3; Alan Crawford, *Thunder on the Right: The "New Right" and the Politics of Resentment* (New York: Pantheon Books, 1980), 162.

5. John C. Green et al., *Religion and the Culture Wars: Dispatches from the Front* (London: Rowman & Littlefield 1996), 20.

6. Donald H. Gill, "Will the Bible Get Back into School?" *Eternity*, May 1964, 10; Bill Rose, "Reagan Charts Course," *Oakland (CA) Tribune*, 25 March 1967; "Reagan on God and Morality," *CT*, 2 July 1976, 39.

7. Charles Grutzner, "Anti-Red Crusade Rallies at Garden," *NYT*, 29 June 1962; Paul Kengor, *God and Ronald Reagan: A Spiritual Life* (New York: Regan Books, 2004), 105; Ronald Reagan, "We Will Be a City upon a Hill," Speech, Conservative Political Action Conference, Washington, DC, 25 January 1974, http://reagan2020.us/speeches/City_Upon_A_Hill.asp; John F. Stacks, *Watershed: The Campaign for the Presidency, 1980* (New York: Times Books, 1981), 194; Ronald Reagan for President Campaign Brochure, "Let's Make America Great Again," www.4president.org/brochures/reagan.pdf.

8. Bruce Nesmith, *The New Republican Coalition: The Reagan Campaigns and White Evangelicals* (New York: Peter Lang, 1994), 40, 74–75.

9. Rosemary Thomson, *Withstanding Humanism's Challenge to Families: Anatomy of a White House Conference* (Morton, IL: Traditional Publications, 1981), 139–141; Sally Saunders, "Reagan Agrees to Debate in State," *Greenville News*, 31 January 1980; Carol Griffee, "Stop 'Bellyaching,' Get Out the Vote, Preachers Are Urged," *Arkansas Gazette*, 6 August 1980.

10. 1980 Republican Party Platform, www.presidency.ucsb.edu/showplatforms .php?platindex=R1980; Dawn Chase, "Moral Majority Goals Outlined by Falwell," *RTD*, 3 August 1980; William H. Elder III, "The New Right: Is It Right or Wrong?" *Light*, August–September 1980, 10.

11. "Falwell Describes Advice Offered Candidate Reagan," Religious News Service, 24 July 1980, "Jerry Falwell" folder, G. Archer Weniger Files, BJU.

12. Anthony Lewis, "Political Religion," *NYT*, 25 September 1980; "Baptist Leader Criticized for Statement about Jews," *NYT*, 18 September 1980; Matthew C. Moen, *The Transformation of the Christian Right* (Tuscaloosa: University of Alabama Press, 1992), 36; Erling Jorstad, *The Politics of Moralism: The New Christian Right in American Life* (Minneapolis: Augsburg, 1981), 95.

13. Steven R. Weisman, "Carter and Reagan Comments Tangle Campaigns in a Controversy Surrounding Evangelical Group," *NYT*, 10 October 1980.

14. Anthony Lewis, "Religion and Politics," *NYT*, 18 September 1980.

15. Lewis, "Religion and Politics"; Howell Raines, "Reagan Is Balancing 2 Different Stances," *NYT*, 4 October 1980; George J. Church, "Politics from the Pulpit," *Time*, 13 October 1980, 34.

16. Nesmith, *The New Republican Coalition*, 77; Reagan campaign press release, "Ronald Reagan Announces the Formation of the Family Policy Board," [1 October 1980], "Family Policy Advisory Board, 1980–1981" folder, box 36, Weyrich Papers, AHC.

17. Matthew C. Moen, *The Christian Right and Congress* (Tuscaloosa: University of Alabama Press, 1989), 45; Weisman, "Carter and Reagan Comments."

18. Mark Silk, *Spiritual Politics: Religion and America since World War II* (New York: Simon & Schuster, 1988), 164; William Martin, *With God on Our Side: The Rise of the Religious Right in America* (New York: Broadway Books, 1996), 216–217; Mann, "Preachers in Politics," 26.

19. Ruth Murray Brown, *For a "Christian America": A History of the Religious Right* (Amherst, NY: Prometheus Books, 2002), 159; "Religious Right Goes for Bigger Game," *USN*, 17 November 1980, 42; Jorstad, *Politics of Moralism*, 100.

20. Church, "Politics from the Pulpit," 35; "Religious Right Goes for Bigger Game," 42.

21. Arthur H. Miller and Martin P. Wattenberg, "Politics from the Pulpit: Religiosity and the 1980 Elections," *Public Opinion Quarterly* 48 (1984): 305.

22. Corwin Smidt, "Evangelicals and the 1984 Election: Continuity or Change?" *American Politics Quarterly* 15 (1987): 431; Sara Diamond, *Roads to Dominion: Right-Wing Movements and Political Power in the United States* (New York: Guilford Press, 1995), 173; Lyman Kellstedt et al., "Faith Transformed: Religion and American Politics from FDR to George W. Bush," in *Religion and American Politics: From the Colonial Period to the Present*, ed. Mark A. Noll and Luke E. Harlow, 2nd ed. (New York: Oxford University Press, 2007), 272–273.

23. Transcript of interview with Ed Dobson conducted for the television documentary *With God on Our Side*, Lumiere Productions (New York), 30 November 1995, 30 (used with the permission of William Martin).

24. Adam Clymer, "Conservatives Gather in Umbrella Council for a National Policy," *NYT*, 20 May 1981; Minutes of the Quarterly Meeting of the Council for National Policy, 13–14 September 1981, "Council for National Policy, 1983–1990" folder, box 36, Weyrich Papers, AHC; Council for National Policy, Program for Annual Conference, Dallas, TX, 29 and 30 May 1987, "Council for National Policy, 05/28–30/1987, Anatole, Dallas, TX" folder, Carl Anderson Files, OA17969, RRPL.

25. "Transition Notes," *WP*, 20 January 1981, A3; "Bible Passages at Inaugurations," Hauenstein Center for Presidential Studies, www.gvsu.edu/hauenstein/index.cfm?id=5FA0D9C5-B592-1C67-202B4E267EE96256; "'Let Us Begin an Era of National Renewal': President Reagan's Inaugural Address," *NYT*, 21 January 1981.

26. Edwin Warner, "New Resolve by the New Right," *Time*, 8 December 1980, 27.

27. Jerry Schneider, "Fundamentalists Spurn Immorality," *San Francisco Herald*, 31 January 1981; Lynn Rosellini, "How Conservatives View U.S. Posts," *NYT*, 21 June 1982.

28. Keith Skrzypczak, "Moving Ahead: Christian Right Eyes New Goals in Wake of 1980 Campaign Success," *Tulsa Tribune*, 20 June 1981; Jon Margolis, "The American Conservatives' Two Faces," *Chicago Tribune*, 12 July 1981.

29. "Around the Nation," *Chicago Daily Law Bulletin*, 15 July 1981 and 17 September 1981; Adam Clymer, "Right Wing Seeks a Shift by Reagan," *NYT*, 6 September 1981.

30. Marjorie Hyer, "'Christian Right' Optimistic: Seeking a Born-Again America," *San Francisco Chronicle*, 31 January 1981.

31. Matthew C. Moen, *The Christian Right and Congress* (Tuscaloosa: University of Alabama Press, 1989), 100; *CD*, January 1981, 79.

32. "Religious Right Goes for Bigger Game," *USN*, 17 November 1980, 42; "Falwell Says Budget, Taxes Should Come First on Hill," *Washington Star*, 20 April 1981; David Nyhan, "New Right Preparing for Battle against Sex, Violence on TV," *BG*, 22 November 1980.

33. Cal Thomas to James Baker, 9 October 1981, "Moral Majority (2)" folder, OA24448, box 10, Morton C. Blackwell Files, RRPL.

34. Michael Briggs, "Bob Jones Calls Reagan 'Traitor to God's People,'" *Chicago Sun-Times*, 1 March 1982.

35. Stan Hastey, "'New Right' Leaders Express Disappointment with Reagan," *Baptist Press*, 29 January 1981, 4.

36. *MMR*, November 1984, 21.

37. Ibid.

38. George W. Cornell, "Religious Groups Protest Reagan's Welfare Cuts, Defense Costs," *WP*, 6 March 1982; Morton C. Blackwell to Cal Thomas, 25 March 1982, "Moral Majority (3)" folder, OA24448, Blackwell Files, RRPL.

39. "Lear TV Ads to Oppose the Moral Majority," *NYT*, 25 June 1981; American Civil Liberties Union, Advertisement, "If the Moral Majority Has Its Way, You'd Better Start Praying," *NYT*, 23 November 1980; Kenneth A. Briggs, "Rabbi Attacks Aims of Moral Majority," *NYT*, 23 November 1980; UPI, "Moral Majority Hit as Bar to Black Progress," *Washington Star*, 11 April 1981; James H. Cleaver, "Moral Majority Draws Fire and Praises," *Los Angeles Sentinel*, 13 August 1981; "62% of Voters in Poll Hold Unfavorable View of Falwell," *RTD*, 6 October 1985; Thomas C. Bridges, "The Influence of the Moral Majority in Virginia Politics" (M.A. thesis, James Madison University, 1986), 85.

40. "Humbard: 'Jesus Wouldn't Get Into Politics,'" *Lansing (MI) Journal*, 30 May 1981; Marguerite Michaels, "America Is Not God's Only Kingdom," *Parade*, 1 February 1981, 6.

41. Skrzypczak, "Moving Ahead"; "An Interview with the Lone Ranger of Fundamentalism," *CT*, 4 September 1981, 25; Jerry Falwell, "The Maligned Moral Majority," *Newsweek*, 21 September 1981, 17; Cleaver, "Moral Majority Draws Fire and Praises," 10; James S. Tinney, "The Moral Majority: Operating under the Hood of Religious Right," *Dollars and Sense*, June–July 1981; Dudley Clendinen, "Rev. Falwell Inspires Evangelical Vote," *NYT*, 20 August 1980.

42. Chuck Fager, "Falwell and Co.—On the Skids . . . Or Speeding Up?" *In These Times*, 5–11 May 1982, 6; Jere Real, "What Jerry Falwell Really Wants," *Inquiry*, 3–24 August 1981, 13–14; Michael Reese, "Jerry Falwell's Troubles," *Newsweek*, 23 February 1981, 24; Robert Scheer, "Right's Reverend: Moral Majority's Jerry Falwell Finds Celebrity Status Brings Profit, Problems," *San Jose Mercury News*, 8 March 1981; Lisa Solod, "The *Nutshell* Interview: Jerry Falwell," *Nutshell*, September/October 1981, 41.

43. "Moral Majority Divided on Many Political Tactics," *Spokane (WA) News*, 6 May 1982.

44. Bill Peterson, "Conservative Critique Charges the Administration with Moderation," *WP*, 22 January 1982; Cal Thomas, "Reagan Must Address Key Social Issues," *CD*, May 1982.

45. Howell Raines, "Reagan Endorses Voluntary Prayer," *NYT*, 7 May 1982; Francis X. Clines, "Abortion Foes, Hailing Reagan Efforts, Plan to Renew Stalled Drive," *NYT*, 17 September 1982; "Reagan Joins Prayer Fight," *Baton Rouge Sunday Advocate*, 26 September 1982.

46. Stan Hastey, "White House Backed Prayer Amendment Bill," *Baptist Standard*, 7 July 1982, 3; Morton Blackwell to Richard Bridges, 21 July 1982, "School Prayer (1)" folder, OA9087, box 7, Morton Blackwell Files, RRPL; Charles Austin, "Baptist Meeting Backs School Prayer Amendment," *NYT*, 18 June 1982; Southern Baptist Convention, "Resolution on Prayer in Schools," June 1982, www.sbc.net/resolutions/amResolution.asp?ID=862; Helen Parmley, "McAteer Emerges as Mover, Shaker of Religious Right," *Dallas News*, 10 July 1982.

47. George Bush, Transcript of Remarks to the Southern Baptist Convention, New Orleans, LA, 13 June 1982, "School Prayer (4)" folder, OA9087, box 7, Blackwell Files, RRPL; Baptist Press, "Bush Endorses Religious Right," *Southern Baptist Advocate*, August/September 1982, 4.

48. Mary Battiata, "Bush Visits Falwell, Wins Praise, Support," *WP*, 14 April 1983.

49. Roy C. Jones, "Draper Denounces Hatch Amendment," *MMR*, October 1983, 1, 8; Telegram from Pat Robertson to Ronald Reagan, 9 September 1983, "Education: Religion (School Prayer, Tuition Tax Credits [2])" folder, OA9081, box 6, Blackwell Files, RRPL; Jerry Falwell, Direct Mail, 29 February 1984, "Moral Majority—School Prayer, Feb./March 1984" folder, PFAW; Robert P. Dugan, Jr., Testimony to Senate Judiciary Committee, 29 July 1982; Gary Jarmin to Morton Blackwell, 20 July 1982, "Prayer in Schools (2)" folder, OA9086, box 7, Blackwell Files, RRPL.

50. Martin Tolchin, "11 Short of Passing," *NYT*, 21 March 1984; Helen DeWar, "Senate Sets Back Antiabortion Cause," *WP*, 29 June 1983; Ronald Reagan, Remarks in Briefing for Right-to-Life Leaders, 30 July 1987, "Pro Life" folder, OA19224, box 4, Gary Bauer Files, RRPL.

51. Garry Clifford, "His Critics Speak Out and Jerry Falwell's Home Base Becomes a Flock Divided," *People*, 10 January 1983, 38; "Social Agenda Stalemate," *WP*, 27 December 1982; Philip J. Hilts, "U.S. to Stop Funding Groups That 'Actively Promote' Abortion," *WP*, 14 July 1984; "President Signs Bill to Assist Students' Religious Groups," *WP*, 12 August 1984; Ronald Reagan to Pat Robertson, 3 May 1983, "Robertson, Rev. Pat" folder, WHORM Alpha File, RRPL.

52. Kenneth A. Briggs, "Criticism of Reagan by Religious Leaders Rises," *NYT*, 8 December 1981; Richard Halloran, "Bishops Joining Nuclear Arms Debate," *NYT*, 4 October 1982; National Association of Evangelicals Press Release, Results of Gallup Survey of Evangelical Views on the Nuclear Arms Race, 5 July 1983, "Nuclear Freeze (1)" folder, OA9088, box 8, Blackwell

Files, RRPL; UPI, "Falwell Sets Freeze Fight as Principal Goal of '83," *WT*, 14 March 1983; Brad Kutrow, "Falwell Takes Aim at Freeze," *Lynchburg News*, 16 March 1983.

53. Haynes Johnson, "A Preacher for 'Peace through Strength,' or, Maybe, the Bomb," *WP*, 3 April 1983; CBN promotional mailing, 20 April 1982, "Robertson, Rev. Pat," WHORM Alpha File, RRPL; Jerry Falwell, Direct Mail, 17 June 1982, "Moral Majority—Nuclear freeze, 6/17/82" folder, PFAW; Jerry Falwell, Direct Mail, 3 May 1985, "Moral Majority—'Star Wars' Letter, 5/3/85" folder, PFAW; Kutrow, "Falwell Takes Aim at Freeze."

54. Robert P. Dugan, Jr., to James A. Baker III, 3 December 1982, "National Association of Evangelicals, March 8, 1983 (6)" folder, box 19, Anthony "Tony" R. Dolan Files, RRPL; Robert P. Dugan, Jr., to Ronald Reagan, 3 December 1982, "National Association of Evangelicals, March 8, 1983 (6)" folder, box 19, Dolan Files, RRPL; Robert P. Dugan, Jr., to Anthony R. Dolan, 25 February 1983, "National Association of Evangelicals, March 8, 1983 (7)" folder, box 19, Dolan Files, RRPL.

55. Ronald Reagan, Remarks at the Annual Convention of the National Association of Evangelicals, 8 March 1983, www.americanrhetoric.com/speeches/ronaldreaganevilempire.htm.

56. William Bole, "The Christian Right Eyes the Republican Party," *Interchange Report*, Winter–Spring 1985, 10; John Herbers, "Moral Majority and Its Allies Expect Harvest of Votes for Conservatives," *NYT*, 4 November 1984.

57. Myra MacPherson, "Falwell: Big-Time Politics from the Pulpit of Old-Time Religion," *WP*, 27 September 1984; "Convention Schedule," *WP*, 22 August 1984; Jerry Falwell, *MMR*, July 1984, 1.

58. Bole, "The Christian Right Eyes the Republican Party," 11; John Rees, "The Religious Right's Dr. Tim LaHaye," *Review of the News*, 8 August 1984, 36–37.

59. "Religious Right Makes Political Arena Its Major Battleground," *LAT*, 29 March 1986; ACTV brochure advertising conference, "How to Win an Election, to be held in Washington, D.C., 15–17 October 1985," "ACTV" folder, carton 7, Sara Diamond Collection on the U.S. Right, Bancroft Library, University of California at Berkeley.

60. Ellen M. Rosenberg, *The Southern Baptists: A Subculture in Transition* (Knoxville: University of Tennessee Press, 1989), 183; Bruce Nesmith, *The New Republican Coalition: The Reagan Campaigns and White Evangelicals* (New York: Peter Lang, 1994), 120; Stratos Patrikios, "American Republican Religion? Disentangling the Causal Link between Religion and Politics in the US," *Political Behavior*, 30 (2008): 368; Corwin Smidt, "Change and Stability among Southern Evangelicals," in *Religion in American Politics*, ed. Charles W. Dunn (Washington, DC: Congressional Quarterly, 1989), 147–159.

61. "Thunder on the Right: The Growth of Fundamentalism," *Time*, 2 September 1985.

62. Francis A. Schaeffer, *A Christian Manifesto* (Westchester, IL: Crossway Books, 1981), 36, 89, 93.

63. Barry Hankins, *Francis Schaeffer and the Shaping of Evangelical America* (Grand Rapids, MI: William B. Eerdmans, 2008), 202; Schaeffer, *Christian Manifesto*, 61–62, 73; Francis A. Schaeffer, "The Secular Humanist World View versus the Christian World View and the Biblical Perspectives on Military Preparedness," Speech, Washington, DC, 22 June 1982, folder 6, OTH 1-1, LUA.

64. Victoria Rosenholtz, "American Fundamentalism in the Independent Baptist Tradition" (Ph.D. diss., University of Pennsylvania, 2000), 212; Daymon Johnson, "Reformed Fundamentalism in America: The Lordship of Christ, the Transformation of Culture, and Other Calvinist Components of the Christian Right" (Ph.D. diss., Florida State University, 1994), 160; John Schlesinger, "Francis Schaeffer Speaks at LBC," *President's Newsletter* (Liberty Baptist College), 5 March 1982, folder 1, OTH 1-1, LUA; Francis Schaeffer, "The Christian Manifesto," transcript of *Old-Time Gospel Hour* broadcast, 21 March 1982, OTGH 492, FM 3-5, LUA; Frank Schaeffer, *Crazy for God: How I Grew Up as One of the Elect, Helped Found the Religious Right, and Lived to Take All (or Almost All) of It Back* (New York: Carroll & Graf, 2007), 339.

65. Cal Thomas, Moral Majority Radio Report Broadcast transcript, 24 July 1984, folder 2, MOR 3-1, LUA; Thomas, MMRRB transcript, 26 March 1984, folder 2, MOR 1-3, LUA.

66. Franky Schaeffer, *Bad News for Modern Man: An Agenda for Christian Activism* (Westchester, IL: Crossway Books, 1984), 143.

67. Susan Friend Harding, *The Book of Jerry Falwell: Fundamentalist Language and Politics* (Princeton, NJ: Princeton University Press, 2000), 131; Tammi Ledbetter, "Franky Schaeffer Demands," *Southern Baptist Advocate*, July/August 1984, 8; "New CLC Materials Deal with Abortion," *Baptist Standard*, 25 December 1985, 7; Tammi Reed Ledbetter, "Conservative Resurgence Focused SBC's Pro-Life Stance," *Baptist Press*, 22 January 2004, www.bpnews.net/bpnews.asp?ID=17486.

68. J. P. McFadden to Ronald Reagan, 1 November 1983, PR014-09 183970, Public Relations Files, RRPL; Fred F. Fielding to J. P. McFadden, 7 November 1983, PR014-09 183970, Public Relations Files, RRPL; Ronald Reagan, *Abortion and the Conscience of a Nation* (Nashville: Thomas Nelson, 1984).

69. Nancy T. Ammerman, "SBC and New Christian Right," *SBC Today*, February 1988, 4; Ray Waddle, "Baptist Support of Bork Hit," *Nashville Tennessean*, 1 September 1987; Jerry Falwell, "A Hero's Story," *Liberty Report*, May 1988, 3–4.

70. "Defensively Speaking," *Liberty Report*, April 1987, 35; "INF Treaty Will Leave Europe Defenseless," *Liberty Report*, June 1988, 27.

71. "Just Say No to Astrology," *Charisma and Christian Life*, September 1988, 29; *Capital Report with Dr. Tim LaHaye*, June 1988, "ACTV (American Coalition for Traditional Values)" folder, box 7, Sara Diamond Collection on the U.S. Right, Bancroft Library, Berkeley, CA.

72. John Dillin, "U.S. Conservatives on the March: Religious Right Optimistic," *CSM*, 19 March 1986; Laura Stepp, "Falwell Quitting as Moral Majority Chief," *WP*, 4 November 1987.

Chapter 10

1. William Martin, *With God on Our Side: The Rise of the Religious Right in America* (New York: Broadway Books, 1996), 290; Allen Hertzke, *Echoes of Discontent: Jesse Jackson, Pat Robertson, and the Resurgence of Populism* (Washington, DC: Congressional Quarterly, 1993), 159; Fred Barnes, "Rarin' to Go: Pat Robertson Hears the Call," *New Republic*, 29 September 1986, 15; Phil Gailey, "Evangelist's Draw Stings G.O.P. Rivals," *NYT*, 29 May 1986.

2. "CBN's Pat Robertson Looks to 1988, and Beyond," *CD*, August 1985, 4, 12; James M. Johnston, "Religious Right Still Going Full Steam," *Milwaukee Sentinel*, 18 January 1986; Pat Aufderheide, "The Next Voice You Hear," *Progressive*, September 1985, 34, 37; Jon Margolis and Bruce Buursma, "Evangelist Listens for Presidential Call," *Chicago Tribune*, 3 November 1985, 13.

3. Kirk Kidwell, "Marion Gordon 'Pat' Robertson: The Lawyer-Turned-Businessman-Turned-Evangelist Wants to Be President," *New American*, 29 February 1988, 44; John McGee, "Pat Robertson Plans Freedom Council's Challenge to ACLU," *Newsday*, 8 November 1985; Sara Diamond, "Pat Robertson's Central America Connection," *Guardian*, 17 September 1986; Paul Weyrich, "Conservatism's Future: Pat Robertson," *CD*, August 1985, 13.

4. Cory SerVaas and Maynard Good Stoddard, "CBN's Pat Robertson: White House Next?" *Saturday Evening Post*, March 1985, 54, 106–109.

5. Kidwell, "Marion Gordon 'Pat' Robertson," 44; James M. Penning, "Pat Robertson and the GOP: 1988 and Beyond," in *The Rapture of Politics: The Christian Right as the United States Approaches the Year 2000*, ed. Steve Bruce, Peter Kivisto, and William H. Swatos, Jr. (New Brunswick, NJ: Transaction Publishers, 1995), 106–107.

6. Wayne King, "Robertson, Displaying Mail, Says He Will Join '88 Race," *NYT*, 16 September 1987; Kidwell, "Marion Gordon 'Pat' Robertson," 44.

7. "What They Say about Pat Robertson," *CD*, August 1985, 9–10; Justin Watson, *The Christian Coalition: Dreams of Restoration, Demands for Recognition*, 2nd ed. (New York: St. Martin's Press, 1999), 35; John J. Fialka, "Robertson's Presidential Bid Invites Scrutiny of His Economics Credentials," *WSJ*, 26 December 1986.

8. Bill Kling, "Robertson, Religious Leaders Powwow on Presidency," *WT*, 22 November 1985; Barnes, "Rarin' to Go," 14.

9. Bob Secter, "Robertson Tries to Distance Himself from TV Clerics," *LAT*, 6 July 1987; Dan Morgan, "Evangelicals a Force Divided," *WP*, 8 March 1988, 9; Walter V. Robinson, "Minister Quits Kemp Campaign," *BG*, 8 December 1987, 1; Ralph Z. Hallow, "Falwell Renews Pledge to Support Bush in '88," *WT*, 14 November 1986.

10. Clyde Wilcox, *God's Warriors: The Christian Right in Twentieth-Century America* (Baltimore: Johns Hopkins University Press, 1992), 172, 176–177, 185.

11. Francis J. Connolly, "The Secular Side of Pat Robertson," *Boston Phoenix*, 12 February 1988; Barnes, "Rarin' to Go," 15; Hubert Morken, *Pat Robertson: Where He Stands* (Old Tappan, NJ: Fleming H. Revell, 1988), 24; Howard Phillips, "Pat Robertson Adds Perspective," *CD*, January 1986, 17, 19–20;

John J. Fialka, "Robertson's Presidential Bid Invites Scrutiny of His Economics Credentials," *WSJ*, 26 December 1986; Kidwell, "Marion Gordon 'Pat' Robertson," 45–47.

12. Doug Hill, "Preacher for President?" *TV Guide*, 15 March 1986, 35 (emphasis in original).

13. Jonathan Alter, "Pat Robertson: The TelePolitician," *Newsweek*, 22 February 1988, 18.

14. Evans and Novak, "Pat Robertson, Kingmaker"; Martin, *With God on Our Side*, 275–276, 284, 289.

15. Wayne King, "The Record of Pat Robertson on Religion and Government," *NYT*, 27 December 1987; Alter, "Pat Robertson," 18; "Church and State," *WT*, 19 June 1986.

16. David S. Broder, "Robertson Says High Court Not Preeminent," *WP*, 27 June 1986.

17. Phillips, "Pat Robertson Adds Perspective," 18.

18. Ibid., 18, 20; Wilcox, *God's Warriors*, 176.

19. Watson, *The Christian Coalition*, 40–41; Alter, "Pat Robertson," 19.

20. E. J. Dionne, Jr., "Dole Wins in Iowa, with Robertson Next," *NYT*, 9 February 1988; Dionne, "Gephardt Is Second," *NYT*, 17 February 1988; Alter, "Pat Robertson," 18; R. W. Apple, Jr., "Bush Takes Resounding Victory in First of the Southern Primaries," *NYT*, 6 March 1988; Michael Oreskes, "Runaway in G.O.P.: Vice President Carries 16 States in Long Stride toward Objective," *NYT*, 9 March 1988.

21. Allen D. Hertzke, "Harvest of Discontent: Religion and Populism in the 1988 Presidential Campaign," in *The Bible and the Ballot Box: Religion and Politics in the 1988 Election*, ed. James L. Guth and John C. Green (Boulder, CO: Westview Press, 1991), 22; Lyman A. Kellstedt et al., "Religious Tradition, Denomination, and Commitment: White Protestants and the 1988 Election," in Guth and Green, *The Bible and the Ballot Box*, 145; Matthew C. Moen, *The Transformation of the Christian Right* (Tuscaloosa: University of Alabama Press, 1992), 110.

22. Martin, *With God on Our Side*, 289; Duane Murray Oldfield, *The Right and the Righteous: The Christian Right Confronts the Republican Party* (Lanham, MD: Rowman & Littlefield, 1996), 145; Randy Frame, "Were Christians Courted for Their Votes or Beliefs?" *CT*, 17 February 1989, 38; Malcolm Gladwell, "Jerry Dumps George," *New Republic*, 24 November 1986, 15–16; Larry Witham, "Bush Bolsters Evangelical Voters," *WT*, 22 August 1988.

23. Marjorie Williams, "Falwell and the Faithful," *WP*, 13 August 1988.

24. Curt Smith, "A Kinder Nation: President-Elect George Bush," *Eternity*, December 1988, 9; Garry Wills, *Under God: Religion and American Politics* (New York: Simon & Schuster, 1990), 76–85, 154–164.

25. E. J. Dionne, Jr., "Voters Delay Republican Hopes of Dominance in Post-Reagan Era," *NYT*, 10 November 1988; Larry Witham, "Bush Bolsters Evangelical Voters," *WT*, 22 August 1988.

26. Michael Oreskes, "Bush Position on Art Group Evokes Protests from Right," *NYT*, 23 March 1990; Charles Colson, "Look Who's in the Rose Garden," *CT*, 16 July 1990, 64; "The Good News, Bad News Cabinet," *FFC*, February

1989, 4; Linda Greenhouse, *Becoming Justice Blackmun: Harry Blackmun's Supreme Court Journey* (New York: Henry Holt, 2005), 204–206; Pat Robertson, *The New World Order* (Dallas: Word, 1991), 37.

27. Henry Locke, "Reaction to Falwell," *Chicago Defender*, 26 August 1985; Erling Jorstad, *The New Christian Right, 1981–1988: Prospects for the Post-Reagan Decade* (Lewiston, NY: Edwin Mellen, 1987), 159–162; Gladwell, "Jerry Dumps George," 15.

28. Larry Witham, "Falwell Quits as Moral Majority Head," *WT*, 4 November 1987; Jim Auchmutey, "Jerry Nims' Career Takes a Right Turn," *AJC*, 27 November 1987; Peter Steinfels, "Moral Majority to Dissolve, Says Mission Accomplished," *NYT*, 12 June 1989.

29. Russell Chandler, "Religious Right Makes Political Arena Its Major Battleground," *LAT*, 29 March 1986; Robert Dreyfuss, "The Reverend Doomsday," *Rolling Stone*, 19 February 2004; Rob Boston, "If Best-Selling End Times Author Tim LaHaye Has His Way, Church-State Separation Will Be Left Behind," *Church and State*, February 2002, 9; John Taylor, "Pat Robertson's God, Inc.," *Esquire*, November 1994, 81; "Scandals Bring Hard Times for Nation's TV Evangelists," *NYT*, 6 October 1989.

30. Steve Bruce, *The Rise and Fall of the Christian Right: Conservative Protestant Politics in America, 1979–1988* (New York: Oxford University Press, 1988); Michael D'Antonio, *Fall from Grace: The Failed Crusade of the Christian Right* (New York: Farrar, Straus and Giroux, 1989); R. Gustav Niebuhr, "Why 'Moral Majority,' a Force for a Decade, Ran Out of Steam," *WSJ*, 25 September 1989; Martin Mawyer, "The Religious Right: Waxing Cold?" *Liberty Report*, January 1988, 6.

31. LaHaye, "Has the Church Been Deceived?" n.d. [1985], "ACTV" folder, carton 7, Sara Diamond Collection on the U.S. Right, Bancroft Library, University of California at Berkeley; Walt Harrington, "What Hath Falwell Wrought?" *WP Magazine*, 24 July 1988, 26.

32. Francis A. Schaeffer, *A Christian Manifesto* (Westchester, IL: Crossway Books, 1981), 89, 93; Jerry Falwell, "Strengthening Families in the Nation," sermon transcript, Atlanta, GA, 1982, "Speeches 1982" folder, FAL 5-1, LUA.

33. James Risen and Judy L. Thomas, *Wrath of Angels: The American Abortion War* (New York: Basic Books, 1998), 205–239; Faye Ginsburg, "Rescuing the Nation: Operation Rescue and the Rise of Anti-Abortion Militance," in *Abortion Wars: A Half-Century of Struggle, 1950–2000* (Berkeley: University of California Press, 1998), ed. Rickie Solinger, 227–250.

34. "OR Founder Terry Unabashed," *CT*, 10 September 1990, 49.

35. Charlotte Lowe Allen, "Anti-Abortion Movement's Anti-Establishment Face," *WSJ*, 8 December 1988; "Pro-Lifers Plan Second National Rescue," *Charisma and Christian Life*, April 1989, 31.

36. AP, "Abortion Foes Jailed in Atlanta," *NYT*, 30 July 1988; Allen, "Anti-Abortion Movement's Anti-Establishment Face"; Jerry Schwartz, "400 Are Arrested in Atlanta Abortion Protests," *NYT*, 5 October 1988.

37. Allen, "Anti-Abortion Movement's Anti-Establishment Face"; Risen and Thomas, *Wrath of Angels*, 284–285.

38. "A Time to Disobey?" *FFC*, June 1989, 14.

39. Risen and Thomas, *Wrath of Angels*, 127; Jerry Falwell, Direct Mail, 20 December 1988, "Moral Majority—Moral Majority Direct Mail—Abortion —1988" folder, PFAW (emphasis in original); Lorri Denise Booker, "250 Protest Falwell Talk on Abortion," *AJC*, 10 December 1988.

40. "Rebuffed by Courts, Antiabortion Chief Regroups," *NYT*, 5 March 1990; Risen and Thomas, *Wrath of Angels*, 357.

41. Anson Shupe, "Prophets of a Biblical America," *WSJ*, 12 April 1989.

42. Shupe, "Prophets of a Biblical America"; "Anti-Abortion Group Spreads Anti-Semitic, Theocratic Message," *Church and State*, September 1994, 20.

43. Colonel V. Doner, "A Personal Word," *Chalcedon Report*, November 1994, 5–7 (emphasis in original).

44. Nina J. Easton, *Gang of Five: Leaders at the Center of the Conservative Crusade* (New York: Simon & Schuster, 2000), 201–210.

45. Watson, *The Christian Coalition*, 42; Easton, *Gang of Five*, 125, 128, 130.

46. Mark O'Keefe, "Christian Coalition Expands Its Agenda," *Charisma*, October 1993, 64–66; Ralph Reed, *Politically Incorrect: The Emerging Faith Factor in American Politics* (Dallas, TX: Word, 1994), 26; Easton, *Gang of Five*, 201–202.

47. Easton, *Gang of Five*, 200, 203–205.

48. Reed, *Politically Incorrect*, 2–3; "Robertson Regroups 'Invisible Army' into New Coalition," *CT*, 23 April 1990, 35; Watson, *The Christian Coalition*, 52–53; Frederick Clarkson, "The Christian Coalition: On the Road to Victory?" *Church and State*, January 1992, 4.

49. Easton, *Gang of Five*, 213–215; Watson, *The Christian Coalition*, 56–57.

50. Russell Chandler, "Robertson Moves to Fill Christian Right Vacuum," *LAT*, 15 May 1990; Pat Robertson, Christian Coalition Direct Mail, 25 October 1989, "Christian Coalition, 1989–1990" folder, PFAW; Tom Minnery, "Why the Left Needs Censorship," *FFC*, 23 July 1990, 4.

51. Chandler, "Robertson Moves to Fill Christian Right Vacuum"; Hertzke, *Echoes of Discontent*, 182; "Robertson Regroups 'Invisible Army' into New Coalition," *CT*, 23 April 1990, 35.

52. Barry M. Horstman, "Christian Activists Using 'Stealth' Tactics," *LAT*, 8 April 1992.

53. Clarkson, "Christian Coalition," 5; Mark O'Keefe, "Robertson's Phone Corps Boosted GOP," *(Norfolk) Virginian Pilot Ledger-Star*, 9 November 1991.

54. Frederick Clarkson, "Inside the Covert Coalition," *Church and State*, November 1992, 6; O'Keefe, "Robertson's Phone Corps Boosted GOP."

55. Clarkson, "Christian Coalition," 5.

56. Pat Robertson, Christian Coalition Direct Mail, 1 January 1992, "Christian Coalition—Direct Mail" folder, PRA.

57. Clarkson, "Christian Coalition," 4–5; Clarkson, "Inside the Covert Coalition," 6.

58. Michael Isikoff, "Christian Coalition Steps Boldly into Politics," *WP*, 10 September 1992; Hertzke, *Echoes of Discontent*, 184.

59. Norman Podhoretz, "Buchanan and the Conservative Crackup," *Commentary*, May 1992, 33; Ronald Smothers, "Bush Gets Two Cheers from Religious Right," *NYT*, 10 March 1992.

60. Dan Hoover, "The VP Issue: Keep Quayle, Religious Conservatives Urge Bush," *Greenville News*, 24 July 1992; Jessica Lee, "Bush Back to Fundamentals," *USA Today*, 3 March 1992; "Evangelicals Offer Uneasy Support for Bush," *CT*, 6 April 1992, 85; "Excerpts from Vice President's Speech on Cities and Poverty," *NYT*, 20 May 1992; E. J. Dionne, Jr., "Quayle Takes Aim at 'Cultural Elite,'" *Chicago Sun-Times*, 10 June 1992; Robin Toner, "Bestow Nomination," *NYT*, 20 August 1992; Chris Black, "Buchanan Beckons Conservatives to Come 'Home,'" *BG*, 18 August 1992.

61. Peter Applebome, "Religious Right Intensifies Campaign for Bush," *NYT*, 31 October 1992; Sheryl McCarthy, "Now It's a 'Sin' to Vote for Clinton," *Newsday*, 19 October 1992.

62. Lyman A. Kellstedt et al., "Religious Voting Blocs in the 1992 Election: The Year of the Evangelical?" *Sociology of Religion* 55 (1994): 311, 317.

63. John F. Persinos, "Has the Christian Right Taken Over the Republican Party?" *Campaigns and Elections*, September 1994, 22; David von Drehle and Thomas B. Edsall, "Life of the Grand Old Party," *WP*, 14 August 1994.

64. William Martin, *With God on Our Side: The Rise of the Religious Right in America* (New York: Broadway Books, 1996), 340–341; Michael Schaffer, "Say a Prayer for the Christian Coalition," *USN*, 28 May 2001, 25; R. Gustav Niebuhr, "Why 'Moral Majority,' a Force for a Decade, Ran Out of Steam," *WSJ*, 25 September 1989, 1.

65. Paige L. Schneider, "The Impact of the Christian Right Social Movement on Republican Party Development in the South" (Ph.D. diss., Emory University, 2000), 97–98.

66. Ibid., 116–117, 140.

67. Jeffrey H. Birnbaum, "The Gospel according to Ralph," *Time*, 15 May 1995, 30.

68. Deal W. Hudson, "Ralph Reed on Catholics," *Crisis*, November 1995, 18–22; Mark O'Keefe, "Christian Coalition Expands Its Reach," *(Norfolk) Virginian Pilot Ledger-Star*, 23 April 1993; transcript of interview with Ralph Reed conducted for the television documentary *With God on Our Side*, Lumiere Productions (New York), 23 October 1995, 56 (used with the permission of William Martin).

69. Randall A. Terry, "The Sell-Out of the Christian Right," *Loyal Opposition*, Summer 1994; People for the American Way, "The Two Faces of the Christian Coalition," September 1995, www.electric-escape.net/rr/two-faces?

70. Martin, *With God on Our Side*, 330; Schaffer, "Say a Prayer for the Christian Coalition," 25; Ralph Reed, Jr., "Casting a Wider Net: Religious Conservatives Move Beyond Abortion and Homosexuality," *Policy Review*, 65 (Summer 1993): 31; Dan Balz and Ronald Brownstein, "God's Fixer," *WP*, 28 January 1996.

71. Joe Maxwell, "Randall Terry Attacks Religious Right," *CT*, 12 September 1994, 61; Balz and Brownstein, "God's Fixer."

72. Dan Gilgoff, *The Jesus Machine: How James Dobson, Focus on the Family, and Evangelical America Are Winning the Culture War* (New York: St. Martin's Press, 2007), 18–23.

73. James C. Dobson, *Dare to Discipline* (Wheaton, IL: Tyndale House, 1970); John Dart, "Religion a Force in Conservative Protestant America," *LAT*, 2 April 1988.

74. Dirk Johnson, "Rise of Christian Right Splits a City," *NYT*, 14 February 1993; Dale D. Buss, "Focusing on the Family with James Dobson," *American Enterprise*, November 1995, 43ff; Marc Fisher, "The GOP, Facing a Dobson's Choice," *WP*, 2 July 1996.

75. Dale Buss, *Family Man: The Biography of Dr. James Dobson* (Wheaton, IL: Tyndale House, 2005), 153; Briefing on Participants in Discussion of White House Conference on Families, 11 April 1980, "Projects—Miscellaneous Completed" folder, box 108, Public Outreach, Robert L. Maddox Papers, JCL.

76. White House memos from Gary L. Bauer to Frederick J. Ryan, Jr., 31 August, 15 September, and 21 October 1987, "Dobson Photo-Op, 11/10/1987" folder, box 1, OA17952, Juanita Duggan Files, RRPL.

77. Gilgoff, *Jesus Machine*, 31–32; Buss, *Family Man*, 154–155.

78. Susan Crabtree, "The Long Shot," *Salon*, 8 November 1999, http://archive.salon.com/news/feature/1999/11/08/bauer/index.html; American Values Web site, www.ouramericanvalues.org/bauer_main.php; Gary Bauer to Edwin L. Harper, 18 May 1982, "Pro-Life (2)" folder, OA12450, box 11, Morton Blackwell Files, RRPL.

79. Gilgoff, *Jesus Machine*, 117–118.

80. Peter Steinfels, "No Church, No Ministry, No Pulpit, He Is Called Religious Right's Star," *NYT*, 5 June 1990; "Family Research Council: A Vigorous Voice in Washington," *FFC*, January 1989, 15; Buss, *Family Man*, 347.

81. Tom Minnery, "Taking the Pledge," *FFC*, November 1988; Mike Yorkey, "George Bush's Faith," *FFC*, January 1989, 1; "Reclaiming the Airwaves," *FFC*, May 1989, 14–15; Tom Hess, "Repairing the Damage: What Kind of Supreme Court Justices Should George Bush Be Scouting These Days?" *FFC*, July 1989; Tom Minnery, "Why the Left Needs Censorship," *FFC*, 23 July 1990, 4; "What Did Quayle Really Say?" *FFC*, 20 July 1992, 6; "Bush Renews Courtship of the Religious Right," *LAT*, 15 August 1992.

82. Philip S. Gutis, "Small Steps toward Acceptance Renew Debate on Gay Marriage," *NYT*, 5 November 1989; "Foes of Civil Rights Bill Mount 11th-Hour Drive," *NYT*, 22 March 1988; Gilgoff, *Jesus Machine*, 34–35; Warren Epstein and Rick Ansorge, "The Ministry of Influence," *Colorado Springs Gazette-Telegraph*, 8 March 1993.

83. Buss, *Family Man*, 150–151, 157; Gilgoff, *Jesus Machine*, 35; "Focus Founder to Serve on National Commission," *Colorado Springs Gazette-Telegraph*, 16 December 1994; Martin, *With God on Our Side*, 343.

84. Gustav Niebuhr, "Advice for Parents, and for Politicians," *NYT*, 30 May 1995; Adele M. Stan, "Power Preying," *Mother Jones*, November/December 1995, 44; Martin, *With God on Our Side*, 341, 343–344.

85. Howard Kurtz et al., "Dole, Reed, Schlafly and Abortion," *WP*, 24 December 1995; R.W. Apple, Jr., "G.O.P. 'Peace Candidate,'" *NYT*, 8 June 1996; Gustav Niebuhr, "G.O.P. Candidates Divide Religious Right," *NYT*, 19 January 1996.

86. Jason DeParle, "A Fundamental Problem," *NYT*, 14 July 1996; AP, "Abortion Debate Divides GOP," *Greensboro News Record*, 7 August 1996; David E. Rosenbaum, "The Platform: G.O.P.'s Moderates Accept an Accord on Abortion Issue," *NYT*, 8 August 1996; Karen Ball, "Reed Bent with the Wind," *New York Daily News*, 7 August 1996.

87. Jamie C. Ruff, "Tapes Put Falwell in Spotlight," *RTD*, 18 August 1994; Mark O'Keefe, "Christian Stations Boom with Emphasis on Politics," *Norfolk Virginian-Pilot*, 6 February 1994.

88. "Clinton Criticizes Two of His Critics: Falwell, Limbaugh," *Seattle Times*, 25 June 1994; E. J. Dionne, Jr., "Sleaze on the Right," *WP*, 28 June 1994; Philip Yancey, "The Riddle of Bill Clinton's Faith," *CT*, 25 April 1994, 26–27.

89. Mike Dorning, "Senate Fails to Overturn Veto of 'Partial Birth' Abortion Ban; GOP Sees Vote as Campaign Issue," *Chicago Tribune*, 27 September 1996; Marc Fisher, "Judgment Day: Christian Right Looks Down on Abortion Loss as Political Winner," *WP*, 27 September 1996.

90. "Graham: 'President Was Wrong,'" *Baptist Courier*, 16 May 1996; Fisher, "Judgment Day."

91. Gilgoff, *Jesus Machine*, 103, 112; Gustav Niebuhr, "Voters of Various Faiths Return to Democratic Fold," *NYT*, 9 November 1996; Mike Dorning and James Warren, "Labor Regains Relevance; Conservative Christians Flex Their Muscle," *Chicago Tribune*, 7 November 1996.

92. Laurie Goodstein, "Conservative Christian Leader Accuses Republicans of Betrayal," *NYT*, 12 February 1998; Sasha Abramsky, "Tales from America 3: Vote Redneck," *Observer* (London), 27 October 1996.

93. Goodstein, "Conservative Christian Leader Accuses Republicans of Betrayal"; Ralph Z. Hallow, "Family Activist Fires Another Broadside at Hill Republicans," *WT*, 27 March 1998; Benjamin Domenech, "Dobson's Choice: Why the Conservative Outsider's Agenda Worries GOP Leaders," *WP*, 19 April 1998.

94. Ralph Z. Hallow, "Dobson Hears Appeals of House Conservatives," *WT*, 20 March 1998; Michael Gerson, Major Garrett, and Carolyn Kleiner, "A Righteous Indignation," *USN*, 4 May 1998.

95. Ralph Z. Hallow, "GOP Vows to Push Religious-Right Issues," *WT*, 10 April 1998.

96. Gilgoff, *Jesus Machine*, 114–116; Alison Mitchell, "Fretting over Grip on House, G.O.P. Courts Conservatives," *NYT*, 9 May 1998.

97. Ralph Z. Hallow, "GOP, Activists Agree on Legislative Goals," *WT*, 9 May 1998; Louise D. Palmer, "For Gay Rights, a Tough Road Ahead," *BG*, 24

July 1998; "For Our Rights, a Sigh of Relief," *St. Petersburg Times*, 14 November 1998.

98. Richard L. Berke, "Christian Coalition Looking to Ex-Lawmaker as Leader," *NYT*, 11 June 1997.

99. James Traub, "A Curse on the House," *NYT*, 28 February 1999; Frederick Clarkson, "The Clinton Contras' Smoke and Mirrors," *In These Times*, 3 May 1998; Alison Mitchell, "Fund-Raising Furor: Clinton Agenda Is Hindered," *NYT*, 17 March 1997; Richard L. Berke, "Patience Guides a Calculated G.O.P. Response," *NYT*, 8 February 1998.

100. Laurie Goodstein, "The Testing of a President," *NYT*, 20 September 1998; James C. Dobson, "The President, 'That Woman Miss Lewinsky,' and the American People," *Focus on the Family Newsletter,* September 1998, www.focusonthefamily .com/docstudy/newsletters/A000000802.cfm; Paul M. Weyrich, "The Culture War Is Lost. Now What?" *Sacramento Bee*, 24 February 1999.

101. Cal Thomas and Ed Dobson, *Blinded by Might: Can the Religious Right Save America?* (Grand Rapids, MI: Zondervan, 1999), 26, 80.

Chapter 11

1. Steve Benen, "Pat's Plot Thickens," *Church and State*, March 1999, 7.

2. George F. Will, "A Conservative on Bush's First 100 Days," *Pittsburgh Tribune Review*, 29 April 2001 (emphasis in original).

3. David D. Kirkpatrick, "The Evangelical Crackup," *NYT Magazine*, 28 October 2007; E. J. Dionne, Jr., *Souled Out: Reclaiming Faith and Politics after the Religious Right* (Princeton, NJ: Princeton University Press, 2008), 4.

4. Robert Draper, *Dead Certain: The Presidency of George W. Bush* (New York: Free Press, 2007), 3–15; Mary Leonard, "No Shying Away from God Talk in Campaign," *BG*, 23 December 1999; David M. Shribman, "GOP Hopefuls Court the Right," *BG*, 8 June 1999; AP, "Dobson Warns Bush to Take Hard Line on Abortion," *Colorado Springs Gazette*, 15 March 1999; Jim Yardley, "The 2000 Campaign: The Governor's Speech; Bush's Words to Conservative Group Remain a Mystery," *NYT*, 19 May 2000; Anthony Lewis, "A Simple Question Reveals Much about George W. Bush," *Austin American Statesman*, 1 December 1999; Maureen Dowd, "Playing the Jesus Card," *NYT*, 15 December 1999.

5. Stephen Mansfield, *The Faith of George W. Bush* (New York: Penguin, 2003), 67–72.

6. Ibid., 107–111.

7. Ibid.; Deborah Caldwell, "An Evolving Faith," *Christian Ethics Today*, 2 April 2003, www.christianethicstoday.com.

8. Helen Kennedy, "Senator Catapults into Lead in S.C. Poll," *New York Daily News*, 4 February 2000; Anne E. Kornblutt and Yvonne Abraham, "Touting Conservative Themes, Bush Shifts Tone in S.C.," *BG*, 3 February 2000.

9. "Leader: Candidates Mishandled Religion," *Augusta (GA) Chronicle*, 9 March 2000; Alison Mitchell, "McCain Hopeful Bauer Backing Delivers Christian Conservatives," *NYT*, 17 February 2000.

10. "Text of Bush's Letter to Cardinal O'Connor," *NYT*, 28 February 2000.

11. Jill Abramson, "The Religious Right vs. McCain," *NYT*, 5 March 2000; Jerry Falwell, "Falwell Confidential" mass e-mail, 18 February 2000, "Falwell Confidential" folder, FAL 2-1, LUA.

12. "Falwell and Dobson Condemn Bauer Endorsement of McCain," *PR Newswire*, 18 February 2000.

13. Richard L. Berke, "Bush Halts McCain in South Carolina by Drawing a Huge Republican Vote," *NYT*, 20 February 2000.

14. "Excerpt from McCain's Speech on Religious Conservatives," *NYT*, 29 February 2000; David Barstow, "McCain Calls Leaders of Christian Right 'Evil,'" *NYT*, 1 March 2000.

15. Hanna Rosin and Dana Milbank, "A Political 'Heretic' Is Cast Out," *WP*, 25 March 2000; Kevin Sack, "Remarks Rally Christian Right against McCain," *NYT*, 3 March 2000; "Leader: Candidates Mishandled Religion"; Frank Bruni, "The Arizona Senator: McCain Apologizes for Characterizing Falwell and Robertson as Forces of Evil," *NYT*, 2 March 2000.

16. Richard S. Dunham, "Bush's Avenging Angel," *Business Week*, 21 February 2000, 154; Laurie Goodstein, "The Religion Issue: Bush's Jesus Day Is Called Insensitive and a Violation of the First Amendment," *NYT*, 6 August 2000; David Grann, "Where W. Got Compassion," *NYT*, 12 September 1999.

17. Amy E. Black et al., *Of Little Faith: The Politics of George W. Bush's Faith-Based Initiatives* (Washington, DC: Georgetown University Press, 2004), 75–99; Wendy Murray Zoba, "Youth Has Special Powers," *CT*, 5 February 2001; Lucia Mouat, "Reformer Wins Templeton Award," *CSM*, 18 February 1993; "Evangelical Environmentalism Comes of Age," *CT*, 11 November 1996. For examples of *Christianity Today*'s coverage of evangelical social activism, see Christine J. Gardner, "Raising Funds while Helping the Poor," *CT*, 11 January 1999; Belinda Pollard, "Christians Oppose Threats to Welfare," *CT*, 26 April 1999; Bill Yoder, "The Case for Compassion," *CT*, 6 March 2000; Sheryl Henderson Blunt, "Networking against Poverty," *CT*, 3 April 2000; "Grassroots Activism Delivers Debt Relief," *CT*, 4 December 2000.

18. Larry Witham, "Tennessean No Stranger to Matters of Religion," *WT*, 14 August 2000; Jim Wallis, "What's an FBO?" in *What's God Got to Do with the American Experiment?* ed. E. J. Dionne, Jr., and John J. DiIulio, Jr. (Washington, DC: Brookings Institution, 2000), 151; Barrie McKenna, "Bush and Gore Join the Party of God," *Globe and Mail* (Toronto), 2 September 2000.

19. Witham, "Tennessean No Stranger to Matters of Religion"; McKenna, "Bush and Gore Join the Party of God"; David Firestone, "The Nation: What Hath God Wrought? Lieberman and the Right," *NYT*, 3 September 2000; Larry Witham, "Lieberman Gets Unusual Amen Corner," *WT*, 9 September 2000.

20. Ralph Z. Hallow, "Evangelical Vote Could Decide Election," *WT*, 26 October 2000; John Dillin, "Growing Gap at Ballot Box: Religious vs. Secular Vote," *CSMr*, 29 January 2001; Lyman Kellstedt et al., "Faith Transformed: Religion and American Politics from FDR to George W. Bush," in *Religion and American Politics: From the Colonial Period to the Present*, ed. Mark A. Noll and Luke E. Harlow, 2nd ed. (New York: Oxford University Press, 2007),

273; Thomas B. Edsall, "Robertson Quits Political Post," *WP*, 6 December 2001; Larry Witham, "Religion's Role Seen as Greater in 2000," *WT*, 26 January 2001; Richard L. Berke, "Aide Says Bush Will Do More to Marshal Religious Base," *NYT*, 12 December 2001.

21. John Gizzi, "Right Still Likes Bush," *Human Events*, 20 August 2001, 1, 3; Gary Schneeberger, "Seven Points of Fight," *FFC*, March 2001, 18.

22. Michael Iserkoff, "Taxing Times for Robertson," *Newsweek*, 21 June 1999; Ralph Z. Hallow, "Christian, but No Longer a Powerful Coalition," *WT*, 14 March 2001; Edsall, "Robertson Quits Political Post"; Alan Cooperman and Thomas B. Edsall, "Christian Coalition Shrinks as Debt Grows," *WP*, 10 April 2006.

23. AP, "Ministry Needs Funds, Dobson Says," *Denver Post*, 15 May 2001; Eric Gorski, "Problems Put Focus in a Tricky Position," *Colorado Springs Gazette*, 21 October 2000.

24. Dan Gilgoff, *The Jesus Machine: How James Dobson, Focus on the Family, and Evangelical America Are Winning the Culture War* (New York: St. Martin's Press, 2007), 148–149; Terry Mattingly, "Voices of Religious Right Carefully, Tactfully Supporting Bush," *Knoxville News Sentinel*, 25 August 2001; Ralph Z. Hallow, "Religious Right Loses Its Political Potency," *WT*, 20 May 2001.

25. Chris Mondics, "Setbacks for Ashcroft on His Social Agenda," *Philadelphia Inquirer*, 21 April 2002; Sheryl Henderson Blunt, "The Unflappable Condi Rice," *CT*, September 2003, 43–48; Gary Scheeberger, "On a Roll," *FFC*, June 2001, 15; Esther Kaplan, *With God on Their Side: How Christian Fundamentalists Trampled Science, Policy, and Democracy in George W. Bush's White House* (New York: New Press, 2004), 5, 34–166; Gary Scott Smith, *Faith and the Presidency: From George Washington to George W. Bush* (New York: Oxford University Press, 2006), 383.

26. Paul Kengor, *God and George W. Bush* (New York: HarperCollins, 2004), 159–172; Smith, *Faith and the Presidency*, 369–372.

27. Official White House Website, "Promoting a Culture of Life," www.whitehouse .gov/infocus/achievement/chap15.html (accessed 11 March 2008); Ron Hutcheson, "Bush OKs Law Limiting Abortion," *Philadelphia Inquirer*, 6 November 2003; Amy Goldstein, "Bush Signs Unborn Victims Act," *WP*, 2 April 2004; Kaplan, *With God on Their Side*, 210; Richard L. Berke, "The President's Decision: The Constituencies; Bush Appears to Have Straddled a Divide," *NYT*, 11 August 2001.

28. Black et al., *Of Little Faith*, 9–11.

29. Pat Robertson, "Faith-Based Initiatives Pose Some Problems," n.d., www.patrobertson.com/newscommentary/faithbasedinitiatives.asp; Laurie Goodstein, "Bush Aide Tells of Plan to Aid Work by Churches," *NYT*, 8 March 2001.

30. Hallow, "Religious Right Loses Its Political Potency."

31. Laurie Goodstein, "After the Attacks: Finding Fault," *NYT*, 15 September 2001.

32. Mark Galli, "Now What?" *CT*, 22 October 2001, 24; Alan Cooperman, "Ministers Asked to Curb Remarks about Islam," *WP*, 8 May 2003.

33. George W. Bush, Address on the White House South Lawn, 16 September 2001, www.globalsecurity.org/military/library/news/2001/09/mil-010916-usia4 .htm; Bush, Address at the FBI, 10 October 2001, http://avalon.law.yale.edu/ sept11/president_043.asp.

34. George W. Bush, Address to a Joint Session of Congress and to the American People, 20 September 2001, www.whitehouse.gov/news/releases/2001/09/ 20010920-8.html.

35. Kaplan, *With God on Their Side*, 7; Steven Waldman, "Heaven Sent: Does God Endorse George W. Bush?" *Slate*, 13 September 2004, www.slate.com/ id/2106590/; Dana Milbank, "Religious Right Finds Its Center in Oval Office," *WP*, 21 December 2001; "The Buzz," *World*, 6 October 2001.

36. Jane Lampman, "New Scrutiny of Role of Religion in Bush's Policies," *CSM*, 17 March 2003; Jan Cienski, "War Puts Bush in a Religious Quandary: Churches Oppose Attack," *National Post* (Canada), 11 February 2003; "The Buzz," *World*, 22 and 29 March 2003; Bill Broadway, "Evangelicals' Voices Speak Softly about Iraq," *WP*, 25 January 2003.

37. Jim Remsen, "Faith and War Support Linked," *Philadelphia Inquirer*, 8 March 2003; Brad A. Greenberg, "Poll: Christian Support for War Declining," *Ontario (CA) Inland Valley Daily Bulletin*, 12 September 2005; Alan Fram, "AP Poll: Most See Iraq War as Failure," *Huffington Post*, 11 September 2007, www .huffingtonpost.com/huff-wires/20070911/us-iraq-ap-poll/.

38. Michael Cooper, "The Republican Running Mate: Cheney's Remarks on Marriage Irk Conservatives," *NYT*, 10 October 2000; Kaplan, *With God on Their Side*, 148–151.

39. Gilgoff, *Jesus Machine*, 161–162.

40. Cheryl Wetzstein, "Group Wants Marriage Defined in Constitution," *WT*, 13 July 2001; Gilgoff, *Jesus Machine*, 141–144.

41. James C. Dobson, "Marriage on the Ropes," *Focus on the Family Newsletter*, September 2003, www.focusonthefamily.com/docstudy/newsletters/A000000771 .cfm#footnote39.

42. Ibid.

43. Sheryl Stay Goldberg, "White House Avoids Stance on Gay Marriage Measure," *NYT*, 2 July 2003; Mary Leonard, "Campaign 2004: Gay Marriage Stirs Conservatives Again," *BG*, 28 September 2003; Gilgoff, *Jesus Machine*, 139–140; Southern Baptist Convention, "Resolution on Same-Sex Marriage," June 2003, www.sbc.net/resolutions/amResolution.asp?ID=1128.

44. Sheryl Gay Stolberg, "Democratic Candidates Are Split on the Issue of Gay Marriages," *NYT*, 16 July 2003; Jane Lampman, "Gay Marriage: An Issue That Divides the Faithful," *CSM*, 21 November 2003.

45. Bill Sammon, "Bush Cool on Measure to Ban Gay 'Marriage,'" *WT*, 3 July 2003; Stephen Dinan, "Bush Stance 'Not Clear,'" *WT*, 18 December 2003; Katharine Q. Seelye, "Conservatives Mobilize against Ruling on Gay Marriage," *NYT*, 20 November 2003.

46. David D. Kirkpatrick, "Conservatives Using Issue of Gay Unions as a Rallying Tool," *NYT*, 8 February 2004; George W. Bush, State of the Union Address, 20 January 2004, www.whitehouse.gov/news/releases/2004/01/20040120-7

.html; Mike Allen and Alan Cooperman, "Bush Backs Amendment Banning Gay Marriage," *WP*, 25 February 2004.

47. Kirkpatrick, "Conservatives Using Issue of Gay Unions."

48. Walter Shapiro, "Ohio Churches Hope Marriage Ban Prods Voters to Polls," *USA Today*, 27 September 2004; Paul Farhi and James V. Grimaldi, "GOP Won with Accent on Rural and Traditional," *WP*, 4 November 2004.

49. Alan Cooperman and Thomas B. Edsall, "Evangelicals Say They Led the Charge for the GOP," *WP*, 8 November 2004; Mara R. O'Connor, "The Incredible Popularity of *The Purpose-Driven Life*," *Enlightenment Magazine*, June–August 2005, www.wie.org/j29/purpose-driven.asp; Hanna Rosin, "Redeem the Vote Spreads the Election-Year Gospel," *WP*, 29 October 2004.

50. George W. Bush, Address to the Southern Baptist Convention, 15 June 2004, www.multied.com/elections/2004/2004mainelec/Bushspeeches/faithbased .html; David D. Kirkpatrick, "Bush Allies Till Fertile Soil, among Baptists, for Votes," *NYT*, 18 June 2004.

51. Gilgoff, *Jesus Machine*, 245–250; Amy Sullivan, *The Party Faithful: How and Why Democrats Are Closing the God Gap* (New York: Simon & Schuster, 2008), 115–152.

52. Daniel Williams and Alan Cooperman, "Pro-Choice Politicians 'Not Fit' for Communion," *WP*, 24 April 2004; Julian Coman, "Don't Allow Kerry to Take Communion, Vatican Chief Tells U.S. Catholic Bishops," *Sunday Telegraph* (London), 11 July 2004.

53. Alan Cooperman and Thomas B. Edsall, "Evangelicals Say They Led Charge for the GOP," *WP*, 8 November 2004; "The Triumph of the Religious Right—American Values," *Economist*, 13 November 2004.

54. Farhi and Grimaldi, "GOP Won with Accent on Rural and Traditional"; Cooperman and Edsall, "Evangelicals Say They Led Charge for the GOP"; Dana Milbank, "Deeply Divided Country Is United in Anxiety," *WP*, 4 November 2004.

55. Audrey Hudson, "President's Domestic Agenda to Include Marriage Amendment," *WT*, 8 November 2004; Susan Schmidt, "Furor Continues over Specter Comments on Nominees," *WP*, 8 November 2004.

56. Bob Powers, "Nearly Half of All Americans Listen to Christian Radio," NRB, [2005], www.nrb.org/partner/Article_Display_Page/0,,PTID30877 8%7CCHID568026%7CCIID1985332,00.html; "Conversation: Left Behind," *Online News Hour*, PBS, 20 December 2004, www.pbs.org/newshour/bb/ religion/july-dec04/apocalypse_12-20.html; David D. Kirkpatrick, "College for the Home-Schooled Is Shaping Leaders for the Right," *NYT*, 8 March 2004. For an analysis of contemporary evangelicals' leadership positions in cultural, academic, and political institutions, see D. Michael Lindsay, *Faith in the Halls of Power: How Evangelicals Joined the American Elite* (New York: Oxford University Press, 2007). For information on Patrick Henry College, see Hanna Rosin, *God's Harvard: A Christian College on a Mission to Save America* (Orlando, FL: Harcourt, 2007).

57. Frank Rich, "The Plot against Sex in America," *NYT*, 12 December 2004; David D. Kirkpatrick, "Some Backers of Bush Anticipate a 'Revolution,'" *NYT*, 4 November 2004.

58. Debra Rosenberg, "Church Meets State," *Newsweek*, 13 November 2006.

59. Charles Babington, "Frist Urges End to Nominee Filibusters," *WP*, 25 April 2005.

60. Mitch Frank, "Terri Schiavo: The Legal Struggle," *Time*, 4 April 2005; David D. Kirkpatrick, "Conservatives Invoke Case in Fundraising Campaigns," *NYT*, 25 March 2005; Ronald Brownstein, "The Death of Terri Schiavo," *LAT*, 1 April 2005; James C. Dobson, "Life, Death and Judicial Tyranny," *Focus on the Family Action*, April 2005, www.focusaction.org/Articles/A000000020.cfm.

61. David D. Kirkpatrick, "A Year of Work to Sell Roberts to Conservatives," *NYT*, 22 July 2005; Thomas B. Edsall, "Conservatives Rally for Justice," *WP*, 15 August 2005.

62. James Moore and Wayne Slater, *The Architect: Karl Rove and the Dream of Absolute Power* (New York: Crown, 2006), 229–232; Gilgoff, *Jesus Machine*, 228–234; Marvin Olasky, "Blessed Are the Meek," *World Magazine*, 15 October 2005.

63. Gilgoff, *Jesus Machine*, 232–237; David D. Kirkpatrick, "Endorsement of Nominee Draws Committee's Interest," *NYT*, 10 October 2005.

64. Demian McLean, "Specter to Ask Whether Rove Gave Assurances on Miers," Bloomberg.com, 9 October 2005, www.bloomberg.com/apps/news?pid=10 000103&sid=avIE5l2P51sI; Gilgoff, *Jesus Machine*, 237–241.

65. David D. Kirkpatrick, "Conservatives Are Wary over President's Selection," *NYT*, 4 October 2005.

66. David D. Kirkpatrick, "Rejected by Evangelical Base, Politician Ponders Next Role," *NYT*, 22 July 2006; Dawn Turner Trice, "Hear That Thud? It's the GOP's Latest Scandal," *Chicago Tribune*, 9 October 2006; Colleen Slevin, "Colo. Minister Admits 'Sexual Immorality,'" *WP*, 6 November 2006; Jonathan Darman and Andrew Murr, "Morality Tale: A Pastor's Fall from Grace," *Newsweek*, 13 November 2006.

67. "Polls Find Shifts by Young Evangelicals," *Christian Century*, 30 October 2007, 15; Wayne Slater, "Young Evangelical Voters Diverge from Parents," *Dallas Morning News*, 15 October 2007; Robin Rogers and Peter Goodwin Heltzel, "The New Evangelical Politics," *Society* 45 (2008): 413; Lester Feder, "Explaining McCain's Success among Evangelicals," *Huffington Post*, 20 January 2008, www.huffingtonpost.com/lester-feder/explaining-mccains-succe_b_82378.html.

68. Laurie Goodstein, "Religious Voting Data Show Some Shift, Observers Say," *NYT*, 9 November 2006; David D. Kirkpatrick, "In Ohio, Democrats Show a Religious Side to Voters," *NYT*, 31 October 2006; "Ted Strickland," *WP*, 9 November 2006.

69. Susan Milligan, "Democrats Eye Softer Image on Abortion," *BG*, 19 December 2004; James E. Clyburn, "How Faith Works for Democrats," *WP*, 2 June 2006; David D. Kirkpatrick, "Consultant Helps Democrats Embrace

Faith, and Some in Party Are Not Pleased," *NYT*, 26 December 2006; David D. Kirkpatrick, "Democrats Turn to Leader of Religious Left," *NYT*, 17 January 2005; Jim Wallis, *God's Politics: Why the Right Gets It Wrong and the Left Doesn't Get It* (New York: HarperCollins, 2005).

70. Lisa Miller and Richard Wolffe, "Finding His Faith," *Newsweek*, 21 July 2008; Barack Obama, "'Call to Renewal' Keynote Address," 28 June 2006, http://obama.senate.gov/speech/060628-call_to_renewal/.

71. Franklin Foer, "Beyond Belief: Howard Dean's Religion Problem," *New Republic*, 29 December 2003; Ruth Marcus, "The New Temptation of Democrats," *WP*, 23 May 2006; E. J. Dionne, Jr., "Message from a Megachurch," *WP*, 5 December 2006.

72. Alan Cooperman, "Church Is Urged to Disinvite Obama," *WP*, 30 November 2006; Marcus, "New Temptation of Democrats."

73. Robert E. Webber, *The Younger Evangelicals: Facing the Challenges of the New World* (Grand Rapids, MI: Baker Books, 2002); Cathleen Falsani, "Bono's American Prayer," *CT*, March 2003, 38–44; "Polls Find Shifts by Young Evangelicals," 14-15; Liane Hansen's Interview with Richard Cizik, National Public Radio, 10 February 2008, www.npr.org/templates/story/story.php?storyId=18854833.

74. Jane Lampman, "Evangelicals Find the Center," *CSM*, 18 March 2008; Adelle M. Banks, "Dobson, Others Seek Ouster of NAE Vice President," *CT*, 2 March 2007.

75. White House memo on Focus on the Family, [November 1988], Mariam Bell Files, OA17973, "Focus on the Family (Physician), 17 November 1988 (1)," RRPL; Art Toalston, "Southern Baptists Laud James Dobson, Focus on the Family at 25-Year Mark," Baptist Press, 1 August 2002, http://jmm.aaa.net.au/articles/4716.htm; David John Marley, *Pat Robertson: A Life* (Lanham, MD: Rowman & Littlefield, 2007), 97; Laurie Goodstein, "Even Pat Robertson's Friends Are Wondering," *NYT*, 8 January 2006.

76. "CBS/AP, "Falwell Was 'Old Guard' of Religious Right," CBS News, 16 May 2007, www.cbsnews.com/stories/2007/05/16/national/main2811835.shtml; Press Release from the Evangelical Climate Initiative, "Evangelical Leaders Increase Pressure on Capitol Hill to Enact Prudent Federal Climate Policy," 11 October 2007, www.evangelicalclimateinitiative.org/pub/ECI%20Capitol%20Focus%20News%20Release%2010-11-07.pdf; Neela Banerjee, "Southern Baptists Back a Shift on Climate Change," *NYT*, 10 March 2008; "A Southern Baptist Declaration on the Environment and Climate Change," [2008], http://baptistcreationcare.org/node/1.

77. Kirkpatrick, "Evangelical Crackup"; Dan Balz, "McCain Reconnects with Liberty University," *WP*, 14 May 2006; David D. Kirkpatrick, "In a Surprise, Pat Robertson Backs Giuliani," *NYT*, 8 November 2007; "Christian School Dean Plans to Back Romney," *WSJ*, 16 October 2007; Ralph Z. Hallow, "Republican '08 Options Disappoint Evangelicals," *WT*, 16 April 2007.

78. Zev Chafets, "The Huckabee Factor," *NYT Magazine*, 16 December 2007; David D. Kirkpatrick, "Shake, Rattle and Roil the Grand Ol' Coalition," *NYT*, 30 December 2007.

79. Laurie Goodstein, "For a Trusty Voting Bloc, a Faith Shaken," *NYT*, 7 October 2007; Jim Wallis, "What's Next for Mike Huckabee?" *Huffington Post*, 6 March 2008, www.huffingtonpost.com/jim-wallis/whats-next-for-mike-huck_b_90300.html; Chris Sillizza and Shailagh Murray, "The Man Who Helped Start Huckabee's Roll," *WP*, 2 December 2007; Michael D. Shear and Perry Bacon, Jr., "Iowa Chooses Huckabee, Obama; Evangelicals Fuel Win over Romney," *WP*, 4 January 2008.

80. Ralph Z. Hallow, "Bauer Urges 'Open Mind'; Supports Bid by Thompson," *WT*, 13 October 2007; Kirkpatrick, "Shake, Rattle and Roil the Grand Ol' Coalition"; David D. Kirkpatrick, "Young Evangelicals Embrace Huckabee as Old Guard Balks," *NYT*, 13 January 2008.

81. Shailagh Murray, "Same-Sex Marriage Ban Is Defeated," *NYT*, 8 June 2006; Hallow, "Republican '08 Options Disappoint Evangelicals."

82. "Full Text of Obama Remarks at Messiah," Pennlive.com, 13 April 2008, www.pennlive.com/midstate/index.ssf/2008/04/full_tex_of_obama_remarks_as_m.html.

83. Transcript of Saddleback Civil Forum, Lake Forest, CA, 16 August 2008, http://transcripts.cnn.com/TRANSCRIPTS/0808/16/se.02.html.

84. American Presidency Project, 2008 Democratic Party Platform, 25 August 2008, www.presidency.ucsb.edu/ws/index.php?pid=78283; Suzanne Sataline, "Democratic Convention: From Prayer to 'Faith Caucuses,' Party to Show Religious Side," *WSJ*, 25 August 2008; Naomi Schaefer Riley, "The Weekend Interview with Rick Warren: What Saddleback's Pastor Really Thinks about Politics," *WSJ*, 23 August 2008; Jim Wallis, "A Step Forward on Abortion," "God's Politics" blog, 14 August 2008, http://blog.beliefnet.com/godspolitics/2008/08/a-step-forward-on-abortion-by.html.

85. Elisabeth Bumiller, "Palin Disclosures Spotlight McCain's Screening Process," *NYT*, 2 September 2008; Transcript of Brian Goldsmith's Interview with Richard Land, CBS News, 8 August 2008, www.cbsnews.com/stories/2008/08/08/politics/politicalplayers/main4331863.shtml; David D. Kirkpatrick, "McCain's Effort to Woo Conservatives Is Paying Off," *NYT*, 3 September 2008.

86. Eric Adler, "Palin's Presence on Ballot Sways Some Religious Conservatives but Not All," *Kansas City Star*, 17 September 2008; George Bryson and Richard Mauer, "Nation Examines Palin's Beliefs," *Anchorage Daily News*, 7 September 2008; "Misunderstanding Sarah," *CT*, November 2008, 23.

87. Kirkpatrick, "McCain's Effort to Woo Conservatives Is Paying Off"; Teresa Watanabe, "Evangelicals Differ on Whether Palin's Career Fits Biblical Model," *LAT*, 1 October 2008; AP, Eric Gorski, "Choice of Pro-Life Palin Energizes Evangelicals," *South Florida Sun-Sentinel*, 31 August 2008.

88. Pew Forum on Religion and Public Life, "Inside Obama's Sweeping Victory," 5 November 2008, http://pewresearch.org/pubs/1023/exit-poll-analysis-2008; Pew Forum on Religion and Public Life, "Voting Religiously," 5 November 2008, http://pewresearch.org/pubs/1022/exit-poll-analysis-religion; Pew Forum on Religion and Public Life, "A Look at Religious Voters in the 2008 Election," 10 February 2009, http://pewresearch.org/pubs/1112/religion-vote-2008-election; Laurie Goodstein, "Obama Made Gains among Younger

Evangelical Voters, Data Show," *NYT*, 6 November 2008; Steven Waldman, "Evangelicals Made Up a BIGGER Part of the Republican Coalition This Time," Beliefnet, 10 November 2008, http://blog.beliefnet.com/stevenwaldman/2008/11/evangelicals-made-up-a-bigger.html.

89. Lyman A. Kellstedt and John C. Green, "The Politics of the Willow Creek Association Pastors," *Journal for the Scientific Study of Religion* 42 (2003): 554, 559; Robert Wuthnow, *After the Baby Boomers: How Twenty- and Thirty-Somethings Are Changing the Future of American Religion* (Princeton, NJ: Princeton University Press, 2007), 174–177; Public Religion Research, Faith and American Politics Survey, 2008, www.faithinpubliclife.org/tools/polls/faps/; E. J. Dionne, Jr., "The New Evangelical Politics," *WP*, 19 August 2008.

90. Shayne Lee and Phillip Luke Sinitiere, *Holy Mavericks: Evangelical Innovators and the Spiritual Marketplace* (New York: New York University Press, 2009), 129–148; Timothy C. Morgan and Tony Carnes, "Purpose Driven in Rwanda," *CT*, October 2005; David Van Biema, "The Global Ambition of Rick Warren," *Time*, 18 August 2008; Tina Daunt, "Cause Celebre: No Answer to Their Prayers," *LAT*, 20 December 2008; Sally Quinn, "Pastor Rick's Evolution," *WP*, 20 January 2009; Michael Paulson, "Effort to Surmount Polarizing Debates Backfires on Pastor," *BG*, 19 January 2009.

91. Jeff Zeleny and David D. Kirkpatrick, "Obama's Choice of Pastor Creates Furor," *NYT*, 20 December 2008; Barbara Bradley Hagerty, "Rick Warren: The Purpose-Driven Pastor," *Weekend Edition*, NPR, 18 January 2009, www.npr.org/templates/story/story.php?storyId=99529977; Tony Barboza, "Gay-Rights Backers Protest Pastor's Inauguration Role," *LAT*, 19 January 2009.

abortion (*continued*)
  secularism and culture wars, linked
    to, 116
  Southern Baptists on, 115, 117–19,
    155–58, 209–10
  therapeutic, 112–15
  women's rights and, 117, 156
  younger evangelicals on, 275
Abramoff, Jack, 194, 267
L'Abri (The Shelter), Switzerland, 138,
    140, 141
abstinence-only sex education, 253
Abzug, Bella, 143, 144, 146, 147
ACCC (American Council of Christian
    Churches), 38, 39, 66, 84, 92
Acheson, Dean, 20, 57
ACLU (American Civil Liberties
    Union), 198, 254
ACTV (American Coalition for
    Traditional Values), 206, 222
Afghanistan War, 255
African Americans. *See also* civil rights
  abortion rates of, 227
  gay rights and, 234
AIDS, 249, 251, 270, 275
Alabama Baptist, 63, 66
Alford, Dale, 60
Alito, Samuel, 266
Allen, Jimmy, 66, 192
Almond, Lindsay, Jr., 46
American Civil Liberties Union
    (ACLU), 198, 254
American Coalition for Traditional
    Values (ACTV), 206, 222
American Conservative Union, 136,
    165
American Council of Christian
    Churches (ACCC), 38, 39, 66, 84,
    92
American ideals, identification of
    Protestant Christianity with
    conservatism, Christian Right's
    adoption of concept of, 58–59
  exceptionalism, American, doctrine
    of, 176–77, 187, 188, 189
  by fundamentalists, 41–42, 48

  by Graham, 24, 41
  Kennedy election and anti-
    Catholicism, 50–52
  in Nixon-McGovern election of
    1972, 101
  prophetic speculation, patriotism
    replacing, 19
  by Reagan, 187, 188, 189, 205
  September 11, 2001 and war on
    terror, 254–55
American public's morality, Christian
    Right doubts regarding, 244
Americans United for Separation of
    Church and State, 50, 67
Andelin, Helen, 110
anti-Semitism. *See* Jews and Judaism
Arlington Group, 258, 259, 266
Armey, Dick, 242
Armstrong, Orland K., 55
Ashcroft, John, 252
Association of Volunteers for Educa-
    tional Responsibility in Texas
    (AVERT), 82–83
astrology, Nancy Reagan's reliance on,
    211
atheism
  communism linked to, 18, 21, 24,
    26, 42, 96
  education and, 18, 62, 66, 134,
    201
  secularism and culture wars linked
    to, 17, 18, 96
AVERT (Association of Volunteers for
    Educational Responsibility in
    Texas), 82–83
Ayer, William Ward, 12

Baker, Howard, 66, 196
Baker, James, 196–97
Bakker, Jim and Tammy Faye, 149,
    178, 182, 195, 217
Baldwin, James, 135
Baptist Bible Fellowship (BBF), 42, 48,
    177
Baptist Bible Tribune, 48, 64, 70, 80,
    116, 134

Ostbyu, Sandra, 167
Osteen, Joel, 269
Otis, George, 124
Overstreet, Harry and Bonaro, 71
Oxnam, G. Bromley, 50

PACs (political action groups), 168–69, 175
Paige, Rod, 252
Palin, Sarah, 8, 9, 274–75
Palmer Raids, 18
Panama Canal Treaty, 123, 173
parochial schools, 63–64, 164
Parsley, Rod, 260
partial-birth abortion, 241, 242, 253
The Passion of the Christ (Gibson, 2003), 262
Patrick Henry College, 262–63
patriotism. *See* American ideals, identification of Protestant Christianity with
Peale, Norman Vincent, 50, 51, 54
Pelosi, Nancy, 269
Pentecostals and charismatics, 6, 51–52, 178, 179–82, 216
People for the American Way, 198, 254
Phillips, Howard, 167–68, 171, 174, 180, 194, 241–42
Phillips, Kevin, 98
Pitts, Joseph, 243
Playboy, 24, 81, 126–27, 129, 171, 180
pledge of allegiance, addition of "under God" to, 26, 62
political action groups (PACs), 168–69, 175
political liberalism. *See* liberalism, political
Pollard, Ramsay, 52
Pollution and the Death of Man (Schaeffer, 1970), 138
pornography
    Bryant's campaign against, 150
    Cold War efforts to control, 24
    in conventional view of development of Christian Right, 2
    Dobson's campaign against, 239

Falwell on, 172
    mobilization of Christian Right against, 3, 81–82
Powell, Colin, 251
prayer in schools
    Bryant's campaign for, 150
    communism, as defense against, 62, 63
    constitutional amendment to restore, 65, 66, 75, 181, 200, 202, 203, 214
    in conventional view of development of Christian Right, 2
    failure of Christian Right to legislatively affect, 8
    Goldwater on, 75
    Kennedy administration, *Engel* decision during, 62–64
    Reagan years, 188, 191, 200, 201, 202, 203
    Republican backing of, 1, 7, 75
    Robertson's support for, 214
    Schempp decision and, 64–67
premillennial dispensationalism, 15, 35, 42
Presbyterian Church (US), 30
Pressler, Larry, 154
private schools
    fundamentalist schools, development of, 85, 296–97n43
    home schooling, 239, 262
    IRS directive to investigate civil rights issues at, 163–64, 190, 197
    parochial schools, 63–64, 164
    Reagan Republican platform to support, 189–90
    vouchers for, 136, 217
pro-life movement. *See* abortion
Prohibition, 2, 3, 11–12, 14, 15, 36
prophetic speculation
    in 1930s, 3, 15
    on communism and Soviet Union, 18
    mass market appeal of, 161
    patriotism displacing, 19